MW01000209

Tony Stead • Linda Hoyt

Explorations *in* Nonfiction Writing

Grade
2

*first*hand

HEINEMANN

DEDICATED TO TEACHERS

DEDICATED TO TEACHERS

*first*hand
An imprint of Heinemann
361 Hanover Street
Portsmouth, NH 03801-3912
firsthand.heinemann.com

Offices and agents throughout the world

©2010 by Tony Stead and Linda Hoyt. All rights reserved.

Except where noted, no part of this book may be reproduced in any form or by any electronic or mechanical means, including information storage and retrieval systems, without permission in writing from the publisher, except by a reviewer, who may quote brief passages in a review.

"Dedicated to Teachers" is a trademark of Greenwood Publishing Group, Inc.

Cataloguing-in-Publication data for this book is available from the Library of Congress.

Explorations in Nonfiction Writing, Grade 2
ISBN-10: 0-325-03780-9   ISBN-13: 978-0-325-03780-6 (Lesson Book)
ISBN-10: 0-325-03775-2   ISBN-13: 978-0-325-03775-2 (Guide)
ISBN-10: 0-325-03782-5   ISBN-13: 978-0-325-03782-0 (Big Book of Mentor Texts)
ISBN-10: 0-325-03143-6   ISBN-13: 978-0-325-03143-9 (kit)

Cover photographs: Bill Miller
Design and production: Small Planet

Printed in the United States of America

14   13   12   11   10   VP   1   2   3   4   5   6

Explorations *in* Nonfiction Writing

CONTENTS

VL Indicates Power Writes that focus on Visual Literacy

       Topic Selection Sheet, Ongoing Monitoring Sheets,
      Daily Planners, and Individual Evaluation Records

Introduction to
Explorations in Nonfiction Writing

from Tony and Linda

We undertook the creation of this resource because we both have devoted many years to opening the door to nonfiction for teachers and students. We believe that children should be surrounded by nonfiction reading and writing from the very beginning. Not only does nonfiction reflect real-world demands—to meet standards, to communicate information, to build world knowledge—but exploring nonfiction can also capitalize on our youngest learners' curiosity, their fascination and willingness to learn about the world around them.

In a climate of inquiry and research, nonfiction writing flourishes. Facts and information provide an infinite pool of ideas to write about. Writing for a specific audience and purpose—to inform, narrate or retell, instruct or lay out a procedure, respond, or persuade—gives momentum to those ideas.

Immersion in nonfiction writing does not happen by chance. It requires a dynamic teaching environment in which nonfiction writing is regularly and explicitly taught, not touched upon occasionally or extrapolated from a creative writing process. The unique features and thinking that go into creating nonfiction texts demand teacher modeling and gradual release of responsibility for writing and learning to the students.

Perhaps most important, nonfiction writing has the power to transform a classroom: to generate energy and excitement in all learners and to meet every writer where he or she is, no matter how experienced or inexperienced. When children are constantly engaged in thinking and drawing and writing about what they are learning, knowledge sticks.

Tony Stead

Linda Hoyt

We believe that young writers deserve:

▶ Extended, in-depth writing projects that allow them iterative practice of the entire writing process

▶ Brief, intensive writing tasks that build their fluency in writing a variety of text types

▶ Opportunities to study mentor texts— professional models and models constructed with their teacher—in order to discover the characteristics and features of a variety of written forms

▶ Authentic writing experiences—messages they want to communicate to an audience they care about for a real purpose—that infuse them with enthusiasm for writing

▶ Time to research topics they are passionate about—to immerse themselves in print and other media, to ask and answer questions, to explore collaboratively and independently

▶ Clearly scaffolded instruction that begins with teacher guidance and culminates in the students' independent approximation of a form

▶ Assessment with explicit expectations that makes students partners in their own learning: self-assessment for writers, formative and summative assessment for teachers

▶ Frequent opportunities to share and celebrate their accomplishments as writers

The Extended Writing Units (EWUs) and Power Writes you find in each section of this lesson book are meant to be teaching models, not prescriptions. It is essential to remember that the topics presented in each are simply suggestions—possibilities for you to consider. You may want to take advantage of the organization and content provided and use them just as they are written. However, we also encourage you to personalize them and make them your own!

The real goal of this resource is to give you examples that assist you in linking nonfiction writing to the interests of your students and your curriculum. The following walk-throughs will highlight the teaching framework for all the lessons. By all means, use this framework to teach whatever content works for your class. If an Extended Writing Unit is on bears but you have terrific resources and a curriculum goal that focuses on life cycles of insects— change it! Slip your own topic into the session framework, and go for it! The structure and focus points of the Extended Writing Unit will work just as well with your topic as the topic you find here. If a Power Write is about writing directions on *How to Blow Bubbles,* feel free to switch it to *How to Solve a Math Problem, How to Play Safely on the Playground,* or *How to Read a Book.*

We would love nothing more than to hear how you have personalized the EWUs and Power Writes to create a powerful support system that is finely tuned to the needs of your students and your curriculum. When you infuse a strong writing emphasis into content learning, your students will remember more while at the same time thriving in an atmosphere where writing is a tool for content retention.

Tony Stead and Linda Hoyt

Getting Ready to Teach
Explorations in Nonfiction Writing

To make informed decisions about how to use this resource, what to teach first, and how to integrate nonfiction writing into your classroom practice, you need to know that the *Explorations in Nonfiction Writing* lessons are organized by writing purpose and that you have two kinds of lessons to choose from.

WRITING PURPOSES

The first thing you'll notice as you thumb through this resource is its organization around critical nonfiction writing *purposes*. (See *A Guide to Teaching Nonfiction Writing, Grades K–2*, for an expanded discussion.) The lessons in each of the tabbed sections focus clearly on one of these purposes.

- INFORM to provide information: describe, explain, give the reader facts, tell what something looks like, summarize

- INSTRUCT to tell the reader how to do something: outline a process, detail a procedure

- NARRATE to draw the reader into an event or sequence of events to provide insights into the life of a person, other living thing, or situation: personal narratives are about the writer's own experience; nonfiction narratives are about a person, thing, or event outside the writer

- PERSUADE to influence the reader to take action or to subscribe to a belief

- RESPOND to express ideas about a text or topic; to engage in critical, evaluative thinking; may include a specific prompt or format

EXTENDED WRITING UNITS AND POWER WRITES

Next, you'll find that within each of these tabbed sections, there are two different kinds of exploration.

1. Extended Writing Units

Each Extended Writing Unit (EWU) outlines a two- to four-week writing project during which children research, write, and publish a particular form for a given purpose. Most units are comprised of about ten 40- to 60-minute sessions. An "Inform" unit, with a focus on report writing, includes roughly twenty sessions. You may adapt EWUs to any topic for which you have resources or a curriculum need.

Every EWU follows the same gradual-release teaching model: the first week or two are spent on a whole-class project, rich in teacher modeling and collaborative writing; the next week or two focus on individual projects in which writers apply the whole-class experience to their own independent writing. Throughout the EWU sessions, you will notice the familiar routines you expect to see in a writing workshop.

2. Power Writes

Following the EWU in each section is a collection of Power Writes. These brief, cross-curricular writing experiences are designed to be taught in a single teaching session and linked to your curriculum in science, social studies, math, language arts, and so on. Power Writes offer opportunities for increasing cross-curricular writing volume through brief experiences with a wide variety of text types. Power Writes serve as a springboard for using the target text type again and again as a tool for solidifying cross-curricular understandings.

Like EWUs, Power Writes gradually release responsibility to the student. They begin with explicit teacher modeling and think-alouds before moving to guided and then independent practice.

INFUSING *EXPLORATIONS* INTO YOUR CURRICULUM

The lessons in *Explorations in Nonfiction Writing* can be used to support a variety of instructional purposes in the content areas as well as in language arts. The important goal is to provide your writers with the full spectrum of purposes and text types for nonfiction writing—across the curriculum. Doing a single report on animals is simply not enough to build nonfiction writing power in your students.

Following are three models for ways you might integrate *Explorations* into your classroom. No matter which way you choose, it is critical to note that the order of the tabbed sections (alphabetical) and the lessons within them (Extended Writing Units first, then Power Writes) is not meant to be prescriptive. That is, you are not meant to work from beginning to end in this collection, starting your year with the report in the Inform Extended Writing Unit and ending your year with a Respond Power Write. (In fact, since the Inform project is the longest and most challenging, you'll likely choose another to begin with.) Nor do you need to start a unit on narration, for example, with the EWU. These are resources from which you may pick and choose depending on the requirements of your curriculum.

USE *EXPLORATIONS* AS THE FOUNDATION OF YOUR WRITING CURRICULUM

If you want to strengthen your students' nonfiction writing, it is helpful to begin with Extended Writing Units and identify those you plan to teach. Then, map out a year-long plan for how they will fit into your curriculum. There are six EWUs in your resource guide, so if you do one per month, you can select at least two units to revisit—with a new topic as the focus. You can arrange the units in any order that best matches your learners and your curriculum.

The sample year-long plan that follows lays out one possible scenario. As you review it, notice that this plan provides for two EWUs for Personal Narrative and Informational Report as these two text types are of high utility for writers. The combinations you create and the order in which you present them to your students have endless possibilities.

	OCTOBER	NOVEMBER	DECEMBER	JANUARY	FEBRUARY	MARCH	APRIL	MAY
EWUs	Personal Narrative	Procedural Text	Informational Report	Persuasive Letters	Personal Narrative (self-selected)	Response	Nonfiction Narrative	Informational Report (self-selected)
Power Writes	Throughout the year to teach, reinforce, and refresh							

Sample Year-Long Plan: Using Extended Writing Units and Power Writes to Teach One Purpose Per Month

Note: Samples of grade-specific year-long plans can be found on the *Resources* CD-ROM.

If you are making *Explorations in Nonfiction Writing* your core writing curriculum, you have a choice of where to start. Some teachers like to start with an Extended Writing Unit, and then use Power Writes to ensure that skills and strategies built during the EWU are supported all year long. Power Writes keep writers tuned up and ready to go with a wide variety of text types, ensuring that nonfiction writers don't forget the writing traits and understandings they developed during an EWU.

Other teachers like to begin nonfiction writing through Power Writes as these lessons are quick and easy, yet they are filled with intentional instruction that launches writers into the text type. Power Writes provide explicit teacher modeling of the features and the form, then propel writers into guided practice as they generate nonfiction writing in response to their learning. Once writers have done several Power Writes, you will find that they have developed momentum that will launch them easily into an in-depth Extended Writing Unit.

So, you can start with an Extended Writing Unit and use Power Writes to extend and secure learning. Or, you can start with Power Writes to build momentum for a longer study with an Extended Writing Unit. You are in the driver's seat!

SLIP *EXPLORATIONS* INTO YOUR EXISTING WRITERS WORKSHOP

Both Extended Writing Units and Power Writes can slide easily into your existing writers workshop, providing rich diversity within your existing workshop format. If you have a writers workshop up and running already, you might

▸ use an Extended Writing Unit as a change-of-pace replacement for a unit of study

▸ try out an EWU between two established units of study

▸ teach Power Writes to add depth to a unit of study

Again, map out the year-long plan for your writers workshop and identify the places that a nonfiction *Explorations* unit might contribute to what you are already doing or provide some variation. In the sample year-long plan below, we matched EWUs to an established writers workshop curriculum and specified a choice of Power Writes with the same writing purpose. Once mapped this way, all your choices will align with your core writing curriculum. You can choose to use *Explorations* as additional enhancements or as alternatives to your established plan.

	OCTOBER	NOVEMBER	DECEMBER	JANUARY	FEBRUARY	MARCH	APRIL	MAY
Writers Workshop	Personal Narrative		Writing Craft	Author Study	Procedures		Poetry	Fiction
EWUs	Personal Narrative	Narrative Nonfiction	Informational Report	Response	Procedural Text	Informational Report		Narrate
Power Writes	Any from the Narrate section	Any from the Narrate section	Any from the Inform section	Any from the Respond section	Any from the Instruct section	Any from the Inform section	Poetry in a variety of sections	Any from the Persuade section

Sample Year-Long Plan: Using Power Writes and EWUs as Alternatives or Additions in Writers Workshop

EMBED *EXPLORATIONS* INTO EVERY LEARNING EXPERIENCE

Nonfiction writing is a natural and important aspect of content area learning, and *Explorations in Nonfiction Writing* lends itself to enhancement of all curriculum activities. Extended Writing Units can go hand in hand with social studies or science units, providing a platform for expressing new concepts and ideas. In addition to the traditional science or social studies report (the Inform EWU), writers might *narrate* a bit of the history they are studying, create a flyer to *persuade* the school to care for the environment, *respond* to a historical fiction read-aloud, or *instruct* another class how to do a science experiment. Embedding an ongoing EWU into a content area unit does triple duty. It provides sustained writing instruction; it consolidates content area learning; and, perhaps most important, it provides a purposeful learning experience. Students have reasons to write. Writers have reasons to learn.

Power Writes are especially easy to infuse into every dimension of the learning day. Most Power Writes can be completed in a single session, so you will find that they merge easily into math, science, social studies—even read-aloud and snack time. The goal with Power Writes is to create opportunities for short bursts of writing in every subject area, every day. If you set aside just five minutes of every time segment and write to remember, write to wonder, write to understand—you will see a difference in both content retention and writing expertise.

Note: See grade-specific examples of ways you might integrate Power Writes and Extended Writing Units into your learning day on the *Resources* CD-ROM.

SETTING UP YOUR CLASSROOM FOR *EXPLORATIONS*

To optimize your teaching of nonfiction writing, you will want to plan your space, set up a system for keeping track of your writers' work, find and organize resources to support research, and establish "thinking partners" to give each student a writing buddy. The "Setting the Stage for Nonfiction Writing: Scaffolds for Success" section of *A Guide to Teaching Nonfiction Writing, Grades K–2*, provides a wealth of practical, classroom-savvy management ideas. In addition, for a look into an inquiry-based classroom where all of these structures are in play, check out the two DVDs in *Nonfiction Writing: Intentional, Connected, and Engaging*, also published by Heinemann.

SPACE

Explorations in Nonfiction Writing operates best in a classroom that supports children's curiosity, talk, collaboration, and concentration as well as your own teaching flexibility.

You need space:

▸ to gather the whole class for focused instruction

▸ to pull a small group together for a differentiated lesson

▸ to circulate among writers, coaching and encouraging

▸ to confer with individuals about their writing

Writers need space:

▸ to research their topics

▸ to work together in pairs and small groups

▸ to write on their own

▸ to confer one-to-one with their teacher

Plan for your whole-group instruction first, making sure you can seat the class comfortably for a focused minilesson, and then plan the table or desk grouping for your own small-group lessons or individual writing conferences. Next, seat writers at tables or clusters of desks to encourage collaboration and sharing. Finally, organize the space for your research stations and carve out some corners for children to write on their own or share with a friend.

RESEARCH STATIONS

Gathering resources—books, pictures, objects, and the like—about the topic or topics students are learning and writing about in specific locations in the classroom helps organize and focus information gathering. Not only do research stations provide specific locations for specific topics, but also they allow you to disperse resources across several areas of your classroom to provide spaces in which writers can productively engage with a variety of media tools to collaborate, share information, and learn together.

Stations may be organized by topic (fish at one station, frogs at another) or by medium:

▸ Books and magazines

▸ Pictures, photographs, and models

▸ Realia or observations

▸ Computer and Internet

▸ Listening station

▸ DVDs and video

The Resources section at the back of this book provides extensive guidance in setting up, managing, and teaching children to use research stations, including setting up task management boards, using research notebooks or folders, and showing writers how to record information from the stations' resources.

If your classroom is small, don't worry! You can still utilize research stations by placing resources in tubs that teams can take to their tables or place on the floor while engaging in a "station."

WRITING AND RESEARCH FOLDERS OR NOTEBOOKS

If a sustained writing effort is part of your classroom, you probably already have a system for keeping track of writers' ongoing work and for archiving finished pieces in a portfolio. If not, *A Guide to Teaching Nonfiction Writing, Grades K–2*, provides a mini-course in organizing a writers workshop. You'll at least want to set up and teach children to manage their own writing folders—and to store them in a central location where you can regularly review their work (and keep the work safe from hazard and loss!).

Beyond writing folders and notebooks, a specially designated research notebook or folder is a good idea for each project explored in the nonfiction writing classroom. State standards as well as the Common Core standards make it clear that nonfiction writers are expected to develop a wide array of strategies for researching and organizing nonfiction information. In an Extended Writing Unit especially, significant amounts of time are dedicated to research so that your writers are empowered with facts and data to infuse into their whole-class and independent projects. In the Resources section at the back of this lesson book, you'll find specific descriptions of a variety of research tools—notebooks, folders, concept webs, R.A.N. charts, and so on—that will enhance your writers' information gathering.

THE R.A.N. STRATEGY: READING AND ANALYZING NONFICTION

The R.A.N. chart (first explored in *Reality Checks: Teaching Reading Comprehension with Nonfiction K–5*. Portland, ME: Stenhouse.) is a foundational tool for organizing information during Extended Writing Units, in particular the Inform report-writing unit. The chart is used throughout a research project to record and categorize information on the go. The R.A.N. chart helps writers in two critical ways: first, to be aware of and critically examine their thinking, and second, to organize their research information in preparation for writing.

The following annotated R.A.N. chart for an exploration on the topic of bears shows how it works. (A full explanation and teaching notes for using this chart with primary-grade writers appears in the Resources section at the back of this lesson book.) Before students begin researching a topic, they first record—on sticky notes or cards—what they think they already know about it, their prior knowledge (column 1). As they research, they gather facts to support or contradict their prior knowledge (columns 2 and 3), to add new facts to their knowledge base (column 4), or to generate questions they want to answer with their research (column 5) and regularly come back to categorize their information on the R.A.N. chart. In doing so, they take care to post their information next to the appropriate subtopics—on this example, "look like," "live," "eat," and

Headings ⟶ Categories ↓	1 What we think we know	2 Yes, we were right or Confirmed information ✓	3 We don't think this anymore or Misconceptions ✗	4 New learning	5 Wonderings ?
What bears look like	Children state information they think to be correct about bears (prior knowledge)	Children read to confirm prior knowledge about bears	Children read to discard incorrect prior knowledge about bears	Children read to locate additional information about bears	Children raise questions about bears based on the new information gathered
Where bears live					
What bears eat					
Other great facts					

R.A.N. chart for a class report on bears

"other great facts")—which you have identified to reflect the resources you have available or the demands of your curriculum.

The R.A.N. chart's true power is its use as a tool for organizing facts and ideas in preparation for writing. The R.A.N. chart facilitates the transition from research information to a logical, topically organized report. Each of the subtopics in the left column of the chart can become the heading for a section of the report. The facts next to that subtopic can be re-examined and selected (or not) for the final report.

THINKING PARTNERS

TURN &TALK You'll notice in the following sample lessons that writers are asked to Turn and Talk at key moments during the focused minilesson or during sharing and reflecting.

Whether you assign thinking partners yourself or let writers choose their own, it helps to establish the partnerships before the lesson so that partners can sit together. The moment of turning and talking is then completely focused on the target learning. There is no time wasted searching for a conversation partner. The distributed discourse of a Turn and Talk—first between thinking partners and then shared with the group—empowers language use and improves content retention.

Thinking partners can also be useful collaborators during researching, peer editors during revising and editing, and colleagues during publishing. If you choose to make significant use of thinking partnerships, you might want to pair students for social reasons (for example, a more focused learner with a more active one) or for instructional reasons (a strong writer with a challenged one).

Teaching
Explorations in Nonfiction Writing

Explorations in Nonfiction Writing provides teaching tools and models the methodology for integrating nonfiction writing into your school day. As you roll up your sleeves and prepare to utilize *Explorations* with your students, you'll want to become familiar with what it offers.

THE RESOURCES

Explorations in Nonfiction Writing provides four key resources:

▸ this book drives instruction with classroom-based teaching models

▸ a *Resources* CD-ROM packaged with this book contains printable versions of support materials for students and teachers

▸ a *Big Book of Mentor Texts* supports the sessions with exemplary writing models for students to emulate

▸ *A Guide to Teaching Nonfiction Writing, Grades K–2*, lays out the professional underpinnings of effective teaching of nonfiction writing with primary grade writers

EXPLORATIONS IN NONFICTION WRITING LESSON BOOK

In this tabbed, spiral-bound lesson book, you will find Extended Writing Units (EWUs) and Power Write lessons organized according to the major purposes for which nonfiction writing is created: Inform, Instruct, Narrate, Persuade, and Respond. Behind each purpose tab is an EWU (two EWUs in the narrative section) and a collection of Power Writes, all focused on writing a particular form to meet that writing purpose.

Extended Writing Units

Each Extended Writing Unit (EWU) in the lesson book outlines a two- to four-week writing project during which children research, write, and publish a particular form for a given purpose. Most units are comprised of about ten 40- to 60-minute sessions. An "Inform" unit, with a focus on report writing, includes roughly twenty sessions. EWUs may be adapted to any topic for which you have resources or a curriculum need.

Every EWU follows the same gradual-release teaching model: the first week or two are spent on a whole-class project, rich in teacher modeling and collaborative writing; the next week or two focus on individual projects in which writers apply the whole-class experience to their own independent writing. Throughout the EWU sessions, you will notice the familiar routines you expect to see in a writing workshop.

Power Writes

Following the EWU in each section is a collection of Power Writes. These brief, cross-curricular writing experiences are designed to be taught in a single teaching session and linked to your curriculum in science, social studies, math, language arts, and so on. Power Writes offer opportunities for increasing cross-curricular writing volume through brief experiences with a wide variety of text types. They serve as a springboard for using the target text type again and again as a tool for solidifying cross-curricular understandings.

At least two Power Writes in each purpose section highlight visual sources of communication—photographs, labeled diagrams, drawings, and the like—in the mentor texts and in the nonfiction writing that writers construct. Look for the visual text label in this lesson book's organizing charts and table of contents to locate these important lessons.

Like EWUs, Power Writes gradually release responsibility to the student. They begin with explicit teacher modeling and think-aloud before moving to guided and then independent practice.

BIG BOOK OF MENTOR TEXTS

This richly-crafted collection of texts is used throughout the EWUs and Power Writes to show writers exemplary models of various text forms. The texts showcase enlarged print and beautiful visuals so your young writers can easily access high-quality linguistic features, text features, visuals, and nonfiction content. With these models, your writers will soon be writing like experts!

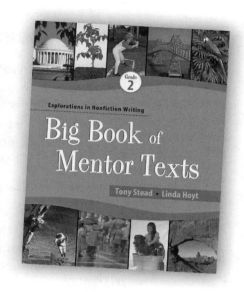

RESOURCES CD-ROM

All of the selections in the *Big Book of Mentor Texts* are on the CD-ROM so you can easily print the selections for the enjoyment of your students both at school and at home. Stored on this disk you will also find a wide array of ready-to-use, printable writing tools like Personal Word Walls, Picture Alphabet Cards, and Editing and Revising Checklists, as well as teaching tools like Ongoing Monitoring Sheets, Self-Assessment forms, and so on.

A CD-ROM icon at the corner of a facsimile tells you this resource is printable from the CD-ROM.

A GUIDE TO TEACHING NONFICTION WRITING, GRADES K–2

This guide is loaded with tips and tools for helping you launch an exciting adventure with nonfiction writing. You will find a rationale for why nonfiction writing is so important to the future of the students we serve, explanations of the unique features of nonfiction texts, help with setting up and managing a writers workshop, ideas for conducting effective writing conferences, and a vast array of additional information to make your class's nonfiction writing experiences powerful.

THE LESSONS

As you take a look at the following pages from an Extended Writing Unit and a Power Write, you will notice the harmony in their routines. The three-part lesson structure is identical in both EWUs and Power Writes and follows the gradual release of responsibility model: 1. Focused Minilesson (teacher-directed, student-engaged); 2. Writing and Coaching (student-driven, teacher-guided); and 3. Sharing and Reflecting (student-centered, teacher-supported).

1. Focused Minilesson

The lesson guides you to set the stage for your writers and focus attention on specific learning tasks. This may be done by interacting with the *Big Book of Mentor Texts*, by thinking aloud and creating a piece of modeled writing, or by engaging nonfiction writers more deeply with their research or writing strategies.

2. Writing and Coaching

There is no replacement for time to write. For our learners to become proficient writers, they need lots of writing time. During Writing and Coaching, children research, draw, write, meet with partners, confer, and join guided-writing or shared-writing sessions. They are active, engaged—and writing! Nor is there any replacement for your own time to circulate among your writers, observing, praising, questioning, giving hints, making notes for future minilessons, or calling small groups together. You will find many tips for management and conferring in *A Guide to Teaching Nonfiction Writing*.

3. Sharing and Reflecting

This is a time to consolidate the learning. Partners or individuals share the drawing, writing, and research they have done, consider the learning goals of the session, and consider how they can continue to move forward as nonfiction writers. You will want to take this opportunity to summarize and restate the teaching points in the lesson as well as asking partners to turn and talk about their work. In the Power Writes, a summary chart icon reminds you to create a chart of the text features (listed at the beginning of the lesson) that you have taught.

TURN &TALK EWUs and Power Writes also share abundant opportunities for partners to turn and talk. This is important. If you call on only one student, only one learner is thinking, using language, and taking responsibility for understanding. On the other hand, if you pose a question and ask all students to turn to a thinking partner, suddenly all writers are engaged— thinking, using language, and taking responsibility for understanding.

Extended Writing Units (EWUs)

An Extended Writing Unit is designed to be taught over two weeks to a month. It first guides writers through discovery of a specific text structure and its features, then models the writing process through creation of a collaborative class project, and finally turns the process just learned over to students to publish their own individual projects. An EWU can be planned to support any unit of study—in math, science, or social studies—that requires collecting and organizing information in order to convey it to an audience.

The overview to each EWU provides:

▸ a description of what this particular unit is about, a chart laying out the teaching and learning tasks in each three-part session, and ideas for adapting the EWU to other topics and forms

▸ specific guidance for advance preparations: charts to make, research stations and notebooks to set up, a standards rubric to plan for, and the like

▸ ways to make the unit most effective before, during, and after teaching

Each EWU has two parts:

▸ a class project—five to ten 40- to 60-minute sessions—when writers work together supported by extensive teacher modeling from research to final published project to create a text

▸ an individual project—also five to ten 40- to 60-minute sessions—when writers work more independently to create the same kind of text using a new topic

Every session in both the class and individual projects follows the same three-part procedure.

A SESSION FROM AN EXTENDED WRITING UNIT

Headers tell you where you are in the Extended Writing Unit.

The **lesson title** and a **brief description** let you know what happens in the session.

Checking the **materials list** ahead of time assures that you won't be caught without a key resource.

Time estimates give you a sense of how the session may unfold, but it is important to note that sessions can easily be adjusted to match the needs of your students. If your writers need more time along the way, you can stretch the session across more than one day. If your writers are whizzing along and don't need all the time allocated in the session, by all means move on. The times provided are all approximate.

---

20 INFORM : Extended Writing Unit

SESSION 4
Researching and Drafting

Students continue to record information from multiple sources as they practice writing facts in their own words.

MATERIALS
- *Big Book of Mentor Texts:* "The Sonoran Desert," pages 2–9
- Research stations
- Research notebooks or paper
- Whole-class R.A.N. chart
- Sticky notes and pencils

FOCUSED MINILESSON *(drafting)*
15 MINUTES

■ Focus the learning: *In this session, we're going to continue researching from different sources and writing down the important information we find. But this time we're going to try very hard to record the information in our own words. We'll learn why this is an important skill, and then we'll practice it during our writing time. We'll also learn what to do when we find that information we thought we knew actually is not correct.*

TURN &TALK *Writers, why do you think it's important to write facts in your own words? Turn to your partner and talk about it.*

■ Summarize for students some of what you heard from the partner discussions: *I heard a few of you say that it is not right or fair for one person to copy exactly what another person has written. Someone else said that we can understand and remember facts better if we put them in our own words. These are both excellent reasons!*

■ Show students page 5 of the mentor text. Think aloud as you model stating facts in your own words: *Here, the author has written that a spadefoot toad "lives in muddy pools left by the storms." If I can say it in my own words, I can be sure I understand what the author means. I'm going to say, "The storms make a muddy pool. A muddy pool is a great place for a toad to live." When you are looking for a new way to write something, it helps to talk to a partner about it. Then try writing it. Remember, you want to use ideas from your research in your reports. But you need to use your own words and not the author's.*

■ Read other facts from the page.

TURN &TALK *Use your own words to tell your partner a fact from this page.*

■ Prepare students for their research time: *Today, when you are at your research stations, try to use your own words to record the facts you find.*

---

1 At the beginning of every session, a teacher-directed **Focused Minilesson** invites writers to explore the features of a text or models some aspect of the writing process. A mentor text from the *Big Book of Mentor Texts* provides the initial model for text features, language features, and conventions.

Session 4 : CLASS PROJECT 21

- Discuss the "Misconceptions" heading on the R.A.N. chart: *As you do your research, you may find that some things you thought you knew actually are not right. A misconception is something we thought was right that turns out to be incorrect. If you find that your information was not correct, you can move it from "What We Think We Know" to "Misconceptions" on our R.A.N. chart.*

WRITING and COACHING *(prewriting, drafting)*
25 MINUTES

- Have students continue to research and write information in their research notebooks. Remind them to use their own words rather than the author's words to record information.

- As you circulate around the room, encourage students to use pictures, diagrams, bullet points, and labels to summarize ideas from their research. Then, when it's time to write the report in complete sentences, they will have no choice but to use their own words!

- Have students choose their favorite or most important facts, record them on sticky notes, and then place them on the class R.A.N. chart in the correct categories.

SHARING and REFLECTING 3
15 MINUTES

TURN &TALK *Show your partner information you collected about rain forests. Which piece did you choose to put on our R.A.N. chart?*

- Read through all the confirmed facts and new facts. Help students identify information that is repeated and discard it.

TURN &TALK *Did you learn anything at your research station today that would tell you to move a sticky note from "What We Think We Know" to "Yes, We Were Right"? Is there anything that you want to move from "What We Think We Know" to "Misconceptions"?*

- Reinforce the idea that when we say things in our own words, we understand and remember them better: *I think you are going to remember the things you learned today for a long time. You wrote your facts using your own words instead of copying the author's words. When you can restate the facts in your own words, you show that you understand the information.*

- *You're becoming expert researchers! In our next session, we'll delve more deeply into our research to be sure that we've provided our readers with exciting information.*

TIP for Conferring with Individuals and Small Groups

Gather into a small group any students who struggle with putting information in their own words. Use a book that includes rain forest facts. Guide students to share their restatement of facts with the small group as you provide reinforcement and feedback. Then encourage students to use their own words to record the information in their notebooks.

The **stage in the writing process** at which writers are most likely working appears next to each lesson section heading. See *A Guide to Teaching Nonfiction Writing, Grades K–2,* for a full explanation of each stage and some sample lessons.

Teaching **TIPS** provide explanations, advice, and ideas for managing and tailoring the session to all students.

TURN &TALK

Regular **Turn and Talks** give writers a chance to consolidate and share understandings.

Teaching language in italics gives you a model for how you might think aloud, explain, or guide students' participation.

---

2 During **Writing and Coaching**, students research and write on their own. Over time, they collect, organize, write, revise, and edit information for the text they are creating. During this independent work time, you confer with individuals and small groups as needed.

3 At the close of each day's lesson, **Sharing and Reflecting** on their work prompts writers to discuss progress, lingering questions, and goals for the next step in the process. Facilitate this conversation, helping students consolidate knowledge and summing up important teaching points for the day.

CONSIDERATIONS FOR IMPLEMENTING EXTENDED WRITING UNITS

Teachers who have piloted the Extended Writing Units (EWUs) in their classrooms have shared valuable insights. Following is their advice for managing efficient, effective extended writing units.

Collaborate.

▸ Where possible, team up with the colleagues and implement the units at the same time. This will enable you to share resources as well as plan and evaluate the units together. Your students will also be able to share their class and individual projects with other classes that have explored similar text types and topics.

▸ Take advantage of the expertise of your school or town librarian. Alert your librarian in advance so he or she can assemble a cart of related books and periodicals—and perhaps videos and a website list—that can support your writers' research.

Plan ahead.

▸ Read the entire series of sessions ahead of time so you know what's coming up. This will assist you in assembling resources, choosing teaching priorities, and planning the timing of your sessions.

▸ Initially, there's a lot of prep work with the research stations, but once they are up and running they will be a powerful means to have students locate information for themselves, rather than being spoon-fed facts. Give yourself a pep talk as you organize your learning environment: you are helping your students become curious, self-motivated learners.

▸ If your EWU is centered on a science or social topic, be familiar with the content. This will enable you to help students gather relevant and accurate information.

Teach routines.

▸ If this is your students' first time working with an extending writing unit, they will need time to get used to the process of investigation. You may need extra sessions to assist them with researching, recording information, and the writing process. Once students are familiar with the routine, you will find that the EWUs will run smoothly.

▸ During every EWU session, there are many opportunities for students to turn and talk. To ensure this works successfully, make sure each writer has a learning partner and guide partners to sit together during focused minilessons and sharing/reflection time. Demonstrate to students how to both share their thinking and listen to their partners.

Focus on teaching priorities.

▸ Remember that you are not trying to accomplish all of your writing goals in one EWU. Be selective about what you concentrate on and go deep rather than trying to achieve too much.

▸ When using the mentor texts for writing instruction, keep the students focused on the strategy or feature you are teaching. Avoid getting lost in the content of the text. The selections in the *Big Book of Mentor Texts* have been designed to represent the text structure and language features of specific text types. If you want to explore the content of the mentor texts further, use your reading and/or content time to achieve this.

▸ When students are writing, many may need assistance at one time. It takes time for students to learn independence. Throughout independent writing time, coach for independence. Teach writers strategies for working on their own instead of waiting for help. For example, when writers are unable to spell a word, show them how to write the letter for the beginning sound, then draw a blank line for the rest of the word and keep going. This will keep writers writing and on the path toward success.

▸ When students are researching, make sure they are not spending all their time finding information. They need quality time to discuss and record their findings. Don't skip the sharing and reflecting time at the end of each session. Often this is the most valuable opportunity for consolidating knowledge.

Be flexible.

▸ Although each EWU session is designed to be accomplished in forty to fifty minutes, it is likely that you'll need to adjust the number of sessions or their duration to fit your students' needs. Use the unit's sessions as the foundation of your teaching, adjusting the time frames as necessary to give your students time to research, draft, revise, edit, and publish.

▸ If something suggested in an EWU doesn't work well, ask yourself what adjustments you can make to ensure it works better next time.

▸ If some of your students are pre-emergent readers, use visual pictures/cues when constructing charts to help them remember what's on the chart.

▸ If you find your students are already knowledgeable about something suggested in an EWU, extend their understandings with deeper demonstrations and discussions.

▸ When students are publishing, don't expect perfection. Celebrate their attempts, but also stretch them to produce their best and take pride in their work.

Integrate writing across the curriculum.

▸ The topics explored in these model EWUs are only suggestions. They are a vehicle for showing how to develop students' skill with and understanding of different text types. Many other topics that suit your students and your curriculum can be substituted for what you see here. With this said, if you select an EWU on a topic that is on your science or social studies curriculum, you will also be able to develop key content understandings through the units.

▸ Although these are writing units, the emphasis on reading is strong. Integrating the reading/writing process is important. Use your read-aloud and shared, guided, and independent reading times to support your extended writing units.

▸ You will find that each time you implement an EWU, you will become more confident and knowledgeable in providing a wonderful series of lessons that will help your students grow as nonfiction writers. Each year, it helps if you select some of the same topics as in past years but also do a couple of new ones based on the class's interests or your curriculum. That way you begin creating another great set of explorations you can repeat in the future. This means you will gradually accumulate resources and become familiar with the supports and challenges of implementing a variety of units.

Power Writes

A Power Write is an introductory lesson designed to be taught in a single 30- to 40-minute block. The lesson begins with your on-the-spot creation of a mentor text accompanied by a think-aloud narrating your thinking process as you write. This focused minilesson allows young writers to see and hear the process of writing a specific form and has the added potential to directly reflect something that is going on in their own school lives. It is easy to see how you might substitute a topic you just studied or an audience (the librarian in place of the principal?) or even a purpose (narrate instead of instruct?) in the lessons provided.

Power Writes are designed to slip into your day as a natural part of your curriculum. When students engage with manipulatives during math, with a multi-media experience in art, with the science experiment you conduct as a group, or with the books and videos you show to help social studies come to life, they are engaging in research that can be turned immediately into a written form. The Power Writes give you ideas for following your curriculum activities with writing lessons that give students a chance to work in a meaningful way with the information they have just learned. Power Writes help you link to the content of your curriculum so that nonfiction writing can become a part of every subject, every day.

Some Power Writes in each section focus on creation of a visual text—a cross section, graph, map, table, labeled diagram, and so on. In addition, each section always includes investigations in which writers work with the layout of a magazine-like spread that requires pleasing, informative placement of pictures, captions, diagrams, and the like to develop students' visual literacy as it develops their ability to create the form.

A POWER WRITE

Headers tell you the purpose and the form the lesson addresses.

The **lesson title** names the writing form, and **a brief description** below it relates the form to the purpose.

The **Features** list calls out the distinctive features of the form that you will want to emphasize for writers.

Teaching language in italics gives you a model for how you might think aloud, summarize, or guide students' participation.

TURN &TALK Brief opportunities to **Turn and Talk** keep children on task, provide access to others' ideas, and give them time to think about what they want to say or write.

Investigation

Investigations use special text features to give information about topics.

FEATURES

- Focused topic with facts
- Two facing pages that form a "spread"
- Visual supports: title, headings, labels, and diagrams
- Text boxes

FOCUSED MINILESSON

Writers, we've learned a lot about ocean life. Today I want to showcase what we know about whales in an interesting form—an investigation. Let's take a look at some investigations in our mentor text. In the Big Book of Mentor Texts, *turn to page 22 or 38. These investigations have different purposes—to persuade and narrate. But let's look at the features to think about the form our investigation might take.*

TURN &TALK *Partners, think together. As you take a closer look at these investigations, what features stand out for you?*

You noticed so many great features! We can definitely pull these into our investigation—title, headings, boxes with text, colors and bold text to set apart different parts of the work. We have a lot of decisions to make. That's why it makes sense to plan an investigation before we put all the information on paper.

Watch as I get started by folding this piece of paper in half to create a center gutter line. I'm writing my title at the top of the page in big letters: Whales: Gentle Giants. *Did you notice that I wrote the title across the center line? Now I am going to make my main illustration cross the middle line, too. Watch as I sketch a whale and add labels for* blowhole, tail, flukes, flippers, *and* upper and lower jaws. *I am drawing lines from the labels to the body parts to be sure that readers can identify each part of the whale.*

Next, I'm making text boxes with space to write whale facts. I'm leaving space on this side of the page to place a map where I can color in the locations of whales around the world. There's some space on this side that's a perfect place to list what whales eat. Once I like how the page looks, I will fill in my text boxes.

After writing: Writers, I planned an investigation that will use features to show information. A title reveals the focus of the content. A big illustration is going to anchor the piece, and labels will give information about whales. The map and other text features will show readers information in a very exciting way!

1 A teacher think-aloud is the heart of every **Focused Minilesson**. Think aloud as you create a writing model that captures the features of the form you are introducing. In keeping with the gradual release of responsibility, this part of the lesson is the most teacher-supported.

Power Write : INVESTIGATION 73

INFORM

Whales: Gentle Giants

upper jaw
blowhole
lower jaw
flukes
tail
flipper
WHALE FACTS
MAP
WHAT WHALES EAT

Modeled Writing

The think-aloud model that begins every Power Write narrates the process of creating a **Modeled Writing** sample. This becomes the mentor text for the lesson.

WRITING and COACHING ②

Writers, we've planned an investigation, but it's not complete. Let's work together to finish this investigation about whales. Students who need support can work independently to create elements for the investigation you started, while more capable writers can plot out the elements of investigations to complete on their own.

SHARING and REFLECTING ③

Writers, your investigations make information jump out at your readers! Using text features helps us show ideas about our topic in a way that is exciting and easy to understand.

ASSESS THE LEARNING

As students create their investigations, note which students are able to use text features. Use the investigations in the mentor text to point out features such as headings and text boxes and to talk about how they are helpful to readers.

SELF-ASSESSMENT

SELF-ASSESSMENT
Informing with an Investigation

YES NO
1. Did you include facts about your topic? ☐ ☐
2. Did you plan your space before you started to write? ☐ ☐
3. Did you use features such as captions, headings, and text boxes? ☐ ☐

An **Assess the Learning** feature in every Power Write frames your evaluation of student work. The accompanying **Self-Assessment** provides a way to focus writers' attention on key conventions and elements of the form.

A **CD-ROM icon** signals a printable resource on the CD-ROM.

A **summary chart icon** reminds you to create a classroom chart of the text features in the lesson for writers to use as a resource.

SUPPORTING AND EXTENDING

▸ Examine layouts in nonfiction magazines, such as National Geographic's *Explorer*. Discuss elements of the magazine layout students might want to include in their own writing.

▸ As you start a unit on a nonfiction topic, have teams begin investigations. As their knowledge expands, students can add to their work. Allow time for finalizing investigations at the end of the unit.

▸ Have students create investigations on topics you are exploring in class. After students have shared their work, bind investigations into class books that students can explore during independent reading time.

A **Supporting and Extending** feature with every Power Write nudges you to repeat this lesson with other topics and to other audiences. The lesson you have just taught is only the beginning.

② Hand over the writing to students as you provide guidance and, if needed, additional teaching during **Writing and Coaching**.

③ Each Power Write ends with a distilled summary of the important teaching points for the day in **Sharing and Reflecting**. Think about giving children the last word here, too, with a Turn and Talk that lets them share what they have learned.

Assessment in
Explorations in Nonfiction Writing

Assessing and monitoring students' competencies as writers is a critical component in planning and implementing a focused, balanced nonfiction writing program. In *Explorations in Nonfiction Writing*, it is a daily occurrence.

Pre-assessment, ongoing monitoring, and final assessment enable you to:

▸ Plan Extended Writing Units, Power Writes, and focused minilessons based on the common needs of the class

▸ Tailor instruction to the needs of each writer through conferences and small-group instruction

▸ Document each student's growth as a writer

▸ Give students an opportunity to see their own growth as writers

WHAT WILL I ASSESS?

You may be embedding nonfiction writing into your content curriculum—writing letters to town officers in a Power Write or writing a persuasive essay to the school principal in a social studies EWU—but resist the temptation to confuse students' content learning with their writing performance. Judge the merits of their writing by how well it reflects the text features and writing traits you have taught.

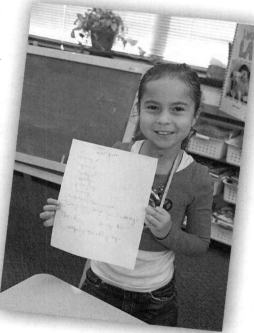

Identifying the specific traits that students need as nonfiction writers is critical. It enables you to provide targeted formal and informal assessments and look at specific attributes and strategies while monitoring students' growth and planning instruction.

Purpose-Centered Writing Rubrics

Every section of this book begins with an introduction to the writing purpose and contains a rubric, Key Skills and Understandings, that is specific to the type of text being studied. This rubric is a helpful tool that will guide your pre-assessment, help you choose focused minilessons, direct your individual student conferences, and help you assess the progress of your writers. Keep the rubric at your fingertips—or use the Ongoing Monitoring Sheet that is a direct copy of the rubric on a tracking form—when teaching Extended Writing Units and when assessing writing products that result from Power Writes. (Full-size copies of the Ongoing Monitoring Sheet can be printed from the *Resources* CD-ROM or found in the Resources section at the end of this book.)

In addition, each Power Write begins with a notation of the critical features of the form or text type that students will be writing and ends with focused summation and assessment of these same features. You always know what it is important for students to know and for you to teach and assess.

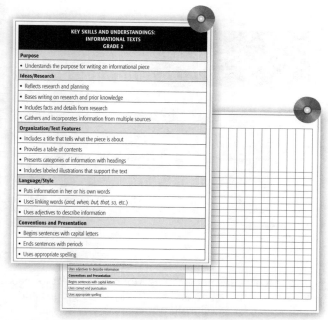

The Key Skills and Understandings rubric and the Ongoing Monitoring Sheet are tools for tracking and teaching for writing progress.

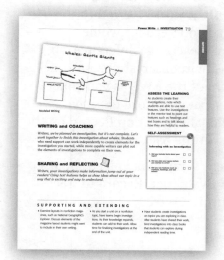

Focusing instruction on the text and visual features of each text type assures writers' effective creation of that text.

WHEN SHOULD I ASSESS?

Explorations in Nonfiction Writing puts the emphasis on formative assessment—ongoing assessment that informs instruction—so assessment permeates every session of an EWU and every Power Write. Instead of building on separate test performances that distract writers from the important business of moving forward in their writing development, *Explorations in Nonfiction Writing* integrates daily, explicit, natural opportunities to gather data, assess understanding, and make plans for specific demonstrations in whole-class, small-group, and individual settings based on identified needs.

Before, During, and After an Extended Writing Unit

The first session of every Extended Writing Unit is a pre-assessment that assesses students' prior knowledge of the purpose and form. This is a writing assignment in which students are asked to generate a piece of writing using the target text type for the EWU before they are provided with instruction. Your analysis of the results will tell you what your students already know—and

ONGOING MONITORING SHEET: INFORMATIONAL WRITING — Names	Alice C.	Lian E.	Erik F.	LaToya H.	Ben J.	Jorge M.	Lars M.	Ayaka S.	Dariel T.	Renat U.	Gabbi W.	Tegan Y.
Purpose												
Understands the purpose for writing an informational piece	3/5	3/7	3/7	3/5	3/7	3/7		3/5	3/9		3/7	
Ideas/Research												
Reflects research and planning	3/5	3/7		3/5		3/7		3/5	3/9		3/7 3/7	
Bases writing on research and prior knowledge												
Includes facts and details from research	3/9	3/9		3/9			3/9					
Gathers and incorporates information from multiple sources												
Organization/Text Features												
Includes a title that tells what the piece is about	3/5	3/7	3/7	3/5	3/7	3/7		3/5	3/9		3/7	
Provides a table of contents	3/5	3/7	3/7	3/5	3/7	3/7		3/5	3/9		3/7	
Presents categories of information with headings												
Includes labeled illustrations that support the text			3/6		3/6		3/6					3/6
Language/Style												
Puts information in her or his own words			3/7				3/7			3/7	3/7	
Uses linking words (and, when, but, that, so, etc.)	3/9							3/9				
Uses adjectives to describe information												
Conventions and Presentation												
Begins sentences with capital letters	3/4	3/4	3/4	3/4	3/4	3/4	3/4	3/4	3/4	3/4	3/4	3/4
Uses correct end punctuation		3/4	3/4			3/4			3/5			
Uses appropriate spelling	3/5					3/5				3/5		

This teacher uses her Ongoing Monitoring Sheet to record what students can do and to identify small groups and individuals for additional instruction.

thus, you do not need to teach—and what they don't know about a particular form and purpose. Analyze writers' work on the pre-assessment sample. The writing samples, evaluated against the unit's rubric, show what writers do and do not understand about the text type. This information scaffolds and supports planning of minilessons to specifically target learner needs, while providing a way to celebrate the understandings that writers bring to the unit of study. **Keep the Session 1 pre-assessment samples.** They provide a powerful and useful before-and-after comparison at the end of the unit.

Use the class Ongoing Monitoring Sheet (copy the full-size version from the Resources section at the back of this book or print a copy from the *Resources* CD-ROM) or a recording form of your own to record the results of your pre-assessment and keep track of the key skills and understandings students need to learn. Use whatever notation system works for you to monitor student performance and to identify what you need for whole-class and small-group instruction or for individual teaching conferences in order to assure understanding. Record pre-assessment observations on your Ongoing Monitoring Sheet and update it throughout the EWU as you collect and review student work. (If you want to keep a separate record of each student's understanding, use copies of the Individual Evaluation Record on the *Resources* CD-ROM and in the Resources section at the back of this book.)

At the conclusion of the unit, analyze each student's individual piece and use the Ongoing Monitoring Sheet or the Individual Evaluation Record to track individual growth. Use these results to inform future units.

With Every Power Write

The Assess the Learning feature of every Power Write lesson provides you with specific tips for looking at students' writing. You can make your assessment part of your observational notes as you circulate amongst writers, helping them during the Writing and Coaching part of your lessons. Or, you might use the tips either to establish the final step in children's daily writing or to guide Sharing and Reflecting.

During Sharing and Reflecting, Assess the Learning offers students a variety of self-assessment opportunities. Children may be asked to compare their writing to the model you created to be sure that their work includes all the features of the target text type. They may be invited to meet with a partner and identify the elements they are most proud of in their writing. In addition, each Power Write contains a self-assessment checklist designed for children. You'll note that this checklist reflects the precise features and understandings that are the focus of instruction. Read more about checklists under Self-Assessment on page xxxiv.

HOW SHOULD I ASSESS?

The ongoing assessment embedded in *Explorations* assumes that you'll want to collect and evaluate student writing often (**formative assessment** to inform your instructional plans), encourage children to look at and become constructive critics of their own writing (**self-assessment** to build writer confidence and independence), and that in the end you will want to have clear evidence that students are becoming more powerful and flexible writers (**summative assessment** to provide a record of growth).

Formative Assessment

Make it a point every day or two to look at writing or the research created by your students so you can assess understanding and decide if some writers need support through additional modeling, re-teaching, a writing conference, and so on. This kind of regular, informal review of work will quickly tell you if all students, or just a few, need additional support in implementing a nonfiction writing strategy. It will tell you what to bring up in the next one-on-one conference, with a small group needing special support, or in a whole-class focus lesson. As noted above, the Ongoing Monitoring Sheet is a convenient place to record and store your ongoing observations for both EWUs and Power Writes.

It is especially important to use what you find in children's writing as an opportunity to celebrate writer strength and see the positives in the work of each child. Even if you only take a few samples per afternoon from Power Writes or EWUs and review them to identify points of growth and learner need, you will be well-informed about the progress of your students and the steps you need to take in lifting them as nonfiction writers.

In addition, writing conferences during the Writing and Coaching part of each day are perfect forums for observing, evaluating, recording, and teaching. A clipboard loaded with your Ongoing Monitoring Sheet or a stack of sticky notes or some other convenient data collector of your choice on which to write notes about each child will set you up to make the most of your side-by-side talks with students. Your review of a child's writing the day before, your notes, or your Ongoing Monitoring Sheet may suggest what you want to examine. Alternatively, you may simply sit down and see what the writer is working on, seizing the moment to praise what he or she is already doing and to suggest one more step toward writing excellence. Consult the Focus on Conferring section in *A Guide to Teaching Nonfiction Writing, Grades K–2*, for tips on effective writing conferences.

Self-Assessment

We know that self-reflection and self-assessment are among the most powerful tools we utilize in education. There are many opportunities for student reflection and self-assessment built into *Explorations*.

▸ Sharing and Reflecting: In both Extended Writing Units and Power Writes, writers pause at the end of each day to consider their learning for the session. They self-assess the facts they gathered, the quality of the revisions they made, the kinds of edits they inserted into their work, or the quality of headings that were featured in their nonfiction writing, monitoring their growth as writers. To facilitate this kind of self-reflection, you will find a Student Self-Reflection Sheet for each writing purpose on the *Resources* CD-ROM.

▸ Self-Assessment Checklists: Every Power Write has a self-assessment checklist that you may elect to have students discuss, or fill out and save in their writing folder for ongoing reflection on personal growth. You may elect to read the checklist aloud and have children think about and discuss it, or you may have writers actually fill it out (a full-size copy is on the *Resources* CD-ROM) and save it in their writing folders for ongoing reflection on personal growth. The interactive nature of the self-assessment increases self-reflection and writers' observation of their own work.

SELF-ASSESSMENT

Informing with an Investigation

	YES	NO
1. Did you include facts about your topic?	☐	☐
2. Did you plan your space before you started to write?	☐	☐
3. Did you use features such as captions, headings, and text boxes?	☐	☐

Self-assessment checklists at the end of every Power Write highlight the key elements writers should be sure to include.

▸ Revising and Editing Checklists: These encourage writers to look critically at their own work. Choose from or adapt the collection of writing and editing checklists on the *Resources* CD-ROM.

Summative Assessment

As suggested in *A Guide to Teaching Nonfiction Writing, Grades K–2*, you will want to maintain a storage folder for children's writing as well as a folder for ongoing work. The storage folder can house the various compositions that result from Power Write lessons as well as final EWU projects. After a few months, writers (and their parents!) can glance through and see the array of different text types they have written, and, more important, you and the writer can look for evidence of growth. Is the child writing more in January than he did at the beginning of the school year? Is she trying more spellings and more features? Are mechanics becoming more conventional? Do later pieces look more "finished"—detailed, neat, illustrated—than earlier pieces, showing that the child has become engaged as a real writer? Document the changes. Comparing work from month to month should give you summative evidence of improvement.

If you have been sure to keep writers' pre-assessment writing samples from Session 1 of an Extended Writing Unit, you have the perfect vehicle for demonstrating growth. Look at the writer's pre-assessment sample and final writing side by side. Consult the Key Skills and Understandings rubric or the Ongoing Monitoring Sheet. What does the writer do now that he or she did not do before? How many elements on the rubric has the writer added to her or his repertoire? Has the writer moved from beginning to use a skill to developing it or from developing a skill to using it with confidence? If you need to give grades, rubrics and the writer's ongoing work will give you plenty of data to inform them.

There is one added benefit to before-and-after writing samples. When writers are presented with their writing from Session 1, the pre-assessment, and asked to compare this and their final writing with the "Features of a Great _____" chart that was built throughout the unit of study, children see for themselves how much they now know about the form of writing under study. The comparison of the writing pieces often results in astonishment for the writers but usually ends in joyful celebration as they recognize their own progress.

Grade 2
Overview of Learning Objectives

Inform

Extended Writing Unit: Report	Mechanics	Features of a Great Report
• Purpose (to inform) • Features • Using a R.A.N. chart • Choosing a topic • Recording prior knowledge • Using multiple sources • Researching • Drafting • Choosing information • Writing facts in your own words • Organizing information under appropriate headings • Adding illustrations with captions and labels that match the text • Rereading, checking for sense, and revising as needed • Making sure every part is correct • Table of contents • Cover	• *Using descriptive adjectives* • *Using linking words to join related ideas* • *Revising for sense* • *Correct spelling* • *Correct punctuation*	• A title tells us exactly what the report will be about. • The report gives us facts. • The report is organized in categories of information. • A table of contents helps readers find information. • The writer uses adjectives to describe things. • Some ideas are joined with linking words. • There are illustrations, captions, and labels that match the information.
Power Write: Friendly Letter to Summarize	• A friendly letter can summarize learning.	*Features of a Friendly Letter to Summarize* • Greeting • Body with topic and important details • Closing and signature
Power Write: Note to Invite	• Invitations are notes that tell readers about upcoming events.	*Features of a Note to Invite* • Greeting • Title of the event • Date, time, and location • Special instructions
Power Write: E-mail to Summarize	• An e-mail shares information with others using current technology.	*Features of an E-mail to Summarize* • Recipient(s) • Short, clear subject line • Greeting • Purpose and details • Closing and name
(VL) **Power Write:** Map	• A map visually represents a place on Earth. • Map symbols and key	*Features of a Map* • Shows how an area would look if viewed from above • Title, symbols, and key • Clearly marked roads/routes

Power Write: Readers Theater	• A Readers Theater piece can convey information in the form of a script. • Colons	*Features of Readers Theater* • Title • Facts about a topic • Script format with speakers' names followed by colons • Parts for "all" and "some"
Power Write: Biography	• A biography tells the facts of a real person's life. • Third-person point of view	*Features of Biography* • Factual information • Third-person point of view (Uses *he* or *she*) • Presents a few highlights of a person's life
VL **Power Write:** Venn Diagram	• Venn diagrams allow you to compare and contrast two subjects.	*Features of a Venn Diagram* • Title • Headings • Two overlapping circles • Facts about each category
Power Write: Class Newsletter	• A class newsletter shares information and informs readers.	*Features of a Class Newsletter* • Title and headlines • Columns • Important information and interesting facts
Power Write: Informational Poem	• Poems can teach about content while using descriptive language.	*Features of an Informational Poem* • Title • Factual information • Descriptive words • Words in lines instead of paragraphs
VL **Power Write:** Investigation	• Investigations use special text features to give information about topics. • Two-page spread	*Features of an Investigation* • Focused topic with facts • Two facing pages that form a "spread" • Visual supports: title, headings, labels, and diagrams • Text boxes

Instruct

Extended Writing Unit: Procedural Text • Purpose (to instruct) • Features • Choosing a topic • Title and materials list • Steps • Action words • Time order • Using numbered steps or time-order words • Using direction words • Adding illustrations that match each step and help readers understand	*Mechanics* • *Action words* • *Time-order words* • *Direction words* • *Numbering steps* • *Byline* • *Handwriting* • *Punctuation*	*Features of a Great Procedural Text* • It lists the things you need. • There is a title that tells what it's about. • It uses descriptive words to make the directions clear. • Pictures help readers understand. • The numbered steps are in order. • Each step starts with a verb. • Illustrations match each step.

Power Write: Procedural Letter	• A friendly letter can provide a procedure for making or doing something. • Time-order words	*Features of a Procedural Letter* • Greeting • Body with words that show time order (*first, next, then, finally*) • Steps to complete a project • Closing and signature
Power Write: How-To List	• A procedural list gives readers step-by-step instructions for completing a task. • Action verbs	*Features of a How-To List* • Title • Numbered steps • Short sentences with action verbs
Power Write: Art Project Directions	• Directions can include illustrated steps for completing an art project.	*Features of Art Project Directions* • Title • Materials list • Numbered steps • Steps that start with verbs
Power Write: Recipe	• A recipe gives readers instructions for cooking or making food.	*Features of a Recipe* • Title • Ingredient list • Numbered steps describing a process • Short phrases using action verbs
VL Power Write: Cross-Section Diagram	• A procedural text can explain how to create a diagram. • Create a cross-section diagram. • Write instructions for creating a cross-section diagram.	*Features of a Cross-Section Diagram with Instructions* • Sketch of the interior of an object • Labels and lines to identify parts • Numbered instructions for creating a diagram
VL Power Write: Column Graph	• A column graph allows readers to compare data. • Create a column graph. • Record the procedure for creating a column graph.	*Features of a Column Graph* • Title • Labels for items and numbers • Rows of sticky notes that form columns
VL Power Write: Investigation	• A visual investigation combines words and pictures to give instructions for making or doing something. • Two-page spread • Text features	*Features of an Investigation* • Title • Two facing pages that form a "spread" • Visual supports: title, headings, and diagrams • Numbered steps and sequence words

Narrate

Extended Writing Unit: Personal Narrative • Purpose (to tell about a real event in the life of the author) • Features • Using the first person • Sequence • Beginning, middle, end • Using powerful adjectives that describe feelings • Ending that focuses on feelings when the event was over • Adding illustrations that enhance the narrative • Title • Cover	*Mechanics* • *Powerful adjectives* • *Feeling words* • *Spelling strategies* • *Complete sentences* • *Punctuation*	*Features of a Great Personal Narrative* • It includes a title. • It tells events in the order they happened. • It has a beginning, middle, and end. • It is told using the word *I*. • It tells how the writer felt. • It tells why the moment was important. • It has a strong ending.
Extended Writing Unit: Biography • Purpose (to tell about a real person's life) • Features • Using the third person • Heroes and heroism • Sequence • Researching to find information • Drafting • Using time-order words • Using interesting words and details • Adding illustrations that support the text • Finishing touches	*Mechanics* • *Time-order words* • *Third-person pronouns* • *Revising for missing words or details* • *Spelling* • *Handwriting*	*Features of a Great Biography of a Hero* • It tells events from the person's life. • It includes interesting facts about the person. • It describes successes and failures. • It shows how the person is a hero. • It tells about the person over time. • It uses third-person point of view. • It tells facts in time order.
Power Write: Personal Narrative	• A personal narrative captures the action, setting, and feelings of a specific moment in time. • First-person pronouns	*Features of a Personal Narrative* • Focus on small event or part of event • Description of feelings and the setting • First-person point of view
Power Write: Retell from a Different Point of View	• A change of point of view allows a retelling from a different perspective.	*Features of a Retell from a Different Point of View* • Title • First-person point of view • Beginning, middle, and ending • Descriptive details
Power Write: Nonfiction Narrative	• Nonfiction narrative often provides factual information through beautifully crafted text. • Descriptive phrases	*Features of Nonfiction Narrative* • Factual information • Descriptive language • Visual images
Power Write: Eyewitness Account	• An eyewitness account is a newspaper-style story of events witnessed firsthand. • Details • Headline	*Features of an Eyewitness Account* • Summarizing headline • Beginning, middle, and end • Details about the event

Power Write: Factual Recount		Features of a Factual Recount
	• A factual recount uses words and sketches or photographs to retell facts about an experience. • Sequence words and phrases • Specific verbs	• Retelling of events with description • Time-order words • Supporting sketches
VL Power Write: Timeline		Features of a Timeline
	• A timeline is a visual way to retell events or show a sequence of events. • Labels and sketches	• Title • Horizontal line with tick marks • Events in sequential order • Captions and/or illustrations
VL Power Write: Investigation		Features of an Investigation
	• A visual investigation combines text and features such as illustrations to present a narrative. • Two-page layout • Adding color	• Title • Two facing pages that form a "spread" • Features such as text boxes, subheadings, and captions • Retelling of a narrative

Persuade

Extended Writing Unit: Travel Brochure	Mechanics	Features of a Travel Brochure
• Purpose (to persuade) • Features • Researching to find and check facts • Drafting • Using descriptive words and persuasive language • Revising and editing facts • Adding illustrations to match each category of information • Revising for clarity and sense • Persuasive openings • Strong closings	*• Persuasive words* *• Matching illustrations to text* *• Capitalization of place names* *• Spelling*	• It includes the name of the place. • It captures your attention with a catchy opening sentence. • It has a powerful ending. • It is organized into chunks or categories of text. • It uses descriptive words that help persuade.
Power Write: Written Argument		Features of a Written Argument
	• A written argument uses opinions and facts to persuade readers to take action. • Strong opening • Strong conclusion	• Strong opening argument that tells your opinion • Reasons that support the argument • Inspiring conclusion that repeats your opinion
Power Write: Persuasive E-mail		Features of a Persuasive E-mail
	• An e-mail can persuade readers with a strong argument and reasons.	• Subject line • Friendly greeting • Opinion or request with supporting reasons • Persuasive ending • Closing and signature
Power Write: Friendly Letter		Features of a Friendly Letter
	• A friendly letter can persuade readers with an argument and supporting reasons. • Strong opening and closing	• Greeting, body, closing, and signature • Persuasive argument • Reasons to support the argument

Power Write: Book Review	• A book review persuades readers with convincing reasons to read a certain book. • Rating a book	*Features of a Book Review* • Title and author • Star rating that shows the writer's opinion • Reasons that support the star rating • Persuasive language
VL **Power Write:** Persuasive Flyer	• A flyer can persuade others by stating an opinion and giving strong reasons for it.	*Features of a Persuasive Flyer* • Single page • Attention-getting opinion statement • Eye-catching art • Reasons to support the opinion • Inspiring conclusion
VL **Power Write:** Graphic Organizer	• A graphic organizer shows both an opinion and reasons to support it.	*Features of a Graphic Organizer* • Title • Boxes and connecting lines • Persuasive argument with reasons
VL **Power Write:** Investigation	• An investigation combines convincing words and supporting pictures in a powerful layout. • Persuasive message • Two-page spread • Text features	*Features of an Investigation* • Headings and text boxes • Two facing pages form a "spread" • Labels and captions

Respond

Extended Writing Unit: Response Poster • Purpose (to respond to a book) • Features • What the writer likes and does not like about the book • Connections the writer made with the book • Strong endings that summarize thoughts and feelings • Adding illustrations that match text • Poster design	*Mechanics* • *Using linking words* • *Using powerful adjectives* • *Editing techniques* • *Proper use of conventions*	*Features of a Great Response* • It includes the title and author. • It tells what the writer likes about the book. • It may tell what the writer dislikes about the book. • It may tell connections that the writer made to the book. • It has an ending that summarizes what the writer thought of the book.
Power Write: Response to a Poem	• A poetry response reveals reactions, opinions, connections, and questions. • Provide evidence to support thoughts.	*Features of a Response to a Poem* • Title and author • Reactions, opinions, and connections with support • Questions
VL **Power Write:** Fact/Opinion Chart	• A good response can include both facts and opinions about a topic.	*Features of a Fact/Opinion Chart* • Detailed statement of fact • Detailed statement of opinion • Supportive illustrations
Power Write: Two-Word Strategy	• Choosing two important words can help us focus our thinking as we respond to text. • Craft sentences to reveal thinking. • Underline focus words.	*Features of the Two-Word Strategy* • Two words at the top of a piece of paper • Focus words used in sentences

Power Write: Friendly Letter	• A friendly letter is one way to respond to a text or to an author's work. • Provide evidence to support your thoughts.	*Features of a Friendly Letter* • Greeting • Body with reactions, opinions, and connections • Closing with signature
Power Write: Information Equation	• Math symbols can connect ideas about a topic and reveal deeper understanding. • Respond to a writing stem.	*Features of an Information Equation* • Words or phrases • Math symbols • Relationships between ideas and concepts • Writing stem: *This is important because* _____.
VL **Power Write:** Sketch to Stretch	• A simple sketch with labels on it captures thinking about a topic. • Important facts and ideas	*Features of a Sketch to Stretch* • Simple one-color sketches • Labels • Facts about a topic
Power Write: Fact-and-Response Grid	• A fact-and-response grid captures responses based on prompts. • Focus on a single fact. • Respond to stems: *I wonder… I think… I feel… I'd like to know…*	*Features of a Fact-and-Response Grid* • Single fact about content • Sentence stems to launch responses about the topic
VL **Power Write:** Investigation	• A visual investigation combines words and pictures to capture a response to a text. • Opinions with supporting facts and details • Two-page spread • Text features	*Features of an Investigation* • Two facing pages that form a "spread" • Text features such as text boxes, headings, illustrations, and boldfaced words • Opinions as well as facts

Informational Writing Projects

Informational texts describe and classify our world. Their purpose is to describe a place, thing, or group of things, rather than to retell a happening or series of events. Often, informational texts give details about such topics as animals, space, plants, weather, geographical features, machines, places, industries, housing, and medicine. Students are most likely to encounter informational text in the form of nonfiction books and reports, but informational text may appear in many formats, including signs, posters, charts, lists, notes, and informational poetry. Informational text often includes illustrations.

CONTENTS

EXTENDED WRITING UNIT

▸ Class Project: Report About the Rain Forest (about 10 days)

▸ Individual Project: Report About Another Habitat (about 10 days)

POWER WRITES

▸ Friendly Letter to Summarize

▸ Note to Invite

▸ E-mail to Summarize

▸ Map

▸ Readers Theater

▸ Biography

▸ Venn Diagram

▸ Class Newsletter

▸ Informational Poem

▸ Investigation

The Big Picture:
Class and Individual Projects

. . . .

During the *class project*, students work together to create a collaborative report about the rain forest. The mentor text "The Sonoran Desert" provides a model of the structure and features of a report. Note that the mentor text is about the desert, not the rain forest. This is to ensure that students will actively research to discover their own information and not just copy the mentor text directly. Students begin by observing features of the mentor text and then use a class Reading and Analyzing Nonfiction (R.A.N.) chart (Figure 1.1) and their research notebooks (Figure 1.2) to gather and organize information about the rain forest. From their notes, students write and illustrate pages for the report. They revise, edit, and publish the report as a class book with a cover, table of contents, and heading pages. They read the report collaboratively, share it with another class, and reflect on what they have learned about report writing.

During their *individual project*, students review the features of a report, choose a topic, and plan, draft, revise, edit, and publish a report—complete with a title, table of contents, headings, and illustrations that match the text. They share their reports with a partner to check for sense and reflect on what they have learned.

	CLASS PROJECT		
Session	**Focused Minilesson**	**Writing and Coaching**	**Sharing and Reflecting**
1	Introduce informational text; choose topics	Draft pre-assessment informational text	What is a report? How is it different from telling a story?
2	Study "The Sonoran Desert"; list features; set up R.A.N. chart title and categories	Record prior knowledge on first page of research notebook, "What I Think I Know"; put favorite idea on a sticky note and place on R.A.N. chart	What prior knowledge did we put on the chart? What is important to include when we write a report?
3	Study "The Sonoran Desert"; use table of contents; tour research stations; discuss research notebook categories	Conduct research; record information in notebooks; choose facts to place on R.A.N. chart	What did you add to the chart? Did we learn anything that confirmed what we thought? Is any information repeated?
4	Study "The Sonoran Desert"; use your own words to state facts; look for misconceptions and move on R.A.N. chart	Continue researching and drafting notes; use your own words to record information; add to R.A.N. chart	What did you add to the R.A.N. chart? Is there information we should move? Using your own words helps you remember what you learn.
5	Study "The Sonoran Desert"; learn about using adjectives to describe information; record wonderings on R.A.N. chart	Continue researching and drafting notes; use adjectives to describe nouns; add to R.A.N. chart	What information did you collect? Share an adjective you used. What wonderings do you have? Is there information we should move or discard?
6	Study "The Sonoran Desert"; learn about linking words (*and, when, but, that, so,* etc.)	Continue researching and drafting notes; add to R.A.N. chart; join facts with linking words	What facts did you add? What linking words did you use? Did you answer any wonderings? Is there information we should move or discard?
7	Study "The Sonoran Desert"; learn about using adjectives and linking words; learn not to use prior thinking unless confirmed	Revise information from the "Yes, We Were Right" and "New Learning" columns; use linking words and adjectives	What did you change? How did you make the writing better?
8	Study "The Sonoran Desert"; learn to check spelling and punctuation before publishing	Edit information revised in previous session	Share edits with a partner. Point out good examples of changes (capital letters, periods, correct spelling).
9	Study "The Sonoran Desert"; focus on illustrations, captions, and labels that match text	Publish pages; illustrate; publish cover, table of contents, heading pages, dedication page	Share pages. Point out favorite things. Collate and bind pages in order.
10	Read finished report; make connections with features chart	Read contributions; celebrate, reflect on what was learned	Share with another class and hold a discussion.

		INDIVIDUAL PROJECT	
Session	Focused Minilesson	Writing and Coaching	Sharing and Reflecting
11	Review features of informational text; see how research notebook is organized; select a topic	Write title on cover; record background knowledge on sticky notes in research notebook	Share with a partner. What prior knowledge do you have?
12	Learn about selecting and recording interesting details	Research and record information in categories; include important and interesting details	What interesting facts did you find? What was confirmed? Share misconceptions, wonderings, answers.
13	Learn to write information in your own words	Continue researching, drafting, revising; write information in your own words	What did you write in your own words? What was confirmed? Share misconceptions, wonderings, answers.
14	Learn to use adjectives to describe information	Continue researching, drafting, revising; use adjectives	Where did you use a great adjective? How did it help your writing? What was confirmed? Share misconceptions, wonderings, answers.
15	Learn to reread and revise	Continue researching, drafting, revising	What did you revise? What was confirmed? Share misconceptions, wonderings, answers.
16	Learn how to edit and use basic proofreaders' marks	Edit for clarity, spelling, punctuation	What edits did you make?
17	Learn to organize, create headings, and publish writing	Begin publishing; use headings	Share a heading you wrote. What information is in that section?
18	Learn to add illustrations, labels, and captions that match text	Continue publishing; use headings; add illustrations, labels, and captions	Share an illustration. How does it help your reader?
19	Learn to design a cover and table of contents	Create a cover and table of contents	Share your cover and table of contents. What does your cover tell readers?
20	Share, celebrate, and display publications	Compare published report with features chart and report from Session 1	How did you improve as a writer? What have you learned about writing a report?

Other Topics and Forms for Informational Writing

Although this model project uses the topic of habitats as a springboard for teaching report writing, the teaching process here can be adapted to many other informational topics and forms. The Power Writes in this section will give you ideas for several such adaptations in addition to those that follow.

Possible Topics

Topics may correlate with content in your science and social studies standards, current events, or class interests.

Science	Social Studies
Insects	Homes
Birds	Our school
Reptiles	Our community
Space	Our country
Earth	Our flag
Plants	Jobs
Trees	Sports
Deserts	The city
Oceans	Farms
Sand	Clothing
Rocks	Food
Sharks	Cultures
Machines	Heroes
Weather	Transportation
Matter and energy	Buildings
Forces and motion	

Possible Forms

Some of these forms are invariably informational (like reports), while others (like notes or poems) can be used for a variety of purposes, including giving information.

Reports	Flow charts
General descriptions (such as planets)	Cause-and-effect charts
Specific descriptions (such as Mars)	Posters
Signs	Newspaper reports
Notes	Magazine articles
Letters	Documentaries
Lists	Diagrams
Explanations	Illustrations
Tables	Poems

Constructing a Reading and Analyzing Nonfiction (R.A.N.) Chart

To prepare for the *class project*, you will need to construct a class R.A.N. chart. Be sure to make it big enough for students to place sticky notes within its sections. Figure 1.1 gives an overview of this chart. Please refer to page xiv in the introduction to this book and page 295 in the Resources section at the end for additional information on constructing and using a class R.A.N. chart. Categories selected by your class may not be identical to those in Figure 1.1.

Figure 1.1: Class R.A.N. Chart for Rain Forests

THE AMAZING AWESOME RAIN FOREST					
HEADINGS → CATEGORIES ↓	What we think we know	Yes, we were right or Confirmed information ✔	We don't think this anymore or Misconceptions 💡	New learning ✖	Wonderings ?
Location	Students state information they think to be correct about the topic	Students research to confirm prior knowledge	Students research to locate additional information not stated in prior knowledge	Students research to discard prior knowledge	Students raise questions based on the new information gathered
Climate					
Animals					
Plants					
Interesting Facts					

Setting Up Your Research Stations

In Sessions 3–6, students will be investigating at research stations and adding information to the class R.A.N. chart. To set up the research stations for the *class project*, you will need to gather books, magazine articles, encyclopedia entries, and websites that feature information about the rain forest—enough material that the whole class can research and take notes simultaneously. Make sure the research materials you gather include close-up photographs of rain forest animals and plants. Try to include books on tape or CD, video clips, and models of rain forest animals and plants. If possible, bring in live specimens of rain forest animals or plants for students to observe. You will need to divide students into groups and have each group visit a different station each day. If you have more than four stations, make adjustments to the number of groups. You may also adjust the number of days allocated for research if you so desire. You may wish to set up a task management board that lists the names of each station and on what days each student will be going there to research.

For the *individual project*, gather similar materials on four habitats of interest to your students. If possible, provide live specimens of animals and plants for students to observe.

Please refer to page xiii in the introduction and page 285 in the Resources section for additional information on setting up and using research stations.

Preparing Research Notebooks

When students are at each research station they will be working collaboratively to find and record information in their research notebooks. A research notebook is simply a collection of pages with a cover. The first page is where students record their background knowledge about the topic. Label the other pages for the categories of information they will research. For the *class project*, set up the research notebooks as shown in Figure 1.2.

Figure 1.2: Sample Research Notebook for the *Class Project*

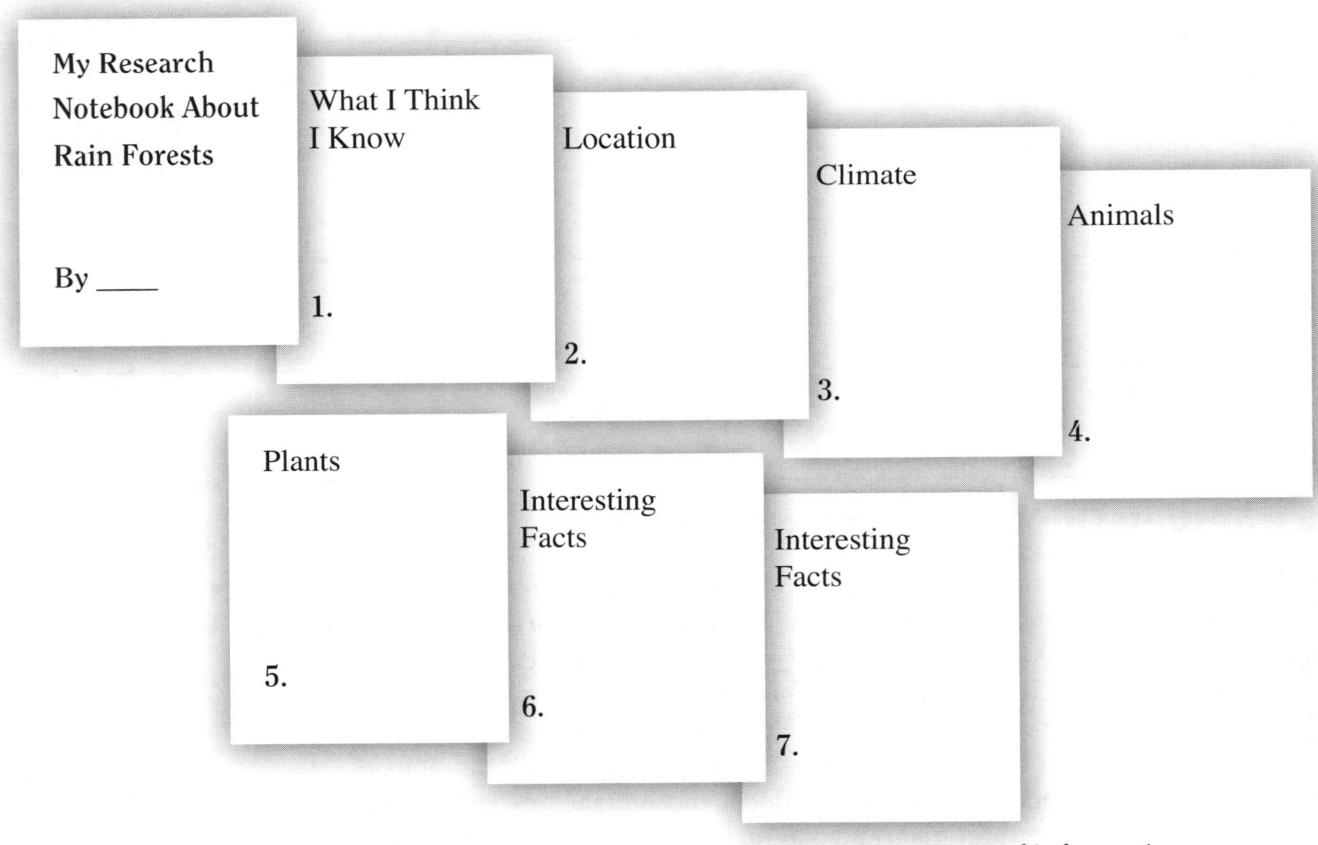

My Research Notebook About Rain Forests

By ____

What I Think I Know

1.

Location

2.

Climate

3.

Animals

4.

Plants

5.

Interesting Facts

6.

Interesting Facts

7.

Note: You may wish to provide two pages for each category of information students will research.

For the *individual project*, give students research notebooks similar to those for the class report but specific to the topic they are exploring, and add pages for "Misconceptions" and "Wonderings," as seen in Figure 1.3.

Figure 1.3: Sample Research Notebook for the *Individual Project*

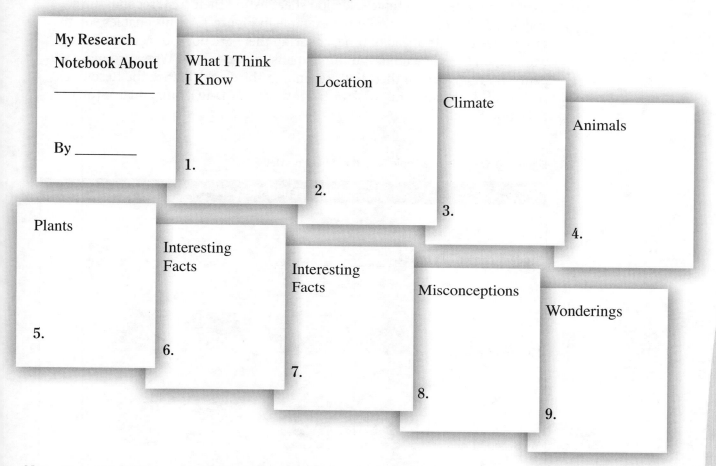

Note: You may wish to provide two pages for each category of information students will research.

Selecting Topics for the Individual Projects

Prior to the individual project, pre-select four or five habitats about which the students can write. Narrowing the choices will allow you to gather resources ahead of time. Have students select the habitat they wish to research. You may want them to fill out a topic selection sheet listing their first, second, third, and fourth choice as shown in the example in Figure 1.4. This enables you to group the students ahead of time, ensuring there are not too many students working on the same topic and thus exhausting resources. When grouping students, try to give them their first, second, or third choice. (See the Resources section at the back of this book or the *Resources* CD-ROM for a blank Topic Selection Sheet.)

Figure 1.4 Example of a Topic Selection Sheet on Habitats

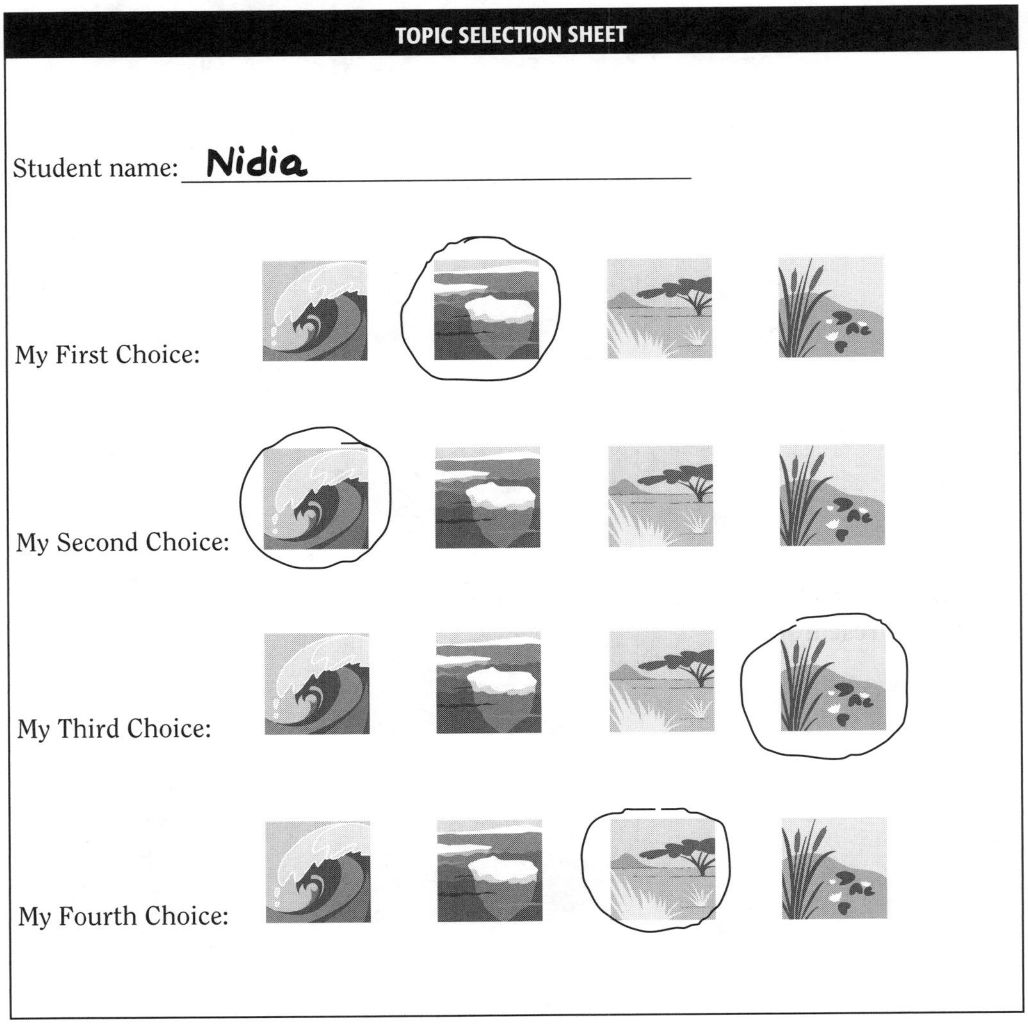

TOPIC SELECTION SHEET

Student name: Nidia

My First Choice:

My Second Choice:

My Third Choice:

My Fourth Choice:

Focusing on Standards

This extended writing unit is designed to teach students about the form and content of informational writing as they apply basic writing strategies. Each of the lessons provides you with suggested demonstrations, but you may wish to tailor your instruction based on the common needs of your own students. The pre-assessment from Session 1 will help you identify these needs.

Before introducing this unit, carefully review the list below so you can keep the lesson objectives in mind as you teach, coach, and monitor students' growth as writers of informational texts.

KEY SKILLS AND UNDERSTANDINGS: INFORMATIONAL TEXTS GRADE 2
Purpose
• Understands the purpose for writing an informational piece
Ideas/Research
• Reflects research and planning
• Bases writing on research and prior knowledge
• Includes facts and details from research
• Gathers and incorporates information from multiple sources
Organization/Text Features
• Includes a title that tells what the piece is about
• Provides a table of contents
• Presents categories of information with headings
• Includes labeled illustrations that support the text
Language/Style
• Puts information in her or his own words
• Uses linking words (*and, when, but, that, so,* etc.)
• Uses adjectives to describe information
Conventions and Presentation
• Begins sentences with capital letters
• Ends sentences with periods
• Uses appropriate spelling

The list is the basis for both the Individual Evaluation Record and the Ongoing Monitoring Sheet shown in Figure 1.5. (Both forms can be found in the Resources section at the back of this book and also on the *Resources* CD-ROM.) Use the Individual Evaluation Form if you want to keep separate records on individual students. The Ongoing Monitoring Sheet gives you a simple mechanism for recording information on all your students as you move around the class, evaluating their work in progress. Use this information to adapt instruction and session length as needed.

Figure 1.5 Individual Evaluation Record and Ongoing Monitoring Sheet

You will also use the Ongoing Monitoring Sheet and/or the Individual Evaluation Record at the end of the unit to record students' growth as writers after comparing their published work from the individual project with the pre-assessment they will complete in Session 1 of the class project.

Planning and Facilitating the Unit

Students will need preparation, coaching, prompting, and support as they move through this extended writing unit. Use the following tips and strategies as needed to ensure each child's success.

Before the Unit:

▸ Each session in this unit is designed to be completed in a day, but you may find that your students need more time. Take the time you need to adequately respond to the unique needs of your students.

▸ Begin building background knowledge about informational texts in general as well as the rain forest (or your class topic) at least a week in advance. Shared reading, guided reading, and read-aloud experiences as well as group discussions will ensure that students are not dependent exclusively on their own research.

▸ As you share informational texts with students, be sure to highlight the title and purpose of the text, categories of information, tables of contents, headings, and illustrations that match the words.

During the Class Project:

‣ Begin each session with a focused minilesson to demonstrate traits in informational writing. The mentor text "The Sonoran Desert" acts as the model to show students the structure and features of a report. You may wish to use other mentor texts to assist you with your demonstrations.

‣ Be sure to model note taking for students as you think aloud about information in reference materials. Use sticky notes to capture your notes about the rain forest. Display the class R.A.N. chart prominently as students work independently in research stations.

‣ As students work independently on their writing and illustrations, note those who are struggling and bring them together in small groups for think-alouds. Show them how you choose what to include, write information in your own words, use adjectives to describe information, and use linking words to join ideas. Talk about and model how you illustrate facts and details. Show how you check sentences for capital letters and periods. If necessary, scribe from students' dictation so they can copy sentences that are written correctly.

‣ Students who seem very confident and who have clearly grasped all of the concepts taught so far can be brought together in a small group to extend their understanding to more challenging work, such as creating a word bank of linking words along with example sentences modeling correct usage.

‣ Students who complete their pages early can work on publishing the cover, table of contents, heading pages, or a dedication page for the class book. They can be research and writing partners for students who are crafting their pages.

‣ Although the lessons provide suggested demonstrations for each session, you may wish to tailor your instruction to meet the common needs of your students. The Ongoing Monitoring Sheet, together with the Individual Evaluation Record, will help you keep track of each student's unique needs. Refer to the section on assessment and ongoing monitoring on pages xxx–xxxv in the introduction to this book for further information.

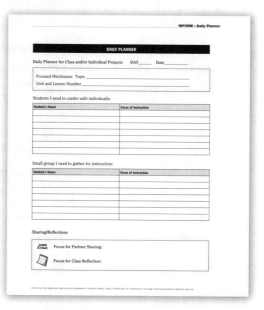

‣ Use the Daily Planner (Figure 1.6, and found on the *Resources* CD-ROM) to plan your own class projects for future explorations based on the needs of your students.

Figure 1.6 Daily Planner

During the Individual Project:

▶ Continue to use the Ongoing Monitoring Sheet and the Individual Evaluation Record to identify topics you'll want to address in the focused minilesson that begins each session. Continue to use the Daily Planner to lay out future explorations based on student needs.

▶ Display the class R.A.N. chart prominently so students can refer to it as they plan their reports and take notes in their research notebooks.

▶ Have students select a habitat (or other topic) from a small number of choices for which you can provide plenty of information at research stations.

▶ Help students identify categories of information to research. If students get stuck, suggest categories such as location, climate, animals, plants, and interesting facts.

▶ Have students record their background knowledge in their research notebooks. As they research, remind them to check their "What I Think I Know" page and move confirmed facts to other pages.

▶ Encourage students to use both background knowledge and new information as they plan their writing and illustrating.

▶ Remind writers to put information in their own words and to use adjectives and linking words. Remind them to discard repeated ideas as they reread their notes.

▶ Some students will benefit from talking about the facts and details to a partner before writing them.

▶ Provide templates for students who need extra support when writing their reports. Include spaces for the title, table of contents, and headings for each page or category of information. Include space for illustrations.

▶ Remind your insecure illustrators that this is not an art project and they will not be graded on the quality of their drawing. Emphasize that stick figures and simple line drawings are perfectly adequate; the important thing is that the drawings reflect and clarify what is written.

▶ Encourage students to label their drawings if time allows. This may be especially helpful to English language learners.

▶ Have writing partners conference with each other often in order to check one another's work for sense and clarity.

▶ You may find it helpful to work on your own informational text along with your students. Then you can use this model as an example during think-alouds.

After the Unit:

▸ Be sure to give students opportunities to share and celebrate their individual writing projects.

▸ Distribute copies of the Student Self-Reflection Sheet (on the *Resources* CD-ROM). Students will benefit greatly from the chance to reflect on their progress during the unit and to hear their classmates' feedback.

▸ Compare students' final writing products with their pre-assessments to evaluate their growth as writers of informational text.

▸ Look at common needs of the class and address these when planning future explorations on informational writing, or through the Power Writes.

▸ Reflect on the strengths and challenges of implementing this series of lessons. How might it be adjusted to maximize student learning?

SESSION 1
Immersion and Pre-Assessment

Students are introduced to informational text and draft simple reports for the pre-assessment.

MATERIALS
• Books and pictures of different habitats
• Paper and pencils

TIP Prepare a content word wall about habitats with matching pictures. This will assist students in spelling words when they draft their information.

FOCUSED MINILESSON *(prewriting)*
15 MINUTES

■ Introduce the unit: *During the next few weeks we are going to work on a type of nonfiction writing that you probably already know something about. We're going to research and write a class report. A report gives detailed information about a specific topic. A report could be about a famous city, a favorite animal, an important invention, or just about anything else you can think of.*

TURN &TALK *How do you think a report is different from a fictional story?*

■ Lead students to the understanding that a report always contains real facts about a chosen topic, while a fictional story is made up and not true.

■ Spark students' interest in the topic they will report on by showing them books and pictures of various habitats.

TURN &TALK *What things do you see in these pictures that are similar? What things are different?*

■ Discuss the definition of a habitat: *Writers, these books and pictures are about different* habitats. *A habitat is an area of the world that has unique features, such as temperature, light, water, animals, and plants. We can use this information to write a report about a habitat.*

TURN &TALK *What habitat could you write about in a report? Tell your partner the name of the habitat and something you know about it.*

■ Encourage a few students to share what they know about habitats. *Writers, you all have great information to share! The facts you know about habitats would make some fascinating reports.*

WRITING and COACHING *(drafting)*
20 MINUTES

■ Ask students to choose a habitat and write about it in a brief report. They should choose a habitat they already know well because there will not be time to do any research for the pre-assessment. The habitat can be a place as familiar as a backyard garden.

■ Remind students that this is just a first try. The main goal at this point is to get ideas down on paper. Students will have the chance to learn more about report writing and can return to their drafts another time.

■ As you circulate around the room, you can keep students focused on their chosen habitats, but try not to provide too much direct support with report writing at this time. That will come in subsequent sessions.

SHARING and REFLECTING
15 MINUTES

TURN &TALK *Show your partner what you wrote. Talk about the information you included.*

■ *Your writing has great ideas! What information in your partner's report did you find the most interesting?*

TURN &TALK *Partners, think together. If someone asked you, "What is a report?" what would you say? How is a report different from a fictional story?*

■ Sum up the purpose of a report. A report tells others information, or facts and details, about a topic. The information is true.

■ Preview the upcoming sessions: *Over the next few days we will write a class report about one of my favorite habitats—the rain forest. We can even make a class book about the rain forest and give it to the librarian to put in the library for other students to read.*

■ After class, evaluate each student's writing using the Ongoing Monitoring Sheet (in the Resources section at the back of this book and also on the *Resources* CD-ROM). Use the results to revise instruction and personalize the lessons in this unit. If you want to keep individual records on students, use the Individual Evaluation Record found on the *Resources* CD-ROM. Please see page xxx of the introduction to this book for more information on the role of pre-assessment.

TIP By second grade, most students should understand the difference between fiction and nonfiction, but a few students may not yet have grasped this difference. If needed, provide additional practice by presenting a mixture of fiction and nonfiction books. Have students categorize the books. For a few titles, have students explain why each is fiction or nonfiction.

SESSION 2
Introduction to the R.A.N. Chart

Students begin to explore the features of a great report and record prior knowledge about rain forests on the class R.A.N. chart.

MATERIALS
- *Big Book of Mentor Texts:* "The Sonoran Desert," pages 2–9
- Chart paper and marker
- Research notebooks or paper
- Whole-class R.A.N. chart (Refer to page 297.)
- Sticky notes and pencils

FOCUSED MINILESSON *(prewriting)*
15 MINUTES

- Before class, you will need to create a whole-class Reading and Analyzing Nonfiction (R.A.N.) chart as discussed on page 297.

- Introduce the topic and the mentor text: *Today we will begin writing our reports. A report is a special kind of writing with unique features. We'll take a look at a report so that we have an idea of its features before we write our class report on rain forests.*

- Show students the cover page of the mentor text and point out the title: *What do you notice about the title? That's a great observation! The title tells readers exactly what the report is about.*

- Point out the table of contents and the headings in the mentor text.

TURN &TALK *Think together, partners. What do you notice about how the information in this report is organized?*

- Add the features you discuss with students to a class features chart and hang it for students' reference.

  - Work with students to develop a title for the whole-class report: *Let's see if we can develop the first feature for our report. Our report is going to be about the rain forest. We need a title for our report.* Elicit students' ideas: *Good idea! We'll call it "The Amazing Awesome Rain Forest."* Write the chosen title at the top of the R.A.N. chart.

  - Discuss the categories of information for the class report: *See how we listed that the information in a report is arranged in categories? That organization helps readers. We want our report to be organized in categories, too. As we do our research, we are going to put our information in categories to make it easier for us to write our report.* Show students how the R.A.N. chart is organized in categories, such as "Location," "Climate," "Animals," "Plants," and "Interesting Facts."

Features of a Great Report

A title tells us exactly what the report will be about.

The report gives us facts.

The report is organized in categories of information.

- Tell students what they will be working on in the rest of this session: *Today we're going to write what we think we know about the rain forest. I use the words "think we know" because sometimes we find out later that our information wasn't quite correct. We'll be able to research to double-check that our facts are right. We will also be able to gather lots of new facts from our research that we can put in our class report.*

WRITING and COACHING *(prewriting)*
20 MINUTES

- Have students record their prior knowledge on the first page of their research notebooks. Then have each student select one favorite fact and write it on a sticky note. Have students place their sticky notes on the class R.A.N. chart under the correct category: "What We Think We Know."

- Provide support for students who struggle with placing their information in the correct category: *Anna, I can see you wrote that you think the rain forest has butterflies. Where will you put this on the R.A.N. chart? That's right—under "What We Think We Know," next to "Animals."*

TIP Remember that it is acceptable for students to write incorrect information, as this is their background knowledge, or what they think they know. They will be able to modify or discard this information as they research.

SHARING and REFLECTING
10 MINUTES

TURN &TALK *Tell your partner about the one piece of information you wrote on your sticky note and placed on the R.A.N. chart.*

- With students' assistance, look at all the information on the class R.A.N. chart to make sure it has been put in the correct category.

- Wrap up by summarizing the features of a report from the chart.

TURN &TALK *Tell your partner what you think is important to include when we write a report.*

- *I heard you mention great features of a report! A report includes facts, and it's organized so that readers have easy access to information. You've listed some great background knowledge about rain forests. In our next session, we'll start researching to confirm that what we think we know about the rain forest is actually correct.*

SESSION 3
Using Multiple Sources

Students use a number of research sources to check their prior knowledge and locate new information for the class report.

MATERIALS
- *Big Book of Mentor Texts:* "The Sonoran Desert," pages 2–9
- Features chart from Session 2
- Research stations
- Research notebooks or paper
- Whole-class R.A.N. chart
- Sticky notes and pencils

FOCUSED MINILESSON *(prewriting)*
20 MINUTES

■ Review the learning from Session 2, and introduce the focus of today's lesson: *During our last session, we put information we thought we knew about the rain forest on our class R.A.N. chart. Today let's find out more! When we discover that the things we thought we knew actually are correct we can move our sticky notes to a new category: "Yes, We Were Right." We will also add any new information we find to the chart under the heading "New Learning."*

■ Model how to use a table of contents as a research tool. *I am especially interested in finding out what plants live in the Sonoran Desert. Watch as I use the table of contents in the mentor text. Notice that the writer has listed topics in the report. Each topic has a page number. Scanning the list, I see that information about plants begins on page 7. The table of contents helps readers find precisely what they need in the report. That's a great feature of a report! Let's add it to our chart.*

■ "Tour" the research stations and demonstrate how to locate information in each one. It may be necessary to have a separate session to achieve this. See page 285 in the Resources section at the back of this book for more information on research stations.

> **Features of a Great Report**
>
> A title tells us exactly what the report will be about.
>
> The report gives us facts.
>
> The report is organized in categories of information.
>
> A table of contents helps readers find information.

- Point out that the research notebooks are organized into categories: *As you take notes, it helps to have your notebook organized into categories. Let me show you how I have organized your notebooks. I made a page for each of the categories on our R.A.N. chart and two for "Interesting Facts" because I'm sure you'll have lots of interesting facts that don't fit into the categories. When you are researching, make sure you put each piece of information in the correct category.*

WRITING and COACHING *(prewriting, drafting)*
25 MINUTES

- Have students go to their designated research stations and begin recording information in their research notebooks.

- Have students choose their favorite or most important facts to record on sticky notes. Then have them place their sticky notes on the class R.A.N. chart in the correct categories.

SHARING and REFLECTING
10 MINUTES

TURN &TALK *Share your research with your partner. Tell him or her which piece of information you selected to put on a sticky note for our R.A.N. chart.*

- Remind students about information they wrote in the previous session under "What We Think We Know." *Did you learn anything today that showed that what you thought yesterday about the rain forest is true? If it is true, let's move it to "Yes, We Were Right."*

- Review the confirmed facts. Model how to discard information that is repeated: *Look what I found under "New Learning." This note says that giant-sized cockroaches live in the rain forest. I can see another note that says the same thing. So, I will take one of the notes off our chart. We need only one note that shows each fact.*

- Wrap up the lesson as you preview the next session: *It was great to use the research stations to confirm our knowledge and to find so much more new information! You'll have more time to add to your learning in our next session.*

TIP Encourage students to raise questions about the information they are recording and to post these under "Wonderings" on the class R.A.N. chart or in their research notebooks.

TIP By second grade, many of your students will be able to work independently in the research stations. Continue to provide support for those who still need help, enlisting parent volunteers to assist you when possible.

SESSION 4
Researching and Drafting

Students continue to record information from multiple sources as they practice writing facts in their own words.

MATERIALS

- *Big Book of Mentor Texts:* "The Sonoran Desert," pages 2–9
- Research stations
- Research notebooks or paper
- Whole-class R.A.N. chart
- Sticky notes and pencils

FOCUSED MINILESSON *(drafting)*
15 MINUTES

■ Focus the learning: *In this session, we're going to continue researching from different sources and writing down the important information we find. But this time we're going to try very hard to record the information in our own words. We'll learn why this is an important skill, and then we'll practice it during our writing time. We'll also learn what to do when we find that information we thought we knew actually is not correct.*

> **TURN &TALK** *Writers, why do you think it's important to write facts in your own words? Turn to your partner and talk about it.*

■ Summarize for students some of what you heard from the partner discussions: *I heard a few of you say that it is not right or fair for one person to copy exactly what another person has written. Someone else said that we can understand and remember facts better if we put them in our own words. These are both excellent reasons!*

■ Show students page 5 of the mentor text. Think aloud as you model stating facts in your own words: *Here, the author has written that a spadefoot toad "lives in muddy pools left by the storms." If I can say it in my own words, I can be sure I understand what the author means. I'm going to say, "The storms make a muddy pool. A muddy pool is a great place for a toad to live." When you are looking for a new way to write something, it helps to talk to a partner about it. Then try writing it. Remember, you want to use ideas from your research in your reports. But you need to use your own words and not the author's.*

■ Read other facts from the page.

> **TURN &TALK** *Use your own words to tell your partner a fact from this page.*

■ Prepare students for their research time: *Today, when you are at your research stations, try to use your own words to record the facts you find.*

■ Discuss the "Misconceptions" heading on the R.A.N. chart: *As you do your research, you may find that some things you thought you knew actually are not right. A misconception is something we thought was right that turns out to be incorrect. If you find that your information was not correct, you can move it from "What We Think We Know" to "Misconceptions" on our R.A.N. chart.*

WRITING and COACHING *(prewriting, drafting)*
25 MINUTES

■ Have students continue to research and write information in their research notebooks. Remind them to use their own words rather than the author's words to record information.

■ As you circulate around the room, encourage students to use pictures, diagrams, bullet points, and labels to summarize ideas from their research. Then, when it's time to write the report in complete sentences, they will have no choice but to use their own words!

■ Have students choose their favorite or most important facts, record them on sticky notes, and then place them on the class R.A.N. chart in the correct categories.

SHARING and REFLECTING
15 MINUTES

TURN & TALK *Show your partner information you collected about rain forests. Which piece did you choose to put on our R.A.N. chart?*

■ Read through all the confirmed facts and new facts. Help students identify information that is repeated and discard it.

TURN & TALK *Did you learn anything at your research station today that would tell you to move a sticky note from "What We Think We Know" to "Yes, We Were Right"? Is there anything that you want to move from "What We Think We Know" to "Misconceptions"?*

■ Reinforce the idea that when we say things in our own words, we understand and remember them better: *I think you are going to remember the things you learned today for a long time. You wrote your facts using your own words instead of copying the author's words. When you can restate the facts in your own words, you show that you understand the information.*

■ *You're becoming expert researchers! In our next session, we'll delve more deeply into our research to be sure that we've provided our readers with exciting information.*

TIP for Conferring with Individuals and Small Groups

Gather into a small group any students who struggle with putting information in their own words. Use a book that includes rain forest facts. Guide students to share their restatement of facts with the small group as you provide reinforcement and feedback. Then encourage students to use their own words to record the information in their notebooks.

SESSION 5
Researching and Drafting

Students continue to research and write facts in their own words, focusing on the use of descriptive adjectives.

MATERIALS
- *Big Book of Mentor Texts:* "The Sonoran Desert," pages 2–9
- Whole-class R.A.N. chart
- Features chart
- Research stations
- Research notebooks or paper
- Sticky notes and pencils

FOCUSED MINILESSON *(prewriting, drafting)*
15 MINUTES

■ To focus on vivid descriptions, read aloud the first paragraph about the bark scorpion on page 6 of the mentor text.

> **TURN &TALK** *Partners, think together. What words does the author use to show what the bark scorpion looks like?*

■ *You noticed some descriptive words:* small, dangerous, long, *and* sharp. *These words help us create pictures in our minds. Descriptive words are called* adjectives. *Good reports use adjectives that help readers visualize what something is really like.*

■ Using some of the information from the R.A.N. chart, identify three or four nouns.

> **TURN &TALK** *Tell your partner some adjectives we could use to describe these words. Choose words that would create pictures in your mind.*

■ Have several students share their thinking with the class.

■ *Today, as you research, think of adjectives you would use to describe something. You can get some great ideas by looking at pictures. Here's a picture of an arrow frog. I might use words like* bright *or* brilliant *to describe its colors.*

■ Return to the "Features of a Great Report" chart. *I think we have discovered a new feature of good reports. Let's add it to our list of features.*

■ Discuss the "Wonderings" heading on the R.A.N. chart: *Sometimes when I research, I read something that is so interesting it makes me ask more questions about it. I read that an anaconda can swallow prey larger than its head! I wonder how it can open its mouth wide enough to do that. I'm going to place this question under the heading "Wonderings" on our R.A.N. chart. If you have questions as you research, write them on sticky notes and put them on our R.A.N. chart under the heading "Wonderings."*

Features of a Great Report

A title tells us exactly what the report will be about.

The report gives us facts.

The report is organized in categories of information.

A table of contents helps readers find information.

The writer uses adjectives to describe things.

WRITING and COACHING *(prewriting, drafting)*
25 MINUTES

■ Send students to research stations to record information in their notebooks. Encourage them to use vivid adjectives to describe nouns as they write information in their own words.

■ Have students choose their favorite or most important facts to record on sticky notes. Then have them place each sticky note in the correct category on the class R.A.N. chart.

■ Help students raise "wonderings" from information they are collecting and write their questions on sticky notes to place on the class R.A.N. chart.

SHARING and REFLECTING
15 MINUTES

TURN &TALK *Show your partner the information you collected today. Tell your partner a great adjective you used to describe something.*

■ Ask volunteers to tell you if there was anything they learned that made them wonder or ask more questions.

■ Have students move any information they were able to prove in their research from "What We Think We Know" to "Yes, We Were Right."

■ Ask if any of the information that students thought they knew actually turned out to be incorrect. Move these sticky notes to "Misconceptions." Remind students that they do not want to include misconceptions in their reports, as misconceptions would mislead their readers!

■ Read through all the confirmed and new facts. Have students help you identify information that is repeated; discard the repeats.

TIP for Conferring with Individuals and Small Groups

If students struggle with using adjectives, convene a small group to brainstorm a "word bank" of adjectives that might be used to describe an animal, a plant, or a place. Display the word bank in a prominent place in the classroom so that all students can use this resource if they get stuck. Encourage students to add to this tool as they research in future sessions.

SESSION 6
Researching and Drafting

Students continue researching and writing facts in their own words, focusing on using linking words to join related ideas.

MATERIALS
- *Big Book of Mentor Texts:* "The Sonoran Desert," pages 2–9
- Research stations
- Features chart
- Research notebooks or paper
- Whole-class R.A.N. chart
- Sticky notes

TIP Some second graders may not be ready for more sophisticated linking words. At this stage, it may be enough to focus on combining simple words and ideas using the word *and*. Enlist students who are ready to use more sophisticated linking words in helping you create a word bank of linking words along with example sentences modeling correct usage.

FOCUSED MINILESSON *(drafting)*
15 MINUTES

■ Introduce the session: *In our last session, you did a fantastic job of making your writing better by adding descriptive adjectives. Those words really made your writing sparkle! Today we are going to learn how to make our writing sound better and flow more smoothly.*

■ Read this sentence from page 3 of the mentor text *"The Sonoran Desert"*: *"They are home to many kinds of plants and animals."* Here, I can see that the author put two facts in one sentence.

TURN &TALK *Think with your partner. What word did the author use to join these facts?*

■ *Yes, the author used the word* and *to join the two facts. She could have said, "They are home to many kinds of plants. They are home to many kinds of animals." Instead, she used the word* and *to make those two sentences one. Doesn't that sound better?*

■ Provide other examples of linking words, such as *and, but, or,* and *so.* List the words on chart paper and have students identify the words in the mentor text. Discuss what ideas are linked with each of the words.

■ Work with students to identify some facts on the R.A.N. chart that can be joined in one sentence. As you join sentences, replace the two facts with one sticky note that includes both, using linking words: *I notice that I have two sentences about the poison dart frog. "Poison dart frogs are tiny" and "Their poison could kill 100 people." Watch as I combine these sentences with the linking word* but: *Poison dart frogs are tiny, but their poison could kill 100 people."*

■ *We have discovered another feature of good report writing! Great writers use linking words to connect related ideas. Let's add it to our chart.*

■ Set students up for successful research: *Today will be your last day researching. When you write down your new facts, try to connect them with linking words whenever you can.*

WRITING and COACHING
(prewriting, drafting)
25 MINUTES

- Send students to research stations to record information in their notebooks.

- Have students choose their favorite or most important facts to record on sticky notes. Then have them place each sticky note in the correct category on the class R.A.N. chart.

- Students who struggle with the proper use of linking words may be finding it difficult to identify related ideas. Use think-aloud language as you offer support: *These two facts have something in common. They both list plants that can be found in the rain forest. What if you used the word "and" to link the facts together? Give it a try, and see if you can make one smooth sentence.*

> **Features of a Great Report**
>
> A title tells us exactly what the report will be about.
>
> The report gives us facts.
>
> The report is organized in categories of information.
>
> A table of contents helps readers find information.
>
> The writer uses adjectives to describe things.
>
> Some ideas are joined with linking words.

SHARING and REFLECTING
15 MINUTES

TURN &TALK *Show your partner the information you collected today. Tell your partner which of these facts you placed on our R.A.N. chart.*

- Invite students who connected related facts using linking words to share their sentences with the class.

- Read through all the facts. Help students identify information that is repeated and discard it.

- Ask volunteers if they learned anything new that answered a "wondering" that was posted yesterday. If so, write the answer on a sticky note and place it under "New Learning."

- Ask students if there was any information they thought they knew that today's research proved to be correct. Place these notes under "Yes, We Were Right." Ask if there was any information students thought they knew that turned out to be incorrect. Place these notes under "Misconceptions."

- *You have done an amazing job with your research—your readers will be amazed by all they can learn about the rain forest from your reports! In our next session, we'll take all our great information and start to write our reports.*

SESSION 7
Revising

Students revise information on the R.A.N. chart, as they continue to focus on using adjectives and linking words that can improve their writing.

MATERIALS
- *Big Book of Mentor Texts:* "The Sonoran Desert," pages 2–9
- Whole-class R.A.N. chart
- Paper and pencils

FOCUSED MINILESSON *(revising)*
15 MINUTES

- Focus the learning: *We've been working on writing notes that contain plenty of adjectives and using linking words to join facts that are related. In this session, we'll practice both of those strategies as we revise some of the notes on our class R.A.N. chart.*

- Model how to revise a sentence using an example of your own writing or from the R.A.N. chart. *Here I wrote, "In the rain forest there are frogs. In the rain forest there are butterflies." I'm going to revise this using adjectives and linking words to make my writing sound better. Watch as I revise: "In the steamy rain forest there are poisonous frogs and colorful butterflies." See how I've used the adjectives* steamy, poisonous, *and* colorful *to make my writing sound better? I also used the joining word* and *to link two facts about rain forest animals.*

- Select two more pieces of information from the mentor text or the R.A.N. chart.

  TURN &TALK *Partners, think together. How can we use a linking word to join these facts? How can we use adjectives to make the writing stronger?*

- Have several partners share their thinking with the class.

- Set a purpose for today's work: *Today, we are going to be revising the information under the headings "Yes, We Were Right" and "New Learning." We are not going to use the information that is still under "What We Think We Know," because we aren't sure if it's right. That doesn't mean the information is wrong. We just aren't sure enough to write it in our reports. We are certainly not going to use our misconceptions, because we know they are not true.*

TIP Students need to understand that nonfiction writers may discard prior thinking because they are unable to validate what they previously thought.

WRITING and COACHING (revising)
25 MINUTES

■ Divide the class into pairs. Each pair will be responsible for revising two pieces of information from the "Yes, We Were Right" and "New Learning" categories on the R.A.N. chart. If you have sticky notes left over, give them to early finishers to revise.

■ Have pairs write their revisions on paper and then discard the sticky notes. Support students by using questioning strategies as you circulate around the room: *Based on the research you've done, can you tell me how you picture the trees in the rain forest? What size are they? What colors? Is there any other way to describe them? Those are great adjectives that you can add to this note!*

■ Emphasize that students may not find many opportunities to use linking words because only certain types of sentences can be combined sensibly. When they do use linking words, remind the students to read back their final sentence to be sure it makes sense.

TIP Some students may struggle with using both linking words and adjectives. If this is the case, have them concentrate on using only one strategy.

SHARING and REFLECTING
5 MINUTES

■ Have pairs meet with other pairs to share their revisions.

TURN &TALK *Explain what you changed to make the writing better.*

■ Read through some of the revised notes. Point out good examples of changes that were made: *I like the way you used strong descriptions of the kapok trees. I really get a sense of what it would be like to stand underneath one!*

■ *You've really improved those notes by adding adjectives and looking for places where it made sense to use linking words. In our next session we'll focus on improving our writing by making it clearer for our readers.*

SESSION 8
Editing the Report

Students check spelling and punctuation before publishing their writing in final form.

MATERIALS
- *Big Book of Mentor Texts:* "The Sonoran Desert," pages 2–9
- Features chart
- Revised information from Session 7
- Publishing materials

FOCUSED MINILESSON *(editing)*
20 MINUTES

■ Preview the session: *Soon our report will be a book that we can read and share with other people! We can then give it to the librarian to put in our school library for other students to read. But before we show it to others, we want to make sure all of our spelling and punctuation is correct. That's what we'll work on in this session.*

■ Use sentences from the mentor text to model correct use of end punctuation: *When we write, we want to make sure we show where one sentence ends and another begins. That helps our writing make sense to our readers. A capital letter is a signal that we're starting a new sentence. A punctuation mark signals the end. But punctuation marks can also tell a reader what kind of sentence it is. Let's look at this information about the tortoise. When the writer says, "The tortoise also has a large pouch inside its body that works like a tank to store water," it's a fact the author wants to tell us. A fact ends with a period. In the next sentence, he writes, "The tortoise can go for months without taking a drink!" The exclamation mark shows that the author is amazed about that fact. It is amazing, isn't it?*

■ Show students another page from the mentor text.

TURN &TALK *Tell your partner what punctuation the author has used on this page and explain how it helps the reader.*

■ Discuss strategies for checking spelling: *If you aren't sure about the spelling of a word, say the word and stretch out the sounds. Do the letters match the sounds of the word? You can also look at the content word wall, or ask a friend. And if you are still stumped, I will come around and help you.*

WRITING and COACHING *(editing)*
20 MINUTES

■ Set the purpose for today's work: *Today, you will be checking the spelling and punctuation of the sentences that you revised yesterday. Work together to check carefully and make changes. Remember, we aren't changing the ideas. At this stage, we are checking punctuation and spelling.*

■ Have students work with their partners from Session 7 to edit the information they revised in that lesson.

■ Model various strategies for spelling, such as: *Orchids are flowers that grow in the rain forest. I'm not exactly sure how to spell* orchids, *though. I wrote so fast when I was researching that I can't read my own writing! I spelled* orchid *o-r-k-i-d. That's how the word sounds, but it doesn't look quite right to me. I'm thinking about other words I know with the /k/ sound, like* chorus *and* choir. *In those words, /k/ is spelled with* ch. *So I'm trying to spell again: o-r-c-h-i-d. That looks correct, but just to be safe, I'll underline the word so I remember to return to it and then, when I'm done editing, I'll take a look in a dictionary or in the reference source just to double-check.*

■ Early finishers can begin designing pictures for the front and back covers of the class book.

SHARING and REFLECTING
5 MINUTES

■ Have pairs of students share with other pairs the edits they made.

■ Read through some of the edited notes. Point out good examples of changes that were made: *Here is a great example of writing correct sentences. I see that you have started with a capital letter and ended with a period. I also like the way you fixed your spelling. That is so much easier to read. Nice work!*

■ *You have done an amazing job of writing a variety of sentences with different end punctuation! Your spelling makes your messages clear to your readers, too. In our next session, we'll put more touches on our reports that will excite our readers!*

TIP for Conferring with Individuals and Small Groups

Gather into a small group any students who struggle with editing for end punctuation. You might look through the mentor text again to focus on declarative, interrogative, and exclamatory sentences. Have students sort sentences and take a closer look at end punctuation.

SESSION 9
Getting Ready to Publish

Students add illustrations with captions and labels to their reports in preparation for publishing the class book.

MATERIALS
- *Big Book of Mentor Texts:* "The Sonoran Desert," pages 2–9
- Features chart
- Revised and edited information from Session 8
- Plain printer paper, pencils, markers

FOCUSED MINILESSON *(publishing)*
15 MINUTES

■ Focus the learning: *In this session we'll learn how illustrations with labels and captions can make it easier for readers to understand what our words are saying. Then we'll draw pictures to go with the categories we've been working on.*

■ Display the mentor text and explain that matching appropriate illustrations to text is an important feature of a great report: *Do you see how the pictures in each section of this report help us better understand the words? This part talks about how the plants in the desert provide animals with shelter. The picture near it shows us an example of what that looks like. Here, words and pictures work together to make it easier for us to understand what the author has written.*

TURN &TALK *What sorts of illustrations might you use to help your readers better understand what you have written? Tell your partner.*

■ Explain that captions and labels can make it even easier for readers to understand what is shown in a photograph or an illustration. If possible, show students examples of labeled drawings or pictures with captions from a range of nonfiction sources: *Sometimes captions and labels repeat what has already been said in the text, but sometimes they contain brand new information. We have discovered another feature of a great report. Let's add it to our chart!*

Features of a Great Report

A title tells us exactly what the report will be about.

The report gives us facts.

The report is organized in categories of information.

The writer uses adjectives to describe things.

Some ideas are joined with linking words.

There are illustrations, captions, and labels that match the information.

WRITING and COACHING *(publishing)*
30 MINUTES

■ Have students remain in the pairs from the previous few sessions. Distribute printer paper, and have each pair sketch one or more illustrations for their section of the report: *As you work on your drawing, ask yourself: Does this illustration match the information? Would labels make it clearer? Should I add a caption to give my reader more information about what my drawing shows?* In the next session, students will cut out the illustrations and add them to their reports as they publish.

■ You might suggest that partners discuss what they will draw and where it will go in the report before actually sketching it on the publishing paper. Partners can provide feedback on whether the illustration matches the text or makes it easier to understand.

■ Remind reluctant artists that they do not have to draw perfect pictures. The important thing is that they show their understanding of matching illustrations to text.

■ Encourage students to sketch in pencil first, and then go over their pencil lines with markers to add depth and color.

SHARING and REFLECTING
5 MINUTES

■ Have each pair share their work with another pair. Encourage them to tell each other what they like most about each other's illustrations.

■ Choose a few student samples to share with the class: *I really love this drawing of the whole rain forest that you added to your first page, Daniella. It gives a wonderful picture of the subject of your report that I can keep in my mind as I read the rest.*

■ Sum up the session and preview the next: *You've all drawn wonderful illustrations that I know will help our readers better understand our reports. I can't wait until tomorrow, when we will write our reports in our best handwriting and paste our drawings where they best belong!*

SESSION 10
Publishing, Sharing, and Celebrating

Students publish their final reports before sharing them with classmates and celebrating their accomplishments as writers of informational text.

MATERIALS
- Features chart
- Publishing materials
- Revised and edited information from Session 8
- Students' illustrations from Session 9

TIP Seeing the product of their research fully realized in the form of a final report will help students see themselves as serious writers. This will give them the confidence to move on to their individual reports.

FOCUSED MINILESSON *(publishing)*
15 MINUTES

■ Introduce the session: *We're finally ready to publish our report. This means that we will create the final copy that we will be proud to show to others. It must be clear, easy to read, and organized so others can use it to find information. We're also going to use our best handwriting to write the words and make sure that every part is correct.*

TURN &TALK *Writers, what do we need to add to our report before it's really finished? Talk it over with your partner.*

■ Display the features chart as you review: *Let's take one last look at our chart to find out what we still need to include. We don't have a title for our class report yet, but that will go on a separate cover that we'll make later. We do have categories for the information in our report, but we'll need to make headings in the report that tell what kind of information is in each category. We should also have a table of contents so our readers will know where to find each category. Other than these things, which we'll do later, we are ready to publish!*

■ Impress on students the importance of using their best handwriting. This will help reinforce the idea that this is a final, published piece that will be ready by others.

■ Although the whole-class report was a group effort, it's important to recognize and validate students' individual contributions to the project so they know they are capable of handling the individual project that comes next.

WRITING and COACHING *(publishing)*
20 MINUTES

■ Pass out publishing materials and have pairs work together to publish their section of the report, leaving room for the illustrations they drew in Session 9. Support them as they write and position the illustrations, offering hands-on help as well as positive feedback.

■ Early finishers may work with you on the cover, table of contents, section headings, and any other elements you'd like to add, such as a dedication page or a glossary. Alternatively, you could add another session so the class could work in small groups to add these specific text features.

■ Collate all of the published pages in the correct order. Add the cover, title page, table of contents, and so on, then bind.

SHARING and CELEBRATING *(publishing)*
10 MINUTES

■ Celebrate the class report by having individual students share their contributions with the class. As they do, connect with the features listed on the "Features of a Great Report" chart. *You did a great job of using vivid adjectives when describing a parrot. This is a very important feature of a great report!*

TURN &TALK *If another student was working on a report and asked you for help, what would you say a great report should include? Tell your partner your ideas.*

■ Invite another second-grade class to join you for a second reading of the report. After the reading, hold a discussion about the rain forest. This will reinforce students' understanding of the purpose of an informational report as they see others using their information. Present the report to the librarian or display it in a prominent place in the classroom so other students can view it.

TIP After the whole-class project, the rain forest report can provide a useful model for students' individual projects. Students can use the report as a reference to support and guide them as they become more confident in their own writing.

SESSION 11
Launching the Individual Project

Students review the features of a great report and record their prior knowledge about their chosen habitat.

MATERIALS
- Features chart from class project
- Research notebooks
- Pencils
- Sticky notes
- Topic Selection Sheet (see *Resources* CD-ROM)

TIP Have students fill out a Topic Selection Sheet ahead of time, listing their first, second, and third choices. This will allow you to group students ahead of time, ensuring there are not too many students working on the same habitat and thus exhausting resources.

TIP If you did not have adequate time to build students' background knowledge about habitats prior to starting this unit, some may worry that they don't know enough to fill out this section of the research notebook. Reassure these students that it's okay if they don't have prior knowledge to record. That's why research is so important!

FOCUSED MINILESSON *(prewriting)*
20 MINUTES

■ Explain to students that today they are going to begin drafting their own reports. Inform students that as they write their reports, you will be working on your own report alongside them. Select a different habitat than those the students are investigating. This will ensure that students don't copy the facts that you use in demonstrations: *A habitat has unique features, such as temperature, weather, animals, and plants. I've visited an alpine tundra before in the Rocky Mountains—I remember how amazed I was at how many different kinds of birds and other animals lived there! I already know a little bit about the alpine tundra, so I'm going to choose* alpine tundra *as the topic of my report.*

■ List other habitats on the board, and have each student choose one.

TURN &TALK *Think back to our report on rain forests. Tell your partner the features that we included in that report. Explain how these features help our readers.*

■ Refer students to the "Features of a Great Report" chart as you reflect together on what to include in a report: *Make sure you use these features when you write your own report.*

■ Think aloud as you reflect on how the research notebooks are organized: *Now I need to get ready to start my research. The research notebooks are already organized into categories like the ones we had when we did our class project: "Location," "Climate," "Animals," "Plants," and "Interesting Facts." This will help me keep my information organized. The first page of my notebook is reserved for information I think I already know about my habitat, which is the alpine tundra. The last page is set aside for misconceptions. There is also a page called "Wonderings" in case I have any questions as I research.*

TURN &TALK *What do you think you already know about your habitat? Tell your partner.*

■ Briefly discuss some of the information partners shared before students begin to write.

WRITING and COACHING *(prewriting, drafting)*
25 MINUTES

■ Have students write their report titles on the cover of their research notebooks. Students may want to record topics and determine their titles when they've finished writing.

■ Have students record what they think they know about their habitat on sticky notes and place these notes on the first page of their notebooks. Later, when they confirm any of these facts, they can move them under the correct category in the research notebook. If they find that any of their background knowledge was a misconception, they can move it to the last page of the notebook.

■ If students have any questions, they can record these on the "Wonderings" page in the research notebook.

SHARING and REFLECTING
5 MINUTES

TURN &TALK *Show your partner an important piece of information that you wrote today about your habitat.*

■ Have one or two students share their information with the class.

■ Tell students what they will be working on next: *Over the next four sessions, you will be going to research stations to gather new information about your habitat. You will also be thinking about the information you wrote today under the heading "What I Think I Know." You will need to research to see if you can confirm any of this information. If you can, you will be able to move it forward and use it in your report. If you find that your information was incorrect, you can move it to "Misconceptions." As you research, you may also have some questions. If you do, write them on the "Wonderings" page in your research notebook.*

SESSION 12
Researching and Drafting

Students begin to research their habitats and record the most interesting facts they can find.

MATERIALS
- Features chart
- Research stations (books, magazines, Internet resources)
- Research notebooks
- Pencils
- Sticky notes

TIP Students need to understand that they should not record every fact they find when researching. Modeling how you select the most interesting facts will assist them with this process.

FOCUSED MINILESSON *(prewriting, drafting)*
15 MINUTES

■ Focus the learning: *In today's session, we'll begin our research on the habitats we've chosen, and we'll learn how to take notes that will guarantee that our reports are as interesting for our readers as they can be.*

■ Explain to students that they should not attempt to write down every fact they come across. Instead, they should focus on locating information about their habitat that will be the most interesting to readers. *When I look through this book on the alpine tundra, it tells me a lot of information. I want to be sure that I select the best information for my report. On this page, the author has listed lots of animals that live on the alpine tundra. I can't write about all of them, so I'll choose the four animals that interest me the most. If I find them interesting, my readers probably will, too!*

TURN &TALK *Why shouldn't I write about every animal that lives on the alpine tundra? Talk it over with your partner.*

■ Have some of the students share their thinking with the class. Provide positive affirmations to their responses: *Yes, Henry, that's right. Too much information can be overwhelming to readers and will make my report so long that people won't want to read it. So let's choose only the most important or most interesting information for our reports.*

WRITING and COACHING *(prewriting, drafting)*
25 MINUTES

■ Review the research stations, and remind students to record their information directly into their research notebooks in the correct categories.

■ Encourage students to share the facts they select with a partner before writing them in their research notebooks. Partners can give each fact a quick thumbs up or thumbs down depending on how interesting or important they think it is.

■ If you have only a few computers in your classroom, have students work at them in pairs or even groups of three. This will ensure that everyone gets a chance to do computer-based research and also is a great way to get students talking about the information they find.

SHARING and REFLECTING
5 MINUTES

TURN &TALK *Think for a moment about the interesting facts that you discovered today during your research. Tell your partner. Explain to him or her why you think each fact is interesting.*

■ Use this opportunity to celebrate the information students have discovered: *Raul, I see you've discovered that the apple snail is the snail kite's only food. So, if the apple snail is endangered, those snail kites may have trouble finding food. That's fascinating! I wonder what other animals depend on each other in wetlands. That might be a great question to put in the "Wonderings" section of my research notebook.*

TURN &TALK *Show your partner any information that you thought you knew and that was confirmed by your research. Tell your partner if you had any misconceptions. Did you have any new "wonderings"?*

■ After students have shared their research discoveries, prepare them for the upcoming session: *You have already discovered some great information about habitats! I'm sure you're anxious to learn even more. You'll have another chance to visit the research stations, confirm what you know, and add to your learning about habitats.*

TIP for Conferring with Individuals and Small Groups

Provide support for students in adding details that can make their writing more interesting: *Look at the information that you wrote today. You've said here that there are polar bears in the arctic and that they are big. I'm sure your readers are going to want to know how big they are. Do you think this is an important detail? Maybe that's something you could add to your writing.*

SESSION 13
Writing in Their Own Words

Students research, draft, and revise their notes as they practice writing information in their own words.

MATERIALS
- Research stations
- Research notebooks
- Features chart
- Pencils
- Sticky notes

TIP Some students may be reluctant to write a word that they aren't sure how to spell. Tell students that when they are gathering information, or writing it in their own words, it's fine if some words aren't spelled correctly. It's more important that they get the information down, especially if it's something they think is very interesting. Tell them they will have plenty of time to correct their spelling later.

FOCUSED MINILESSON *(drafting)*
15 MINUTES

■ Introduce the session: *Writers, today we'll focus on a really important part of writing from research—putting information in our own words—and you'll have a chance to practice in your research notebook.*

■ Remind students of their work on the class project and why they worked so hard to write information in their own words: *When we wrote our report on rain forests, we tried to write in our own words, didn't we? Even though we got our information from books, magazines, and other sources, writing in our own words showed that we understood the facts and made our writing more interesting because our unique personalities came through.*

■ Being able to write facts from research in one's own words is an important, but sometimes difficult, skill. You will want to model writing information in your own words: *Here, I read that in the tundra "the marmot eats as much as it can in the summer to store up fat to survive through the winter." How can I say that in my own words? I'm going to put the book down and think about what I have learned. Then I will tell my partner. I'll say, "The marmot eats all summer. That way, it will have plenty of fat to live on during the long, cold winter." Now I will write this in my research notebook.*

■ Prepare students for independent writing: *Today, when you are researching, try to use your own words when taking notes. It sometimes helps to think about the information first and then tell a friend before writing it, like you just saw me do. This way, you can show your unique personality when you write and also show that you understand the information. It's important not to copy the author's words.*

WRITING and COACHING *(prewriting, drafting)*
25 MINUTES

TIP Bring together students with similar needs for small-group instruction. This will help you reach all of the students who need support.

- Have students continue to research and draft their reports, being sure to record information in the correct categories in their notebooks.

- Students are likely to need lots of help with writing information in their own words. Enlist parent helpers, if possible, and model frequently. Be sure to praise all efforts: *Great, Tanisha! You've found a wonderful way of expressing that thought! You've captured the information using your words and not the author's.*

SHARING and REFLECTING
5 MINUTES

- Discuss the information students gathered during today's research. Exhibit particularly skillful examples in which students expressed information in their own words.

TURN &TALK *Show your partner a piece of research that you put in your own words. Tell your partner something you wrote that makes you proud.*

- Have one or two students share their notes with the class. Encourage students to give feedback about what they liked about the notes.

TURN &TALK *Show your partner any information you thought you knew that you were able to confirm. Tell your partner if you had any misconceptions. Did you have any new "wonderings"? Were any of your previous questions answered?*

- *One fantastic part of the research process is that, when you find new information, wonderings come up. You think of new questions as you learn more! In our next session, you'll return to the research stations. You may want to focus on answering some of the intriguing questions that have come up in your research.*

SESSION 14
Drafting and Revising

Students research, draft, and revise their notes, focusing on using vivid adjectives that make their writing come alive.

MATERIALS
- Research stations
- Research notebooks
- Pencils
- Sticky notes

TIP At this age, students may rely on "overused" adjectives, such as *good, great, nice,* and so on. Try bringing students together in small groups to spark their thinking. Show each group a photograph of a habitat, then ask them to work together to brainstorm a list of vivid adjectives that describe the habitat in the picture. Record adjectives on a class chart.

FOCUSED MINILESSON
(drafting, revising)
15 MINUTES

■ Recall with students how they made the class report on the rain forest more interesting and inviting by using strong adjectives to describe information: *When we wrote our report on the rain forest, we tried to use sparkling adjectives that helped our readers form pictures in their minds.*

■ Model for students how to add describing words to enhance information: *I was amazed at how the mountain goat can walk along the sides of tricky cliffs and rocks in the alpine tundra. I wrote, "The sure-footed mountain goat has tiny dewclaws on its feet to help it climb." I used the adjective* sure-footed *to emphasize that the mountain goat is a very skillful climber. This word creates a strong mental picture for me, a goat that is climbing in hazardous places but is able to navigate the rough terrain with the unique claws on its feet.*

TURN &TALK *Partners, think together. What adjectives can you use to make your writing better?*

■ Give students a few minutes to review their notebooks to see if they can find a sentence that can be improved with an adjective. If time allows, brainstorm and chart with the class a list of adjectives that can be used to describe plants, animals, and their habitats.

■ Prepare students for independent writing: *Today, when you do your research and write your notes, try to think of great adjectives you can use to make your writing sound more inviting. Be sure that your adjectives are precise!*

WRITING and COACHING *(drafting, revising)*
25 MINUTES

- Have students continue to research, draft, and revise their notes. Guide students in recording information in the correct categories in their notebooks.

- Help students discover new adjectives to describe information. Remind them to use the class chart of adjectives if they are stumped. More advanced students may use a thesaurus to find new describing words. Encourage students who are struggling to consult with their partners about where adjectives might improve their writing. Consider making it a class expectation that students consult a partner before asking for your help.

SHARING and REFLECTING
5 MINUTES

- Discuss the information students gathered during today's research. Share sentences that contain especially vivid adjectives.

  TURN &TALK *Show your partner the notes you created today and any place in your writing where you added a great adjective. How did it help your writing?*

- Have one or two students share their notes with the class. Encourage students to give feedback about what they liked most in the research they did today.

  TURN &TALK *Show your partner information that you thought you knew that you were able to confirm. Tell your partner if you had any misconceptions. Did you have any new "wonderings"? Were any of your previous questions answered?*

- Sum up the session and prepare students for the next. *Writers, the adjectives you've added today really make your habitats come to life. In our next session, we'll continue to revise our work and make it even more powerful.*

TIP for Conferring with Individuals and Small Groups

Begin to introduce adverbs to students who appear to have mastered the use of adjectives. Make a list of adverbs with the students and then have them go back and add some to their drafts.

SESSION 15
Revising Information

Students reread their writing, checking for sense and revising as needed.

MATERIALS
- Research stations
- Research notebooks
- Features chart
- Pencils
- Sticky notes

FOCUSED MINILESSON *(revising)*
15 MINUTES

- Introduce the session: *Have you ever written something, put it away, and then come back to it later? If so, you may have noticed that one or more of your sentences didn't make sense. In this session we will learn why it's so important to reread our writing before considering it final, and we'll practice on our report drafts.*

- Review with students what it means to revise one's writing: *Once you've written something the first time, it's always a good idea to read it to yourself to make sure that it says what you want it to say and to check that no words have been left out. When you read it to yourself, listen carefully to the words and try to imagine what it would sound like to someone else who is unfamiliar with the habitat and is learning about it for the first time.*

- Model the revision process by reading a sample of your own writing out loud and making necessary revisions: *Here I wrote about plants on the tundra: "It's windy on the tundra plants low to the ground." I remember the idea that I had when I wrote this, but now that I read it, I see that I've left out some words.* Demonstrate using a caret to insert missing words: *Now this makes much more sense: "It's windy on the tundra, so plants grow low to the ground." Taking the time to read our writing ensures that we've included all the words so that readers can understand our ideas! When you take your notes today, read them back to be sure you're not missing important words and that your writing makes sense.*

- Have students look over their notes to prepare for their research: *Do any of your categories need more notes? Think about the research you need to do today so that you have a balanced report with information about all the categories.*

  TURN &TALK *Tell your partner which category in your report needs more information. Where might you look to find this information?*

- Remind students to keep using vivid adjectives as they draft notes from their research: *Remember how we talked yesterday about using great describing words? Don't forget to keep using these as you draft your information. Refer to our chart if you need some ideas.*

WRITING and COACHING *(drafting, revising)*
25 MINUTES

- Have students continue to research, draft, and revise their research notes, which will form the basis for their reports. Guide students in recording information in the correct categories in their notebooks.

- Help students discover new adjectives to describe information. Encourage them to work with their partners to read aloud what they have written to see if it makes sense and sounds right.

SHARING and REFLECTING
5 MINUTES

- Discuss the information students gathered during today's research. Show students an example of a good revision that you observed during the writing period: *I noticed that Susan was reading back something she had written, and she found a great way to write it better. Susan, you wrote, "Killer whales hunt seals. Diving under the ice." This didn't make sense to you, so you were able to link the two thoughts. Can you read your revision? "Killer whales hunt seals that dive under the ice." That sounds great, Susan!*

TURN &TALK *Show your partner a strong revision that you made today.*

- Have one or two students share their notes with the class. Encourage students to give feedback about what they liked about the pages.

TURN &TALK *Tell your partner if any of the information that you thought you knew was confirmed. Did you have any misconceptions? Did you have any new "wonderings"? Were any of your previous questions answered?*

- *You've done a fantastic job of making your words come alive for your readers. One thing you've done particularly well is to look back at your work to be sure it sounds right, makes sense, and delivers your message in the best possible way. In our next session we'll make sure that our spelling and punctuation are correct.*

TIP Some students may have a tendency toward repetition, using the same phrases and sentence structures over and over again. Encourage these students to listen for repetition as they are reading their writing to themselves, and challenge them to find new ways to write the same information. You might create model sentences with different structures, such as compound sentences or sentences with openers. Encourage students also to insert a question now and then or to show strong feelings with an exclamation.

SESSION 16
Editing

Students edit their reports to prepare them for publishing, focusing on using correct punctuation and spelling.

MATERIALS
• Research notebooks
• Publishing materials: paper, pens
• Pencils

TIP Introduce students to a few proofreaders' marks, such as a caret for inserting text. Tell them that this is how professional writers and editors edit their work. Create a classroom chart with some basic proofreaders' marks along with example sentences demonstrating their use.

TIP If students have not left enough space between lines, they may have trouble inserting carets and editing marks. These students will benefit from having erasers on hand when they are editing and from reminders about using spacing when they write.

FOCUSED MINILESSON *(editing)*
15 MINUTES

■ Tell students what they will be working on today: *You've all come up with some great research on your habitats and found interesting ways to describe the information in your reports. Today we are going to edit our writing to make sure it is correct before we publish our reports.*

■ Explain what it means to edit one's writing: *When we edit our writing, we concentrate on finding the little "bugs," like mistakes in spelling and punctuation. We know our ideas and descriptions are great—but now we want to make sure everything is correct because when we publish our reports, other people will want to read them. For example, we want to make sure every sentence begins with a capital letter and ends with the right punctuation mark.*

■ On the board, write two sentences that have errors in punctuation and spelling. Model editing the first sentence, using editing marks: *I see here that I spelled* wildflower *wrong. The* w *comes before the* o. *I'm going to cross out* wildflower *by drawing one line through it. Then I'm going to write the correct spelling above it.* Then have students turn and talk about errors in the other sentence.

TURN &TALK *What's wrong with this sentence? What do we need to fix? Talk to your partner about what corrections need to be made.*

■ Explain to students that now they will edit what they have already written. They will be making marks on their writing to make corrections, just as you demonstrated.

WRITING and COACHING *(editing)*
25 MINUTES

■ Help students edit their writing. If some have difficulty finding errors in their own writing, bring them together for small-group instruction.

- Remind students that they should read their writing several times to make sure it is correct and easy to understand. Explain that it is sometimes helpful to read for a different type of editing each time. For example, they might read a paragraph once to check spelling and a second time to check punctuation. This kind of focused editing will make it easier to spot mistakes.

- Encourage students to ask each other for help if they are having difficulty with spelling a word. This will contribute to building a community of writers.

TIP As students edit their work, compile a list of words that are misspelled. Some commonly misspelled words may appear in many reports, even if the reports focus on different habitats. Write a list of the words—spelled correctly—for students' reference.

SHARING and REFLECTING
5 MINUTES

TURN &TALK *Turn to your partner and show him or her some of the edits you made today.*

- Invite volunteers to show edits they made to their reports. Allow time to reflect on the importance of editing as part of the writing process: *You have been very careful editors today. This shows that you are serious writers and that you care about the writing you will be sharing with others!*

- Preview what students will be working on next. *Now that you've made your writing clearer for your readers, it's time to get it ready to publish. In our next session, we will begin putting your writing in final form!*

SESSION 17

Beginning to Publish

Students begin to transfer their edited work to publishing paper, organizing it under appropriate headings as they go.

MATERIALS

- Research notebooks
- Features chart
- Publishing materials: paper, pens

TIP Many students may wish to keep the original headings for the research categories, but some may be ready to write more descriptive headings. This will allow them to personalize their writing.

FOCUSED MINILESSON *(publishing)*
15 MINUTES

■ Prepare students for what they will be doing today: *Now we are going to take our edited drafts and write them in final form to create our published work. We are going to use our best handwriting and make sure we include all the corrections we made yesterday.*

■ Explain why headings are important for readers: *Remember how we organized our information about the rain forest into categories before we wrote our report? Each category had a heading to tell readers what that section was about. As we did our research this time, we also organized our information in categories. Now, when we publish our reports, we need to create headings that will tell our readers what information they can find in each section.*

■ Model creating a heading for a category of information: *I've written a lot in my section about where the alpine tundra is located, so I could use "Location" as my heading for that section. But I wonder if I can think of an even better heading. I wrote that the tundra is so high in the mountains that trees can't grow there. So, a better heading for my section on location might be "Land Above the Trees." That sounds much more interesting!*

TURN &TALK *Partners, look over your research categories. What headings are you going to use for each of these categories in your own reports? Share your ideas.*

■ *You have some wonderful ideas for your headings. They tell us what your categories are about and make us want to read on. Now you're ready to start publishing.*

WRITING and COACHING *(publishing)*
25 MINUTES

■ Guide students in transferring their edited drafts onto publishing paper: *Breanna, I noticed that you used a caret to show some words you left out of your draft. When you copy your finished report, be sure that you include those missing words, but not the caret!*

■ Help students write their headings at the top of each section of the report. Bring together students who are struggling with headings to have them brainstorm titles together. You might write the headings on chart paper for students to copy.

SHARING and REFLECTING
5 MINUTES

■ Provide an opportunity for students to share their work: *I noticed that all of you came up with some great headings for your sections. Cameron, you had a really good one for your section on animals of the savannah. Many of your animals were predators, so you called it "Hunters of the Grassland and Their Prey." That makes me want to read further!*

TURN & TALK *Turn to your partner and tell him or her about a heading you wrote. Tell your partner what kinds of information readers can find in that section.*

■ Tell students what they will be working on next: *We'll continue working on our published reports in the next session. We're going to add pictures, captions, and diagrams to help our readers understand our information.*

TIP If sufficient computers are available in the classroom, consider allowing some students to type their published reports. This will be much faster and easier for some students than having to copy their writing legibly. Students can also learn valuable technology skills and may have the ability to place digital photos or maps in their reports.

SESSION 18
Adding Illustrations

Students continue to transfer their edited drafts to publishing paper, adding illustrations that match the text.

MATERIALS
- Research notebooks
- *Big Book of Mentor Texts:* "The Sonoran Desert," pages 2–9
- Publishing materials: paper, pens
- Illustration materials: markers, crayons

TIP Students may need more examples of illustrations with captions and labels. Bring in a variety of nonfiction books or have students investigate the research materials to find these text features. Talk about what makes these features so helpful for readers as you discuss the information shown in each one.

FOCUSED MINILESSON *(publishing)*
15 MINUTES

- Explain the purpose of today's session: *Today we are going to continue publishing our final reports. As we do, we're going to add illustrations to help our readers understand the information.*

- Show students the mentor text: *Remember that illustrations are not there just to look nice! Illustrations should show something that the text is telling us about. Here, you see there is a picture showing the kangaroo rat digging a burrow under a log. And it's right next to a paragraph that describes how this happens.*

- Explain how to add captions and labels to the drawings: *Does anyone remember how a caption helps us? That's right, Mia, it tells us a little about what is shown in the picture. It helps readers understand what they should learn from the picture.*

  TURN &TALK *Find a section in your report that you think might be hard to understand without a picture to help your readers. Now explain to your partner what kind of picture you are going to add, and how it will help readers understand your report.*

- Have students share some of their ideas with the class before they resume publishing.

WRITING and COACHING *(publishing)*
20 MINUTES

- Continue guiding students in transferring their edited writing into the correct categories in their published reports, leaving room for illustrations. Remind students to include a heading for each section.

- When students are finished writing their published text, they can begin adding illustrations. Help them create captions and labels for their pictures. Guide them in placing illustrations near the text so they are truly helpful for readers. Remind students to match pictures to text: *Remember, our reports are about habitats. The polar bear exhibit at the zoo is amazing, but our readers will learn so much more from seeing illustrations of polar bears in their natural environments. Then they will understand why polar bears need blubber to keep warm and special traction on their feet to stay on top of the ice.*

■ If students do not finish their work today, provide additional sessions as needed.

SHARING and REFLECTING
5 MINUTES

■ Provide an opportunity for students to share their work: *You've all made some brilliant illustrations for your reports. The pictures really make your writing come to life!*

TURN &TALK *Turn to your partner and tell him or her about an illustration you created for your report. Tell your partner how that illustration helps your readers understand your report.*

■ Tell students what they will be working on next: *In our next session, we'll to add a cover and a table of contents to help readers find information and use our reports more easily.*

TIP Some students may not be comfortable with their artistic skills. If time is short, allow students to use images from the Internet to illustrate their reports. Challenge them to write their own captions for the pictures and to create labels showing important parts and features.

SESSION 19
Publishing the Cover and Table of Contents

Students create a cover for their reports and a table of contents with entries that match category headings.

MATERIALS
- Examples of informational books
- Research notebooks
- Publishing paper
- Heavy paper for making covers
- Pens, crayons, markers

TIP Some students may have difficulty designing a table of contents. Give these students a preprinted template. Students can then look at their pages and write the page numbers on the template. This extra scaffolding will allow them to create organized reports they can be proud of!

FOCUSED MINILESSON *(publishing)*
15 MINUTES

■ Discuss the goal for this session: *We have lots of wonderful information in our reports now, and we've drawn great illustrations that match the text. It's time to work on our covers and tables of contents. We'll do that today.*

■ *Remember that when a report is published, it becomes available for others to read. These readers need to know right away what the report will be about. A cover will help them find out and make them want to read further. What are some kinds of information you can find on a book's cover? That's right—the title, the author's name, and sometimes a good picture about the subject.*

TURN &TALK *Turn to your partner and tell him or her what ideas you have for your cover. What picture might you include? What other information should you put there?*

■ Show students informational books that have intriguing covers and well-organized tables of contents: *Here's a great book on wetlands. I know what it's about right away by looking at the cover. When I open the cover, there's a table of contents telling me where to find each section. Notice how the headings in the table of contents match the headings within the book.*

TURN &TALK *Turn to your partner and tell him or her what categories you will have in your table of contents.*

■ Send students to write independently so that they can create their covers and tables of contents.

WRITING and COACHING *(publishing)*
20 MINUTES

■ Provide students with heavy paper for making covers. Help them compose descriptive titles for their reports.

■ Help students write page numbers on their finished pages, and guide them in writing the correct page numbers in their tables of contents. Be sure that table of contents entries match headings within the report. Enlist parent helpers to assist as needed.

■ Early finishers can create the illustrations for their covers. Students who need more time can finish up in the next session.

SHARING and REFLECTING
5 MINUTES

■ Provide an opportunity for students to share their work: *You've all made some terrific covers and tables of contents. They invite readers to look inside!*

> **TURN &TALK** *Turn to your partner and tell him or her about your cover and table of contents. Tell your partner how your cover lets readers know what they can expect to find inside.*

■ Tell students what they will be doing next: *In our next session, we will have time to finish our publishing. Then we'll share our wonderful reports with each other.*

SESSION 20
Publishing and Celebrating

Students finish publishing their reports. Then they celebrate their writing and reflect on their growth as writers of informational text.

MATERIALS
- Features chart
- Student reports
- Sample "About the Author" blurbs
- Publishing materials: paper, pencils, crayons, colored pencils, and so on

FOCUSED MINILESSON *(publishing)*
10 MINUTES

- Focus the learning: *In this session we'll finish our covers and tables of contents. Then, if we want, we can add an additional feature called an "About the Author" page. When we're happy with our published work, we'll share our reports with each other.*

- Display and read aloud the sample "About the Author" blurbs you have assembled. *I don't know about you, but when I finish reading a really great nonfiction book, I always want to know something about the person who wrote it. What do you notice about these "About the Author" pages?*

- *That's right. All of these pages tell the author's name, the state that he or she lives in, and some facts about what the author likes to do for fun. Each one also includes a picture of the author, and it lists other books that he or she has written.*

   TURN &TALK *If you decide to write an "About the Author" page for your report, what will you tell about yourself? Talk it over with your partner.*

WRITING and COACHING *(publishing)*
15 MINUTES

- Have students continue to work on their covers and tables of contents. Those who have already finished can help their classmates or may choose to write an "About the Author" page. Encourage these students to draw self-portraits to go with their author blurbs.

- As students finish, bind their reports. If you have access to your school's Internet server, you might want to create a website to display the finished reports. Scan and upload reports to the server, then organize them into an online "encyclopedia." Invite parents to assist students in this effort.

SHARING, REFLECTING, and CELEBRATING
20 MINUTES

- Bring the students together to share their reports. This may happen with the whole class, with partners, or in small groups. Alternatively, you may wish to arrange for students to share their work with another class, or hold a class publishing party and invite parents.

- Display the reports in a place of honor in the classroom. Allow other students to borrow and read the reports during independent reading time.

- Display the features chart from the whole-class project, and lead students in comparing their finished work to the features chart.

TURN &TALK *Tell your partner all the ways you have improved as a writer. What have you learned about writing a report?*

- Remember to look back at students' pre-assessment pieces and to use the Ongoing Monitoring Sheet or the Individual Evaluation Record to document growth and note areas for improvement. Pass out copies of the Student Self-Reflection Sheet found on the *Resources* CD-ROM to assist students as they reflect on their own growth. Finally, be sure to take notes on what worked and what didn't during the unit so you can make adjustments that will maximize student learning. See "After the Unit," page 13, for more information about post-assessment and self-reflection.

TIP Post-assessment is critical if future demonstrations and learning experiences are to extend students' skills as writers of informational text.

Friendly Letter to Summarize

A friendly letter can summarize learning.

Dear First Graders,
We make new friends.
In gym we clim the ropes.
It is not scary.
We made ginger braed houses.
It was supor fun!
We did marble panting.
That was neat!

from,
Julia

FEATURES

- Greeting
- Body with topic and important details
- Closing and signature

FOCUSED MINILESSON

Writers, letters are great ways to share our learning. Today I am going to write a letter that captures our learning about math to share with your parents.

Before we start, let's take a look at a letter a student wrote to summarize learning about science. In the *Big Book of Mentor Texts,* turn to page 10. *I'm noticing that this letter starts with a greeting. Watch as I start my letter the same way:* Dear Parents. *Notice the greeting is at the top of the page, and I follow it with a comma. I'll start writing on the next line.* Read the first paragraph of the letter on page 10.

TURN &TALK *Writers, what do you notice about this part of the letter? Think together as you describe its purpose.*

What great observations! You noticed that the first part of the letter tells what the rest of the letter is about. Watch as I write the first part of my letter: Today we learned how to identify two- and three-dimensional shapes.

TURN &TALK *Writers, describe with your partner one important fact we learned about two- and three-dimensional shapes.*

I'm using your great ideas as I continue writing. Use students' ideas to craft a letter as in the sample. *Now that we've come to the end of our summary letter, we need to end it. Take a look at the mentor text. The science letter ends with the closing:* Your daughter. *That's not the best closing for a letter that I write to your parents. Watch as I write a more business-like closing. Notice that I start the closing on its own line and put my name on its own line:* Sincerely, Mrs. Brent.

Dear Parents,

Today we learned how to identify two- and three-dimensional shapes. We identified shapes such as spheres, prisms, cones, and cubes. We learned that we can find two- and three-dimensional shapes everywhere, such as the circles of tires and the sphere that is a playground ball! Math is all around us!

Sincerely,

Mrs. Brent

Modeled Writing

TURN &TALK *Writers, let's look closely at the model we created. What features do you notice in the letter?*

Use students' ideas to create a features list for a friendly letter that summarizes learning.

WRITING and COACHING

Now it's your turn to write a letter that summarizes learning! Write a letter to your families to tell what you've learned in science this week. Remind students to use the features list as they write. You might provide a form for writers who are struggling. Early finishers can add a sketch to illustrate the concept.

SHARING and REFLECTING

Writers, you should be proud of your letters! Not only did you summarize your learning by starting with the topic and sharing details, you also included all the features that make letters easy for your readers to understand.

TURN &TALK *Writers, if you were going to teach someone else how to write a letter that summarizes, what advice would you give? Share with a partner.*

ASSESS THE LEARNING

Have students compare their letters to the model to assess for inclusion of all the features. Gather small groups to reteach as necessary.

SELF-ASSESSMENT

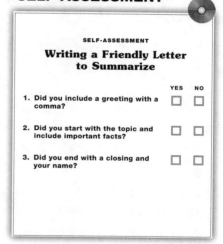

SELF-ASSESSMENT

Writing a Friendly Letter to Summarize

	YES	NO
1. Did you include a greeting with a comma?	☐	☐
2. Did you start with the topic and include important facts?	☐	☐
3. Did you end with a closing and your name?	☐	☐

SUPPORTING AND EXTENDING

▸ Form "Fact Friends" with another second-grade class. Have the students write to their friends about content-area concepts. Writing the letters and reading those written by their Fact Friends will reinforce content-area learning as well as writing skills.

▸ Have students write a letter to you that summarizes what they did over the weekend. Remind them to use all of the features of a letter.

▸ Students can take turns being "class reporter" for the class newsletter. Each "reporter" can write a letter to parents that summarizes learning.

Note to Invite

Invitations are notes that tell readers about upcoming events.

FEATURES

- Greeting
- Title of the event
- Date, time, and location
- Special instructions

FOCUSED MINILESSON

Writers, our open house is coming up. I have a friend who is a teacher in another school, and I want to invite her so that she can see what we are doing in our class.

Watch as I write the greeting Dear *and her name,* Susan, *on the first line of my paper. I write a comma after the greeting. Now comes the important part of the note—the name of the event and all the important details. The event is our second-grade open house, so I am writing a welcoming sentence:* You are cordially invited to our second-grade open house!

An invitation tells our readers the important information at a glance. Invitations are brief and focused just on the event. Instead of writing out a sentence for each important piece of information, I'll make it very easy for my readers to scan. What are the important things to know about an event? The date, time, and place. So I am writing the words, Date, Time, Place, *and following each with a colon. Watch as I complete the invitation.*

TURN &TALK *Is there anything else I should put on my invitation? Turn to your partner and share an idea.*

I heard a great idea to add some special instructions. Come to the front door. I think that's important. My friend might not know which door to use. I also like the idea I heard to R.S.V.P. An R.S.V.P. means that my friend will tell me if she is coming or not. That will help me plan how much juice and food I need for the open house.

TURN &TALK *Partners, think together. What are the important features of an invitation? List them.*

Ask students to share their responses. Create a features list on chart paper that students can use as a guide.

Dear Susan,

You are cordially invited to our second-grade open house!

Date: February 12

Time: 7:00 P.M.

Place: Washington School

Enter through the front door of the school.
Please R.S.V.P.

Modeled Writing

WRITING and COACHING

Choose an event for which your students can write invitations. *Writers, each of you is going to write an invitation to our open house for your family. Remember to use the features list and include all of the important details.* Students who are struggling might benefit from having an invitation form.

SHARING and REFLECTING

Writers, your invitations are so welcoming! I noticed that you remembered to include a greeting, the name of the event, the date, time, location, and special instructions. Your writing focused only on the open house, without giving other information. Great job!

ASSESS THE LEARNING

Have small groups gather to compare their invitations to the modeled writing. As you work with students, notice which students left out important information or included extra information. Reteach the purpose and features of an invitation as necessary.

SELF-ASSESSMENT

SELF-ASSESSMENT
Writing a Note to Invite

	YES	NO
1. Did you include a greeting with *Dear* and the person's name?	☐	☐
2. Did you include a date, time, and place?	☐	☐
3. Did you note special instructions on the invitation?	☐	☐

SUPPORTING AND EXTENDING

▸ Encourage students to write invitations to community members inviting them to a special classroom celebration or to assist with an event such as reading in the classroom.

▸ Provide opportunities for students to write notes that inform (see the *Resources* CD-ROM for "From the Desk of" Notes). Notes that inform might be reminders, such as *Dental Appointment, 2 P.M.* Notes might also be summaries of learning in which students write a note telling their parents what they learned in math, science, or social studies.

▸ Help students learn that notes are helpful communication tools by having them write notes instead of standing in line to tell you something. These notes might be along the line of, "We are out of paper towels." They might also be anecdotes from home that students want to share.

E-mail to Summarize

An e-mail shares information with others using current technology.

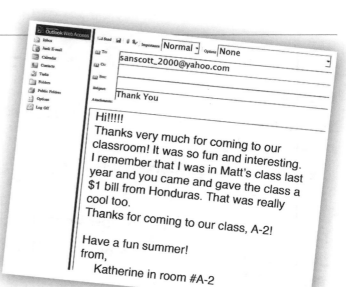

Hi!!!!!
Thanks very much for coming to our classroom! It was so fun and interesting. I remember that I was in Matt's class last year and you came and gave the class a $1 bill from Honduras. That was really cool too.
Thanks for coming to our class, A-2!

Have a fun summer!
from,
    Katherine in room #A-2

FEATURES

- Recipient(s)
- Short, clear subject line
- Greeting
- Purpose and details
- Closing and name

FOCUSED MINILESSON

Before starting the lesson, draw an e-mail "form" on a piece of chart paper, creating a space for the recipient name(s), subject line, and message. You might also project a real e-mail onto a viewing screen using an LCD projection system or electronic whiteboard.

E-mail is a great way to send a message quickly. I want to send the other second grade teachers in the building a note to remind them of our science fair. It would be great if they could bring their students!

Watch as I write the e-mail addresses into the address lines. My next step is to insert a subject line. This is usually very short—just a word or two. I am writing Science Fair. *That doesn't tell everything I need to say, but it gives my reader an idea of what this is about. Now I am ready for a greeting. Watch as I capitalize the first letters in the greeting and write:* Dear Second Grade Teachers. *This is just like a friendly letter.*

TURN &TALK *Evaluate the features of my e-mail so far. What did you see me do as I wrote the e-mail? What will you need to remember when you send an e-mail of your own?*

Now watch as I begin the body of the e-mail. This is where I insert important information: Come join us at the Second Grade Science Fair this Friday in the gym. The science fair begins at 2:00 P.M. We hope to see you and your students there.

Did you notice the information I shared was brief? In an e-mail to inform, tell the facts and stick to the topic. I did not write about anything other than the science fair.

Get ready, here comes the closing. This is where we say goodbye and sign our names. I am thinking that I could write: We hope to see you there! The Scientists in Room 11.

TURN &TALK *Examine this e-mail. Is that the best closing I could write? Is there another closing that might be even better? We really want everyone to come, so we need to get our reader(s) excited. Let's take a look at the closing.*

To: LSandvold@sd134.org

Subject: Science Fair

Dear Teachers,
Come join us at the second grade science fair this Friday in the gym. The science fair begins at 2:00 P.M. We hope to see you and your students there.

We hope to see you there!

The Scientists in Room 11

Modeled Writing

After writing: *Let's take a close look at this e-mail as we create a list of its features. E-mails are a lot like friendly letters! I notice some important features. The e-mail address allows me to send the note to someone else. If the address isn't correct, the e-mail will come back to me! The subject line tells the reader at a glance what the e-mail will be about.*

WRITING and COACHING

Writers, now it's your turn! Write an e-mail to your partner that summarizes a book you have been reading for independent reading. Identify the most important ideas from your reading so your partner knows what your book is about. After you each receive your e-mails, look at the book your partner read and then write back! E-mails are like letters, but they allow us to send information more quickly.

SHARING and REFLECTING

Writers, e-mails are a speedy and fun way to share information. Your e-mails included all the features—address, subject line, brief message, and a closing. The best part is that when we send an e-mail, we usually get a response!

ASSESS THE LEARNING

Have students print copies of their e-mails so you can assess them for correct use of features. If students need assistance in crafting an e-mail, talk over the features and provide additional support.

SELF-ASSESSMENT

SELF-ASSESSMENT

Writing an E-mail to Summarize

	YES	NO
1. Did you include a recipient?	☐	☐
2. Is your subject line short and clear?	☐	☐
3. Did you provide accurate details?	☐	☐

SUPPORTING AND EXTENDING

▸ Research and bookmark websites at which students can e-mail questions to experts. As you search for web-sites, bookmark those that are appropriate for student use.

▸ After students ask the experts, they can e-mail learning partners to tell what they learned.

▸ Gather family e-mail addresses or distribute a note to families giving the access information to a school web-site or server. Allow students to take turns writing a short class newsletter each week about upcoming events to send to or share with families.

Map

A map visually represents a place on Earth.

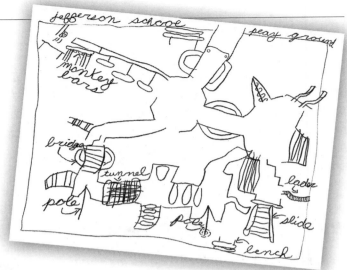

FEATURES

- Shows how an area would look if viewed from above
- Title, symbols, and key
- Clearly marked roads/ routes

FOCUSED MINILESSON

Writers, when I need to find out how to get to a place, I enter the address into a program on my computer that prints out a map for me. The map shows me how to get from my house to where I want to go. Maps are powerful tools!

I want to create an important map today. This map will be a reminder of how we get from our room to the safe place where we gather during a fire drill. Before we start our map, let's look at a map together. In the *Big Book of Mentor Texts,* turn to page 11. *This map shows the trails at a park.*

TURN &TALK *Partners, think together as you look at the map. What features really stand out as you examine it?*

Many of you noticed the title. Watch as I write a title for our map: Fire Drill Map. *That title is short and simple. Others noticed the part called the key. Why is the key important? The map would get crowded if we wrote these parts out every time they occurred on the map. Wouldn't it be complicated if we saw all those words?*

TURN &TALK *Remember, we are drawing a map from our classroom to our safe spot. What things might we show on a key?*

I like the ideas of having symbols for the restrooms and for the exit signs! Watch as I create symbols for these items. I'll put the symbols in the key and write what they stand for next to each symbol.

Now watch as I create the map. I am sketching our classroom and the hallway that leads to the door. I am putting in a space for the area where we meet outside. See the symbols for the restrooms and exit signs? I marked those on the map to help us find our way.

After writing: Let's take a close look at the map as we create a list of its features. The map shows how the area would look from above. We included a title, symbols, and a key. These features make it easy for our readers to understand our map and find their way from one place to another!

INFORM

Fire Drill Map

Modeled Writing

WRITING and COACHING

Writers, now it's your turn! Let's make a set of maps that school visitors could use to find their way around the building.

TURN &TALK *What locations could we map in our school?*

Those are fabulous ideas! We could make maps that show the playground, the route from our classroom to the bus area, even a map of the cafeteria showing the different lines for food and milk. Choose a map to create with a partner. Remind students to draw clear maps that include symbols and keys.

SHARING and REFLECTING

Writers, your maps will be so helpful to school visitors! What makes them so great? Your titles clearly state what the map shows. Your maps are easy to follow. And the symbols show real-life places that visitors will find along the route.

ASSESS THE LEARNING

Have students compare their work to the map you created. If necessary, help students review the relationship between the real locations and the overhead perspective of a map.

SELF-ASSESSMENT

SUPPORTING AND EXTENDING

▸ Have students create maps of the classroom, marking areas for centers, books, supplies, and so on.

▸ Have students create maps of their homes, of their bedrooms, or of simple routes, such as how to get to a familiar location like the library or the home of a friend.

▸ Have students prepare maps of places to explore, such as the South Pole, the Grand Canyon, or local attractions.

Readers Theater

A Readers Theater piece can convey information in the form of a script.

FEATURES

- Title
- Facts about a topic
- Script format with speakers' names followed by colons
- Parts for "all" and "some"

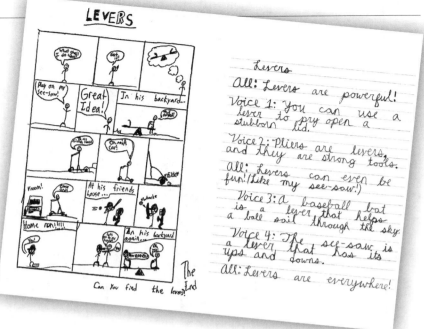

FOCUSED MINILESSON

This lesson is written about simple machines, but you can modify it to fit any content area.

Writers, I want to share this Readers Theater piece with you today! Readers Theater is like a play, with lines that different people speak, but we won't have to use actions or costumes. Instead, we read with expressive voices while we learn something new!

Turn to page 12 in the *Big Book of Mentor Texts*. If time allows, read the entire Readers Theater piece as a class, dividing students into teams for the reading. *Wow! I've learned a lot about polar bears, how about you? This is such a unique format. Instead of reading from a book, we said lines aloud with other readers. What a great way to share a reading experience!*

TURN &TALK *Partners, think together. What makes this form of writing different from others?*

Great observations! You noticed that the "All" parts give a big topic and that the "Team" parts give details. You also noticed an important feature of all Readers Theater scripts. Rather than using quotation marks to show what each person says, a Readers Theater piece says the name of each speaker followed by a colon. When you see the name of a speaker and a colon after it, you know the speaker should say the next part aloud.

Simple Machines are Everywhere

All: There are six kinds of simple machines.

Team 1:   A nail is a wedge that we can pound into wood.

Team 2:   A screwdriver turns the screws that hold something together.

Team 3:   A slide is a ramp that is fun to use.

Team 1:   A teeter-totter is a lever.

Team 2:   A pulley raises the flag in front of the school.

Team 3:   A bicycle rolls on a wheel and an axle.

All: Simple machines are all around — lever, ramp, wheel, screw, wedge, and pulley!

Modeled Writing

We are going to write a Readers Theater piece that captures what we know about simple machines. Watch as I write a part for everyone to speak: All: There are six kinds of simple machines. *Notice that there is a colon after* All. *That shows that all of us will say the line together.*

TURN &TALK *Identify the six types of simple machines. Select examples showing where we find simple machines everyday in our lives.*

I heard some great ideas! Watch as I capture some of them in parts for three teams. I want to name some simple machines in our lives, so I will start with a wedge. Watch as I write: Team 1: A nail is a . . . *Did you notice that I name the speaker and use a colon? Then, I leave a little space before I write my sentence. Team 2 will speak next. Watch my spacing as I write about a screwdriver. Spacing is important when you create a Readers Theater script.*

After writing: *Let's list the features of a Readers Theater piece.*

WRITING and COACHING

Divide the class into small groups. Have each group research and write lines that tell about one simple machine. Have groups work together to perform their completed Readers Theater script. After practicing, they may also want to present to another class.

SHARING and REFLECTING

Writers, the audience is going to learn a lot when you perform your Readers Theater! The script is full of fascinating facts. Each line has a speaker's name, followed by a colon, and then a space before the sentence begins.

ASSESS THE LEARNING

Call students over in their small groups to identify features of the Readers Theater piece in the mentor text and the script they helped create. Reteach the features as necessary.

SELF-ASSESSMENT

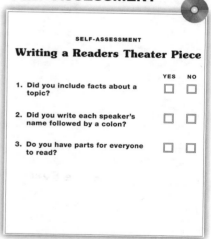

SELF-ASSESSMENT
Writing a Readers Theater Piece

	YES	NO
1. Did you include facts about a topic?	☐	☐
2. Did you write each speaker's name followed by a colon?	☐	☐
3. Do you have parts for everyone to read?	☐	☐

S U P P O R T I N G   A N D   E X T E N D I N G

▶ Have groups work to create a Readers Theater piece about the works of a famous inventor. Each group should give facts about one invention and present it using the features of a Readers Theater script.

▶ Have students develop a Readers Theater piece about a science process or discovery to perform for another second-grade class.

▶ Invite students to create a Readers Theater script that gives information about a person in history, a favorite animal, a health-related topic, and so on.

Biography

A biography tells the facts of a real person's life.

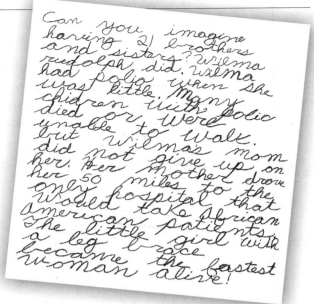

FEATURES

- Factual information
- Third-person point of view (Uses *he* or *she*)
- Presents a few highlights of a person's life

FOCUSED MINILESSON

This lesson focuses on a biography of Wilma Rudolph. (*Wilma Unlimited* by Kathleen Krull would be a great read-aloud to consider.) Adapt the content of the lesson for your class.

Writers, I've really enjoyed learning about Wilma Rudolph. Her story is inspirational! Today, I want to write a biography of Wilma Rudolph. A biography is a true account that presents important moments in someone's life.

Before I start writing, I'll look at a biography to get some ideas of its features. In the *Big Book of Mentor Texts*, turn to page 14. *This is a biography of Nancy Lopez. As I read one page, think about the features of this biography.* Read aloud page 14.

TURN &TALK *Partners, think together. What features on this page really stood out to you as you followed along?*

This is a great introduction to Nancy Lopez's life, isn't it? The writer could have said, "Nancy Lopez was born in 1957." But instead, the writer started with an interesting story that captured our attention. I am going to try to do the same thing in my writing. Watch as I write the start of my biography: Can you imagine wearing a brace on your leg as a child, and then going on to become one of the fastest runners alive? Wilma Rudolph did just that!

TURN &TALK *Writers, think about the life of Wilma Rudolph. What important events should I include in my biography about Wilma Rudolph?*

So far, we're off to a great start! This biography starts with an attention-getting beginning. Watch as I continue: Wilma had polio when she was very young and had to wear a brace on her leg. *Writers, did you notice that in this biography I either write Wilma's name or use the word* she *when I talk about her? This is important in a biography. My next sentence will begin:* Walking was so difficult . . . *Since this is a biography, I need to either write* Wilma *or use the pronoun* she.

TURN & TALK *Think together and select the word that you think would sound best in this sentence. Try the sentence both ways and decide if I should use* Wilma *or* she.

In a biography a nonfiction writer needs to focus on the most important events and challenges in a person's life. So, my next sentence will tell how Wilma got rid of her brace. Watch as I write: Wilma worked . . .

After writing: Let's focus on the features of our biography. A biography captures facts about a real person. Because we write biographies about other people and not about ourselves, we use pronouns like she *and* he *to show that we are writing about others.* List the features of biography for student reference.

Can you imagine wearing a brace on your leg as a child, and then going on to become one of the fastest runners alive? Wilma Rudolph did just that! Wilma had polio when she was very young and had to wear a brace on her leg. Walking was so difficult she couldn't even go to school with her friends. Wilma worked hard to exercise and make her leg strong.

Modeled Writing

WRITING and COACHING

I started Wilma Rudolph's biography, but we know more about her life and the amazing things that she did! It's time for you to continue. Think of the facts you know as you write about her life. Students can use your beginning to complete the biography. More capable writers may craft other powerful beginnings.

SHARING and REFLECTING

Writers, your biographies will help your readers understand the courage of Wilma Rudolph. You included facts and highlights of her life. And you pronouns such as she *and* her.

ASSESS THE LEARNING

As you assess students' biographies, be sure they have included facts rather than fiction. Look for third-person pronouns and note which students may need extra assistance.

SELF-ASSESSMENT

SELF-ASSESSMENT
Writing a Biography

	YES	NO
1. Did you include facts about the person in your biography?	☐	☐
2. Did you use pronouns such as *he, she, they,* and *their*?	☐	☐

SUPPORTING AND EXTENDING

▸ Read a biography that focuses on a single facet of a famous person's life, such as *George Washington's Teeth* by Deborah Chandra and Madeleine Comora or *Martin's Big Words* by Doreen Rappaport.

▸ Students can interview classmates to create biographies. Give students class pictures to add to the biographies, which you can bind into a book.

▸ Have students write biographies of other notable people you study. Students can introduce their biographies and include a prop that exemplifies something about the person.

Venn Diagram

Venn diagrams allow you to compare and contrast two subjects.

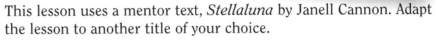

FEATURES

- Title
- Headings
- Two overlapping circles
- Facts about each category

FOCUSED MINILESSON

This lesson uses a mentor text, *Stellaluna* by Janell Cannon. Adapt the lesson to another title of your choice.

Writers, I was fascinated by Janell Cannon's Stellaluna! *It was so interesting to see how Stellaluna was like the birds—and how she was different. Today, I'm creating a Venn diagram. A Venn diagram is a special graphic organizer that helps me compare and contrast two things. Comparing is showing how two things are the same. Contrasting is showing how they are different.*

Watch as I draw two big circles that overlap each other. Notice that these are big enough so that I have room to write in them. Now I need to write headings over each circle. I am going to compare bats to birds, so over one circle, I'm writing Bats. *Over the other circle, I'm writing the heading* Birds.

TURN &TALK *Partners, think together. How is a bat like a bird?*

Bats and birds fly and have wings. See where the circles overlap? Here I write things that are true of both topics.

TURN &TALK *Describe something that is true only of bats. What can bats do that the birds can't do?*

Bats sleep upside down. That is different from birds. Watch as I write this fact in the part of the circle that is under the heading Bats. *This shows that the fact is true only of bats. I heard someone say that the birds land on their feet.*

TURN &TALK *Partners, give me some advice! Where should I put the fact that the birds land on their feet?*

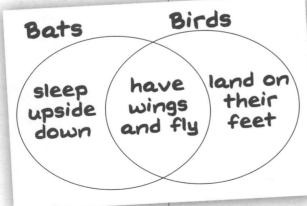

Modeled Writing

You've got the idea! The fact about the birds should go in the circle under the Birds *heading.* As time allows, elicit students' ideas for more facts about bats, birds, or both.

After writing: *Writers, let's take a look at our diagram and list its features. Each of the two circles features facts that describe only the topic in the heading. The place where the circles overlap describes both.*

WRITING and COACHING

Writers, now it's time for you to create your own Venn diagrams. We've learned a lot about owls. Use the Venn diagram to compare owls and bats. Give students pre-printed forms with circles already created. Adapt the assignment for content in your class. *Bats and owls both fly. Since this is true about both animals, where would you write that fact? Exactly—right in the middle where the circles overlap!*

SHARING and REFLECTING

Writers, your diagrams do an amazing job of organizing information to show us how two things are alike and different. You placed facts correctly in your diagrams. And you included a title and headings.

ASSESS THE LEARNING

As students create their diagrams, note which students need extra support to understand where to put the facts. Help them sort the facts into the categories *alike* and *different* for easy placement in the diagram.

SELF-ASSESSMENT

SELF-ASSESSMENT
Making a Venn Diagram

	YES	NO
1. Did you include a title and headings?	☐	☐
2. Did you place facts that describe both topics in the center of your diagram, where the circles overlap?	☐	☐
3. Did you place facts that are different in the correct circles?	☐	☐

SUPPORTING AND EXTENDING

▶ Work with students to create comparing and contrasting sentences based on their Venn diagrams, such as *Bats and birds both ___. While bats ___, birds ___.*

▶ Have students work in teams to create Venn diagrams about science topics, such as solids and liquids or rain and snow. Students can explain their work before placing diagrams in the science center.

▶ Have students create Venn Diagrams comparing themselves with learning partners in the classroom.

Class Newsletter

A class newsletter shares information and informs readers.

FEATURES

• Title and headlines
• Columns
• Important information and interesting facts

FOCUSED MINILESSON

Writers, look at what I got in the mail! This newsletter came from my dentist. My dentist likes to inform her patients about the great things going on in her office.

Our friends and families love to have information about the amazing things we learn in school. Today, we're going to write a newsletter that shares important information with them. Taking a look at my dentist's newsletter, I notice the title, From the Smile Doctor. *I want to grab my readers' attention too, so watch as I write the title:* Extra! Extra! 2M News! *Notice that I center the title at the top of the page.*

Let's take another look at my dentist's newsletter. Here's an article that caught my attention. The headline says "Straight Smiles," and the article under it tells about a new kind of braces.

For our newsletter, I want to start with some text highlighting our science unit about Earth's rotation.

TURN &TALK *Partners, put your heads together. Think of a headline that would really capture readers' attention.*

I heard a lot of great ideas! I am going to write: As the Earth Turns. *Watch where I write it on the page. I want each article to have its own column, so I center the title over a column instead of across the top of the page. Notice that there is a title for the newsletter across the top and now a title for an article at the top of the left column.*

Now for the article. I want to include that it takes 24 hours for the earth to rotate. That is why each day is 24 hours long. Watch as I write: We learned that . . . *Notice how I keep my writing inside the column. Newsletter columns keep articles separate.*

TURN &TALK *Writers, identify additional important ideas about the rotation of the earth that I should include.*

I really like the idea of adding a photograph, because it's hard to picture how this works without seeing it. This visual makes the newsletter even more exciting!

Extra! Extra! 2M News!

As the Earth Turns

We learned that it takes 24 hours for the earth to rotate on its axis. That equals one day and night on Earth. We made a model of Earth, the sun, and the moon with balls and a flashlight. Our model helped us see how Earth turns!

(Here is where I'll put my photo.)

Modeled Writing

After writing: *Let's look at the newsletter and list its features. The newsletter has a title. The article on Earth's rotation is in its own column with a headline. The headline captures our readers' attention and sums up with important details.*

WRITING and COACHING

TURN &TALK *Writers, we have more space! What other news could we share?*

Use students' ideas to generate a topic list. Then have students work independently or with partners to create articles. Compile students' work into a newsletter to send home.

SHARING and REFLECTING

Writers, we can be proud of our class newsletter. Headlines capture our readers' attention. The articles are full of interesting facts. We used columns, too. We've created a great tool for sharing our work!

ASSESS THE LEARNING

As students work, assess their ability to create engaging headlines and capture content. Work with small groups as necessary on topics such as effectively summarizing or writing attention-grabbing headlines.

SELF-ASSESSMENT

SELF-ASSESSMENT

Making a Class Newsletter

	YES	NO
1. Does your newsletter article have an engaging headline?	☐	☐
2. Did you arrange your newsletter in columns?	☐	☐
3. Did you share important information and interesting facts?	☐	☐

SUPPORTING AND EXTENDING

▸ Have students publish book summaries in newsletters. Create headlines for subject areas such as fiction, poetry, science, math, and sports. Place copies of the newsletter in the library.

▸ Have students create newsletters about math. Suggest topics such as famous mathematicians, story problems, math shortcuts, and powerful math strategies.

▸ Divide students into groups and have them create a newsletter about a favorite topic, e.g., Earth Day, volcanoes, current events. Have students deliver the newsletters to another class.

Informational Poem

Poems can teach about content while using descriptive language.

Where'o where is my square?
Blissfully, Cudly blanket
Joyful, family fun, board games
colorful, Creative picturs
Big, black, shiny T.V
Cold, smooth, floor tiles
You can find squares everywhere!

FEATURES

- Title
- Factual information
- Descriptive words
- Words in lines instead of paragraphs

FOCUSED MINILESSON

Writers, I love the descriptive words of poetry. A poem can take a topic and give it words that roll off your tongue and around in your mind, too. I am going to create a poem today based on something we've been learning about in science—states of matter. It might seem odd to write a poem about something like this, but I know we can make it descriptive and exciting.

Before I start writing, I'll look at an informational poem to see how another author created one. In the Big Book of Mentor Texts, turn to page 19: Isn't this interesting? It's a poem about a social studies topic, goods and services! Read the poem to students.

TURN & TALK *Writers, think together. What makes this poem different from a paragraph about goods and services?*

You noticed that a poem has lines instead of sentences that flow together. I am going to start a poem now on states of matter. Watch as I write the first two lines: Rock, block, ice cube, book. / You can really put your hands on solids!

TURN & TALK *What do you think of these lines of the poem? Evaluate my writing so far.*

I heard many of you say that you were looking for more descriptive words. Those would make my writing more interesting, wouldn't they? Let's check back on the mentor text. The writer uses words such as cold, drippy, smiling, shining. Those words

Solids, Liquids, and Gases Matter!

Speckled rock, wooden block, shivery ice cube, thick heavy book.

You can really put your hands on solids!

Goopy honey, sparkling water, thick colorful paint, powerful fuels.

Liquids spread to take the shapes of their containers.

Have you felt the breeze brush your skin? Watched a balloon float in the air?

You can't see gases, but you can see and feel their effects!

Modeled Writing

INFORM

help readers make great pictures in their minds! Watch as I revise: Speckled rock, wooden block, shivery ice cube, thick heavy book. / You can really put your hands on solids!

TURN &TALK *Partners, I want to write about liquids now. What liquids could I describe in a poem? Share some ideas with your partner.*

Honor students' thinking as you create lines about liquids and gases as shown in the sample modeled writing. *Writers, there is one more piece that we need to add to our poem: a title! A title should sum up the poem and capture our readers' attention. Watch as I write at the top and the center:* Solids, Liquids, and Gases Matter!

Capture features of informational poems as you reread the model: *Let's take a look at our poem! It uses lines instead of paragraphs. And even with the use of descriptive words, you can read about real facts. If you didn't know the definition of solids, liquids, and gases, this poem would help you.*

WRITING and COACHING

We read and wrote informational poems. Now it's your turn! Write your own poem with descriptive words and phrases. Students who struggle to get started can use your matter poem and insert other descriptions of solids, liquids, and gases into the lines. More confident writers can create informational poems about other topics.

SHARING and REFLECTING

Writers, you should be proud of what you've done with these poems. You've taken information and made it descriptive and interesting for your readers.

ASSESS THE LEARNING

Have students compare their work to the poem that you created to note features. If necessary, review with students how to insert powerful description into poetry.

SELF-ASSESSMENT

SELF-ASSESSMENT

Writing an Informational Poem

	YES	NO
1. Did you use lines instead of paragraphs?	☐	☐
2. Did you include a title?	☐	☐
3. Does your poem include factual information?	☐	☐
4. Did you use powerful descriptions in your writing?	☐	☐

SUPPORTING AND EXTENDING

▸ At the beginning of a unit, post the topic on a bulletin board. As students read and research, they can post descriptive words and phrases. As a culminating activity, create a poem with the posted words.

▸ Have students write poems to describe a scene from a story they've read.

▸ Ask students to write poems about the same nonfiction topic—habitats, for example. Have them illustrate their poems and help you bind them into a class book.

Investigation

Investigations use special text features to give information about topics.

Polar Bears live in the North Pole. They live in dens.

What they look like

They have blubber under their fur. Polar Bears have white fur. On sunny days the sun gets into their skin. They weigh about 750 pounds to about 1100 pounds.

Polar Bear

What they eat

Polar Bears eat seals, fish, seabirds, and reindeer. Polar Bears are carnivores, which means they eat meat. Their favorite food is ringed seals.

Wow facts

Polar Bears move a lot. When they're first born they can't see. Polar Bears can swim well. They're about four feet tall. They lay on the ground to find seals. They can smell three feet away. Polar Bears have webbed feet and sharp claws.

FEATURES

- Focused topic with facts
- Two facing pages that form a "spread"
- Visual supports: title, headings, labels, and diagrams
- Text boxes

FOCUSED MINILESSON

Writers, we've learned a lot about ocean life. Today I want to showcase what we know about whales in an interesting form—an investigation. Let's take a look at some investigations in our mentor text. In the Big Book of Mentor Texts, turn to page 22 or 38. These investigations have different purposes—to persuade and narrate. But let's look at the features to think about the form our investigation might take.

TURN &TALK *Partners, think together. As you take a closer look at these investigations, what features stand out for you?*

You noticed so many great features! We can definitely pull these into our investigation—title, headings, boxes with text, colors and bold text to set apart different parts of the work. We have a lot of decisions to make. That's why it makes sense to plan an investigation before we put all the information on paper.

Watch as I get started by folding this large piece of paper in half to create a center gutter line. I'm writing my title at the top of the page in big letters: Whales: Gentle Giants. *Did you notice that I wrote the title across the center line? Now I am going to make my main illustration cross the middle line, too. Watch as I sketch a whale and add labels for* blowhole, tail, flukes, flippers, upper jaw, *and* lower jaw. *I am drawing lines from the labels to the body parts to be sure that readers can identify each part of the whale.*

Next, I'm making text boxes with space to write whale facts. I'm leaving space on this side of the page to place a map where I can color in the locations of whales around the world. There's some space on this side that's a perfect place to list what whales eat. Once I like how the page looks, I will fill in my text boxes.

After writing, list features of an investigation as you point them out on the model: Writers, I planned an investigation that will use features to show information. A title reveals the focus of the content. A big illustration is going to anchor the piece, and labels will give information about whales. The map and other text features will show readers information in a very exciting way!

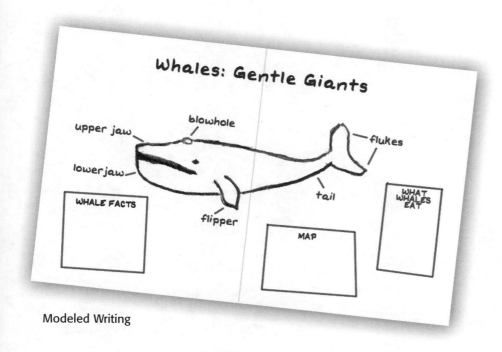

Modeled Writing

WRITING and COACHING

Writers, we've planned an investigation, but it's not complete. Let's work together to finish this investigation about whales. Students who need support can work independently to create elements for the investigation you started, while more capable writers can plot out the elements of investigations to complete on their own.

SHARING and REFLECTING

Writers, your investigations make information jump out at your readers! Using text features helps us show ideas about our topic in a way that is exciting and easy to understand.

ASSESS THE LEARNING

As students create their investigations, note which students are able to use text features. Use the investigations in the mentor text to point out features such as headings and text boxes and to talk about how they are helpful to readers.

SELF-ASSESSMENT

SUPPORTING AND EXTENDING

▸ Examine layouts in nonfiction magazines, such as *National Geographic Explorer*. Discuss elements of the magazine layout students might want to include in their own writing.

▸ As you start a unit on a nonfiction topic, have teams begin investigations. As their knowledge expands, students can add to their work. Allow time for finalizing investigations at the end of the unit.

▸ Have students create investigations on topics you are exploring in class. After students have shared their work, bind investigations into class books that students can explore during independent reading time.

Procedural Writing Projects

Procedural or instructional texts tell the reader how to make something, do something, complete a process, or accomplish any task that requires several steps. Students are most likely to encounter procedural text in the form of directions on schoolwork, instructions on how to use something, or instructions for playing a game. Procedural text may appear in many formats, including directions on schoolwork or forms, rules for games, recipes, map directions, care directions, instructions for assembly, and user guides.

- -

CONTENTS

The Big Picture:
Class and Individual Projects

. . . .

During the *class project,* students work together to create a collaborative procedural text on how to draw a crab. The mentor text "How to Draw a Dolphin" provides a model of the structure, features, and language of a procedural text. Note that the mentor text is about how to draw a dolphin, not a crab. This is to ensure that students will actively research to discover their own information and not just copy the text directly. Students begin by observing these elements in the mentor text and then use their research notebooks to organize information about crabs and various drawing techniques in order to plan and draft the materials, illustrations, and steps needed for their group work. Finally, students collaborate on publishing their final procedural text and arrange for students in another class to follow the instructions in order to assess how effective the class how-to really is.

During their *individual project*, students review the features of a procedural text, choose a topic for their own procedural writing, and plan, draft, revise, edit, and publish "how-to" instructions—complete with a materials list, numbered steps, and illustrations. Writing partners follow each other's directions to test for accuracy.

CLASS PROJECT			
Session	**Focused Minilesson**	**Writing and Coaching**	**Sharing and Reflecting**
1	Introduce procedural text; choose topics	Draft pre-assessment procedural text	How are our procedural texts the same? Different?
2	Study "How to Draw a Dolphin"; list features; use descriptive words while taking notes	Craft title and materials list; conduct research; take notes	Are our materials lists complete? Do titles tell what procedure is about?
3	Study "How to Draw a Dolphin"; notice strong descriptions and steps to follow	Continue research and note taking; begin to draft steps	How did we explain the first part of drawing a crab? Why was our research so important?
4	Study "How to Draw a Dolphin"; notice action words (verbs), numbered steps, and illustrations	Revise steps for clarity, order, and strong verbs;	What processes did we use to write our steps? Can our partners follow them? Did we start with action words?
5	Study "How to Draw a Dolphin"; notice that the steps make sense; check work against features chart	Edit, revise, and publish final procedural text; try out with others; celebrate, reflect on what was learned	Share with another class. Celebrate efforts and display finished texts.

INDIVIDUAL PROJECT			
Session	**Focused Minilesson**	**Writing and Coaching**	**Sharing and Reflecting**
6	Review features of procedural text; choose a topic	Write title and draft materials list in research notebook	Do our titles tell what the text is about? Are our materials lists complete?
7	Analyze modeled writing; notice time-order words and numbered steps	Draft directions/steps; share with partner	How have we organized our texts? What can we do to make our directions clearer?
8	Learn to revise for complete steps and time order	Revise drafts for clarity and order; discuss revisions with partner	What did we discover by revising our work? What changes did we make?
9	Learn to create illustrations that match the text	Publish title, byline, and materials list; add illustrations; share	How do illustrations improve our directions? How can we make them better?
10	Learn to revise for punctuation and legible handwriting	Publish drafts with legible handwriting, correct punctuation, and illustrations that match text	What features of procedural text have we included in our writing? Evaluate against checklist.

Other Topics and Forms for Procedural Writing

Although this model project uses the topic "how to draw" as a springboard for teaching procedural writing, the teaching process here can be adapted to many other procedural topics and forms. The Power Writes in this section will give you ideas for several such adaptations in addition to those that follow.

Possible Topics

Topics may correlate with content in your science and social studies standards, current events, or class interests.

▸ How to make a favorite food (popcorn, bumps on a log, tacos, etc.)

▸ How to make a sandwich

▸ How to play a game (tag, t-ball, computer game, etc.)

▸ How to get somewhere (from the classroom to ____)

▸ How to have a good book discussion

▸ How to take care of something (a dog, your shoes, etc.)

▸ How to cross the street safely

▸ How to look up a word (in a dictionary, online)

▸ How to wrap a gift

▸ How to keep a younger person happy (baby, toddler, etc.)

▸ How to be a good classmate or friend

▸ How to do a science experiment

▸ How to clean your bedroom

▸ How to grow a flower

Possible Forms

Some of these forms are invariably procedural (like game directions or recipes), while others (like letters or lists) can be used for a variety of purposes, including procedures.

▸ Signs

▸ Recipes

▸ Brochures

▸ Maps

▸ Directions

▸ Diagrams

▸ Illustrations

▸ Flow charts

▸ Advertisements

▸ Notes

▸ E-mail messages

▸ Letters

▸ Posters

▸ How-to lists

Setting Up Your Research Stations

For the *class project,* you will need to gather books, magazine articles, encyclopedia entries, and websites that feature crab anatomy for research stations—enough material that the whole class can research and take notes simultaneously. Make sure the research materials you gather for this project include plenty of close-up photographs, diagrams, and plastic models of crabs if available. Also include books or posters that name shapes, as well as books of drawing instructions, so that students can generalize from these artistic how-to's to their own efforts. If possible, provide books or other resources recorded on tapes or CDs. Do not, however, include specific instructions for drawing a crab.

In addition to the mentor text, you will need two or three simple how-to texts, each with just 3 or 4 procedural steps, to use as models during Session 1. If the samples you find in published books do not have the relevant features (materials list, steps), you may want to draft these simple models yourself. You'll find plenty of ideas to get you started in the "Possible Topics" section on page 77. Another set of instructions, perhaps a little more complicated, with illustrated steps, will help you convey the importance of illustrations during Session 3.

For the *individual project,* you will not need to assemble research materials because students will be writing simple procedures for things they already know how to do.

Please refer to page xiii of the introduction to this book and page 285 in the Resources section at the end for additional information on setting up and using research stations.

Focusing on Standards

This extended writing unit is designed to teach students about the form and content of procedural writing as they apply basic writing strategies. Each of the lessons provides you with suggested demonstrations, but you may wish to tailor your instruction based on the common needs of your own students. The pre-assessment from Session 1 will help you identify these needs.

Before introducing the unit, carefully review the list below so you can keep the lesson objectives in mind as you teach, coach, and monitor students' growth as writers of procedural texts.

KEY SKILLS AND UNDERSTANDINGS: PROCEDURAL TEXTS GRADE 2
Purpose
• Understands the purpose for writing a procedural piece
Ideas/Research
• Reflects research and planning
• Bases writing on research and prior knowledge
• Includes facts and details from research
• Gathers and incorporates information from multiple sources
Organization/Text Features
• Includes a title that tells what is to be done or made
• Provides a list of materials
• Presents steps in a logical sequence
• Supports the text with illustrations or diagrams
Language/Style
• Uses descriptive words to make directions clear
• Includes time-order words (*first, next, then, last*)
• Begins each step with an action verb (*put, mix, cut, take,* etc.)
Conventions and Presentation
• Begins sentences with capital letters
• Uses correct end punctuation
• Begins each step in the process on a new line

The list is the basis for both the Individual Evaluation Record and the Ongoing Monitoring Sheet shown in Figure 2.1. Both forms can be found in the Resources section at the back of this book and on the *Resources* CD-ROM. Use the Individual Evaluation Record if you want to keep separate records on individual students. The Ongoing Monitoring Sheet gives you a simple mechanism for recording information on all your students as you move around the class, evaluating their work in progress. Use this information to adapt instruction and session length as needed.

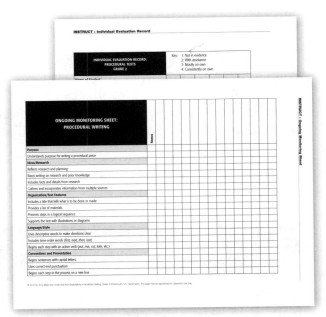

Figure 2.1 Individual Evaluation Record and Ongoing Monitoring Sheet

You will also use the Ongoing Monitoring Sheet and/or the Individual Evaluation Record at the end of the unit to record students' growth as writers after comparing their published work from the individual project with the pre-assessment they will complete in Session 1 of the class project.

Planning and Facilitating the Unit

Students will need preparation, coaching, prompting, and support as they move through this extended writing unit. Use the following tips and strategies as needed to ensure each child's success.

Before the Unit:

▸ When planning your teaching, bear in mind that each session in this unit is designed to be completed in a day. However, you will likely find that your students need more time for certain activities. Take the time you need to adequately respond to the unique needs of your students.

▸ Begin building background knowledge about procedural texts in general as well as crabs and crab anatomy at least a week in advance. Shared reading, guided reading, and read-aloud experiences as well as group discussions will ensure that students are not dependent exclusively on their own research.

▸ As you share procedural texts with students, be sure to highlight the purpose of the text, numbered steps, use of action verbs to begin steps, and illustrations that match the words.

During the Class Project:

▸ Be sure to model note taking for students as you think aloud about information in reference materials. Use chart paper to capture your notes about what crabs look like, and display the model prominently as students work independently in research stations.

▸ Students may benefit from an organizer they can use to capture their thoughts. Leave space for a materials list and steps. Consider allowing students to choose between an organizer with time-order words and one with numbers for the steps.

▸ Provide templates for students who need extra support when writing their directions. Include spaces for the title, byline, materials list, numbered steps, and accompanying illustrations.

▸ As students work independently on their drawing instructions, note those who are struggling and bring them together in small groups for think-alouds. Show them the sections of the crab's body and use descriptive words to explain the shapes you see. If students need support to write their directions, scribe from their dictation and let them copy or paste the sentences onto their publishing paper.

▸ Students who seem very confident and who have clearly grasped all of the concepts taught so far can be brought together in a small group to extend their understanding to more challenging work, such as using reference sources to take notes, or creating a list of rules for capitalization. Students who complete their work early can work with partners to test their directions.

▸ Although the lessons provide suggested demonstrations for each session, you may wish to tailor your instruction to meet the common needs of your students. The Ongoing Monitoring Sheet together with the Individual Evaluation Record will help you keep track of each student's unique needs. Refer to the section on assessment on pages xxx–xxxv in the introduction to this book for further information.

▸ Use the Daily Planner (Figure 2.2, and found on the *Resources* CD-ROM) to plan your own class projects for future explorations based on the needs of your students.

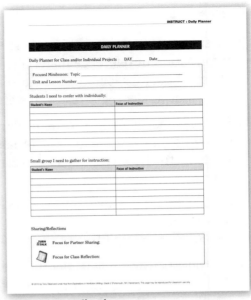

Figure 2.2 Daily Planner

During the Individual Project:

▸ Continue to use the Ongoing Monitoring Sheet and the Individual Evaluation Record to identify topics you'll want to address in the focused minilesson that begins each session. Continue to use the Daily Planner to lay out future explorations based on student needs.

▸ Help students select simple procedures that are easy to describe. Students should be able to easily envision and remember each step in the procedure. If students get stuck, suggest procedures such as brushing one's teeth or washing the family dog.

▸ Encourage students to act out the steps in the procedure they are writing about in order to ensure the correct sequence.

▸ Some students will benefit from saying the steps out loud to a partner before writing them.

▸ Remind your insecure illustrators that this is not an art project and they will not be graded on the quality of their drawing. Emphasize that stick figures or simple line drawings are perfectly adequate; the important thing is that the drawings reflect and clarify what is written.

▸ Encourage students to label their drawings if time allows. This may be especially helpful to English language learners.

▸ Have writing partners conference with each other often in order to check one another's work for sense and clarity.

▸ You may find it helpful to work on your own procedural text along with your students. Then you can use this model as an example during think-alouds.

After the Unit:

▸ Be sure to give students opportunities to share and celebrate their individual writing projects.

▸ Distribute copies of the Student Self-Reflection sheet (on the *Resources* CD-ROM). Students will benefit greatly from the chance to reflect on their progress during the unit and to hear their classmates' feedback.

▸ Compare students' final writing products with their pre-assessments to evaluate their growth as writers of procedural text.

▸ Look at common needs of the class and address these when planning future explorations on procedural writing, or through the Power Writes.

▸ Reflect on the strengths and challenges of implementing this series of lessons. How might it be adjusted to maximize student learning?

SESSION 1
Immersion and Pre-Assessment

Students are introduced to procedural text and draft a simple procedure for the pre-assessment.

MATERIALS
• 2–3 very simple procedural texts, enlarged if possible
• Paper and pencils

TIP Help your students connect procedural writing with real-life reasons: *When I went to the beach last weekend, my dog stayed with my friend. So I wrote down everything she needed to do to take care of my dog.* When you provide real-life reasons, you help your students see that procedural texts have a purpose and an audience. You give them a context for writing.

FOCUSED MINILESSON *(prewriting)*
20 MINUTES

■ Introduce students to the purpose of procedural texts by mentioning a procedural text you have recently used in class: *Remember when we were playing a new game last week? We weren't sure of the rules. How did we figure it out? That's right—we followed directions! Directions are a special kind of writing called procedural text. A procedure tells how to make or do something.*

TURN &TALK *Partners, put your heads together. Talk about a procedural text you've used recently. How did it help you make or do something?*

■ After listening to students' examples, praise their understanding as you reiterate the purpose: *I heard you mention some great procedural texts, such as recipes, directions for playing a game, and a procedure for making a craft project. All of these examples teach you how to make or do something!*

■ Show students additional examples of procedural texts. Ask them to identify the purpose of each piece and what the reader will learn from reading it.

TURN &TALK *We are going to write procedural texts. Turn to your partner and tell him or her something that you could describe how to make or do in a procedural text.*

■ Capture students' ideas on chart paper. If students get stuck, suggest simple procedures such as brushing their teeth, washing the family dog, or making a cheese sandwich.

■ Let students know their goal for writing: *Choose one of the ideas from our list to focus on as you write a procedure. Remember, your text should tell your readers how to make or do something.*

WRITING and COACHING *(prewriting, drafting)*
20 MINUTES

- After students have identified their topics, they should draft their pre-assessment pieces. Remind them that their goal is to show what they know about writing procedural text.

- Encourage students to ask each other for assistance before asking you. This will help create a community of writers in your classroom and will give you more time to reach the students who need your help the most.

SHARING and REFLECTING
10 MINUTES

TURN &TALK *Share your procedural text with your learning partner. How are your texts the same? How are they different?*

- Sum up what students have learned, focusing on the purpose of procedural text: *As I listened to your conversations, I heard some great ideas for things to make or do that you wrote about as procedural text! During the week, we'll learn more about what makes a clearly written and engaging procedural text. It will be interesting to think about how we can make our work engaging and easy for our readers to understand.*

- After class, evaluate each student's writing using the Ongoing Monitoring Sheet in the Resources section at the back of this book and on the *Resources* CD-ROM. Use the results to revise instruction and personalize the lessons in this unit. If you want to keep individual records on students, use the Individual Evaluation Record on the *Resources* CD-ROM. Do not make corrections or marks on students' work.

- Please see the introduction to this book for more information on the role of the pre-assessment.

TIP If students seem anxious as they get started, empathize with them: *When I try a new kind of writing, I can get nervous. But I just make a first effort using what I know. Then when I learn more, I can fix my first draft or write an even better one.* Showing students that writing is an evolving process will give them confidence and insight into the writing process. It will also reassure students who may be struggling with this first attempt.

TIP Reflective thinking (and, when possible, reflective writing) following any kind of lesson helps students to more fully internalize their experiences and their new knowledge. Also, during reflective discussion, children hear other students' experiences and pick up things they may have missed the first time around. Time spent in reflection is always worth it!

SESSION 2
Identifying Features, Researching, and Writing

Students identify features of a procedural text and begin to research and write their titles and materials lists.

MATERIALS
- *Big Book of Mentor Texts:* "How to Draw a Dolphin," pages 24–27
- Chart paper and marker
- Research notebooks
- Pencils
- Research materials: books, pictures, movies, and book-marked websites

---

Features of a Great Procedural Text

It lists the things you need.

There is a title that tells what it's about.

TIP If necessary, help students identify and describe the features of the mentor text, but resist listing features for them. Discovery is an experience like no other. When students discover things for themselves, they won't soon forget them.

FOCUSED MINILESSON *(prewriting)*
25 MINUTES

- Focus the learning: *In our last session, we learned the purpose of a procedural text—to teach our readers how to make or do something. We use procedural texts all the time! Today, we'll look more closely at procedural text to see what makes it so special and what we need to include in procedural texts of our own.*

- Explain using the mentor text: *When I'm going to write a kind of text that's new to me, it helps me to look at what a more experienced writer has done. Let's take a look at a great procedural text to see what features it has.*

- Display the mentor text and read aloud the title. Invite students to share some prior knowledge about dolphins. Read the names of the parts of dolphins as you point to the completed diagram on page 24. Then read the mentor text aloud.

  TURN &TALK *Partners, think together. What do you notice about the mentor text that you'd want to include in your own procedural texts?*

- As students share the features they have identified, begin a features chart. Because students will be writing titles and materials lists, focus on those characteristics. If you would like, adapt the lesson to focus on a diagram that matches content your class is studying.

- *For our procedural text, we are going to write about how to draw a crab. Since we are not crab experts, we are going to have to do some research and take some notes. We will use these research materials to describe how to write about drawing a crab.*

  TURN &TALK *Since we are writing a procedural text about drawing a crab, what kind of information will we need? Talk it over with your partner.*

- Invite students to share their ideas, discussing things they will need to know, such as what a crab looks like, part by part and shape by shape.

TURN &TALK *Partners, take a closer look at the materials list in the mentor text. Talk together about what you notice about how it's written.*

■ *You noticed that the materials list is just that—a list. It's not a group of sentences. And because it doesn't have sentences, you don't need to include capital letters at the beginnings of the lines.*

WRITING and COACHING *(prewriting, drafting)*
25 MINUTES

■ Have students craft their titles and materials lists before starting their research and note taking. Circulate around the room encouraging students to imagine themselves completing the task in order to visualize all of the materials they will need.

■ Have students choose research materials from which to take notes on crabs. Have them record the key parts of a crab they will need to include in their directions. Ask them to look at and record the shape of these parts. Remind them to focus on what they will need to know in order to write their procedural texts. Guide them as needed: *I notice that you found some fascinating information about what crabs eat. But for this text, we're focusing on how to draw a crab. What body part does a crab use to catch food? That's right, a crab uses its claws to catch food. Claws are an important body part to draw.*

SHARING and REFLECTING
10 MINUTES

TURN &TALK *Share your writing with your partner. Make sure your partner has included all the materials needed to draw the crab.*

■ *Your titles are simple and to-the-point, and your materials lists are complete. In our next session, we'll take a look another look at features and continue writing our procedures!*

TIP Students may mention capitalization "dos and don'ts" as a result of the discussion. When students make connections between what they are learning and what they already know, the new learning will have deeper meaning for them. If time allows, work with students to create and post a list of rules for capitalization with real-life examples. In the next session, students can add to this list when they look at the steps in the mentor text.

TIP You might provide a title frame for English language learners or struggling writers, such as *How to _____*. Help them fill in the title with the purpose of the procedural text. Remind them to center titles at the top of the page.

SESSION 3
Researching and Writing

Students identify additional text features, continue their research, and begin to draft the steps in their procedures.

MATERIALS
- *Big Book of Mentor Texts:* "How to Draw a Dolphin," pages 24–27
- Chart paper and marker
- Research notebooks with notes about crabs
- Features chart from Session 2
- Publishing materials: blank sheets of paper, markers, crayons, and so on

---

Features of a Great Procedural Text

It lists the things you need.

There is a title that tells what it's about.

It uses descriptive words to make the directions clear.

Pictures help readers understand.

The numbered steps are in order.

FOCUSED MINILESSON *(prewriting, planning)*
20 MINUTES

- Introduce the session: *Now that you've written a title and materials list, you're ready to start drafting the steps in your procedure. Before you do, let's take another look at the mentor text.*

- Turn to "How to Draw a Dolphin" on pages 24–27.

  TURN &TALK *Partners, what do you notice about the language and the structure of this text? Describe the language you see.*

- *You noticed that a procedural text has strong description. If the directions were not descriptive, it would be hard for readers to follow them. It's so important to name those shapes, to tell how to make the lines, and so on. The more specific your writing is, the better your readers' drawings will be. You also noticed that the writing has steps. Steps tell what to do in the order that the steps need to be done. This helps the reader follow the directions.*

- Explain to students that they will continue to research as they draft their steps, and that they should use descriptive words when taking notes. Use chart paper to model note taking as you think aloud: *Watch as I use these great pictures of crabs and my reference materials to take notes on what a crab looks like. This picture shows the crab's body, and I will describe it by naming the shapes I see:* The body looks like a triangle with one tip cut off and a round opposite side.

  - Leave the model where students can see it as they work independently. *You can use this note-taking model as you work to take notes about what crabs look like.*

  - Tell students that if they finish their research, they can start drafting their steps today.

WRITING and COACHING *(prewriting, drafting)*
25 MINUTES

■ Have students continue their research to be sure that they know what a crab looks like and can give instructions for drawing one. As you circulate around the room, make sure that every student has studied a picture or physical representation of a crab as part of his or her research.

■ Students who have finished their research may begin drafting the steps in the procedure.

■ Have students draw their crabs first, then think about each step before drafting.

SHARING and REFLECTING
10 MINUTES

TURN &TALK *Partners, share the work that you've done today. How did you instruct your readers to start their crab drawings?*

■ Reaffirm the work that students have done so far: *You've done a fantastic job with taking what you've learned about crabs and using that knowledge to create directions! That research was so important because you needed to be able to visualize a crab before you could teach someone else to draw one. In our next session, you can continue your steps.*

TIP If students are struggling to decide what to write, bring them together for small-group sessions. Think aloud as you identify the sections of a crab's body. Say the names of the body parts and describe their shapes. You might also pull together more capable writers for small-group lessons on using reference sources to take notes.

SESSION 4
Drafting the Steps

Students continue drafting the steps in their procedures, focusing on features, illustrations that match text, and action words.

MATERIALS
- *Big Book of Mentor Texts:* "How to Draw a Dolphin," pages 24–27
- Research notebooks
- Features chart

FOCUSED MINILESSON *(prewriting)*
15 MINUTES

- Focus the learning: *So far, we've taken great notes about crabs and started to draft the steps needed to draw one. In this session we're going to make our steps better by reviewing the features of procedural text and making sure we use them in our writing. Let's take another look at the mentor text.*

  TURN &TALK *Partners, think together. What do you notice about the steps in the mentor text procedure?*

- After you listen in, reiterate the features of the procedural text: *I heard you mention some great features! Each of the steps has a number. The steps are in order. The illustrations match the text, too. Let's add these features to our chart.*

- Point out the language used in the steps: *Writers, I've noticed that the steps all start the same way. What do you notice about them? Exactly! Each step starts with an action word, a verb. Directions are active—they tell you what to do. So each step has an action word that tells you what to do.*

  TURN &TALK *Partners, take another look at the illustrations. What do you see that you'd like to use in your own procedural text?*

- *Yes, you noticed that each step has an illustration. The illustrations make the steps easier to understand. Because we're teaching our readers how to draw something, showing them each drawing step is incredibly helpful!*

- Tell students they will continue drafting the steps. Remind them that for each step, they should start with a number and a verb that tells the reader what to do.

Features of a Great Procedural Text

It lists the things you need.

There is a title that tells what it's about.

It uses descriptive words to make the directions clear.

Pictures help readers understand.

The numbered steps are in order.

Each step starts with a verb.

Illustrations match each step.

WRITING and COACHING *(drafting, revising)*
20 MINUTES

■ Have students work on their steps, paying close attention to the features discussed in the minilesson. If they began writing their steps in the last session, they can revise them to include numbers, strong verbs, and illustrations. If they have not yet started, they can draft their steps, applying the features of strong procedural texts. Students can write their directions on a new page after their title and materials list.

SHARING and REFLECTING
10 MINUTES

TURN &TALK *Partners, talk about the process you used to create the steps. What advice would you give writers of procedural texts?*

■ After listening in, praise the strategies and advice students discussed: *I heard some great advice for other writers. You said that it helps to act out the steps so you can be sure about the order of your procedure. You thought hard about what your reader will have to do so you could decide what action words to use. And you added drawings to help make the directions clear. I've heard a lot of fantastic strategies. You worked hard to put the steps in the correct order and to make sure that each had its own number. I heard some of you mention starting each step with a verb. That is so helpful for your readers—it tells them exactly what to do.*

■ Sum up the concepts covered in this session and set the stage for what will follow: *You've drafted great steps that have numbers, start with action words, and contain illustrations that match the text. In our next session, we'll finish our procedures and share them with classmates.*

TIP You may want to keep research materials on hand in case students need to refer back to them to refresh their memories or add to their notes. Allow early finishers to work with partners to test their directions. Partners should trade directions and try to follow them to make sure they work.

SESSION 5
Publishing and Celebrating

Students complete their procedural texts, share their work, and celebrate their accomplishments.

MATERIALS
- *Big Book of Mentor Texts:* "How to Draw a Dolphin," pages 24–27
- Features chart
- Publishing materials: paper, pencils, crayons, colored pencils, and so on

TIP Check that students are not feeling discouraged by the editing and revising process. Point out that writers go through the process of editing and revising to polish their work for their audiences. By showing enthusiasm for these steps, you help students become invested in improving their writing. This will help them be proud of their finished texts!

FOCUSED MINILESSON *(editing, revising)*
10 MINUTES

- Focus the learning: *In this session, we will edit and revise our procedural texts to make them easy for our readers to understand. Then we will publish and share our work.*

- Display the mentor text: *Before this text could go in a book, the writer needed to check it to be sure it made sense. The writer went through the process of editing. Today, you'll take a closer look at your own writing to make sure it's the best that it can be.*

  TURN &TALK *Partners, what do you want to look for as you review your procedural texts before publishing and sharing them? List ideas together.*

- Students may focus on features that are particular to this writing form, such as starting each step with a verb and a capitalized letter, leaving end punctuation off the materials list, and so on. Students should also look carefully at their illustrations to be sure that they match each part of the text.

- Reiterate that the features chart is a great place to start with the revision process: *Our features chart can serve as a checklist for us. Look at each item on the chart and then check for that feature in your writing. Reread, checking for one feature at a time.*

- Model this process for students, using the procedure you have written on the chart paper: *Watch as I examine my procedural text one last time. I'm going to scan each sentence with my finger, looking for features as I read. I see my title, and I see the steps I wrote, each one numbered and each one starting with an action word. I see that I have included illustrations, but this one doesn't look right. It doesn't really match the step, does it? So I'm going to erase this illustration and replace it with a new drawing that better explains the step. Now I think my procedure is perfect, and I'm ready to share!*

WRITING and COACHING *(editing, publishing)*
30 MINUTES

■ Have students edit and revise by making their directions clear, by checking each step for a number and an action word, and by making sure their illustrations match the text.

■ Praise students for changes they are making: *You made each direction even clearer—now your readers will be able to draw crabs on their own! Your adjustment to your illustration will help your readers know what shapes to use when they draw their own crabs. Fantastic work!*

■ Allow adequate time for students to publish their procedures. This may require an additional session.

SHARING and REFLECTING
15 MINUTES

■ Have students share their work with another class. Each student can pair up with another student and assist the partner as needed.

TURN &TALK *Reflect with your partner about the procedural texts that we created. In what ways were they similar or different? What have you learned about good procedural writing?*

■ Invite volunteers to share their thoughts. Students may notice that writers described different physical directions for drawing a crab; for example, drawing from the center outward or top to bottom.

■ Celebrate students' efforts and display the finished procedural texts in an art or science center. *Your procedural texts will help other students draw crabs. Why? Because you included all the features of great directions—numbered steps that begin with action words, a materials list, and illustrations. You should be proud of how easy these procedures are to follow!*

TIP One of the best ways to revise directions is to try to follow the directions to see if they make sense! Have students trade directions with one another to see if they can follow the procedures in the texts.

TIP If time allows, follow up by discussing other reasons for writing procedural texts. This will help students focus on features of procedural texts while getting them to think about the procedures they may want to write about during the individual project.

SESSION 6
Launching the Individual Project

Students reflect on the features of procedural texts, select topics for the individual project, and begin their drafts.

MATERIALS
- Features chart from class project
- Research notebooks
- Chart paper

TIP Encourage writing and thinking across the curriculum. You can incorporate math content by encouraging students to write steps for solving specific types of problems. Reference content from health class by suggesting topics such as "How to Brush Your Teeth." You can incorporate language arts by suggesting topics such as "How to Use Capital Letters." Include the arts by suggesting topics such as "How to Tap a Rhythm" or "How to Make a Paper Flower."

TIP Some students may benefit from an organizer (found on *Resources* CD-ROM) they can use to capture their thoughts. Leave space for a materials list and then a numbered list so that students can write the procedural steps in order as they plan.

FOCUSED MINILESSON *(prewriting)*
25 MINUTES

- Introduce the session: *Last week we worked as a class to create excellent procedural texts. This week you will work individually to write a procedural text on a topic of your choice. We'll start today by reviewing the features of a great procedural text, choosing our topic, and writing the title and materials list. Then you can get started!*

- Direct students' attention to the features chart developed in the class project: *Let's read the features of a great procedural text together. You used all these features in our class project on how to draw a crab. Now you're going to use them in your individual projects.*

  TURN &TALK *Think together. Talk with your partner about something that you know how to do that will be a great topic for a procedural text.*

- Capture students' ideas on chart paper. If they suggest ideas that are too involved, help them make adjustments: *You know how to do so many different things. Be sure to choose a topic that you know well enough to be able to tell others how to do it.*

- Model how to create a title for your procedural text: *I know it's important to do a good job when we brush our teeth, so that's the topic I chose.* Write a title and your byline prominently on the chart paper: *How to Brush Your Teeth by Miss Fellers.*

- *My title tells readers what the procedural text is about. The byline tells them who wrote the instructions.*

- *The first part of a procedural text is the materials list. I am thinking about the things I need to have on hand so I can brush my teeth. I know that I need a toothbrush and toothpaste.* Write these items on your modeled writing. *Do I need anything else?* Add student suggestions. *Great thinking! You really thought through the process. Remember that as you draft, you can add more items that you may have forgotten. Sometimes as we write, we remember things we left out!*

  TURN &TALK *What materials will your readers need to complete the tasks in your procedural writing? List some ideas with your partner.*

WRITING and COACHING *(prewriting, drafting)*
15 MINUTES

- Have students write their titles and materials lists in their research notebooks.

- Provide support as needed, using language that guides students toward their own discoveries: *That's an interesting title, Annabelle, but I'm not sure what your directions want me to do. Why don't you give it another try, but this time start with the words "How to . . ."* Manny, have you acted out your procedure so you could write down the necessary materials as you go along? That might help you remember better.*

SHARING and REFLECTING
10 MINUTES

TURN &TALK *Partners, think together as you evaluate your work. Does your title tell your readers what the text is about? Is your materials list complete?*

- Sum up the day's learning and preview the next session: *You created titles that are very descriptive and let your readers know exactly what's in store for them. Your materials lists include the important things your readers need to complete the tasks. During our next session, you will start drafting the steps in your directions.*

TIP for Conferring with Individuals and Small Groups

Gather students who struggle to write a materials list. Guide the group through a simple visualization exercise: *Close your eyes and imagine you are about to (tie a shoe, make a bed, and so on). What do you have in front of you? What else will you use? Put those items on your list!*

SESSION 7
Drafting the Steps

Students work on their drafts, focusing on numbered steps or time-order words.

MATERIALS
• Research notebooks
• Chart paper and marker

TIP If you provide an organizer for this portion of the procedural text, consider allowing students to choose between one with words and one with numbers. English language learners, for example, may find it easier to use a list with numbers rather than time-order words. Students will naturally gravitate toward one or the other. Either will provide students with the organization they need.

FOCUSED MINILESSON *(drafting)*
15 MINUTES

■ Focus the learning: *In our last session, we focused on the first features of a procedural text—the title and the materials list. Now we'll focus on drafting the steps in our procedures to make sure they are organized and easy to follow.*

■ Think aloud as you provide a modeled writing about your steps: *I'm ready to begin writing my directions for* How to Brush Your Teeth. *I'm going to pretend that I am doing it right now.* Pantomime as you think aloud: *First, I get the toothbrush wet. Oh! That is the first step in my directions!* Write the step on the chart paper: *First, get the toothbrush wet.*

■ Pantomime and then write the second step: *Next, put a bit of toothpaste on the brush.*

TURN &TALK *Look at the first words in my steps. Talk about these words with your partner. What do they tell my readers?*

■ *You noticed that these words tell my readers the order in which they should do the steps. Those words are called "time-order words." Without them, the steps could be confusing!* Begin a list of time-order words on chart paper, and help students discover additional time-order words (*first, next, then, after that, finally,* and so on). As students discover other time-order words, they can add them to the list. Post the chart for reference throughout the exploration.

■ *How else could we tell our readers what to do first, second, and third? That's right—we could put numbers in front of all the steps. Time-order words and numbers are both good ways to keep our steps organized so that readers aren't confused.* On a new sheet of chart paper, write your steps again, using a numbered list. *Notice that when I use numbers, I don't use time-order words. I need to choose **either** time-order words **or** numbers. When I use numbers, I start each step with an action verb.*

TURN &TALK *Think together about the steps in your procedure. Are any of them out of order? Now is the time to adjust them.*

WRITING and COACHING *(drafting)*
20 MINUTES

■ Have students work on drafting the steps in their procedures. Provide assistance for students who are stuck: *I see that after step 3, you kind of lost your train of thought and haven't been able to write what comes next. I'll bet you'll remember what comes next when you pretend to be doing the steps! Let's act out the process together. Let's hold up a finger for each step and keep going when we get to three!*

■ In addition to acting out steps, many students will benefit from talking through the steps in their procedures before putting them on paper.

SHARING and REFLECTING
10 MINUTES

TURN &TALK *Share your steps with your partner. Partners, do you have suggestions for making the steps clearer?*

■ Sum up the learning from today's session: *I noticed that some of you organized your steps with numbers, and some of you used time-order words to organize your steps. Both of these are great organizational tools! You should be proud of how you organized the steps for your readers. They will be able to easily follow these procedures to make or do something.*

TIP Provide procedural texts you have gathered, such as directions for board games, recipes, and so on. Struggling students can see the mesh of instructions and organizational tools. Early finishers can examine these texts—they'll be inspired when they see reminders of how practical and important procedural texts are in real life!

SESSION 8
Revising and Editing

Students revise and edit their drafts, checking for complete steps and time order.

MATERIALS
- Research notebooks
- Your modeled writing

FOCUSED MINILESSON *(drafting, revising)*
15 MINUTES

- Focus the learning: *In the last session, you did a great job of drafting your directions. The numbered or time-ordered steps you wrote will guide your readers so they can follow the steps themselves. Now we're ready to revise our procedures so we can be sure they are as good as they can be.*

- Model revising your own directions: *Let's look back at my directions. I think that after I brush, I will need to rinse my toothbrush.* Add this step to your directions list: *So I have added, "After that, rinse your toothbrush and put it away."*

- *Adding details to the directions is also important. If people didn't know how to brush their teeth, I'm not sure they could follow the instructions the way that I wrote them. Give it a try and see what you think!* Lead students to pantomime: *It would make a lot more sense if I wrote* how *to brush teeth. How about if I wrote:* Brush your teeth with a gentle motion, up and down on each tooth. *Those directions might make more sense now with the additional details.*

- Have students work on revising their procedures for complete steps and time order: *Here's another draft I started! This one is a procedure for making a peanut butter sandwich. Here are the steps:* 1. Put peanut butter on a slice of bread. 2. Put jelly on a slice of bread. 3. Put the slices of bread together.

  TURN &TALK *Partners, analyze my directions. Do I need to make any revisions?*

- *Great observations! You noticed that a step is missing. I can use a caret mark to add in the step:* Gather materials. *Then each step needs a new number. I heard a few of you suggest that the directions need a materials list. That's a great idea, too! Then I won't need my first step to be about gathering materials.*

WRITING and COACHING *(drafting, revising)*
15 MINUTES

■ Have students revisit their drafts to add additional steps or to revise them so that all of the steps are complete, in time order, and make sense. Encourage students to read the steps out loud to themselves, act them out, share them with a partner, or use any other strategies that will ensure that their writing is clear and understandable.

■ When you conference with individual students, always check for understanding by asking them to restate what they are going to be working on.

TIP If students have difficulty putting their steps into words, encourage them to first tell you or a partner what the step is or act it out. After saying or doing the action aloud, many students will find it easier to write.

SHARING and REFLECTING
10 MINUTES

TURN &TALK *What did you discover when revising your procedure? Tell your partner one change you made that improved your procedure and made it easier to follow.*

■ Praise various types of revisions: *I think it is great that Garrett changed the order of his steps when he realized they would not work. That is an important change! Tiffany improved her writing by removing something from the materials list that her readers do not really need. Did anybody add something to his or her materials list?*

■ Sum up the learning: *In this session you worked hard to revise your procedures so they are clear and easy to follow. Now you're ready to start publishing!*

SESSION 9
Publishing the Title, Byline, and Materials List

Students review the role of illustrations in a procedural text and add illustrations to their titles and materials lists before publishing them.

MATERIALS
- Research notebooks
- Publishing materials: paper, pencils, crayons, colored pencils, and so on
- Chart paper
- Printed illustrations from magazines and the Internet

TIP Some students will struggle with illustrating. Reassure them that the illustrations do not have to be perfect. Even a quick sketch will help readers better understand the directions. As an alternative, allow students to search for illustrations in magazines or at bookmarked websites. They can cut out and glue the art to their pieces.

FOCUSED MINILESSON *(revising)*
15 MINUTES

- Introduce the minilesson on the use of illustrations in procedural text: *The procedural texts we wrote for the class project,* How to Draw a Crab, *included many wonderful illustrations, didn't they? In this session, we're going to talk about why illustrations are so important, and we'll add illustrations to our titles and materials lists before publishing them.*

  TURN &TALK *Turn to your learning partner, and discuss what job illustrations do in a procedural text. How do illustrations help your readers?*

- *I heard some great comments on illustrations. You remembered that illustrations can show what happens at each step in a procedure. You said that if you are writing directions for making something, illustrations can show what materials are needed and what the finished product will look like. Many of you also said that illustrations can make it easier for readers to know what to do as they follow a procedure.*

- Write your title and byline on a fresh sheet of chart paper, and model adding illustrations: *Watch as I draw a bright, healthy smile next to my title. This will help my reader know exactly what my procedure is all about!*

- Write your materials list on the chart paper under your illustrated title: *Now I'm going to draw a picture of each item my readers will need in order to brush their teeth. Remember: The illustrations we add should make it easier for readers to use our procedural text.*

  TURN &TALK *Partners, take another look at my illustrations. Do they give you ideas about how to illustrate your own title and materials list? Tell your partner one of your ideas.*

WRITING and COACHING *(revising, publishing)*
25 MINUTES

■ *Now it's your turn! On a clean sheet of publishing paper, carefully write your title, byline, and materials list. Add illustrations to help your reader more easily follow your procedure.*

■ *As you work, ask yourself, "Does this illustration support my step? Will my readers understand what I am showing?"*

SHARING and REFLECTING
10 MINUTES

■ Having students offer both positive feedback and suggestions for improvement creates a community of writers in which students are able to offer constructive feedback and become more accepting of others' ideas.

■ Model appropriate feedback: *These pictures in your materials list are fantastic! I'll be able to gather everything I need before I even begin to make the paper flowers. I'm a little confused about what the flower should look like after I complete step 3, though. If you drew the shape of the petal next to the directions, I'd know exactly what to do in that step!*

TIP If students are unsure of what to illustrate, revisit the mentor text: Do you see how the writer drew the dolphin at each step? That's so helpful! If the picture showed the whole dolphin, I might not be able to figure out how the writer got from the beginning to the end. But showing each step in order makes it clear what the dolphin looks like at each step. How can your illustrations show the steps in your procedure?

SESSION 10
Publishing the Steps

Students publish the steps in their procedural texts, focusing on handwriting and punctuation. Then they share their work and celebrate their accomplishments.

MATERIALS

- Research notebooks
- Publishing materials: paper, pencils, crayons, colored pencils, and so on
- Features chart from class project
- Chart paper

TIP If some of your students struggle with handwriting, facilitate their publishing by rewriting the students' steps on sentence strips. Students can then copy the sentences, one by one, on publishing paper or simply glue the sentence strips onto the paper. This will keep them focused on understanding and producing procedural texts without becoming frustrated by their handwriting efforts.

FOCUSED MINILESSON *(revising, editing)*
15 MINUTES

- Focus the learning: *In our last session, we illustrated and published our titles, bylines, and materials lists. Today we will publish the steps in our procedures and we'll use correct punctuation and our best handwriting as we work.*

- Neatly write the steps in your procedure on a large piece of chart paper. As you write, lead students to recognize your consistent use of capitalization and end punctuation: *Watch as I write the steps in my procedure about how to brush your teeth. What do you notice about how my sentences begin and end? That's right! Every sentence begins with a capital letter, even if it comes after a number. And every sentence ends with a period. Do you see any question marks or exclamation points in my procedure? No, because my directions are statements about what readers should do and when they should do it. So the sentences end with periods.*

TURN &TALK *What about handwriting? Turn to your learning partner and give one reason why neat handwriting matters when you're writing directions.*

- *I heard some great comments! You said that neat handwriting is important because readers won't be able to follow the steps correctly if they can't read them. You also said that sometimes the steps in a procedure help readers know what to do to stay safe in an emergency. It's very important to be able to read those kinds of directions, isn't it? So make sure your handwriting is as neat as it can be.*

WRITING and COACHING *(revising, publishing)*
25 MINUTES

■ Have students carefully write the steps in their directions on publishing paper, paying close attention to punctuation and legible handwriting, and adding illustrations as needed: *Are you ready to publish your steps now? Write them carefully and neatly on your publishing paper—and don't forget to start each step with a capital letter and end each step with a period.*

■ Remind students of the illustrations they added to their materials lists in the last session, and encourage them to illustrate some or all of the steps in their procedures as well.

■ Create a community of learners by having students work with partners: *What's the best way to know if our directions work? That's right! We need to try them. Work with your partner to try each other's directions. Listen as your partner reads each step aloud. If the materials you need are here in the classroom, try to follow your partner's steps; otherwise, just act them out. Tell your partners which steps need to be clearer. Are any steps missing?*

SHARING, REFLECTING, and CELEBRATING
10 MINUTES

TURN &TALK *Share your drafts with your partners. Partners, what did you appreciate most about the text you read?*

■ After students share, name some specific details that really caught your eye: a particularly clever way to break down the steps; the persistence to include many steps; new ideas about what materials to use; well-crafted sentences; detailed drawings; and so on.

■ Let students know that you will be binding their procedural texts into a class book that they can share with other students in other classes. Consider inviting another class into your room for a read-aloud from the class book in which your students' accomplishments can come to life.

■ Remember to look back at students' pre-assessment pieces and to use the Ongoing Monitoring Sheet or the Individual Evaluation Record to document growth and note areas for improvement. Pass out copies of the Student Self-Reflection Sheet found on the *Resources* CD-ROM to assist students as they reflect on their own growth. Finally, be sure to make notes on what worked and what didn't during the unit so you can make adjustments that will maximize student learning. See "After the Unit," page 83, for more information about post-assessment and self-reflection.

TIP Early finishers might help you create a cover for the class book of procedural texts. You might also allow early finishers to write a quick procedural text on how to write a procedural text! Post these for the rest of the class to read and enjoy.

TIP Another way to help students solidify their learning is to have them teach somebody else what they know: *At home tonight, show your family what you've learned about procedural text. Find a recipe or printed directions for a favorite game, and point out the title, materials list, and numbered steps. Everyone will be proud that you've learned so much!*

Procedural Letter

A friendly letter can provide a procedure for making or doing something.

Dear Anne,

Sorry I couldn't write to you in so long. Just in case you need to know how to put on nail polish so it stays on a long time, here's how you do it.

• First you file your nails so they are nice and shinny.

• Second you add your clear coat

• Third you paint the color of nail polish you want on.

• And last you add another clear coat

That is how you do it. I hope your nails look pretty all summer long.

Love,

Eva

FEATURES

- Greeting
- Body with words that show time order *(first, next, then, finally)*
- Steps to complete a project
- Closing and signature

FOCUSED MINILESSON

Writers, I really enjoyed making our clay pots together! I know Mr. Britton's class would enjoy the same activity. I am going to write a letter to him today to explain the process to him.

Watch as I start my letter: Dear Mr. Britton. *The greeting of the letter ends with a comma, and it all sits on one line. Notice that when I start the letter, I'll write on the next line on the paper. Now watch as I continue:* My class made clay pots. Your students will enjoy making pots, too! Here are the instructions. First, roll modeling clay into a long snake.

TURN &TALK *Writers, take a close look at my letter so far. What do you notice about my instructions?*

A lot of you noticed an important word—first. That word helps organize the steps. Rolling the clay is the first step of the procedure. Words like first *will help us keep the steps in order as we write.*

TURN &TALK *Partners, think together. After you roll the clay, what should you do next? Describe the step together.*

After you roll the clay, you should make the base of your pot. Watch as I write the next step, starting with a time-order word: Next, coil the clay to make the base of your pot.

Continue writing the steps of the process. *Writers, I want to end the letter with a great conclusion and a friendly closing with my signature. Watch as I write:* Let me know if you have any questions about this fun project! Enjoy, Mr. Siegel. *Notice that this last sentence ends the letter with a positive statement that wraps up the instructions. I wrote my closing and my name on two separate lines at the end of the letter.*

Dear Mr. Britton,

My class made clay pots. Your students will enjoy making clay pots, too! Here are the instructions: First, roll modeling clay into a long snake. Next, coil the clay to make the base of your pot. Then coil the clay to make the sides of the pot. Finally, smooth out the sides to finish the pot. Let me know if you have any questions about this fun project!

Enjoy,

Mr. Siegel

Modeled Writing

INSTRUCT

Capture the features of a procedural friendly letter in a chart as you examine the model with students: *Let's take a close look at the letter so we remember its features. The letter has the parts that all friendly letters share: greeting, closing, and signature. But because this letter gives directions, I included the steps in the order they need to be done. Each step begins with a time-order word.*

WRITING and COACHING

Writers, now it's your turn! You know how to make and do all sorts of things! Write a letter to a partner in another class. Explain a procedure that you're familiar with. You can deliver and read your letters when you're finished. Writers who need additional scaffolds will benefit from a list of time-order words and having your modeled writing in a highly visible place.

SHARING and REFLECTING

Writers, your letters with directions are fantastic! I see that you each have a greeting and a closing. Even more important, you organized your steps using time-order words so that your readers know exactly what to do to follow your procedures.

ASSESS THE LEARNING

After students have completed their letters, ask each to identify features of a friendly letter and directions in their own work. Identify writers who would benefit from a small-group lesson focused on the features.

SELF-ASSESSMENT

SELF-ASSESSMENT
Writing a Procedural Letter

	YES	NO
1. Did you include a greeting, heading, and signature?	☐	☐
2. Did you include time-order words that organize the steps?	☐	☐

S U P P O R T I N G   A N D   E X T E N D I N G

▸ Have students write letters to their parents explaining a school procedure, such as where to enter the building or what to do on open house night.

▸ After completing a science experiment, have students write letters to partners to explain the procedure of the experiment. Partners can offer feedback.

▸ Students can write letters to friends explaining how to get to their homes or to a local place, such as a park, from school. Have partners try the directions.

How-To List

A procedural list gives readers step-by-step instructions for completing a task.

FEATURES

• Title
• Numbered steps
• Short sentences with action verbs

FOCUSED MINILESSON

Write *How to Do a Fire Drill* on chart paper. *Writers, when we have a fire drill, we follow a procedure to stay safe. We have to follow the steps in order. A list will help us remember the procedure.*

TURN &TALK *Turn to your learning partners and tell them what to do first when we evacuate, or leave, our classroom safely during a fire drill.*

I heard an important step: line up quietly at the door. Watch as I write this step first. If we write our list in order, lining up quietly is the first thing that we do. Since this step is first, I write the number 1 in front of it. I use the action verb: line up. Action verbs can sound a little bossy, but that's OK! Instructions tell someone how to do something. It makes sense to start each step with a verb.

Another step I heard was to turn off the lights and shut the windows. I am writing that as the second step, so I start with the number 2.

TURN &TALK *Writers, what else do you notice about my steps? Share your observations with your partner.*

Some of you noticed that each sentence is short. If procedural texts have too many words, they are hard to follow. We keep them brief so that our readers can follow the instructions. Continue modeling the steps for doing a fire drill. Emphasize the action verbs, the numbers that keep the steps in order, and the brief sentences that help readers focus on what to do.

After writing: *Let's take a look at my list. My readers will definitely know what to do during a fire drill. Each step has a number to keep the steps in order. All the steps start with action verbs. Each step is brief.*

TURN &TALK *Turn to your learning partner. Point out a feature of the procedural text that you want to remember when you write your own list.*

How to Do a Fire Drill

1. Line up quietly at door.

2. Turn off lights and shut windows.

3. Shut classroom door behind us.

4. Walk quickly and quietly to class meeting place.

5. Stand quietly while the teacher takes attendance.

6. Wait for the fire department or principal to give the "all clear."

7. Stay in line and return quietly to the classroom.

Modeled Writing

As students share their ideas, write the features on chart paper. Remind students to refer to the features list as they write their own how-to lists.

WRITING and COACHING

What other procedures would a visitor or a new student to our class need to know? Let's brainstorm a list. After students have contributed ideas, ask them to each choose a topic for creating a procedural list. As students work independently, prompt their thinking by asking questions: *How are you keeping steps in order? What kinds of words start each step?*

SHARING and REFLECTING

Writers, your instructions are wonderful. You each wrote a title, numbered steps, and short sentences with action verbs. Your procedural texts wil be crystal clear for our classroom visitors!

ASSESS THE LEARNING

Gather the procedural lists and assess students' use of the features. If students need assistance with numbered steps, provide a procedural text with the instructions out of order. Students can place them in order as you assess their understanding of sequence and using numbers to indicate order.

SELF-ASSESSMENT

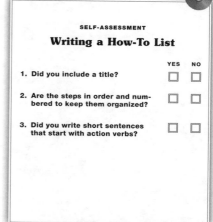

SELF-ASSESSMENT
Writing a How-To List

	YES	NO
1. Did you include a title?	☐	☐
2. Are the steps in order and numbered to keep them organized?	☐	☐
3. Did you write short sentences that start with action verbs?	☐	☐

SUPPORTING AND EXTENDING

▸ Have students create procedural texts that tell how to solve a math problem or how to read a book. Have students exchange their work and test each other's instructions.

▸ Have students create posters for safety and health that tell how to wash hands, how to exit a school bus safely, or how to sneeze without spreading germs.

▸ Encourage students to create flow charts that show how to set up an aquarium, a terrarium, or a cage for a class pet.

INSTRUCT

Art Project Directions

Directions can include illustrated steps for completing an art project.

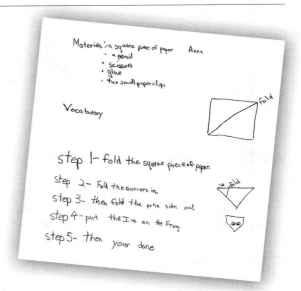

FEATURES

- Title
- Materials list
- Numbered steps
- Steps that start with verbs

FOCUSED MINILESSON

Adapt the content of this lesson to an art project that your class has recently completed.

Writers, our spider crafts were a fun way to cap off our study of arachnids. They look great! I know another class might want to do this same project, so I'm writing directions to share. Watch as I start with a very important part, the materials list: paper plate, construction paper, glue, googly eyes, single hole punch, string. *Notice that I set the list apart with the heading,* Materials. *This will help my readers gather all the supplies before starting the project.*

TURN &TALK *Think together, partners. What are the steps we followed in creating our spiders?*

The first thing we did was cut eight strips of construction paper. Since that is the first step, I'm labeling it with a 1 and placing a period after it. I'm writing the first step in the project: Cut 8 strips of construction paper to make legs. *Writers, notice that the step starts with a verb:* cut. *Instructions can sound a little bossy! But they tell our readers exactly what to do. Now watch as I write the second step:* 2. Put 8 dots of glue around the plate.

TURN &TALK *Writers, in directions we write the verb first. So far we have used* cut *and* put. *Think together and select a verb that would be a good beginning for our next step.*

I agree that our next step should begin with glue. *That is a perfect verb for this step. Watch as I write a number 3, place a period, and then write,* Glue the . . .

TURN &TALK *What is the next step? Give me advice about what to write and which features to use.*

Continue the steps shown in the modeled writing. As you write, explicitly model how to number the steps and start each step with a verb: *Writers, these directions need a title. What title shall I add? Let's keep it simple. Watch as I write at the top of the directions:* Make a Googly-Eyed Spider! *I'm also sketching what the finished spider looks like. That will help anyone who decides to do this project.*

Make a Googly-Eyed Spider!

Materials
paper plate
construction paper
glue
googly eyes
single hole punch
string

1. Cut 8 strips of construction paper to make legs.

2. Put 8 dots of glue around the plate.

3. Glue the legs onto the plate to make 8 spider legs.

4. Glue the googly eyes to the top and center of the plate.

5. Punch a hole in the plate.

6. Thread a string through the hole to hang the spider.

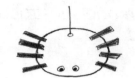

Modeled Writing

Review the model with students as you create a list of features: *Writers, these directions are going to be easy for readers to follow! Why? Because the materials list will help them gather what they need in advance. The steps are numbered so that they are easy to follow, and they begin with strong action verbs.*

WRITING and COACHING

What art project do you know how to make? Write a set of directions that a classmate could follow. If students struggle to write directions without context, do a project together that students can write about. You might also provide students with a form to use, with room for a materials list and numbers after which they can write steps. Encourage students to draw pictures of finished projects.

SHARING and REFLECTING

Writers, the attention to detail on your directions is amazing. From a clear materials list to organized numbered steps that start with active verbs, you have set up your readers for success with their projects.

ASSESS THE LEARNING

Have small groups gather to compare their finished sets of directions with the model. If necessary, conduct small group sessions with students who need assistance understanding time order or starting sentences with action verbs.

SELF-ASSESSMENT

SELF-ASSESSMENT **Writing Directions for an Art Project**	YES	NO
1. Did you include a title and numbered steps?	☐	☐
2. Did you write a materials list for your project?	☐	☐
3. Does each step start with a verb?	☐	☐

SUPPORTING AND EXTENDING

▸ Have students write directions for an art project they can do with kindergarten or first-grade students. Then have students do the project with their younger buddies!

▸ Students can use the same format to write about a science experience. Encourage them to use the form to write a lab report to tell the steps in an experiment.

▸ Have students use the format to write directions for playing an active game. They can post their directions in the gym or make copies to distribute to students in other classes.

Recipe

A recipe gives readers instructions for cooking or making food.

FEATURES

- Title
- Ingredient list
- Numbered steps describing a process
- Short phrases using action verbs

FOCUSED MINILESSON

Writers, I love cooking and making special meals for my family. A recipe is a special kind of procedural text. It tells how to make food. My family enjoys salads. I am going to write a recipe for a salad that I could share with anyone who wants to know how to make it. Watch as I write the title first: Super Salad!

TURN &TALK *Writers, what do you know about recipes? What else do I need to write?*

These are mouth-watering ideas! If our readers want to make our favorite foods, they first need a list of ingredients. Notice that as I write my ingredients, I make a list instead of a paragraph. I write the amount of each ingredient, too. If we added too much or too little of an important ingredient, it could be a disaster!

Now I can start listing the steps. Watch as I number the first step: 1. Wash and dry the vegetables. *Putting numbers on the steps keeps them in order and helps keep the cook organized. It can also prevent disasters in the kitchen! Now it's time for the second step:* Tear up the lettuce.

TURN &TALK *Writers, what do you think of my next step? Share what you notice with a partner.*

A few of you noticed that I did not put a number on the second step. That's important to add! My step could be a little more detailed too. I'm revising it to say: Tear the lettuce into bite-sized pieces and place into a large bowl. *Now the cook knows exactly what to do!*

Coconut bananas

You need:

1 orange
2 bananas
1 cup coconut

Directions

1. Cut bananas into chunks
2. Cut the orange. Squeeze juice onto plate
3. Roll banana chunks in juice
4. Roll banana chunks in coconut.

Super Salad!

1 head of lettuce
2 tomatoes
1 carrot
ranch dressing

1. Wash and dry the vegetables.

2. Tear the lettuce into bite-size pieces and place into a large bowl.

3. Dice tomatoes into small squares.

4. Slice the carrot.

5. Sprinkle tomatoes and carrots over lettuce.

6. Toss with ranch dressing.

Did you notice that each step starts with a verb? Wash, dry, *and* tear *are the actions the cook needs to take. I start each step with an action verb as a I write.*

Continue writing the recipe. Emphasize that you are using numbered steps, the steps are in order, and each step starts with an action word.

After writing: *Writers, let's take a close look at the features of a recipe. The title tells what food is being prepared. All the ingredients are listed first—this makes it easy for the cooks to gather what they need! The steps are in order, and each numbered step starts with a verb.* Note the features on a chart that students can use for reference.

WRITING and COACHING

Now it's your turn to write a recipe! What are some healthy snacks that you know how to make at home? Invite students to share their ideas. If students need prompting, suggest ideas like sandwiches, trail mix, and so on. As students write, help them clarify their directions as necessary. Students who struggle to get started may benefit from a "recipe card" form.

SHARING and REFLECTING

Writers, your recipes sound delicious! I can't wait to try them out. You remembered titles and ingredient lists. You used numbered steps, short phrases, and action verbs. I'll put the recipes in a take-home cookbook for you to share with your families.

ASSESS THE LEARNING

Students can gather in small groups to compare their recipes to the modeled writing. Asses for features: title, ingredient list, and numbered steps that begin with action verbs.

SELF-ASSESSMENT

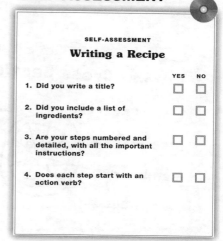

SELF-ASSESSMENT
Writing a Recipe

	YES	NO
1. Did you write a title?	☐	☐
2. Did you include a list of ingredients?	☐	☐
3. Are your steps numbered and detailed, with all the important instructions?	☐	☐
4. Does each step start with an action verb?	☐	☐

S U P P O R T I N G   A N D   E X T E N D I N G

▸ Read a book that features food, such as Helen Cooper's *Pumpkin Soup,* Tomie dePaola's *Strega Nona* or *Pancakes for Breakfast,* or Marcia Brown's *Stone Soup.* Students can write recipes based on their reading.

▸ Have students research traditional meals enjoyed by their families. Ask them to write the recipes to share with the class. Use the recipes for a cultural cooking activity.

▸ As a science project, demonstrate how to grow salt crystals. Have students write the "ingredients" and the steps to grow the crystals. Share the recipes with another class.

Cross-Section Diagram

A procedural text can explain how to create a diagram.

FEATURES

- Sketch of the interior of an object
- Labels and lines to identify parts
- Numbered instructions for creating a diagram

FOCUSED MINILESSON

Adapt this lesson for content in your class.

Writers, scientists often use a special diagram called a cross section *when they are writing about the internal workings of a plant, an animal, a thunderstorm, or even the earth! A cross section allows you to see inside of something. When we look at the outside of this lemon, we see a bright yellow skin. Watch what happens when I cut it in half. Now we are seeing a cross section of the inside of the lemon. Notice the segments? See how they are divided into little pie-shapes by a thin membrane?*

Watch as I create a cross section and sketch the interior of the lemon. My cross-section diagram needs to show the inside of the lemon with as much detail as possible. Look closely—now I will add labels and draw a line from each label to the part of the diagram that I have just identified.

TURN &TALK *Partners, look closely at my cross-section diagram and identify its features. What makes this different from an illustration or a picture? What are the features that make a cross section unique?*

Now that we've created this diagram, I want to use it to instruct others how to make cross-section diagrams of their own. This cross-section is such a powerful example, it would be great to include a text box with instructions right on this page.

TURN &TALK *Share your thinking. Describe the procedure that we followed to create the cross-section diagram. What did we do first?*

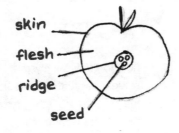

Modeled Writing

The first thing that we did was to cut the apple in half and then take a close look at the inside. Watch as I write that as my first step: 1. Observe what the object looks like from the inside. *What did we do next? We drew a picture of that view.* Continue modeling how to write the procedure. List each step with a number.

After writing: *Let's take a look at the cross-section diagram and the procedure. I drew what the lemon looks like from the inside. I added labels to name each of the parts. Our cross-section diagram gives an inside view! Then, together, we crafted a fantastic procedure so that others can make cross-section diagrams of their own.*

WRITING and COACHING

Show writers examples of books that include cross-section diagrams and examine how professional writers have woven them into their work. For example, display the cover of Gail Gibbons's *From Seed to Plant*. Have students use the procedure they created with you to create cross-section diagrams of plants, trees, fruits, or other elements related to your classroom content.

SHARING and REFLECTING

Your cross-section diagrams are informative because you did a fantastic job of following a procedure for creating them! You showed objects from the inside. Connecting labels to the objects reveals each part and keeps the diagram organized.

ASSESS THE LEARNING

Have students compare their work to the diagram you created. Note which students may need to examine additional examples of cross-section diagrams to successfully create diagrams of their own. Have them retell the procedure and listen in for gaps in their thinking.

SELF-ASSESSMENT

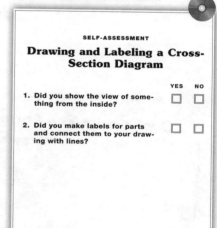

SELF-ASSESSMENT
Drawing and Labeling a Cross-Section Diagram

	YES	NO
1. Did you show the view of something from the inside?	☐	☐
2. Did you make labels for parts and connect them to your drawing with lines?	☐	☐

S U P P O R T I N G   A N D   E X T E N D I N G

▸ Provide students with a rich array of reasons to create cross-section diagrams. They could illustrate the parts of a tree, their skin, a growing plant, the network of tunnels in an ant hill, and so on.

▸ Show students cross-section diagrams in books about the human body. Discuss how these cross-section diagrams help them understand things that cannot safely be cut apart.

▸ In a study of the earth or geology, invite students to create cross sections showing different layers of soil, rock, sand, the earth's core, and so on.

VISUAL LITERACY

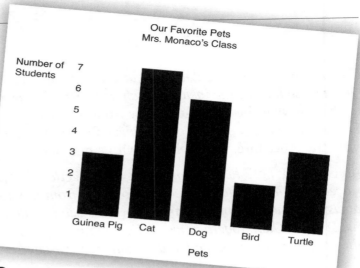

Column Graph

A column graph allows readers to compare data.

FEATURES

- Title
- Labels for items and numbers
- Rows of sticky notes that form columns

FOCUSED MINILESSON

Writers, a column graph is a great way to compare data. We've had a lot of success in creating and using column graphs, so as we create a column graph today, let's capture our steps in a procedural text. Then we can share that procedure with others.

Start a column graph on chart paper. *My first step in creating a column graph is to craft a title that will let readers know what data is being compared. We're going to graph our favorite zoo animals, so watch as I add that as a title:* Our Favorite Zoo Animals! *I'm also recording on a second piece of chart paper our procedure:* 1. Create a title for the column graph. *Notice that I am numbering the steps to keep them in order and make the procedure easy to follow.*

Let's get started making the graph! Let's vote for our favorite animals in this group of animals. Take a class vote. *Let's look at our results:* Lion—5, Bear—4, Monkey—8, Elephant—7.

Let's start with lions. I am going to count five sticky notes to represent each vote. I find the label for lion and place the first sticky note at the bottom. Then I add the other sticky notes above it to make a column. See how the top of the column lines up with the number 5? That shows that five people in our class like lions the best.

Now I want to add a column for bears.

TURN &TALK *Partners, think together. What should I do next? Name the steps.*

Now you're really thinking! Watch as I count four sticky notes to represent each vote for bears. I'm placing them above the label for the bear. They line up to make a column.

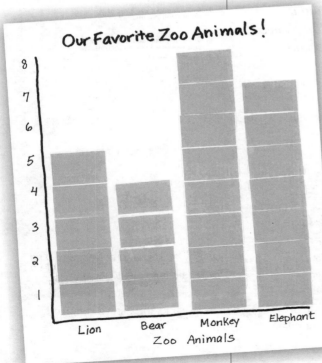

Modeled Writing

Record the steps that students suggest as you model creating the procedure, being sure to include numbers and steps that start with verbs. Then have students help you complete the graph for the remaining votes.

After writing, capture the features of a column graph in a chart as you examine the model with students: *Let's take a look at our column graph to remind ourselves of its features. A title tells our readers what we're graphing: our favorite zoo animals. We have clear labels for the columns and numbers. We have a column for each zoo animal that shows how many people like that animal best. Take one last look at the procedure.*

TURN &TALK *Partners, evaluate our procedure. Do you think a reader could use our procedure to create a column graph? Describe what you might change in this procedural text.*

WRITING and COACHING

Writers, we've created a graph for zoo animals. Now it's your turn to use our procedural text to create a graph for favorite pets. Take a class vote of favorite pets to provide data for the graph. Keep it simple by using just a few pets and having students choose from the small group.

TURN &TALK *Take a look at our finished graph. Evaluate our work. What features did we include? How did our procedural text help you as you created the graph?*

SHARING and REFLECTING

Your work shows data at a glance! You used the labels to place your sticky notes in the correct spots. Your column graph shows how many classmates prefer each kind of pet. And the procedure we created will assist other writers with making column graphs.

ASSESS THE LEARNING

Observe as students create columns on the graph. If students are unsure of the process, work with small groups to help them line up the data with labels to make accurate graphs.

SELF-ASSESSMENT

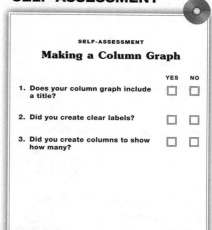

SELF-ASSESSMENT
Making a Column Graph

	YES	NO
1. Does your column graph include a title?	☐	☐
2. Did you create clear labels?	☐	☐
3. Did you create columns to show how many?	☐	☐

SUPPORTING AND EXTENDING

▸ Give teams other topics to use as the basis for column graphs, such as eye or hair color, favorite weather, or favorite foods.

▸ Have students write individual procedures for creating another type of graph, such as a pie graph or a line plot. Students can share their procedural texts with learning partners in other classes.

▸ Work with students to track the temperature over a period of a week or two. Have them create column graphs to show the data. The labels on the bottom should represent days, while the labels on the side represent degrees. Use the column graph with students to examine temperature trends over time.

Investigation

A visual investigation combines words and pictures to give instructions for making or doing something.

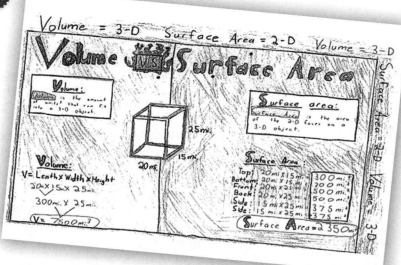

FEATURES

- Title
- Two facing pages that form a "spread"
- Visual supports: title, headings, and diagrams
- Numbered steps and sequence words

FOCUSED MINILESSON

Writers, I have a favorite fall activity to do with my family—making a scarecrow. I want to create instructions so that you could try this fun activity with your own families! I'm using a special format—a visual investigation. It's a mini-report that fits just right on two pages. Let's take a look at an investigation with instructions before we start. Turn to page 28 in the *Big Book of Mentor Texts. Isn't this investigation amazing? Making drums like this looks like a lot of fun!*

TURN &TALK *Analyze this investigation. What did you notice about page layout, spacing, and how the directions are arranged? What did this author do to provide instruction on how to make a cajon?*

Writers, many of you noticed the title that goes across the two pages. Watch as I write Make a Scarecrow. *Notice that this title spreads across the top of the two pages, right over the gutter line. We call the two pages a "spread."*

Watch me start by sketching a scarecrow that goes across both pages of the spread. I will add labels and a title, and I'll create a space for several text boxes. I want one text box to be a set of numbered steps, just like the numbered steps in the mentor text. Another text box will have different ideas about scarecrows from around the world. A box for a materials list is a great idea, too! Notice I am writing a quick note in each box so I can remember what I plan to include. Once I like the way the page looks, I can begin to write sentences for the text boxes, then add captions or labels and color.

After writing: *Writers, let's take a look at this investigation. The steps to instruct are clearly planned with organizing numbers. Special text boxes are ready for facts to make this investigation more exciting!* As you discuss the features with students, capture their thinking on a chart you can display for reference.

WRITING and COACHING

Writers, think of something you know how to make or how to do that you could show in an investigation with steps, such as making a friendship bracelet, building a sand castle, jumping rope, shooting baskets, or caring for a pet.

Provide sheets of 11" x 17" paper with folds in the center to represent gutters. Guide students as they plan their use of space. After planning their space, students can add their own text and color.

SHARING and REFLECTING

Writers, your investigations show the steps in sequence so they are easy to follow. Even more important, you made your investigations visually interesting to excite your readers about trying the process themselves. Your text features make this process really come to life!

ASSESS THE LEARNING

As students create their investigations, note which students may need help using text features. Refer to the mentor text as you discuss features.

SELF-ASSESSMENT

SELF-ASSESSMENT

Instructing with an Investigation

	YES	NO
1. Did you include accurate information?	☐	☐
2. Did you use the space in an interesting way?	☐	☐
3. Did you include features such as captions, headings, and diagrams?	☐	☐
4. Did you include numbered steps or sequence words in the instructions?	☐	☐

SUPPORTING AND EXTENDING

▸ Have students write investigations to instruct on classroom activities, experiments, or procedures. Share with first-grade students so they know what to expect in second grade.

▸ Have students work in teams to write investigations about science experiments or procedures, like how to use a balance. Display them in the science center for reference.

▸ Collect individual investigations in blank books so each student has a record of his or her progress as a writer as well as a lovely collection of writing that summarizes topics of study across the year.

Narrative Writing Projects

Narrative writing projects focus on two areas: personal narrative and nonfiction narrative. The purpose of both is to entertain and inform the reader. A *personal narrative* is written in the first person. It often focuses on a brief episode and includes personal reflection. The purpose is to retell events in order, including details and words that show the writer's feelings. Personal narrative can take many forms including autobiographies, personal reflections, diary entries, diagrams, illustrations, and poetry. A *nonfiction narrative* is written in the third person. The events are factual and told in time order, but the information is woven into a narrative format with a beginning, middle, and end. Narrative nonfiction can take many forms including true stories, news reports, observation logs, diagrams, illustrations, and poetry.

. . . .

CONTENTS

EXTENDED WRITING UNIT

▸ Class Project: Personal Narrative of a Class Experience (about 5 days)

▸ Individual Project: Personal Narrative of a Personal Experience (about 6 days)

▸ Class Project: Biography of Amelia Earhart (about 5 days)

▸ Individual Project: Biography of a Real-Life Hero (about 5 days)

POWER WRITES

▸ Personal Narrative

▸ Retell from a Different Point of View

▸ Nonfiction Narrative

▸ Eyewitness Account

▸ Factual Recount

▸ Timeline

▸ Investigation

The Big Picture:
Class and Individual Projects

Personal Narrative

The extended writing unit begins with class and individual projects for *Personal Narrative*. During the *class project,* students write personal narratives of a class experience. The mentor text "Grandma's Surprise" acts as a model to show students the structure and features of a personal narrative. Students observe features in the mentor text that will help them write their narratives. Then they recount a class experience, focusing on sequence and true information. You will need to ensure the class experience happens prior to the writing project. It could be a field trip, an author tea, or something as simple as a walk. The unit uses an animal visit the class had. Students draft, revise, and publish personal narratives of the class experience. Each child's narrative has a beginning, middle, and end. Students' finished narratives are bound into a class book. Students use the features chart as they share and reflect on their personal stories.

During their *individual project,* students review the features of a personal narrative, choose an episode from their own life to write about, and draft, edit, and publish a personal narrative. Writing partners read each other's drafts and give feedback to improve narrative qualities. Students publish their personal narratives as books. They share and reflect on their finished pieces.

Nonfiction Narrative

The extended writing unit continues with class and individual projects for *Nonfiction Narrative*. During the *class project,* students write a collaborative biography of a real-life heroic figure. The unit focuses on Amelia Earhart. Note that you may choose a different person to fit content your class is learning. The mentor text "Nancy Lopez" acts as a model to show students the structure and features of a biography. Students observe features in the mentor text that will help them write their biography of Earhart. Then they work in small groups to research and write sections of the biography. Their finished pieces may be combined to produce a class display or collated to create a class book.

During their *individual project,* students review the features of a biography. Then they choose another real-life hero, research their subject, and draft, edit, and publish a biography. Students choose how they will publish their final biography. For example, they may create a poster or booklet to showcase the biography or post it to a class or school website. Students share and reflect on their finished pieces.

PERSONAL NARRATIVE CLASS PROJECT			
Session	**Focused Minilesson**	**Writing and Coaching**	**Sharing and Reflecting**
1	Introduce personal narrative text; choose topics	Draft pre-assessment personal narrative	Share your personal narrative with your partner. What did you find easy about writing it? What was challenging?
2	Study "Grandma's Surprise"; chart features; plan writing	Begin drafting	Read your writing to your partner. How were your descriptions and feelings similar? What differences did you notice?
3	Study "Grandma's Surprise"; focus on beginning, middle, ending, feeling words	Continue drafting and revising; focus on feeling words and beginning, middle, ending	Share what you wrote. Did you include the same details? Did you have the same or different feelings?
4	Study "Grandma's Surprise"; focus on punctuation, dialogue	Revise and edit	Tell your partner what changes you made. How did the changes improve your writing?
5	Study "Grandma's Surprise"; focus on title, illustrations	Illustrate and publish; create cover and bind class book	Read, celebrate class book. What have you learned about writing a personal narrative?
PERSONAL NARRATIVE INDIVIDUAL PROJECT			
Session	**Focused Minilesson**	**Writing and Coaching**	**Sharing and Reflecting**
6	Review features of personal narrative text; choose topic; focus on beginning	Draft, revise, and edit the beginning	Read your beginning to your partner. What do you like about your partner's beginning?
7	Study modeled writing; focus on the middle; learn to use adjectives for feelings and emotions	Draft, revise, and edit the middle	Share the middle part. Find words your partner uses to describe feelings. How do they compare to feelings in your work?
8	Study modeled writing; focus on a strong ending	Draft, revise, and edit the ending	Read the ending to your partner. Partners, what events and feelings did you hear about?
9	Study modeled writing; focus on getting ready to publish	Revise, edit narrative	Share a change that you made. Why did you make that change?
10	Study modeled writing; focus on how illustrations bring the narrative to life	Create an illustration for each part (beginning, middle, ending)	Partners, how did adding illustrations make your narratives easier to understand?
11	Focus on publishing and creating a cover	Create cover; publish personal narrative	Read in small groups. What makes your personal narratives so great?

NONFICTION NARRATIVE CLASS PROJECT		
Session / **Focused Minilesson**	**Writing and Coaching**	**Sharing and Reflecting**
1 — Introduce biography; choose topics	Draft pre-assessment biography	Share your biography. Which parts of the person's life did you write about?
2 — Study "Nancy Lopez"; chart features; create class timeline	Begin researching; take notes and stick on class timeline	Share a fact/note from your research. Where on the timeline does it belong?
3 — Study "Nancy Lopez"; focus on third person point of view, time-order words	Finish researching and taking notes to fill timeline	Share information. How do we decide whether to keep a note or not?
4 — Study "Nancy Lopez"; focus on turning facts into interesting details	Small groups draft different parts of the biography	Share what your group wrote. What time-order words did you hear? How do you know it's written in the third person?
5 — Study "Nancy Lopez"; focus on illustrations	Small groups publish their section and create an illustration	Share; celebrate. Review biography traits. Which do you understand best?
NONFICTION NARRATIVE INDIVIDUAL PROJECT		
Session / **Focused Minilesson**	**Writing and Coaching**	**Sharing and Reflecting**
6 — Review features of biographies; choose topic; create planner	Begin researching and drafting; add details to facts on planner	Share an interesting note with your partner. What is fascinating about this fact?
7 — Study modeled writing: learn to add time-order words	Continue researching and drafting; add time-order words and dates	Share what you wrote. How did you put your information in order?
8 — Study modeled writing: focus on using third-person point of view	Finish researching to complete planner	Read facts to your partner. Do you hear the third-person point of view? Do you need to change pronouns?
9 — Study modeled writing: learn to turn notes into sentences	Begin drafting and editing; use one section of notes to draft one part of biography	Read your favorite part to the class. Partners, what did you edit and why?
10 — Study "Nancy Lopez"; focus on how pictures support information	Illustrate and publish	Present final biographies. What traits do you see? How are biographies of the same person similar and different?

Other Topics and Forms for Narrative Writing

Although these model projects use personal recounts and biographies as springboards for teaching narrative writing, the teaching process here can be adapted to many other narrative topics and forms. The Power Writes in this section will give you ideas for several such adaptations in addition to those that follow.

Possible Topics

Topics may correlate with content in your science and social studies standards, current events, or class interests.

Personal Narrative	**Nonfiction Narrative**
My trip to the museum	My favorite:
My trip to the zoo	author
Going to the park	sports hero
My birthday	All about:
A time when I was scared	my pet
A time when I was sad	my brother/sister
My vacation	A day in the life of:
My first day of school	a firefighter
Losing my first tooth	my teacher
A surprise	a farmer
Visiting my grandparents	Explanations using the narrative form
Playing with my friends	such as:
Going to a party	How a spider catches a fly
Trick-or-treating on Halloween	How a snake sheds its skin
A special celebration	The life cycle of a frog
What I like to do best	The life cycle of a tree
	The water cycle
	Where maple syrup comes from
	How a road is made

Possible Forms

Some possible forms of narrative include:

Retell	Autobiography	Illustration
Recount	News report	Postcard
Explanation	Storyboard	Letter
Personal story	Observation log	Poster
Biography	Diagram	Poem

Gathering Your Materials and Setting Up Research Stations

For the *personal narrative class project*, students will be writing about an event the class has experienced together. The unit uses a visit from an animal as a focus. You could choose any experience your class has shared, from taking a walk to having a special day. It will be helpful to have photographs or pictures from the class event on hand to help students recall their experience and generate ideas and details for their narratives.

The personal narrative mentor text is "Grandma's Surprise" from the *Big Book of Mentor Texts*. For Session 1, you will also need examples of diary or journal entries and a biography so students can compare personal narratives to other nonfiction narratives. You will point out that a personal narrative is a brief account of the writer's own experience, while a nonfiction narrative may be told by someone else.

There is no research component to the *personal narrative individual project;* students can write about any episode in their lives. You may want to have examples of published personal narratives available so students can see how illustrations support the text and convey details and feelings.

The *nonfiction narrative class project* is a collaborative biography of a real-life heroic person. The unit focuses on Amelia Earhart. Note that you may choose another person who fits your content or students' interests. If you select someone local, you may be able to arrange for an in-person interview. Set up research stations around the library or classroom. Gather a wide variety of materials about the selected person, including books, periodicals, encyclopedia entries, videos, and printouts from bookmarked websites. Include information on tape or CD and recorded interviews if possible. Divide the materials among research stations. Students can rotate from station to station to collect information. Give students sticky notes or cards and tape for their note taking so they can place their notes on a class timeline.

The nonfiction narrative mentor text is "Nancy Lopez" from the *Big Book of Mentor Texts*. For Session 1, you will also need a biographical article about a heroic person. The unit defines a hero as someone who overcame a problem or showed courage in the face of difficulty, not merely someone who is famous. Children's encyclopedias, books, magazines, and the Internet are great sources for biographies. Choose a person whose accomplishments will interest your students.

For the *nonfiction narrative individual project*, you will need to set up research stations on four or five people of interest to your students. Rather than having students select their own heroes, you might want to pre-select the biography subjects for students to write about. Narrowing the choices will allow you to gather resources ahead of time and will enable you to tie the biography subjects to a content area being studied, such as pioneers. Give students an opportunity to write down their first, second, third, and fourth choice. Try to give them either their first, second, or third choice when grouping. Stock research stations with resources like those for the class project.

Please refer to the research section on pages 285–307 for additional information on setting up and using research stations.

Focusing on Standards

These extended writing units are designed to teach students about the form and content of both personal narrative and nonfiction narrative as they apply basic writing strategies. Each of the lessons provides you with suggested demonstrations, but you may wish to tailor your instruction based on the common needs of your own students. The pre-assessment from Session 1 will help you identify these needs.

Before introducing the unit, carefully review the list on the next page so you can keep the lesson objectives in mind as you teach, coach, and monitor students' growth as writers of nonfiction narrative.

KEY SKILLS AND UNDERSTANDINGS: NARRATIVE WRITING GRADE 2

Purpose

• Understands the purpose for writing a narrative piece (a true story)

Ideas/Research

• Generates ideas

• Tells about event/s or time

• Gives the reader factual information

• Includes engaging related details

Organization/Text Features

• Includes a title that relates closely to the narrative

• Relates an event or sequence of events in time order

• Includes a beginning, middle, and end

• Includes pictures that match text

• Includes labels and captions on pictures

Language/Style

• Uses first person for personal narratives

• Uses third person for nonfiction narratives

• Uses a consistent verb tense

• Uses interesting action words

• Uses descriptive words and phrases

• Uses sequence words and phrases (*at first, soon,* etc.)

Conventions and Presentation

• Uses complete sentences

• Uses regular and irregular verb forms correctly

• Uses strategies to help with spelling

• Capitalizes the pronoun *I*

• Uses capital letters to start sentences

• Uses punctuation marks to end sentences

The list on the previous page is the basis for both the Individual Evaluation Record and the Ongoing Monitoring Sheet shown in Figure 3.1. (Both forms can be found in the Resources section at the back of this book and on the *Resources* CD-ROM.) Use the Individual Evaluation Record if you want to keep separate records on individual students. The Ongoing Monitoring Sheet gives you a simple mechanism for recording information on all your students as you move around the class, evaluating their work in progress. Use this information to adapt instruction and session length as needed.

You will also use the Ongoing Monitoring Sheet and/or the Individual Evaluation Record at the end of the unit to record students' growth as writers after comparing their published work from the individual project with the pre-assessment they will complete in Session 1 of the class project.

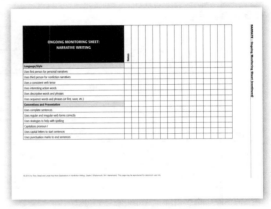

Figure 3.1

Planning and Facilitating the Unit

Students will need preparation, coaching, prompting, and support as they move through this extended writing unit. Use the following tips and strategies as needed to ensure each child's success.

Before the Unit:

▸ When planning your teaching, bear in mind that each session in this unit is designed to be completed in a day. However, you will likely find that your students need more time for certain activities. Take the time you need to adequately respond to the unique needs of your students.

▸ Begin building background knowledge about narrative writing at least a week in advance. Shared reading, guided reading, and read-aloud experiences as well as group discussions will ensure that students are well prepared to write personal and nonfiction narratives.

▸ As you share nonfiction narratives with students, be sure to highlight the purpose of the piece, real events, exciting details, time order (beginning, middle, end), and illustrations that support the text.

‣ For the *personal narrative class project*, choose a class experience to focus on. Gather photographs and materials that will jog students' memories and help them generate ideas and details for their writing.

‣ For the *personal narrative individual project*, think ahead about a personal experience you can share as the mentored writing model. The unit example is a first flight on an airplane.

‣ For the *nonfiction narrative class project*, choose a biographical subject who will appeal to your students and fit content you are studying. The unit focuses on Amelia Earhart. Be sure you can find research material to support your students' exploration.

‣ For the *nonfiction narrative individual project*, you may wish to pre-select four or five biographical subjects students can choose from. This will ensure that you can provide research materials to support students' choices.

During the Class Project:

‣ Begin each session with a focused minilesson to demonstrate traits in narrative writing. The mentor text "Grandma's Surprise" acts as the model to show students the structure and features of a personal narrative. The mentor text "Nancy Lopez" acts as a model to show students the structure and features of a nonfiction narrative. You may wish to use other mentor texts to assist you with your demonstrations.

▸ For the *personal narrative class project*, students may find it easier to draw first. They can add words or a sentence to their picture to tell what happened. You can also give students photographs from the event. Writers can put the pictures in order and write or dictate captions.

▸ For the *nonfiction narrative class project*, students will work in groups to write the biography. Each group will take notes from the class timeline and use them to write sentences. You will assign revising and editing jobs to group members.

▸ Create a bank of sequence words and phrases such as *first, at the beginning, next*, and so on. You can add to this word chart throughout the unit.

▸ Help English language learners build their vocabulary of feeling words. Chart words from the mentor text and words students might be likely to use in their narratives. You may wish to partner beginning English language learners with more proficient speakers.

▸ As students work independently on their writing, note those who are struggling and bring them together in small groups for additional support. For the personal narrative, ask questions and use photographs to help children recall their experience. For the nonfiction narrative, offer guidance for choosing research materials, taking useful notes, and writing about just an event or two in the person's life.

▸ Students who seem very confident and who have clearly grasped all of the concepts taught so far can be brought together in a small group to extend their understanding to more challenging work such as adding transitions, descriptive details, and dialogue.

▸ Early finishers can work together to check for feeling words, logical order, and a structure with a beginning, middle, and end. They can work on the cover of the class book. They can be partners for students who are still writing.

▸ Help students focus their publishing efforts on a few conventions for which they are ready. A simple editing checklist can help them focus on specific points and monitor their own work.

▸ Although the lessons provide suggested demonstrations for each session, you may wish to tailor your instruction to meet the common needs of your students. The Ongoing Monitoring Sheet (Figure 3.1, below), together with the Individual Evaluation Record will help you keep track of each student's unique needs. Refer to the section on assessment and ongoing monitoring on pages xxx–xxxv in the introduction to this book for further information.

▸ Use the Daily Planner (Figure 3.2, below) to plan your own class projects for future explorations based on the needs of your students. A blank Daily Planner can be found on the *Resources* CD-ROM.

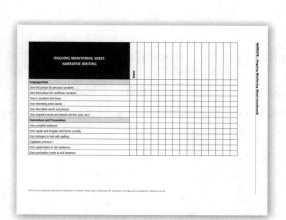

Figure 3.1

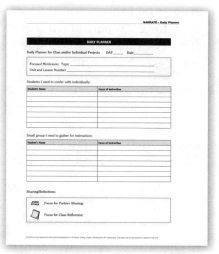

Figure 3.2

During the Individual Project:

▸ Continue to use the Ongoing Monitoring Sheet and the Individual Evaluation Record to identify topics you'll want to address in the focused minilesson that begins each session. Continue to use the Daily Planner to lay out future explorations based on student needs.

▸ Some students will be more comfortable drawing first and then writing to label or tell what happened. Drawing and then labeling their pictures may be especially helpful to English language learners. You can help them extend their syntax and understanding of first-person and third-person point of view through focused questioning and models.

▸ Some students will benefit from saying their ideas aloud to a partner before drawing or writing them.

▸ Display the word charts or provide copies so all students can see the words and use the charts as they draft and revise.

▸ For the *personal narrative*, monitor students' topic selections. Be sure they choose an authentic, personal experience with a beginning, middle, and end. If students have trouble narrowing ideas, you can suggest wide categories with sentence stems like *I was excited when I___* or *The first time I ____, I felt___*. If students need more support for writing, pull them into a small group and ask questions to activate their thinking about what to write or draw for each part of their story. Help students stay focused on the purpose of a personal narrative: telling events in order, including details and words that describe feelings.

▸ For the *nonfiction narrative*, use a planner to help students keep events in order. Create sections such as *Growing Up, Middle Years, Later Years,* and *Amazing Facts!* If some students need more support for writing, pull them into a small group to focus on finding useful facts and writing or drawing the main events in the person's life.

▸ Encourage students to use new and interesting words and not to worry about spelling and mechanics as they are drafting. Assure them that there will be time for editing and revision later.

‣ If some students are ready for more challenging work, pull them together into a small group and extend the focus on transitions, action verbs, or describing words. Be sure to focus on just one aspect of their writing at a time.

‣ Students who finish early can look back at photographs or research materials to make sure they have included true information in time order. Early finishers can also provide feedback on partners' text or illustrations.

‣ Have writing partners conference with each other often in order to check one another's work for sense and clarity.

‣ You may find it helpful to work on your own narrative piece along with your students. Then you can use your model as an example during think-alouds.

After the Unit:

‣ Be sure to give students opportunities to share and celebrate their individual writing projects.

‣ Distribute copies of the Student Self-Reflection Sheet (on the *Resources* CD-ROM). Students will benefit greatly from the chance to reflect on their progress during the unit and to hear their classmates' feedback.

‣ Compare students' final writing products with their pre-assessments to evaluate their growth as writers of narrative.

‣ Look at common needs of the class and address these when planning future explorations on narrative writing, or through the Power Writes.

‣ Reflect on the strengths and challenges of implementing this series of lessons. How might it be adjusted to maximize student learning?

SESSION 1
Immersion and Pre-Assessment

Students are introduced to personal narrative and draft a brief piece about a personal moment in their own lives for the pre-assessment.

MATERIALS
- Handwritten or published diary or journal entry
- Biography or other example of personal narrative
- Paper
- Pencils

TIP To reinforce the concept that a personal narrative is a text about a real event in the life of the author, compare the diary to other nonfiction narratives, such as a biography, that your class has read. Prompt students to explain the difference: a personal narrative tells about the writer's own experiences. A narrative nonfiction text such as a biography is always told by someone else.

TIP Students may need guidance to keep their topics focused on small moments. If they propose describing a larger experience, such as what they did on vacation, direct them to focus on a smaller but significant aspect of it, such as the first time they swam in the ocean or what it felt like to climb to the top of a tower. Use questions to guide the students, such as: *What was the one thing you remember most about your vacation? What was the best part of your birthday party? What memory do you have that is strongest?*

FOCUSED MINILESSON *(prewriting)*
15 MINUTES

- Start to immerse students in the text type by talking about diaries and journals: *A diary or journal tells about events that happened on different days in someone's life. The person who experienced the events is the writer. Why do you think people would want to keep a diary or a journal? I think you're absolutely correct! A diary is a record of important or memorable events. A journal is a way to share events, too—sometimes scientists publish their journals to show their journey of exploration or their scientific discoveries. This kind of nonfiction writing is called a* personal narrative.

  TURN &TALK *Talk with your partner about things people might write about in a diary, which is one kind of personal narrative. What would you write about if you kept a diary?*

- Encourage partners to discuss their ideas. Point out that students are describing real events that happened to them. Some of these events are very personal and should be kept private. But others are great experiences that are worth sharing!

- Recall entries from a diary you have previously read in class. Lead students into a discussion of important experiences they have had: *In the diary entries I read earlier, the writer told about special moments in time that had happened to her. Now you will each write your own personal narrative about a single experience that was important to you.*

  TURN &TALK *Partners, talk together about experiences that you have had. What experience could you focus on in a personal narrative?*

- Have students identify important personal moments they could write about. Record their ideas on the board. If students struggle to identify important personal moments, prompt them with suggestions: *What is something you have a strong memory about? Can you think of when something important happened to you, like the day you started kindergarten or learned to ride a bike?*

- Tell students they will write a personal narrative about an important moment in their lives. Explain that they may use a topic from the board or choose another.

WRITING and COACHING *(drafting)*
20 MINUTES

- Provide students with paper and pencils. Direct them to begin writing about a memorable event in their own lives.

- Students at this age usually are quite comfortable writing about themselves and most likely will have a lot to say. Provide ample warning as the session draws to a close so students will have time to wrap up their thoughts.

- Encourage early finishers to go back and review their work before handing it in. Then they can go on with other writing activities they may have been working on.

SHARING and REFLECTING
10 MINUTES

TURN &TALK *Take turns sharing what you wrote with your partner. What did you find easy about writing a personal narrative? What was a bit more challenging?*

- As students share their challenges, note the skills they feel they need help with. Emphasize that this was a practice try and that the class will be learning more about personal narratives.

- Sum up today's activity and prepare students for the whole-class project: *You did a great job of writing about a special moment in your life. Next time we will begin writing about a special experience our whole class shared.*

- After class, evaluate each students' writing using the Ongoing Monitoring Sheet (in the Resources section and also on the *Resources* CD-ROM) Use the results to revise instruction and personalize the lessons in this unit. If you want to keep individual records on students, use the Individual Evaluation Record in the Resources section and on the CD-ROM. Do not make corrections or marks on students' work.

TIP If students seem uncertain about how to proceed, encourage them to try their best without coaching them about specific characteristics or providing too much direction. Reinforce the focus of the pre-assessment activity by saying: *Write about a moment in your life that was important to you and that you have a strong memory of.* Reassure them that they will learn much more about personal narratives in upcoming sessions.

TIP For the class project, students will need a common experience they all can write about. Plan an experience that can be the basis for your students' writing. For example, you might focus on a special event, such as a community-service project, a field trip, or a classroom visit with a special guest. The lessons that follow focus on a classroom visit with an animal, but you can adapt the lessons to whatever experience you provide for your students. You will need to ensure that the whole-class experience happens prior to the class project.

SESSION 2
Drafting the Beginning

Students examine the features of a personal narrative and begin to draft the beginning of their own narratives.

MATERIALS
• *Big Book of Mentor Texts:* "Grandma's Surprise," pages 30–35
• Chart paper and marker
• Research folders
• Pencils

FOCUSED MINILESSON *(prewriting)*
25 MINUTES

■ Focus the learning: *You've already tried your hand at writing a personal narrative, and you know that it's not always easy to know what to include in this type of writing. In this session we'll take a look at a personal narrative called "Grandma's Surprise," and we'll use it to help us understand what we should include when writing about a special time.*

■ Invite students to predict what the personal narrative will be about based on its title. Then read the mentor text aloud.

> **TURN &TALK** *Turn and talk with your partner about "Grandma's Surprise." What kinds of features does the boy include when he writes his personal narrative?*

■ Use students' responses to generate features on the chart: *The title tells us what this personal narrative is about, so let's add that to our chart. What happens first? Then what happens? Your responses show us that the boy tells events in the order they happened.* And what about the ending? *He tells us about the important thing he learned on his visit with Grandma. That's a strong ending!* Continue until all features have been identified. Display the chart prominently in your classroom.

> **Features of a Great Personal Narrative**
>
> It includes a title.
>
> It tells events in the order they happened.
>
> It has a beginning, middle, and end.
>
> It is told using the word I.
>
> It tells how the writer felt.
>
> It tells why the moment was important.
>
> It has a strong ending.

■ Tell students that they will be writing a personal narrative about the day an animal came to visit your classroom. (Adapt the lesson if you have chosen to focus on another experience in your classroom.)

TURN &TALK *Talk to your partner about what you remember when we saw the snake. What did you think at first? How did you feel?*

■ Discuss students' responses in order to prepare them to write about the experience.

WRITING and COACHING *(drafting)*
15 MINUTES

■ Have students begin drafting the beginning of their personal narratives. If you have pictures of the animal visit to your classroom (or whatever event you chose), encourage students to use them to recall the moment in time: *Write your beginnings. Focus on what happened and how you felt about it.*

■ As you circulate around the room, remind students that a personal narrative doesn't just describe a moment or event: *A great personal narrative gives readers a strong sense of what it was like for the author to be a part of it. As you think about the very first things that happened during our visit, try closing your eyes to remember how you felt at the time. Write about those feelings!*

SHARING and REFLECTING
10 MINUTES

TURN &TALK *Read your beginning to your partner. How were your descriptions and feelings similar? What differences did you notice?*

■ Discuss what students have written. Refer to the features chart and praise them for incorporating features into their drafts: *I like how you used words that show your feelings about snakes. This is an important part of your narrative because you were a little scared of that snake at first and then ended up really liking it.*

■ Praise students for the work they have already done on their personal narratives. Explain that in subsequent sessions they will be able to continue working on them.

TIP Giving students adequate time to discuss and recall the event or experience they are writing about can make independent writing time more productive. You may wish to have students use graphic organizers to record ideas and then discuss their graphic organizers with a partner. For example, students might write three words that describe the animal and three words that describe how they felt during the visit.

TIP for Conferring with Individuals and Small Groups

If students struggle to get started, prompt them with basic questions, such as: *What animal came to our class? What did it look like? What did you do?* Encourage students who have provided only basic information, such as *I saw a snake. It was yellow,* to expand their thinking. Guide them to expand on their responses with questions such as: *Have you ever seen a snake before? How did you feel when you first saw the snake?*

SESSION 3
Drafting the Middle and Ending

Students explore the importance of sequence in personal narrative and draft the middle and ending of their own narratives.

MATERIALS
- *Big Book of Mentor Texts:* "Grandma's Surprise," pages 30–35
- Features chart from Session 2
- Two colors of sticky notes
- Paper
- Pencils

> ### Features of a Great Personal Narrative
>
> It includes a title.
>
> It tells events in the order they happened.
>
> It has a beginning, middle, and end.
>
> It is told using the word I.
>
> It tells how the writer felt.
>
> It tells why the moment was important.
>
> It has a strong ending.

TIP Provide students with a bank of sequence words and phrases, such as *first, after, at the beginning, next, then, finally,* and *at the end.* You may also wish to use these terms in sentences to elicit students' responses, such as: Then *what happens? What happens* after *that?*

FOCUSED MINILESSON *(prewriting, planning)*
20 MINUTES

- Focus the learning: *During our last session, we talked about the features to include when writing our personal narratives. In this session, we'll look at the mentor text again to see if we can identify the important parts of the text—the beginning, middle, and end.*

- Reread the mentor text.

  > **TURN & TALK** *Partners, think together to identify the parts of a personal narrative. What happens at the beginning, middle, and end of this narrative?*

- Write the words *beginning, middle,* and *end* on sticky notes and invite volunteers to place the notes on those parts of the mentor text: *Good job! You recognized the different parts of the narrative and placed them in the right order. Now think about how you can add a clearer beginning, middle, and end to your own narratives.*

- After you discuss sequence, focus on details that show the boy's feelings in the mentor text.

  > **TURN & TALK** *Turn and talk with your partner about how the boy feels when his parents drop him off at Grandma's house. What other feelings does he have throughout the narrative?*

- Reinforce students' ideas as they share them in discussion: *You did a great job of recognizing that, at first, the boy is a little concerned. He loves his grandma, but this is the first time he's been at her house without his family. He's wondering if the weekend will be boring.* As students identify words and phrases that tell about feelings, have them use a second color of sticky note to mark them in the mentor text.

  > **TURN & TALK** *Discuss with your partner what details about feelings you can add to your own personal narratives.*

■ Regroup and have students share their thoughts. *You've done a great job of identifying feelings. Here is another example of a personal narrative that uses very descriptive words:* At first I was apprehensive, but when I saw how much everyone else enjoyed the visit with the snake, I started to feel courageous. *Aren't those fabulous words?* Apprehensive *definitely brings a picture to readers' minds! So does* courageous!

WRITING and COACHING *(drafting, revising)*
20 MINUTES

■ Have students take out their personal narratives and continue drafting, focusing on the beginning, middle, and end.

■ Encourage students to think about the whole-class lesson: *Make sure your readers know what happened at the beginning, middle, and end of the animal visit. Describe how you felt.*

■ Have early finishers work together to check for feeling words and a structure with a beginning, middle, and an end. Provide them with sticky notes as in the whole-class lesson and have them mark these features on each other's drafts. Then have students use the feedback to help them revise.

SHARING and REFLECTING
10 MINUTES

■ Build a classroom writing community by having students share what they have written so far with one another.

> **TURN &TALK** *Share what you wrote with your partner. Did you include the same details? Did you have the same or different feelings about the experience as your partner?*

■ Invite volunteers with a range of responses to share what they wrote. As students share, recognize their achievement. Respond to their use of features: *You organized your ideas by including a beginning, middle, and end. You described your feelings. That really helps your readers understand what was happening at that moment.*

TIP Help English language learners build their vocabulary of feeling and emotion words. List words from the mentor text and words that students might likely include in their personal narratives, such as *nervous, scared, excited, happy, thrilled, curious, worried,* and *confused.* Then act out the words with exaggerated gestures and facial expressions. You may also want to use pictures from books and magazines and help students match emotion words to the pictures.

TIP for Conferring with Individuals and Small Groups

If you notice that students are struggling to write more of their personal narratives, or they are writing only one sentence per part, use pictures you took of the animal visit for support. Ask questions such as: *Do you remember how you felt when you first saw the snake? What were you thinking about? Did you want to touch the snake? Why or why not? How did you feel about snakes after the classroom visit? Why did you change your mind about these animals?*

SESSION 4
Revising and Editing

Students edit and revise their personal narratives, focusing on correct punctuation.

MATERIALS
• *Big Book of Mentor Texts:* "Grandma's Surprise," pages 30–35
• Research folders
• Paper and pencils

TIP In Spanish, questions and exclamations include inverted punctuation marks at the beginning of sentences in addition to the marks at the end. Be sure Spanish-speaking English language learners understand that in English writing, the punctuation marks are placed only at the ends of sentences.

FOCUSED MINILESSON *(revising, editing)*
25 MINUTES

■ Introduce the session's focus: *You have done such a good job with drafting beginnings, middles, and endings so far. In this session, we're going to learn how punctuation marks such as periods, question marks, and exclamation points can make our writing clearer and more interesting.*

■ Conduct a minilesson on sentence punctuation: *When we write, we're careful that the sentences don't just run into each other. That helps our sentences make sense to our readers. A capital letter is a signal that we're starting a new sentence. Punctuation marks not only signal the ends of sentences, they also help readers understand how a writer feels. When I tell someone a fact, I use a period at the end of a sentence. When I ask a question, I use a question mark. When I want to show excitement, I use an exclamation point.* Using sentences from the mentor text or your own sentences, have students generalize about situations in which a writer would use a period, exclamation point, or question mark.

■ Have students look at the punctuation they have used so far in their personal narratives.

> **TURN &TALK** *Turn and talk with your partner about which sentences in your writing should have periods and which might need exclamation points. How can you tell?*

■ Invite students to share examples of sentences with each type of punctuation. *Great job of figuring out places to use exclamation points! We don't want to overuse them, but a well-placed exclamation point can really add excitement to our writing and share that excitement with readers.*

■ Explain to students that reading back their work can help them revise it: *When we read back something we have written, it can help us find things we should change. We might find places where we need to add more details. We might see spelling that doesn't look correct. Take a moment and read what you have written.*

TURN &TALK *Talk to your partner about something you can change in your personal narrative to make it even better.*

■ Discuss students' ideas for changes they can make. Encourage them to make notes about things they want to change during independent writing time.

■ Have students take out their personal narratives. *You will be revising and editing your work. Remember that reading your work back to yourself can help you find things you want to change.*

WRITING and COACHING *(revising, editing)*
20 MINUTES

■ As students revise and edit, offer support as needed. If students request help with spelling, encourage them to sound out words. You may also help them look for words in a dictionary. Praise their successes as they work: *I see that you changed this period to an exclamation point. Now your readers will really understand how excited you felt. You are paying special attention to spelling. That will ensure that readers understand your narrative.*

■ Don't be afraid to stop the writing workshop if too many students seem to need assistance at one time. Have students work independently on other activities until you have had a chance to conference with everyone who needs your help.

SHARING and REFLECTING
10 MINUTES

■ Have partners share what they changed in their personal narratives.

TURN &TALK *Tell your partner what changes you made. Describe how these changes make your writing clearer and easier for your readers to understand.*

■ Invite different pairs to share the changes they made. Encourage them to reflect on how the changes improved the writing.

■ Help students feel a sense of accomplishment as they reflect on the work they've done: *You've done a lot of good work on your personal narratives. At our next session, we will work on publishing them so we can share them with a wider audience.*

TIP Guide students to understand that a good personal narrative tells events in the correct time order. Encourage students to check for logical order as they reread their work.

TIP for Conferring with Individuals and Small Groups

Revising and editing can be confusing and overwhelming for some students. Providing students with a simple editing checklist can help them focus on specific points and monitor their own work. Then, as you confer with them individually and in small groups, you can refer to points on the checklist: *Every sentence begins with a capital letter. Let's check your sentences. Every sentence also ends with a punctuation mark. Can you check each sentence for punctuation?*

SESSION 5
Publishing and Celebrating

Students add titles and illustrations to their personal narratives, then publish and celebrate their work.

MATERIALS

- *Big Book of Mentor Texts:* "Grandma's Surprise," pages 30–35
- Features chart
- Pictures you took of the animal visiting the classroom
- Pencils and drawing materials

TIP Revisiting the features chart reinforces what students have learned in this session and helps them review their own writing for those features. They will not lose sight of the features as they work through their drafts.

FOCUSED MINILESSON *(publishing)*
15 MINUTES

- Focus the learning: *In this session, we'll work on making our personal narratives even better. We will put them together to make one big book of personal narratives that tell about the snake's visit to our classroom.*

- Display the features chart you've developed. *I notice that the list of features includes a title. Let's take a look at the mentor text again. Read the title with me—*Grandma's Surprise. *That title really captures my attention. When I read it, I want to find out what the surprise is. It's much more intriguing than a title like* Planting a Garden. *That title would give away what happens in the narrative!*

  TURN &TALK *Partners, think together. What would be a great title for our class book? List an idea or two.*

- Invite partners to share their title ideas. Record ideas on the board and allow students to vote for the title of the class book.

- Direct students to the mentor text. Point out the illustrations. *"Grandma's Surprise" has pictures that help show what happens during the boy's experience.*

  TURN &TALK *Talk with your partner about the pictures in "Grandma's Surprise." What do they help you understand?*

- Discuss what students found helpful about the pictures: *These illustrations capture not just what happens, but also the feelings surrounding the event.* Tell students that they can use photographs you took of the snake and their own drawings to support their personal narratives.

- Discuss ideas about illustrations students want to add: *Let's work on publishing your personal narratives. Focus on adding great illustrations. Think about illustrations that match what happens in the text. How can you show your feelings in your illustrations?*

WRITING and COACHING *(publishing)*
20 MINUTES

■ Have students take out their personal narrative drafts. *Today, you will publish your work. You can add pictures that show details and words that tell your readers how you felt. Don't forget to give your narrative an attention-getting title.* Early finishers can help you create illustrations for the cover of the class book. More capable writers can add additional details to their narratives.

■ Remember to use think-aloud language as you provide support. Make your guidance as clear and detailed as possible, but stay focused on the main concept you are trying to teach.

■ When students have finished, bind their personal narratives into a class book. Display their book in a prominent location so they can read others' accounts of the same event.

SHARING and REFLECTING
15 MINUTES

■ Have students share their personal narratives. Point out how unique each student's narrative is, and explain that this is because everyone experiences an event in a slightly different way.

TURN &TALK *What have you learned this week about writing a personal narrative as we've worked together on a class project?*

■ Discuss students' understanding of the features, referring to the chart. Encourage reflective thinking by having partners discuss whether they included the features in their own personal narratives.

■ Celebrate the class's accomplishment: *You did a wonderful job describing the experience we had and expressing your feelings about it. I'm sure you're excited to use all that you've learned to craft another personal narrative.*

■ Try to stay flexible about the amount of time you allow for sharing, reflecting, and celebrating. Don't be afraid to add an extra day if you think it will boost students' confidence in their skills or cement the concepts they've been exploring.

TIP Emphasize that it is students' individual choice whether to add photos and illustrations to their writing and where to place them. This can foster a sense of independence and individual voice and reinforce that writers make many decisions about what to include and not to include in their work. It also helps students think about their audience.

TIP Use the personal narrative instruction to help students understand that writing is a process. Invite them to think back about how their work improved as they expanded it, added more details, and revised it. Explain that students will have an opportunity to use the process to write another personal narrative.

SESSION 6
Launching the Individual Project

Students review the features of a strong personal narrative, discuss and select their topics, and draft the beginnings of their personal narratives.

MATERIALS
• Research folders
• Features chart from the class project
• Paper and pencils

TIP If you notice that students are struggling to think of topics or aren't sure what to discuss, provide the class with sentence frames to use in their discussion, such as: *I remember when I ____. When I ____, I felt ____. I was so excited when I ____.*

FOCUSED MINILESSON *(prewriting)*
20 MINUTES

■ Introduce the individual project: *In this session, you are going to begin writing a new personal narrative. Each of you will choose a topic that captures an experience that only you had.* Prompt students to think about possible topics: *Think back to the mentor text, which focused on a boy's experiences in planting a garden with his grandmother. Think back to our class project, too. Now think about your own experiences! What single event or experience could you write about in a personal narrative?*

TURN &TALK *Partners, share your ideas. What might be great topics for your personal narratives?*

■ Have students share ideas as you record them: *You've identified some interesting topics. Your ideas will be fun to explore as you write your personal narratives!*

■ Explain that students can choose a topic from the board or another topic, such as what they wrote about during the pre-assessment. Display the features chart that you created during the class project. Invite students to reflect on the features they included when they wrote about the class experience: *What comes first in a personal narrative? A personal narrative starts with a beginning.*

■ Model how you would begin a personal narrative: *I want to write about the first time I flew on an airplane. For the beginning of my narrative, I will tell what happened first. "I went to the airport. I pulled my suitcase to the ticket counter. Then I walked through a metal detector. I was excited because I'd never flown before!"*

TURN &TALK *Turn and tell your partner the topic you chose and what happens at the beginning of your personal narrative. How did you feel?*

■ Invite a few volunteers to share their topics and their beginnings. Focus on the feelings students had during the experience.

WRITING and COACHING
(drafting, revising, editing)
15 MINUTES

■ Have students start drafting, focusing only on the beginning of their narratives. Remind them that the beginning is what happened first and that a great personal narrative includes the author's feelings about what happened.

■ After students have finished drafting their beginnings, help them revise and edit. If you have not yet introduced the idea of "writing buddies," this would be a good time to do so. Have students read their drafts to their buddies, who can listen for incomplete thoughts or unclear ideas. Students' writing buddies can be the same as their thinking partners or different.

SHARING and REFLECTING
10 MINUTES

TURN &TALK *What do you like about your partner's beginning?*

■ Recognize students' accomplishments: *Your personal narratives have strong beginnings. They tell your readers what your narratives are about and get them interested in finding out more. You've also done a great job of using words that tell about your feelings.*

TIP To reinforce the structure of a personal narrative, you may wish to provide students with a three-column graphic organizer labeled *beginning, middle,* and *end.* This can help them organize their thoughts, focus on just one part of their narrative at a time, and develop a logical sequence of events. Please see the *Resources* CD-ROM for blank graphic organizers.

TIP for Conferring with Individuals and Small Groups

If students have difficulty writing their beginnings, discuss how the beginning of a narrative provides background and helps a reader understand what's happening. Use a think-aloud to model setting a scene: *The first time I tried Japanese food, I was not sure what to expect. I didn't know if I would like it. A friend took me to a Japanese restaurant.* Ask students what happened before or at the beginning of their event. *Will readers understand what you are writing about? What would help readers understand the beginning of your narrative?*

SESSION 7
Drafting the Middle

Students draft the middle of their personal narrative, focusing on powerful adjectives that really describe their feelings.

MATERIALS
• Research folders
• Features chart from class project
• Chart paper and marker
• Paper and pencils

TIP Support English language learners by having them focus on correctly saying simple sentences containing feeling words before they try to write them. You might have these students practice completing simple sentence frames, such as *I felt _____. I was _____*. After they have mastered simple sentences, they can work on more complex sentence structures.

FOCUSED MINILESSON *(drafting)*
15 MINUTES

■ Introduce the session's focus: *In our last session, you chose a topic and wrote the beginning of your personal narrative. What comes next? That's right—the middle. After you set the scene in the beginning, you'll tell the main part of the narrative in the middle. That's what we'll work on in this session.*

■ Model how you would write the middle of a personal narrative: *Remember my narrative about flying in an airplane for the first time? The beginning included what it was like to get to the airport and how excited I was to fly for the first time. In the middle, I might tell what the plane was like. I could describe what I felt, heard, and saw as the plane took off.*

TURN &TALK *Think about what happened next in the personal event you are writing about. Describe the middle to your partner.*

■ Listen in and provide positive feedback: *Your ideas for the middle are great! You are really thinking about the main part of your narrative and what your readers will find most exciting.*

■ Conduct a minilesson on using adjectives that students might use to describe how they felt in their personal narratives: *When we write about our personal event, we can use words that show how we felt. For example, the first time I flew on an airplane, I felt excited.* Record the word *excited* on chart paper: *What words can you name that show feelings or emotions?* Prompt students as needed. Record their ideas on the chart paper: *You've done a great job identifying words that describe how people feel. Think about how you might weave some of these words into your narratives.*

■ Explain that students will be writing the middle of their personal narratives. Remind them to use adjectives that express feelings as they write.

WRITING and COACHING
(drafting, revising, editing)
20 MINUTES

■ Have students write the middles of their personal narratives. Assist any students who are struggling by having them look back at their beginnings and think about what happened next. If students are using graphic organizers, have them return to their organizers to record their ideas about the middles of their narratives.

■ As students finish writing their middles, have them revise and edit their work. Emphasize the importance of reviewing their work so far to identify words they left out or ideas that aren't clear. Explain that they can also add details about the event.

■ Students at this age may find it difficult to stay focused on a single event or moment in time. As you circulate around the room, check to be sure students have not wandered from the specific event or experience they are describing: *I love the detail in this sentence, Gere, but I think it describes something that happened after the event you're writing about, don't you?*

SHARING and REFLECTING
10 MINUTES

TURN &TALK *Share the middle part of your narrative with your partner. Can you find a part where your partner uses words to describe feelings? Compare the feelings in your partner's work to the feelings in your work.*

■ Have volunteers share sentences that include emotions or feelings. Invite them to discuss the feelings their partner wrote about. Then praise students' success: *You've made great progress in writing your personal narratives. You've expressed how you felt, and I look forward to reading what you write next!*

TIP for Conferring with Individuals and Small Groups

If students struggle to write more than one sentence for the middles of their personal narratives, prompt them to explore and expand on their accounts: *How did you feel when this was happening? You were excited? Why did you feel that way? Let's add a sentence about how you were feeling.* Have struggling students refer to the describing words chart from the Focused Minilesson and check for words they could incorporate into their writing.

TIP If students are comfortable with the process of recording their ideas, show them ways they can mark edits and corrections on their drafts. For example, model using a caret to insert a word that has been left out of a sentence. Explain that when they create their final drafts, they can add missing words.

SESSION 8
Drafting the Ending

Students draft the ending of their personal narratives, focusing on their feelings when the event was over.

MATERIALS
• Research folders
• Features chart
• Paper and pencils

TIP A graphic organizer can be a great help in getting students to think about the ingredients in their endings and ways to describe events. Draw a two-column chart labeled *What Happened* and *How I Felt*. Show students how to jot down ideas from your model. Then encourage them to complete their own charts. Explain that they can use these ideas when writing their endings. Please see the *Resources* CD-ROM for blank graphic organizers.

FOCUSED MINILESSON *(drafting)*
15 MINUTES

■ Focus the learning: *So far you have written the beginning and middle of your personal narrative. You have also learned about including words that describe your feelings and emotions.* Point to the chart and read aloud the last feature: *Today we will work on writing a great ending.*

> **TURN &TALK** *Partners, think together. Why is an ending important?*

■ Provide positive feedback after you listen in on discussions: *I heard some strong discussions about endings. You're right! An ending tells what happened last and explains why it is important.*

■ Conduct a minilesson that focuses on strong endings: *The ending tells what happened last. It is also a place where we can explain what we thought and felt.* Model a sample ending to your personal narrative about flying: *I want to describe what happened at the end as the plane landed. Instead of just writing, "The plane landed," I could write, "Then the plane dropped lower and lower. Everything on the ground seemed larger and larger!" These sentences help the reader picture what happened at the end. I can also write sentences that tell what I felt. "The landing was exciting. It felt like a roller-coaster ride! The plane trip was fun, but I was glad to be back on the ground."*

> **TURN &TALK** *Share with your partner what you will include in your ending. What words might you use to share feelings?*

■ Invite volunteers to share ideas. Praise their creativity: *I like how you expressed excitement. You didn't just say that you were excited, you told why. That brought your personal narrative to life!*

WRITING and COACHING
(drafting, revising, editing)
20 MINUTES

- Have students write the endings of their personal narratives. Prompt students if they need help writing about their feelings: *Can you tell me why this was a special moment for you? After it was over, how did you feel? Were you proud? Pleased? Glad it was over? Those would be good details to add to your personal narrative.*

- Have students independently review their endings and make changes. If students need help spelling, review strategies they can try, such as sounding out words, using a high-frequency word wall, or asking others for help.

SHARING and REFLECTING
10 MINUTES

TURN &TALK *Read the ending of your narrative aloud to your partner. Partners, what events and feelings did you hear about?*

- Invite students to share a variety of feelings from their endings: *Your work is impressive! Writers, you demonstrated a lot of different feelings. Partners, you did a great job of recognizing the feelings in your partner's work.*

- Preview the next session's work: *Your narratives each have a clear beginning, middle, and end. Next time you'll have a chance to polish your work and add some great illustrations.*

TIP Having students revise and edit during each session helps them understand that writing is a process. Point out that drafting is the stage where writers put down their ideas. Then they can revise to make their ideas clearer and improve their language.

SESSION 9
Revising and Editing

Students revise and edit their personal narratives, focusing on their use of features, complete sentences, and correct punctuation.

MATERIALS
• Research folders
• Features chart
• Crayons and colored pencils

FOCUSED MINILESSON *(revising, editing)*
15 MINUTES

■ Introduce the session's focus: *You've each created a strong narrative that captures a moment in your life. You've crafted powerful beginnings, middles, and endings that focus on your feelings. In this session, we'll carefully review our drafts and polish them for publication.*

■ Use your narrative about flying on a plane for the first time as a model for revising and editing: *Now that we have finished drafting our personal narratives, we can read all the parts together to see if it all makes sense. We can also check our sentences. Each sentence needs to tell a complete idea. It needs to start with a capital letter and end with a punctuation mark.*

■ Write these incorrect sentences on the board and read them aloud. Have students suggest changes you should make.

> *the plane started to land. Drops lower and lower.*
> *Everything on the ground seemed larger*

■ Praise students as they identify errors and suggest corrections: *You're right! That sentence should begin with a capital letter.* Point out that students will have the opportunity to look at their writing with a fresh eye.

TURN &TALK *Partners, take a look at your drafts together. What do you want to focus on as you edit?*

■ *Great ideas! Most of you named looking at your sentences to make sure they are complete, but you also talked about making sure that you have written the parts of your personal narratives in order. You mentioned having strong feeling words. You are really thinking about how to make your narratives come to life for your readers.*

TIP Be sure that students understand that editing and revising are not only about finding "mistakes." The larger goal is to make the writing clear and effortless for the reader and to forge a strong connection with the audience so that they can focus on the message.

WRITING and COACHING *(revising, editing)*
20 MINUTES

■ Have students take out their personal narratives. *We've talked about the connection you have with your readers. When you revise and edit, you make that connection even stronger. Why? Because your readers can focus on the message rather than trying to figure out what you are writing! As you revise and edit, ask yourself, "How does this revision make my narrative even easier to understand?"*

■ As you circulate, discuss the types of changes students are making to their narratives.

■ Each time you conference with students, make sure that at the end of the conference, they can tell you exactly what they will work on in their writing. This will let you know if they have internalized the scaffolds you've provided.

SHARING and REFLECTING
10 MINUTES

TURN &TALK *Share with your partner a change that you made to your narrative. Explain why you made the change.*

■ *You made changes that make your narratives clearer and easier to understand. Your readers will appreciate those changes, because they'll be able to focus on your interesting experiences.*

■ Preview the next session's work: *Writers, your changes have made your narratives even more powerful. Next time we'll add some illustrations that show the events and make your narratives come to life right before your readers' eyes.*

TIP for Conferring with Individuals and Small Groups

If students are unsure of what to monitor as they edit and revise, have them collaborate in small groups to create checklists. Record these on a chart for the small group to see. Editing and revising may also be easier if students look for a single type of correction at a time.

SESSION 10
Adding Illustrations

Students learn how illustrations can enhance a personal narrative, then add drawings to their own work.

MATERIALS
• *Big Book of Mentor Texts:* "Grandma's Surprise," pages 30–35
• Research folders
• Features chart
• Examples of personal narratives with illustrations or photographs
• Crayons and colored pencils

TIP The minilesson on illustrations can be used to help students develop a sense of writing for an audience. Encourage students to make the connection between the books they like to read and the narratives they are writing. Would they rather read a book with or without pictures? Why? Point out that thinking about what they like to read can help them be better writers.

FOCUSED MINILESSON *(revising, publishing)*
15 MINUTES

■ Introduce the session: *We're almost ready to publish our personal narratives. But before we get to that, we'll learn about one last feature that we can add to our narratives to make them complete.*

■ Display the features from the class project and review the features of a great personal narrative: *Which of these features do you see in your own narratives? Which is missing? That's right! Your narratives don't have illustrations yet, so they are still incomplete.*

■ Talk about how illustrations can enhance a personal narrative and make the events clearer for readers. Return to the mentor text. *Let's look at two different types of illustrations in "Grandma's Surprise." The illustrations on page 31 don't show real events. They show what the boy was imagining at the time. These pictures are really fun! And they give us a glimpse into what the boy was thinking. Now let's take a look at the illustration on page 35. This one is very realistic—it shows what happens at that part of the narrative. Grandma and the boy take a break from planting. See how they are sweaty and dirty? Those are great details that show us how hard it is to work in a garden on a warm day.*

■ Show students other examples of strong personal narratives that contain illustrations and/or photographs that support the text and reveal the feelings of the writer.

TURN &TALK *Partners, think together about the illustrations and photographs you've just seen. How do they help you understand these personal narratives?*

■ *Great observations! The writers chose to illustrate scenes that captured your attention. They matched illustrations and photographs to the writing. They showed their actions and feelings. You can do that with your narrative, too!*

TURN &TALK *Share your personal narrative with your partner. Partners, point out a place where an illustration could really bring a scene or feelings to life.*

■ *Your illustration ideas are going to add so much to your narratives. Think about how your pictures add to your narrative as you create illustrations or add photographs.*

WRITING and COACHING *(revising, publishing)*
20 MINUTES

- Provide students with drawing paper and supplies for creating illustrations. Encourage them to draw an illustration for each part of the narrative—beginning, middle, and end.

- As you circulate, discuss with students how their illustrations help improve their pieces. You might want to encourage students to discuss their illustration ideas with their partners before starting to draw.

SHARING and REFLECTING
10 MINUTES

TURN &TALK *Partners, think together. How did adding illustrations make your narratives easier for your readers to understand?*

- As a few volunteers share their favorite illustrations, praise students' efforts: *These illustrations don't just look nice, they also help your readers understand the events of your narratives. The way you've portrayed feelings in your illustrations makes your narratives even more exciting!*

TIP English language learners may use their illustrations as a way to express ideas for which they lack vocabulary. Use their illustrations as an opportunity to help these students develop vocabulary and construct sentences: *Elena, that looks like a tooth that is loose. Should we write a sentence about how you lost your loose tooth?*

SESSION 11
Publishing and Celebrating

Students publish their personal narratives, adding titles and covers. Then they celebrate their writing accomplishments.

MATERIALS
- Research folders
- Examples of published personal narratives
- Construction paper or other heavyweight paper, crayons, and colored pencils
- Publishing paper
- Features chart

TIP Allowing students to make decisions about publishing helps them take ownership of their work and build confidence in themselves as writers.

FOCUSED MINILESSON *(publishing)*
15 MINUTES

- Introduce the session: *You've accomplished so much already in writing your personal narratives. In this session, we are going to publish your narratives so you can share them with readers.*

- Talk about the final form the narratives will take: *You have interesting narratives, and you have great illustrations. Now it's time to put it all together. You'll publish your narratives on publishing paper and double-check your illustrations. You want to be sure that your illustrations match your text.*

- *When we publish our writing, we put it in a final form for others to read. We focus on using our best handwriting so that our message is clear. We can also add covers to our books.* Show students captivating book covers from your classroom library.

  TURN &TALK *Partners, what do you notice about these covers? List some features of a fantastic book cover.*

- *I heard many great features of book covers—the title, the author's name, and, most importantly, an engaging or exciting picture that captures readers' attention and tells more about the narrative. When you create covers for your personal narratives, think about these features.*

- Explain that another part of publishing is making choices about format: *When you publish your personal narrative, you can choose to make it a book with several pages. You can also choose where your pictures should go.*

  TURN &TALK *Share with your partner your ideas for publishing your narratives. Partners, what feedback do you have to offer?*

- Validate students' ideas as you listen: *I like the idea of publishing your narratives with several pages since you had so much to say. Adding an illustration to each part—beginning, middle, and end—will keep your narrative fresh and exciting and will help you share important details.*

WRITING and COACHING *(publishing)*
20 MINUTES

- Provide students with construction paper or craft paper to create their covers.

- Have students use their best handwriting to copy and publish their personal narratives on publishing paper. Remind them to place their illustrations (cut out from their work in the previous session) at the appropriate places in their narratives.

- As students finish, bind their covers and pages to make books.

SHARING and REFLECTING
15 MINUTES

- Organize students into small groups. Have students take turns showing their covers, reading their personal narratives, and showing their illustrations. Encourage students to use appropriate vocal register and inflection as they read their narratives by modeling with a narrative of your own.

  TURN &TALK *You should be proud of what you have achieved. With your partner, discuss what makes your personal narrative so great.*

- Have students reflect on the process of writing and the features of their personal narratives. Encourage them to recall their first efforts at personal narratives and evaluate how much they have learned: *Your work is exciting, and you've come a long way. You've included so many important features in your work.*

- Place students' finished books in the classroom library for other students to read during independent reading time.

- Remember to look back at students' pre-assessment pieces and to use the Ongoing Monitoring Sheet or the Individual Evaluation Record to document growth and note areas for improvement. Pass out copies of the Student Self-Reflection Sheet from the *Resources* CD-ROM to help students reflect on their own growth. Finally, be sure to make notes on what worked and what didn't during the unit so you can make adjustments for next time. See "After the Unit," page 131, for more information about post-assessment and self-reflection.

TIP Using the small-group share format ensures that every student will have a chance to share work and experience an appreciative audience.

SESSION 1
Immersion and Pre-Assessment

Students are introduced to the features of a biography, then draft a hero's biography for the pre-assessment.

MATERIALS
• A biographical article about a heroic person from a book, magazine, or the Internet

FOCUSED MINILESSON *(prewriting)*
15 MINUTES

■ Introduce the unit: *In this unit we are going to learn how to write a biography. A biography tells about a real person's life. It is a special kind of nonfiction, called* nonfiction narrative. Nonfiction *means that the information is true.* Narrative *means that the writing has a beginning, middle, and end. A biography is one kind of nonfiction narrative.*

■ Preview a hero's biography. Children's encyclopedias, books, magazines, and the Internet are great sources for providing examples that will immerse students in the genre. During the preview, stress again for students that a biography tells the true account of a real person's life.

■ *Listen as I read a biography of a special person. Some of us might call this person a hero!* Then read the text aloud.

TURN &TALK *What makes someone a hero? Think together with your learning partner.*

■ As partners talk about heroism, lead them to understand that heroism is not the same as fame: *Some heroes are famous, but some are not well known. I think many families have a hero of some kind, somebody who is brave or who works hard to overcome a problem.* You may want to write a definition on the board: someone who overcame a problem or showed courage in the face of difficulty.

■ After defining *hero* with your students, have students share some examples of heroes, and record appropriate ideas on the board or chart paper. Redirect students' thinking when the person named is not real or is not appropriate.

TURN &TALK *Today, we're going to write a biography of a hero. You can choose somebody from our list or a hero you know about. Turn to your partner and tell who you will choose. Why is that person a hero?*

TIP Students may need more help to understand the purpose of nonfiction narrative text. *I love reading comic books! They have great heroes in them who do wonderful things for others. Comic books tell stories, so they are narratives. But comic book heroes are not real; they are fictional. A biography is a form of nonfiction narrative, so it has to be about a real person.*

WRITING and COACHING *(drafting)*
20 MINUTES

■ Remind students that a biography is a special kind of nonfiction narrative that tells about the events in a real person's life. Then, direct them to write a brief biography of their real-life hero.

■ Give students paper and pencils for writing. Allow adequate time for students to draft their biographies.

■ Be sure to emphasize that the purpose of the pre-assessment is to find out how much students already know about writing a biography. They will learn a lot more in upcoming sessions and should just do their best for now.

SHARING and REFLECTING
10 MINUTES

TURN &TALK *Share your biography with your partner. Which parts of the person's life did you write about?*

■ After students have had time to share with their partners, ask for volunteers to share their writing with the class.

■ Invite students to talk about writing a biography: *What did you need to know in order to write about a real person? What would have helped you write today?* If possible, steer the discussion toward research that can support biography writing.

■ Sum up today's learning and preview the next session: *Each of you wrote a special kind of nonfiction narrative today, a biography, and you worked hard doing it. You should be very pleased with your first try. In our next sessions, we'll learn more about the features of a strong biography.*

■ After class, evaluate each students' writing using the Ongoing Monitoring Sheet (in the Resources section and also on the *Resources* CD-ROM). Use the results to revise instruction and personalize the lessons in this unit. If you want to keep individual records on students, use the Individual Evaluation Record in the Resources section and on the CD-ROM. Do not make corrections or marks on students' work.

TIP If students struggle to get started, you might suggest that they make a list of things their heroes did. Can they use their lists to write narratives? Some students may benefit from focusing on just an event or two in a person's life. Students don't need to feel compelled to write about a person's entire life from birth to old age—suggest that students think about a few important, interesting events rather than an entire life.

TIP Listen to students' discussion about their first attempt at biographies. This will help you clarify misunderstandings about the genre and plan for individualized instruction.

SESSION 2
Researching and Taking Notes

Students study the features of a strong biography and research the information they'll need to start drafting the class biography.

MATERIALS
- *Big Book of Mentor Texts:* "Nancy Lopez," pages 14–18
- Chart paper and marker
- Reference material about the chosen subject
- Sticky notes or note cards and tape
- Pencils

FOCUSED MINILESSON *(prewriting)*
25 MINUTES

- Introduce the session: *In our last session, we learned that a biography is a special kind of nonfiction narrative that tells events of a real person's life. Today we will talk about what makes a great biography, and we'll find the information we need to write one as a whole class.*

- Introduce the mentor text. *When we read this biography, think about how the writer captured Nancy Lopez's life. Reading this biography may give us ideas for our own writing.* Read the mentor text aloud.

  TURN &TALK *Talk about the mentor text with your partner. What did the writer include in the biography? Name at least one feature with your partner.*

- Invite volunteers to share, and shape their responses into a features list: *Someone mentioned that the biography told the events of a person's life. Let's record that first.* The features list included here is just a suggestion. Use the responses that your students discover for themselves, making sure that the features will generalize to other biographies.

- Generate excitement for writing biographies: *This account about Nancy Lopez was inspirational! She overcame problems to become the best woman golfer of all time. We're going to work as a class to write yet another inspirational biography to include in our classroom library.* Select a hero from the list that the class created in Session 1, or choose another subject, such as a local hero or a person related to your current content-area curriculum. The class project described here focuses on Amelia Earhart.

Features of a Great Biography of a Hero

It tells events from a real person's life.

It includes interesting facts about the person.

It describes successes and failures.

It shows how the person is a hero.

It tells about the person over time.

■ Create a timeline on chart paper or across the chalkboard and divide it into sections such as: *Growing Up, Middle Years,* and *Final Years.* Include a section called *Amazing Facts.* Explain to your students that they will be doing research about Amelia Earhart and writing their facts on sticky notes. Then they will figure out where each fact goes on the timeline. Remind them to include important information that was highlighted on the features chart.

■ Show students the reference materials they will use to research: *Please use these books, magazines, videos, and websites to find the information you would want in the biography. Remember to record your facts on sticky notes.*

TIP Set up research stations around the classroom. Use a wide variety of materials related to the selected biography subject. Include books, periodicals, videos, websites (bookmarked), and even recorded interviews. Students can rotate from station to station to collect information.

WRITING and COACHING *(prewriting)*
20 MINUTES

■ Direct students to begin their research, using the materials you have gathered. They will write facts on sticky notes and place the notes in the correct sections on the timeline.

■ Students will need varying degrees of support as they research and record information. Plan to have parent helpers assist if possible.

TIP If students have selected a local hero, make arrangements for an in-person interview. This will give students experience using a primary resource as research. Help students prepare focused interview questions in advance to ensure they get the information they need.

SHARING and REFLECTING
10 MINUTES

■ Help students remove redundant pieces of information from the timeline: *I see that we have Amelia Earhart's birthday listed twice here. Let's take one of these sticky notes off so we don't get confused when we write.*

TURN &TALK *Find the most fascinating fact from your research today, and share it with your learning partner. Tell your partner where on the timeline your note belongs.*

■ Listen in on discussions to reinforce students' research and provide encouragement: *You found some fascinating facts about Amelia Earhart and why she is an American hero. Our biography is going to be wonderful and full of amazing information!*

■ Tell students that in the next session they will choose what information to include in the biography.

SESSION 3
Continuing to Research

Students examine additional features of a strong biography and continue their research for the class project.

MATERIALS
- *Big Book of Mentor Texts:* "Nancy Lopez," pages 14–18
- Features chart
- Chart paper and marker
- Reference material about the chosen subject
- Sticky notes or note cards and tape
- Pencils

TIP For students who are ready, provide a minilesson on point of view, perhaps creating a chart showing the pronouns used for each. Refer to the last sentence on page 16 of the mentor text. *How would this sentence change if Ms. Lopez were telling about herself? When we talk about ourselves and use words like* I, me, *and* my, *we use the* **first-person point of view.** *But writers who are completely outside the account use the person's name and words like* she *and* her, he *and* him, they *and* them. *This is called the* **third-person point of view.** *Biographies are always written from the third-person point of view.*

FOCUSED MINILESSON *(prewriting)*
20 MINUTES

■ Focus the learning: *In this session, we'll discover more features of a strong biography, and we'll add more notes to our timeline. Let's start by looking at the mentor text again.*

■ Read a section of the text and then stop: *Does this biography use any words like* I *or* me*? What about* you*? Right! This biography refers to people by using their names and words like* she *and* her, he *and* him, they *and* them. *This is called the third-person point of view. A biography uses third-person point of view because it is a text that one person writes about another person. If we were writing about ourselves, we'd use words like* I *and* me. *Then it would be a personal narrative. Let's add* third-person point of view *to our chart. Attach a list of third-person words to the chart.*

■ Discuss time order in the mentor text: *As I read, think about Nancy Lopez's life and how the writer shows time.* Reread all or part of the mentor text, stopping to point out time-order phrases: (page 14: *eight years old;* page 16: *nine years old, three years later, 12 years old, In 1972, started high school,* and *In her senior year;* page 17: *The year after high school graduation, In 1976,* and *the year after her mother died;* page 18: *Before she turned 30* and *today*).

TURN &TALK *Work together with your partner to discuss time in the biography. When we tell about a person's life, how do we arrange facts?*

■ Listen as students discuss the element of time: *I heard some of you discussing the way the biography uses dates and Nancy Lopez's age to tell about her early life first, then the middle part of her life, all the way forward to the present. This is an important part of a biography! Let's add that to our features chart:* It tells facts in time order.

TURN &TALK *What information will you need in order to show time order in the Amelia Earhart biography? Discuss your answers with your partner.*

■ Lead children to discover that dates are an important way to show time in a biography and that they should include dates whenever possible along with their notes. *Writing dates on your notes will help you place them correctly on the timeline! Today while we're working on our research, double-check the notes you placed there in the last session. Be sure that they are in the correct places on the timeline.*

WRITING and COACHING
(prewriting)
20 MINUTES

■ *It's time to finish our research!* Have students return to the research stations and continue taking notes and placing them in the correct sections on the class timeline.

■ Encourage students to discuss their research findings with their partners to decide whether the facts are important enough to place on the timeline.

SHARING and REFLECTING
10 MINUTES

■ Have students remove duplicate information from the timeline.

TURN &TALK *Some people found similar information. How do we decide whether to keep a note or not? Talk about it with your partner.*

■ After students remove the duplicate information, review the features chart and preview the next session: *In the next session, we will start publishing our biography of Amelia Earhart. I hope you're as eager to get started as I am!*

Features of a Great Biography of a Hero

It tells events from the person's life.

It includes interesting facts about the person.

It describes successes and failures.

It shows how the person is a hero.

It tells about the person over time.

It uses third-person point of view.

It tells facts in time order.

TIP If notes from the last session's research lack dates, assign some students to locate the dates for these events and then repost the notes where they belong. Adding dates will help students write in time order.

SESSION 4
Drafting the Biography

Students begin to draft the biography, focusing on the use of interesting words and details.

MATERIALS
• *Big Book of Mentor Texts:* "Nancy Lopez," pages 14–18
• Features chart with notes attached
• Sentence strips
• Pencils

FOCUSED MINILESSON *(prewriting)*
25 MINUTES

■ Introduce the session: *In this session, we are going to learn more about biographies so we can make ours on Amelia Earhart even better.*

■ Lead students to discover the difference between a list of facts and an interesting account of a person's life: *A few days ago, we learned that the job of a biography is to tell facts about a real person's life. But a biography is more than that! What if I just make a list of facts about Nancy Lopez? I could give the dates and tell what happened. Would that be a biography? Would it be interesting?*

TURN &TALK *Turn and talk with your partner about how the biography of Nancy Lopez is different from a list of facts.*

■ Lead students as they discover the added interest that is included in biographies. Reinforce what they find, such as: *The writer gave dates and information, but by using interesting details, she made the account more engaging for readers and helped us get to know Nancy Lopez.*

■ Take a sticky note from one of the sections on the timeline and read it aloud for students. Then model your thinking as you transform a dry fact into an interesting part of the narrative: *This note says:* Amelia Earhart was born in Kansas in 1897. *I could write the sentence that way, but I want to make it more interesting. How about this:* In 1897, Amy Earhart gave birth to a daughter, Amelia. Amelia was born in her grandfather's home in Kansas. *This gives me an interesting way to start my biography.*

TIP Make a **list of time-order words** with students, and place them on the chart paper related to sequence. Show students that there are many words that can be used to show time order and that using a variety of these words can help them avoid repetition when transitioning from one event to another.

■ Repeat with a note from another category. Guide students in their effort to make the fact an interesting part of the narrative. Emphasize adding details, writing about the events in sequence (see Tip), and referring to the biography subject in the third person.

■ Divide students into groups, one group for each section of information on the timeline. Explain that each group will write one part of the biography. Together, each group will take some of the notes and information and then rewrite them in interesting sentences.

WRITING and COACHING *(drafting)*
25 MINUTES

■ Divide the notes from each section on the timeline among students in the designated group. Give each group sentence strips to write on. *Here are the ideas you should write about. Talk about the details you could add and interesting words you could use. Once you decide on how to write the fact in an interesting sentence, put it on the sentence strip.*

■ Students can work in groups to write their sentences. Encourage them to read their work aloud to other group members and use the feedback they offer to make the sentences even more interesting.

SHARING and REFLECTING
10 MINUTES

■ Ask a volunteer from each group to read a note they used and the sentence they crafted from the note.

TURN &TALK *Listen to the sentences the other groups wrote. What time-order words did you hear? How do you know each sentence is written in the third person?*

■ As students share, listen to their conversations. Ask a few partners to share their comments with classmates.

■ Help students recognize the hard work they have done: *Look at how much you have written today! You thought very carefully about the words you used and the way you wrote them. What do you like best about your writing?*

TIP Assign revising and editing jobs to group members. One group member should check that the group has used the third-person point of view. Another student can choose appropriate time-order words. Another group member can look out for repeated words from one sentence to the next. Give one student a primary thesaurus for finding alternative words to avoid repetition.

SESSION 5
Publishing the Class Biography

Students add illustrations before publishing the class biography. Then they celebrate their success as writers of nonfiction narrative.

MATERIALS
- *Big Book of Mentor Texts:* "Nancy Lopez," pages 14–18
- Chart paper or publishing paper
- Completed sentence strips from Session 4
- Pencils and drawing materials

FOCUSED MINILESSON *(publishing)*
15 MINUTES

■ Focus the learning: *We're almost ready to put our group work together in a published biography. But first, we have some finishing touches to add.*

> **TURN &TALK** *Look at the mentor text again. What does it have that our class biography does not?*

■ Listen in as students share. Lead students to see that the mentor text is illustrated and the class biography is not.

> **TURN &TALK** *The biography of Nancy Lopez included pictures from different times of her life. What pictures could you add to your group's part of our biography on Amelia Earhart? Describe your illustration ideas.*

■ Have groups look back on the portions of the biography that they wrote in the last session: *You figured out what your sentences should say. Now we will write them on chart paper as neatly as possible. Your group will also draw a picture to go with this part of the biography.*

■ Give each group a few sheets of chart paper to use for writing and illustrating their section of the biography and have them work together to publish their section. Or allow each student in the group to write and illustrate one or two sentences on a single sheet of printer paper. The individual pages can then be collated to make the class book.

WRITING and COACHING *(publishing)*
20 MINUTES

■ Give each group a piece of chart paper. The group should write their final section of the biography on the paper and illustrate it.

■ Set a purpose for publishing: *Publishing is the last step of writing. This is where you give your reader your very best handwriting, correct spelling, and your neatest drawings. What you do today makes people want to read your book! And it makes it easy for readers to focus on the important facts about the life of our hero.*

SHARING and REFLECTING
15 MINUTES

■ Ask representatives from each group to read their portion of the biography for classmates. Point out instances where students showed their use of time-order words and third-person point of view: *You certainly knew what you were doing here! This is a great way to show when Amelia Earhart made her first flight.*

TURN &TALK *Think about all of the features of biographies that we talked about this week. Which one do you think you understand the best? Explain it to your partner.*

■ Discuss students' understanding of the features of a great biography by having them share their knowledge.

■ Celebrate your students' success! If your class produced a display on chart paper, invite another group of students into your class and read the display with them. If your students produced a book, arrange for another class to come for a read-aloud.

TIP The finished project may take more than one day for students to complete. Be flexible with the time frame so that students have sufficient time to present their best work. If some groups finish early, allow them to work on other personal writing until the class is ready to move on.

TIP Students may look upon the illustrations as "decorations" to fill space in their books. Talk about how the illustrations can help readers understand the text: *If I read that Amelia Earhart made a "solo flight," I might not know what it means. But this picture shows me that she was the only person flying in her plane. It shows exactly what you mean by a "solo flight." Your illustration can help the reader understand the details in your biography!*

SESSION 6
Launching the Individual Project

Students review the features of a great biography and select a hero to write about in their individual biographies.

MATERIALS
- Features chart from the class project
- Research notebook and planner for each student
- Copy of planner on chart paper
- Reference materials

TIP Rather than having students select their own heroes, you might want to pre-select the biography subjects and allow students to choose from four or five subjects. This will allow you to collect resources ahead of time and will enable you to tie the biography subjects to a content area being studied, such as pioneers.

FOCUSED MINILESSON *(prewriting)*
20 MINUTES

- Focus the session: *Now that we've composed a class biography, we're ready to write our own, individual biographies. But first we'll each select a person to write about and we'll review the features of a great biography.*

- Show students the features chart from last week as you reflect together on what to include in a good biography.

  TURN &TALK *Think back to the biography we wrote about Amelia Earhart. Explain to your partner the features we included.*

- Praise students for their understanding of the features of a biography: *I heard some good ideas about what biographies should include.*

- Review the concept of a real-life hero—someone who has shown bravery in the face of danger or has overcome a difficult problem.

- Share with your students who their audience will be: *This week you will get to write a biography of your own. After you are done, we will post the biographies online at our school's website so that our friends and families can read them! Lots of people will learn from our work this week.* (Adapt the audience depending on your classroom needs.)

  TURN &TALK *Tell your partner whom you want to write about. Why do you think that person is a hero?*

- Record the heroes' names, as well as a few reasons each person would make a good subject for a biography. Then, by a student vote or by your own criteria, narrow down the suggestions.

- Create a planner for students that has separate sections for research, labeled: *Growing Up, Middle Years, Later Years,* and *Amazing Facts!* See the *Resources* CD-ROM for a blank planner.

- Give each student a copy of the planner. As an alternative, you may wish to have students write the category titles on separate pages in their writing notebooks.

■ Remind students about the importance of finding information in each of the categories: *Look at the headings at the top of the pages. These headings help you organize the information that you find into categories. Before you write each note, make sure you have the right section. When you take notes, be sure that you write them in your own words. That way, you'll know that you understand the ideas in the source.*

WRITING and COACHING *(prewriting, drafting)*
20 MINUTES

■ Give students access to research materials. You may choose to set up reference materials in stations for ease of access. Allow students time to locate information and write notes.

■ Remind students to look closely at the photographs and illustrations they find in the research materials and to take notes on the information these visuals convey.

SHARING and REFLECTING
5 MINUTES

TURN &TALK *Share your most interesting note with your partner. What do you find fascinating about this fact?*

■ After students have had time to share with their partners, ask for volunteers to share their findings with the class and reflect together on the research so far.

■ Invite students to talk about the use of the planner and research notebook: *Why is it helpful to write your notes in categories rather than all on one page?*

■ Sum up today's learning and preview the next session: *You started your research today. Are you feeling like you have a good start? I hope so! In our next session, we'll have more time for research and we'll talk about how we can make our work more polished and even better for our readers.*

TIP for Conferring with Individuals and Small Groups

After students have had time to research and record information, give them time to flesh out the notes they took. *Look at what you wrote at the research stations. Take time while the information is fresh in your mind to add more details.*

TIP As students read their writing aloud, they may discover spelling errors. Encourage them to attend to content at this point. If children are worried about spelling and mechanics at this early stage, they will not take risks such as using new and interesting words. Assure them that there will be time for editing and revising later.

SESSION 7

Researching and Drafting

Students continue their research and begin to draft notes for their individual biographies, focusing on the use of time-order words.

MATERIALS

- Chart of time-order words from Session 4
- Research planner and notebooks from Session 6
- Reference materials

FOCUSED MINILESSON *(prewriting)*
20 MINUTES

- Focus the learning: *In our last session, you did a fantastic job of researching the hero you chose to write about. Today, you will do some more research to fill out the categories in your notebooks, and you'll use time-order words when you write your notes.*

- Review the research planner and notebook: *Look back at your research planner. Are there any categories that are empty? Today, try to focus on finding facts for those categories.*

  TURN &TALK *Turn and talk with your partner about your research. What do you need to find today? Where will you look?*

- After talking about research, turn students' attention to the time-order word chart they started during the whole-class project: *How did we use these words in our writing?*

  TURN &TALK *Partners, think together. How were those words useful when we wrote our class biography?*

- *These are great words that let us show the order of events in a biography. Let's take a close look at how we can use these words.* Prepare a chart with facts about a hero, and model and think aloud as you add one or two time-order words to the paragraph. Then, guide students as they add more time-order words: *This is a list of events in the life of my hero, my grandmother. What time-order words could you add to make this biography even easier for readers to understand? Let's try out your suggestions and read to see if the biography makes good sense:* First, my grandmother was raised on a farm and was very poor. Then she moved to a big city. Next, she worked for years to earn money to go to school. Finally, she went to college and became a nurse.

TIP Show students various examples of nonfiction narratives and invite them to look for time-order words. Seeing time-order words in "real" narrative nonfiction texts shows students that writers use these words to organize their thoughts. Examining mentor texts allows students to see craft elements at work and to think about how to incorporate them into their own writing.

WRITING and COACHING *(prewriting, drafting)*
20 MINUTES

■ Have children return to their research. *Let's get back to our research! Remember to try to find facts for each category on your planner and to use time-order words and dates as you draft your notes.*

■ If students are having trouble ordering the events they've written about, encourage them to lay their sticky notes out on the floor and manually arrange them in the correct order. Being able to physically manipulate the events this way may be helpful to certain types of learners.

SHARING and REFLECTING
10 MINUTES

TURN &TALK *Share what you wrote with your partner. Show your partner how you put your information in the correct order.*

■ Listen in on discussions and reinforce use of sequence: *I heard some of you talk about using the dates to put your sentences in the right order. That's a terrific idea. Sometimes you have to use what you already know about common events and when they happen, even if you don't have dates. A person is born first, goes to school next, and so on.*

■ Praise your students' efforts: *I saw a lot of focused research happening today. You were writing down facts and thinking hard about putting events in the right order. You must be very proud of your work today!*

■ Tell students that they will finish researching and drafting notes during the next session so that then they can focus on writing their biographies.

TIP When students have had time to research, give them an opportunity to add dates and time-order words to the information they found. *Remember that your biography will be confusing if your dates are not in order. Look at your notes to show what comes first, second, and so on.*

SESSION 8
Researching and Drafting

Students finish researching and drafting their notes, focusing on use of the third person as they write.

MATERIALS
- *Big Book of Mentor Texts:* "Nancy Lopez," pages 14–18
- List of third-person words from Session 3
- Research planner and notebooks from Session 7
- Reference materials

TIP English language learners may have difficulty understanding the difference between first- and third-person points of view. Gently correct their errors when they speak and write while assisting them by providing model sentences that they can tuck into their writing folders and use for reference.

FOCUSED MINILESSON *(prewriting)*
15 MINUTES

- Introduce the session: *It's time to finish up our research and note taking so we'll have time to edit, revise, and publish our biographies. This is our last session for research, so let's get started.*

- Review the categories students have been researching: *Why is it important to find information for each category in your notebook?* Discuss how the biography would be incomplete without information from each category: *Remember, a biography tells somebody's life story. What would happen if the middle part was left out?* Encourage students to discover that a biography with blanks in the middle would confuse readers. Refer them to the mentor text and the whole-class biography, if necessary, to talk about what would happen if part of the narrative were missing.

- Remind students about using third-person point of view: *Let's take another look at the mentor text. Who is telling this story? The writer is telling this story about Nancy Lopez. How would it be different if Nancy Lopez were telling the story herself? Exactly! She would use words like* I *and* me *that show the first-person point of view. Since the writer is talking about Nancy Lopez, the pronouns are words like* her, she, *and* their.

- Turn students' attention back to researching: *What do you have left to look for today? Pay close attention to the categories that don't have enough information. Focus your research on those areas.*

  TURN &TALK *What categories have you researched well? What information should you focus on today? Share your research plan with your partner. What advice about sources can you give your partner?*

- Remind students that this is their last research session. Monitor students' work frequently, and gather small groups who may need extra assistance.

WRITING and COACHING *(prewriting, drafting)*
20 MINUTES

■ *As you research today, focus on finding facts that will fill out the empty categories in your planner.*

■ As students work, circulate around the room to ensure that all are able to find facts for each category. If you discover that some students are bogged down on researching one category, step in to assist them in moving forward by helping them summarize and move on.

■ Make sure students know that they can work on other activities while waiting for your help. Make a list of activities and discuss them with your students before beginning the writing session.

TIP Give students who are writing about the same person opportunities to share their findings. This will help create a community of learners.

SHARING and REFLECTING
10 MINUTES

TURN &TALK *Listen as your partner reads a few research facts. Do you hear third-person point of view? Help your partner change words such as I to she or he.*

■ After students share information, review the use of third person: *We will be publishing soon. Take a minute to look over the rest of your notes. Is there a place where you need to change* you *or* I *to words such as* he *or* she? *Make those changes now.*

SESSION 9
Drafting, Revising, and Editing

Students use their research notes to draft their biographies. Then they revise and edit their work.

MATERIALS
- Research planner and notebooks
- Features chart

TIP If students have access to computers, give them an opportunity to type their biographies with help from you. Revisions are not as frustrating if children can simply retype rather than erase and rewrite neatly. Also, children will like the clean look of their work when they have produced it on a computer.

TIP Encourage students to review their writing to see if they have been repetitive. Students should look at how they start their sentences. If they find that many of their sentences start the same way, like, "Nancy Lopez played . . ." or "Nancy Lopez won . . . " help students find ways to say the same information in a different way.

FOCUSED MINILESSON *(drafting, editing)*
15 MINUTES

■ Introduce the session: *You've done amazing work on your research! You know so much about your subjects that you'll be able to write narratives that captivate your readers. In this session, you will draft your biographies and edit your work.*

■ Display the chart describing the features of a great biography.

■ *Writers should always think about ways they can improve what they write. As you draft your biography today, look at our list of features and think about the ways you can include these features in your biography.*

■ Provide a modeled lesson in which you transform a note into a sentence for a biography. After you use the note, cross it out so that it will not be used again: *I'm writing about a special hero, my grandmother. I said that she grew up on a farm and that her life was challenging. That is a good fact, but I think I can make it more interesting:* My grandmother grew up on a farm. Sometimes there was so much work that even the young children had to help with the chores. *This is an interesting way to say my fact. Now I am going to cross out my note so that I will not use it again.*

WRITING and COACHING
(drafting, revising, editing)
20 MINUTES

■ Help students put their research notebooks to work: *Begin with one section from your notes and use it to draft one part of your biography. Then move on to the next category. Remember to cross out your notes as you use them so you can see what information you still have to write about. If you move through your categories in time order, your narrative will tell the events of your hero's life from beginning to end!*

■ Be sure to allow enough time for students to revise and edit their writing. To make this process easier, encourage them to write their drafts on lined paper, leaving one or two spaces between each line of text. And consider adding an extra session for drafting if needed.

SHARING and REFLECTING
15 MINUTES

■ Ask volunteers to read favorite parts of their biographies to the class. Point out instances where students showed their use of time-order words and third-person point of view: *You remembered to use the tools we talked about this week! Your pronouns are perfect for writing about someone else rather than yourself. Time-order words are keeping the events organized for your readers.*

TURN &TALK *Show your partner a word or sentence you revised or edited today. What did you change and why?*

■ Have volunteers share some of their revisions and edits. Emphasize that writers revise and edit for many reasons. Maybe they forgot to capitalize the first word in a sentence. Maybe they left out an important idea. Maybe the writer just finds a better way to describe something. There are many great reasons to revise and edit!

TIP Work with students to create an editing checklist based on grammar, spelling, and punctuation rules they have learned in language arts. After students edit their own writing, they can work in pairs and review their partner's writing for errors in mechanics.

SESSION 10
Publishing and Celebrating

Students add illustrations before publishing their biographies. Then they share them with classmates and celebrate their new skills.

MATERIALS
- *Big Book of Mentor Texts:* "Nancy Lopez," pages 14–18
- Completed individual drafts

FOCUSED MINILESSON *(publishing)*
15 MINUTES

- Focus the learning: *You are so close to finishing! All that is left is the publishing. In this last session, we will make our biographies look as good as they sound!*

- Display the mentor text. Prompt students to describe the photographs and discover how they support the text.

  TURN &TALK *Look at the mentor text again. How do you think the writer chose the pictures to include?*

- Listen in as students share. Help them see that the pictures match and support the information on the page: *If the text on a page talks about when Nancy Lopez was young, then the picture shows her when she was young, doesn't it?*

  TURN &TALK *Your biography shows different parts of your hero's life. What pictures would you like to find or draw to match each of the sections you wrote? What about your first section? Talk about it with a partner.*

- Listen in on the students' discussions and highlight some of what you hear: *Oscar and Miguel were just talking about how the pictures in the first part of their biographies will show their heroes as children. A biography usually starts with the person's childhood, so that is an excellent match of pictures to text.*

- Set a purpose for publishing: *This last step of writing, publishing, is very important. Publishing helps you create a biography that looks interesting before your reader even starts reading. Neat writing and interesting pictures do that. Creating a polished piece of writing allows your reader to focus on the great message—your narrative about a real-life hero!*

WRITING and COACHING *(publishing)*
20 MINUTES

■ Give students options for how they might publish their final biography. Students may choose to create a poster or booklet to showcase their biographies, or the biographies can be posted to a class or school website.

■ Keep your expectations for what students can achieve in a publishing session realistic relative to their age and developmental stage. Many students will need an additional session for publishing, so build in the extra time if you think your students will need it.

SHARING and REFLECTING
15 MINUTES

■ Ask students to present their biographies for classmates. Point out how they incorporated the features of a great biography. *I can see that your classmates learned a lot from what you wrote! Using all that you know about writing biographies helped you create a piece of writing with a powerful message. Fantastic work!*

■ After each student shares, have the class name specific examples of features included in the biography.

■ Discuss differences and similarities among biographies written about the same subject: *I noticed that even though these two biographies are written about the same person, each writer chose to include different facts and even gave the same facts in different ways! There is not one right way to say something. Different writers are interested in different things and say things in their own ways.*

■ Remember to look back at students' pre-assessment pieces and to use the Ongoing Monitoring Sheet or the Individual Evaluation Record to document growth and note areas for improvement. Pass out copies of the Student Self-Reflection Sheet on the *Resources* CD-ROM to help students reflect on their own growth. Finally, be sure to make notes on what worked and what didn't during the unit so you can make adjustments for next time. See "After the Unit," page 131, for more information about post-assessment and self-reflection.

TIP If students have access to the Internet and a printer, they can locate photographs to support their writing and print them. This will save time over drawing. It will also give students a sense of pride in their writing by providing a finished look.

TIP If you are interested in creating a class Internet page to display the biographies, enlist the help of parent volunteers to scan and upload student work. You may also want to check with local middle and high schools. Students at these levels often need to log community service hours for honor programs or graduation, and they often have the training and equipment necessary to create a web page.

Personal Narrative

A personal narrative captures the action, setting, and feelings of a specific moment in time.

It was so scary that I was shaking like I was about to fool off a plan and I was so scared that I whoted to run away and I didn't wont to talk.

FEATURES

- Focus on small event or part of event
- Description of feelings and the setting
- First-person point of view

FOCUSED MINILESSON

One of our most important jobs as writers is to create descriptions that help readers join us in reliving a special moment. The goal is to write in a way that allows your reader to follow the action, visualize the setting, and understand the emotions you felt at this moment.

Before I write, let's take a look at a personal narrative to remind ourselves of the features of this type of nonfiction. Turn to page 34 in the *Big Book of Mentor Texts.*

TURN &TALK *Partners, think together. What features of this writing really stood out for you?*

Watch as I create a personal narrative about going down the biggest slide at the water park last summer. I am going to use the words I and my to show that this is about me. I am also going to try to make my feelings about the experience come through in my writing: My teeth were chattering and my heart was slamming against my ribs as I stood at the top of the tower.

TURN &TALK *Partners, as I looked down into that tube, I was scared to death! Does this writing make it clear that I was really frightened? Evaluate my writing and see if my feelings are clear to a reader.*

Now, watch as I continue the narrative. I need to add a description of the water slide so my reader can visualize and understand exactly what I was seeing: Right below my toes was a roaring whirlpool of water that dropped through a thirty-foot column to the ground. *Can you picture the water whirling in a circle as it gushed into this huge tube? I felt like I was being pulled in by a huge vacuum cleaner, and there was a strong wind, too. I will write:* The powerfully twisting waterspout roared like the winds of a tornado and sucked at me like a giant vacuum. Nearly paralyzed with fear, I locked arms with my husband and jumped.

My teeth were chattering and my heart was slamming against my ribs as I stood at the top of the tower. Right below my toes was a roaring whirlpool of water that dropped through a thirty-foot column to the ground. The powerfully twisting waterspout roared like the winds of a tornado and sucked at me like a giant vacuum. Nearly paralyzed with fear, I locked arms with my husband and jumped.

Modeled Writing

TURN & TALK *Let's check and see how I am doing at adding the features of a personal narrative. Evaluate my writing: Did I use I and my? How did I do at showing my feelings and describing the setting?*

After writing, use students' ideas to generate a features list: *Writers, did you notice that this was just a short moment in time? I probably stood at the top of that tower for less than one minute. In a personal narrative, we want to focus on a specific moment and use great writing that helps a reader understand exactly what it was like to be in that place and feel the feelings of the writer.*

WRITING and COACHING

Writers, you have each had experiences where you had strong feelings. Think of a moment when you first rode your bike, all alone. Think of a time when you were about to blow out your birthday candles on a cake or open a special gift. I bet you can remember the feeling you had as you opened your mouth to take a huge bite from your favorite cookie or a plate of macaroni and cheese. Those brief moments make great personal narratives. You just need to remember to help your reader by sharing your emotions and writing great descriptions.

SHARING and REFLECTING

These personal narratives share glimpses in time, and that makes them so focused! In this kind of writing we don't tell all about a vacation or all about school. This is a time to pick a specific moment and crack it open for your reader. You shared descriptions and your feelings. That makes for great personal narratives!

ASSESS THE LEARNING

As you assess personal narratives, be sure students have focused on specific moments, not entire events.

SELF-ASSESSMENT

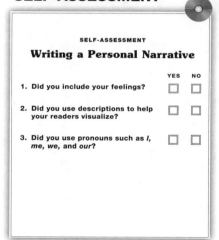

SELF-ASSESSMENT
Writing a Personal Narrative

	YES	NO
1. Did you include your feelings?	☐	☐
2. Did you use descriptions to help your readers visualize?	☐	☐
3. Did you use pronouns such as *I, me, we,* and *our*?	☐	☐

NARRATE

SUPPORTING AND EXTENDING

▸ Invite students to write about specific moments they shared with families. They might also want to add pictures or memorabilia.

▸ Provide opportunities for students to write personal narratives about learning experiences in class. Science experiments, learning a new game in physical education, working with manipulatives in math, or watching a class pet eat its food all provide rich support for personal reflection and written narrative.

▸ Help writers understand that drawing a picture before they write can help them add detail and description to their writing. Expand language capacity by helping them develop descriptive phrases that they can slip into their sentences.

Retell from a Different Point of View

A change of point of view allows a retelling from a different perspective.

I am a rainbow.
I like to play hide and seek.
Spray some water in the sun to find me
you will see my colorful arch.
I am a rainbow.

FEATURES

- Title
- First-person point of view
- Beginning, middle, and ending
- Descriptive details

FOCUSED MINILESSON

This lesson focuses on the behavior of tornadoes, but you can adapt the lesson to fit any content.

Writers, we've learned so much about weather! It's been interesting to read about different kinds of weather patterns, and today I am going to write as though I am a tornado. This means that instead of writing about weather the way a scientist would, I am going to write a narrative as if I were the tornado. I need to start by visualizing roaring winds spinning round and round, smashing houses, and tossing trees like they are matchsticks.

Watch as I begin to write: I am a tornado. My powerful funnel reaches down from the sky like the trunk of an enormous elephant.

TURN &TALK *Partners, think together. Share the visualization that you get from this writing. Use your arms to dramatize the trunk reaching down.*

Listen as I visualize again and identify more facts for my writing. Thinking out loud helped me get my ideas ready. I visualized the rapidly spinning winds inside a huge column. That column isn't straight like a stick; it twists and swirls as it moves. It is so powerful that it acts like a huge vacuum, sucking everything it touches into the cloud. I will write: My roaring winds—like a giant vacuum. . . .

TURN &TALK *Partners, this is a different kind of narrative writing. What features are you noticing?*

After writing, use students' ideas to generate a features list: *There are some very distinct features in this kind of writing. Notice that it begins and ends with* I am a tornado. *It is highly descriptive because it is tightly linked to the visual images we have about tornadoes. It uses the pronouns* I *and* my *to emphasize that as a writer, I am placing myself in the role of the tornado. What could I write for a title?*

I Am a Tornado

I am a tornado. My powerful funnel reaches down from the sky like the trunk of an enormous elephant. My roaring winds — like a giant vacuum cleaner — suck houses, trees, and cars into the air, leaving a trail of destruction. I am a tornado.

Modeled Writing

WRITING and COACHING

Guide writers in reflecting on their research about weather or provide a read-aloud with selections such as *Tornadoes* and *Storms* by Seymour Simon. *Writers, you know a lot about weather. You have gathered facts about hail, lightning, tornadoes, thunder cells, and so much more. As you write today, your challenge is to focus on visualizing a particular kind of weather and writing as though you are lightning, hail, snow, or a gentle spring rain. Remember to begin with* I am a . . . , *and to use pronouns like* my *to show that you are taking the role of this kind of weather.* Pull together any students who are struggling with content to help them remember the details so they can focus on the features.

SHARING and REFLECTING

Writers, today you used the features of a point-of-view narrative. You used first-person pronouns such as I, me, *and* we; *you gave your narrative a clear beginning, middle, and end; and you used amazing descriptions that really brought your writing to life. I can really visualize the type of weather you've chosen to be!*

ASSESS THE LEARNING

Assess for understanding of content as well as the use of first-person point of view. As necessary, provide small-group instruction on first-person pronouns (*I, me, we, us*).

SELF-ASSESSMENT

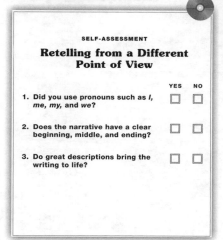

SELF-ASSESSMENT

Retelling from a Different Point of View

	YES	NO
1. Did you use pronouns such as *I, me, my,* and *we?*	☐	☐
2. Does the narrative have a clear beginning, middle, and ending?	☐	☐
3. Do great descriptions bring the writing to life?	☐	☐

NARRATE

SUPPORTING AND EXTENDING

▸ Have students create point-of-view narratives describing the life cycle of a butterfly. Remind them to write from the point of view of the butterfly.

▸ Have students create point-of-view narratives on elements of nature such as a small creek, a raging river, or a hungry eagle.

▸ Provide a read-aloud from *Voices of the Wild* by Jonathan London to learn from this outstanding mentor. For example: *"I am Deer stepping through crisp shadows, twitching ears against deer flies, stretching my neck."*

Nonfiction Narrative

Nonfiction narrative often provides factual information through beautifully crafted text.

Quickly and bravly, the crayfish drarts away from its enimie.
Quikly and aggresivly the crayfish lunges for its prey. Bravely and slowly, the crayfish walks throw another crayfish's taratory.

FEATURES

- Factual information
- Descriptive language
- Visual images

FOCUSED MINILESSON

In advance of the lesson, select a nonfiction narrative such as *Bat Loves the Night* by Nicola Davies, *Tigress* by Nick Dowson, or *Think of an Eel* by Karen Wallace.

Nonfiction narratives are full of facts, but the writer doesn't just report information. The writer deliberately wraps the facts in beautiful language. Listen as I read from Tigress *by Nick Dowson.*

The descriptive language in this nonfiction narrative really stands out. I noticed the descriptive phrase plate-sized paws. *What an image! Visual images are important in a nonfiction narrative.*

TURN &TALK *Partners, think together. Identify descriptive phrases that you think made Nick Dowson's nonfiction narrative beautiful.*

Hungry Parent

high-climbing   yellow-eyed

meat-eating   knife-sharp claws

smells with tongue

In the moonlit clearing, mother tiger's tongue laps out to gather scents. Her knife-sharp claws hold her tightly to the branch of a tall tree as her yellow eyes stay fixed on the watering hole.

Modeled Writing

Watch as I begin a nonfiction narrative about tigers. I start with a list of great descriptive phrases that I can include when I begin my sentences. Here are a few: high-climbing, meat-eating, smells with tongue, yellow-eyed, knife-sharp claws. *I want to write first about how tigers smell with their tongues. Since this is a nonfiction narrative, I will start with the setting:* In the moonlit clearing, mother tiger's tongue laps out to gather scents. *Did you notice that I started with the setting,* in the moonlit clearing, *and then used a comma before I wrote* mother tiger?

TURN &TALK *Partners, examine my writing and the list of phrases. Then think about your prior knowledge about tigers. What else should I include in this nonfiction narrative?*

I want my reader to be able to visualize the action. I started by saying it was a moonlit clearing. Now watch as I focus on the tiger herself. I want to tell about her claws and the fact that she is high up in a tree, so I will write: Her knife-sharp claws . . . . *Writers, could you draw a picture based on my sentence? Can you visualize that mother with her yellow eyes, standing in a tree?*

After writing: Writers, let's focus on the features of this nonfiction narrative. It has facts, it has great descriptive phrases, and it is deliberately designed to help a reader visualize. List the features on chart paper for student reference.

WRITING and COACHING

You know a lot about tigers. With a partner, examine my list of descriptive phrases—or select some of your own—and create a sentence or two that would really help a reader to visualize. You want to write in a way that would make your reader feel like he or she could draw a beautiful picture based on your writing.

SHARING and REFLECTING

Partners, you have created fabulous sentences and used the features of a nonfiction narrative. I can see that you have chosen descriptive phrases to help readers visualize. Plus, you have terrific facts!

ASSESS THE LEARNING

As you assess nonfiction narratives, watch for descriptive phrases, support for visualization, and inclusion of facts. Reteach for students who create fictional stories rather than texts based on factual information.

SELF-ASSESSMENT

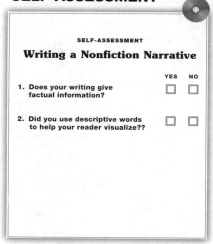

SELF-ASSESSMENT
Writing a Nonfiction Narrative

	YES	NO
1. Does your writing give factual information?	☐	☐
2. Did you use descriptive words to help your reader visualize??	☐	☐

S U P P O R T I N G   A N D   E X T E N D I N G

▸ Provide opportunities for students to read and discuss nonfiction narratives that include rich descriptions and strong visual images. Guide them in making a list of features they want to include in their nonfiction narratives.

▸ As students research favorite animals, guide them in building a rich list of descriptive phrases that they can integrate into their nonfiction writing.

▸ For a unit on the community, have students write highly descriptive non-fiction narratives about community helpers or about a place where community helpers work, such as a fire station, hospital, or school.

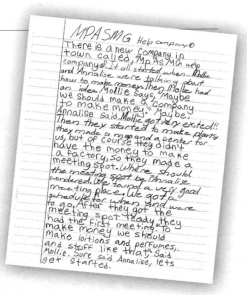

Eyewitness Account

An eyewitness account is a newspaper-style story of events witnessed firsthand.

FEATURES

- Summarizing headline
- Beginning, middle, and end
- Details about the event

FOCUSED MINILESSON

In an eyewitness account, the writer tells about an event that he or she actually got to see. When we read the newspaper, we read eyewitness accounts of events from weather to exciting games! Today, I want to capture a class event, our author tea, in an eyewitness account for our class newsletter.

Watch as I start writing the beginning of the account: Hard-working writers at Elmwood School delighted parents and teachers alike with their fabulous nonfiction writing.

TURN &TALK *Think together, partners. What details might I add so my readers will feel like they went to our author tea?*

Great ideas! In my second sentence, I will name some of the topics. That will make it really clear that I was there and got to hear these wonderful books read aloud. Watch as I write: Audience members learned about the habits of the polar bear cub, the migratory patterns of hummingbirds, the life cycle of a butterfly, and so much more.

TURN &TALK *Writers, evaluate this part of the account. Is my writing making you feel like you were there? Are there other details that would make it clear that this is an eyewitness account?*

I think I need to add something about the feelings and atmosphere at the author tea. That would help my readers know what it was like to be there. Watch as I add: Authors read with expression and excitement, thrilled to share their work. *Now my eyewitness account not only tells what happened, it captures the feelings and events in an exciting way! Watch as I check to be sure I have a beginning, a middle, and an end.*

TURN &TALK *Now it's your turn! Think together. Listen as I read this aloud, and try to visualize the moment. How does my writing help you visualize and understand exactly what it was like to be at the tea?*

Display a newspaper: Writers, I just noticed one more feature that this eyewitness account needs to include—a headline! Newspaper articles have headlines. I could write Amazing Authors, Terrific Tea, Rocking Research, *or* Proud Parents. *Put your heads together and help me think of the best headline for this eyewitness account.*

> ### Amazing Authors!
>
> Hard-working writers at Elmwood School delighted parents and teachers alike with their fabulous nonfiction writing. Audience members learned about the habits of the polar bear cub, the migratory patterns of hummingbirds, the life cycle of a butterfly, and so much more. Authors read with expression and excitement, thrilled to share their work.

Modeled Writing

After writing, gather students' ideas to generate a features list: *So, an eyewitness account needs to have a summarizing headline; a beginning, middle, and end; and details about the event.*

WRITING and COACHING

Writers, now it's your turn to write an eyewitness account. You could write about the thunderstorm we had yesterday, about our assembly this morning, about having a guest author in the library, and so on. Get students started, reminding them to use a narrative structure, with a beginning, middle, and end, and details that give the writing a "you are there" feeling. Some students may benefit from an opportunity to sketch and reflect before they begin to write.

SHARING and REFLECTING

Writers, these eyewitness accounts are definitely newspaper-worthy! Headlines tell the readers what they will read about next, and you have written clear beginnings, middles, and endings. Your choice of details brings the accounts to life!

ASSESS THE LEARNING

Have students gather in small groups to compare their eyewitness accounts to the account you created during the modeled writing. If necessary, reteach for features such as beginning, middle, and end; and descriptive details.

SELF-ASSESSMENT

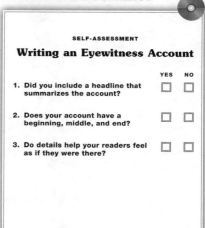

SELF-ASSESSMENT

Writing an Eyewitness Account

	YES	NO
1. Did you include a headline that summarizes the account?	☐	☐
2. Does your account have a beginning, middle, and end?	☐	☐
3. Do details help your readers feel as if they were there?	☐	☐

NARRATE

SUPPORTING AND EXTENDING

▸ Ask students to create eyewitness accounts of a moment of interesting weather, the passing of a fire engine, the bug that joined the classroom, or the surprise when the principal announced that she was going to challenge everyone to a write-a-thon!

▸ Have students partner with kindergarten students. Have your class help the kindergarten students write eyewitness accounts of a special event in their class.

▸ Read author Jon Scieszka's *True Story of the Three Little Pigs* and search for features of an eyewitness account in the retelling by the wolf. Guide students in considering how this kind of writing is helpful in nonfiction.

Factual Recount

A factual recount uses words and sketches or photographs to retell facts about an experience.

Martin and His Words
By Jeremy Neth

We have been learning about Martin Luther King Jr. in room A-10. In his speech "I Have a Dream" he used big words like discrimination, righteousness, freedom and segregation. Those words touched some hearts and others not. He led parades of freedom after they bombed his house and he was put in jail over and over again. He risked his life for others. He gave speeches from Washington D.C. to California. Unfortunately he was shot on a hotel balcony in Memphis Tennessee. He died but his words didn't.

FEATURES

- Retelling of events with description
- Time-order words
- Supporting sketches

FOCUSED MINILESSON

This lesson focuses on a factual recount of observing plant growth. Adapt the lesson sequence to fit content in your class.
A lesson like this may be simpler if students have previously observed and taken notes rather than trying to "reconstruct" events as they write.

Writers, we've planted seeds and observed their growth! Today, I'd like to write a factual recount of our plants' growth. A factual recount is a retelling of actual events. Instead of narrating just with words, I'm including pictures to help my readers visualize events.

Watch as I start by sketching the beginning of our experiment. I am showing the line of dirt and the seed, which we planted below the dirt. Now I'll write what was happening during this part: First, I planted a seed. I made sure to plant it about one inch below the surface. I sprinkled water to moisten the soil.

Writers, notice that I started with a time-order word: first. *Did you notice the details in the writing? I wrote how far below the dirt's surface I planted the seed. And take a look at the verb—*sprinkled. *I could have written* I added water to the soil. *But the verb* sprinkled *is very specific.*

First, I planted a seed. I made sure to plant it about one inch below the surface. I sprinkled water to moisten the soil.

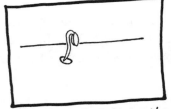

A few days later, the stem poked through the soil. Our plant was growing!

Modeled Writing

TURN &TALK *Partners, think together. A few days after we planted the seeds, what happened? Describe the events.*

I'm drawing a box and sketching the second event in our recount—the day we saw the plant above the soil. I'm writing: We saw the plant above the soil.

TURN &TALK *Writers, what do you think of this part of the recount? Explain with your partner what we might add to our writing.*

We did see the plant above the soil, but I heard some of you suggest adding a word that shows the time order. This writing could be a little more descriptive, too. Great suggestions! Take a look at my revision: A few days later, the stem poked through the soil. Our plant was growing! *Active verbs like* poked *really bring the recount to life!*

After writing: Writers, so far we've created a great factual recount. Our sketches show the events for our readers. And we have some time-order words, first *and* a few days later, *that keep the text organized. Write the features—sketches, captions, and time-order words—on a chart for reference.*

WRITING and COACHING

Once our plant poked through the soil, its growth didn't stop there! What happened next? Draw at least two more pictures that show events in our plants' growth. Write what happened next. It might help some students to have a form with boxes set aside for pictures. English language learners may need a bank of time-order words and phrases to draw from when writing.

SHARING and REFLECTING

Writers, you made this factual recount shine! Your sketches show the plant's growth. Words and phrases like next, later, *and* by the end of the week *organize the events. And your descriptions are wonderfully specific.*

ASSESS THE LEARNING

Have students compare their work to the modeled writing you created. If necessary, reteach such concepts as time order and matching illustrations to writing.

SELF-ASSESSMENT

SELF-ASSESSMENT
Writing a Factual Recount

	YES	NO
1. Did you tell the events using time-order words?	☐	☐
2. Did you draw sketches that support your writing?	☐	☐
3. Did you include specific descriptions?	☐	☐

NARRATE

SUPPORTING AND EXTENDING

▸ Ask students to work with partners to write a factual recount after a field trip or a special class experience in school. Include the factual recounts in the class or school newsletter.

▸ Have students create a factual recount of the steps they took to complete a special math project. Bind recounts into a book to be placed in the math corner.

▸ Encourage students to use the factual recount format to record observations about plants, animals, the weather, and so on.

Timeline

A timeline is a visual way to retell events or show a sequence of events.

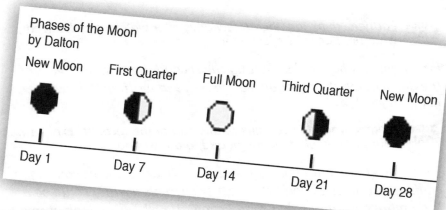

Phases of the Moon
by Dalton

New Moon — Day 1
First Quarter — Day 7
Full Moon — Day 14
Third Quarter — Day 21
New Moon — Day 28

FEATURES

- Title
- Horizontal line with tick marks
- Events in sequential order
- Captions and/or illustrations

FOCUSED MINILESSON

A timeline is a helpful tool that allows writers to show the order in which things occur. Today I am going to create a timeline that shows how the moon changes during one month.

Watch as a I write the title at the top of the page: The Phases of the Moon. *Now I am going to draw the timeline. Watch as I draw a horizontal line, or a line that goes across the page. The timeline needs marks that show units of time. Since there are 30 days in the moon's cycle, I am going to make 30 marks on the timeline. Each line is a day. Notice that I am making them the same distance apart.*

TURN &TALK *Writers, what do you remember about the moon? How does it look at the beginning of its phase?*

Since the moon phases start with the new moon, the new moon will be first. Watch as I write New Moon *under the first mark on the timeline. I'm sketching the new moon, too. The moon looks all dark, so I am drawing a circle and then filling it in.*

About 3 ½ days after the new moon, the moon is in a phase called waxing crescent. *Watch as I count over 3 ½ ticks on the timeline. I'm making a dark mark on that part of the timeline and labeling it* Waxing Crescent. *I will add a sketch to show so you can see the waxing crescent moon right on the timeline.*

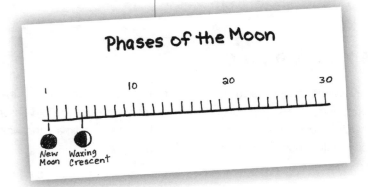

Phases of the Moon

1   10   20   30

New Moon   Waxing Crescent

Modeled Writing

TURN &TALK *Partners, think together as you evaluate my work. What do you notice about the timeline, and the visual way it helps us understand the cycles of the moon?*

After writing, discuss the model as you list its features: *Writers, let's take a look at the timeline. I created a horizontal line with small vertical marks, called tick marks, for each day. I counted the days until the next phase and used labels. The sketches work with the labels to narrate how the moon changes.*

WRITING and COACHING

Writers, our timeline is off to a great start, but the moon has some more phases! I am going to read Seymour Simon's book The Moon *(or another of your selection)* so we can identify the other phases. Each of you will have an opportunity to work with a partner to complete a timeline to show what you have learned about the phases of the moon. Have students work with partners to complete the moon phases timeline. See the *Resources* CD-ROM for a form that presents a master timeline and tick marks already placed so that writers can focus on counting the days and labeling the phases.

SHARING and REFLECTING

Writers, your timelines are great visuals! Each vertical tick mark stands for a day, so it is easy to chart the progress of the moon. Labels and sketches provide important information for your readers.

ASSESS THE LEARNING

As students work, assess to see whether they are able to use the tick marks to count out days and to record events in the order in which they occur.

SELF-ASSESSMENT

SELF-ASSESSMENT

Making a Timeline

	YES	NO
1. Did you include a title?	☐	☐
2. Do vertical tick marks stand for units of time?	☐	☐
3. Are your events in the order in which they happened?	☐	☐
4. Do illustrations and captions explain events?	☐	☐

SUPPORTING AND EXTENDING

▶ Students can create timelines of their own lives. Encourage them to include photographs to show milestones.

▶ Create a working timeline for a science experience such as planting seeds. With each change in the development of the plants, record observations on the timeline.

▶ When you begin a unit of study that focuses on history, biography, or a life cycle, create a large timeline on the bulletin board so that students can contribute events as the unit progresses.

NARRATE

VISUAL LITERACY

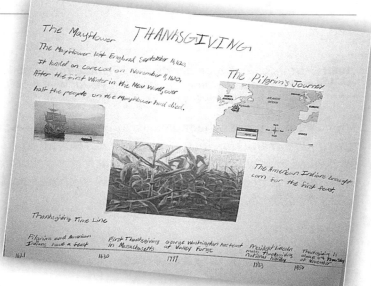

Investigation

A visual investigation combines text and features such as illustrations to present a narrative.

FEATURES

- Title
- Two facing pages that form a "spread"
- Features such as text boxes, subheadings, and captions
- Retelling of a narrative

FOCUSED MINILESSON

Focus on an event that you are studying in your class.

Writers, today I want to create an investigation that is focused on the first Thanksgiving. We've learned the events of the first Thanksgiving, but I want to show them in an interesting and visual way.

Let's take a look at a narrative investigation to see what features are important. Turn to page 20 in the *Big Book of Mentor Texts. This investigation focuses on how the telephone has changed over time.*

TURN &TALK *Partners, think together. What do you notice about the investigation?*

The investigation retells events with different features we would see in a magazine or a great nonfiction book! You noticed many nonfiction text features, like pictures, information in special boxes, headings, and extra facts. When we create an investigation like this, we need to plan our space to be sure we include all the parts of the narrative we want to tell.

Watch as I fold this large piece of paper in half so it looks like two pages. I am writing my title across the top of both pages: The First Thanksgiving. *See how it spreads across the gutter that lies between the two pages? We call these two pages a "spread." Now I am going to anchor my investigation with one big sketch in the middle. The sketch shows the first Thanksgiving dinner.*

Modeled Writing

TURN &TALK *Writers, give me some advice! What events should I show about the first Thanksgiving dinner? Describe them together.*

I heard some great advice! I am leaving space for the events that led up to the first Thanksgiving by sketching boxes where I can draw pictures. I am leaving space for captions, too. Watch as I sketch a boat traveling across the ocean. The boat looks old-fashioned, like in the pilgrims' time. Now I'll write the caption for the illustration: Many ships sailed from England and were never seen again. The voyages were dangerous! Hurricanes, pirates, and sicknesses kept many people from completing the journey.

I noticed that the mentor text uses different colors to set off the headings. When we complete the investigation, we'll add color, too. I am also leaving a spot on the investigation for a cross-section diagram of the Mayflower. *Over on this part of the page, I am leaving a space to draw pictures of the ingredients of the first feast!*

After writing, list features of an investigation as you point them out on the model: *Writers, we have planned for a great investigation that gives our readers information! An illustration in the middle tells what the investigation is about. Each space can show another event, and we can explain those events in captions. We have space for special features, too!*

WRITING and COACHING

Writers, we started a great plan for an investigation. Now let's work together to finish it! Assign students to work independently or with partners to create components of the investigation. More confident writers can plan their own investigations on the same topic.

SHARING and REFLECTING

You've made history come alive with your investigations! The title explains what the investigation is about, and you used headings, illustrations, captions, and special features to capture events.

ASSESS THE LEARNING

As students work, assess their understanding of both the purpose of narrative and of the text features of an investigation. Reteach if necessary by showing students features in nonfiction books and magazines. Talk about how these features support the message of the text.

SELF-ASSESSMENT

SELF-ASSESSMENT

Narrating with an Investigation

	YES	NO
1. Did you retell a story in your investigation?	☐	☐
2. Did you carefully plan how to present information visually?	☐	☐
3. Did you use features such as headings, captions, and illustrations?	☐	☐

SUPPORTING AND EXTENDING

▸ Have students use an investigation to present the biography of a historical figure, classmate, or family member.

▸ Using the mentor text as a model, students can use investigations to trace the development of another invention, such as the bicycle or computer.

▸ Create a narrative investigation on a bulletin board. Have students add events and text features to the bulletin board to create an as-you-go investigation that is shared by the entire class.

NARRATE

Persuasive Writing Projects

Persuasive texts put forward a point of view to influence the reader to take action or to believe something. The purpose may be to convince someone to buy a particular product or to change someone's thinking about a specific issue. Students are most likely to encounter persuasive text in the form of advertisements, posters or articles meant to convince readers to do or think something, and book or movie reviews. Persuasive text may appear in many formats, including bumper stickers, flyers, posters, letters, speeches, debates, essays, editorials, reviews, and poems. Persuasive writing uses both facts and opinions. Persuasive texts are characterized by goals, statements of opinion, supporting facts (evidence), and direct appeal.

CONTENTS

EXTENDED WRITING UNIT
▸ Class Project: Travel Brochures About Our City (about 6 days)

▸ Individual Project: Travel Brochure About _____ (about 5 days)

POWER WRITES
▸ Written Argument

▸ Persuasive E-mail

▸ Friendly Letter

▸ Book Review

▸ Persuasive Flyer

▸ Graphic Organizer

▸ Investigation

The Big Picture:
Class and Individual Projects

· ·

During the *class project*, students work together to research and write travel brochures designed to persuade people to visit their city or town. The mentor text "Washington, D.C." acts as a model to show students the structure and features of a persuasive text. Students begin by observing features in the mentor text and then use their research notebooks to gather information that will help them identify and describe places to visit in their own area. The students learn how to collect, organize, revise, edit, and publish the information into persuasive travel brochures. They discuss ways to distribute and share their brochures to convince people to visit.

During their *individual project*, students review the features of a persuasive text, choose a topic, and use a graphic organizer to research, plan, draft, revise, edit, and publish their own travel brochure for a city of their choice. This piece may take the form of a brochure, booklet, or flyer. Research and writing partners share ideas, read each other's drafts, and give feedback about persuasive qualities. Students share their published pieces with the class and reflect on what they have learned about persuasive writing.

CLASS PROJECT		
Session	**Focused Minilesson**	**Writing and Coaching**	**Sharing and Reflecting**
1	Introduce persuasive text; choose topics	Draft pre-assessment persuasive text	What do you see in your partner's writing that will make people want to visit?
2	Study "Washington, D.C."; list features; focus on organizing information; write categories in research notebooks	"Tour" research stations; begin researching; take notes in categories in research notebooks	Share notes with your partners. What facts would persuade someone to visit our town?
3	Study "Washington, D.C."; focus on persuasive words; start word chart; learn to stretch and spell words	Continue researching, note taking, and drafting; restate facts using persuasive words	Share a descriptive sentence from your writing. What makes it persuasive?
4	Check categories in notebooks. Study "Washington, D.C."; learn to start specific names with capital letters	Research to complete categories; edit to include descriptive words and capital letters (optional: write section beginnings)	How did you revise? What did you improve most about your writing?
5	Study tri-fold brochure; focus on illustrations. Plan headings, illustrations for your brochure	Begin publishing final persuasive text with headings and illustrations on tri-fold brochure	How do your illustrations and text go together? What do you find most appealing about your partner's work?
6	Study mentor texts. Review categories on brochure	Finish publishing brochures	Celebrate and share. What have you learned about what makes a great travel brochure?

INDIVIDUAL PROJECT		
Session	**Focused Minilesson**	**Writing and Coaching**	**Sharing and Reflecting**
7	Review purpose, features of persuasive text; select topic; prepare notebook	Research, take notes, draft information in research notebook	Share notes with partners. Which facts so far are most persuasive? Why?
8	Analyze modeled writing; learn to use persuasive words; learn strategies for spelling words	Continue researching, taking notes, drafting	What tricky word did you use? What strategy did you use to spell it? What is a strong example of a persuasive word?
9	Analyze modeled writing; learn to revise for meaning	Continue researching, taking notes, writing, revising in notebooks	Which facts were most persuasive? What made those facts so convincing?
10	Study "Washington, D.C."; learn to write persuasive openings and closings	Write an opening sentence and powerful ending	Share your opening and closing. What is amazing? How might they be more powerful?
11	Focus on editing, illustrating; make editing checklist; plan brochure with headings	Publish brochure, including headings, text, illustrations; use editing checklist	Share and celebrate. What makes your travel writing so persuasive? What is your favorite feature in your work?

Other Topics and Forms for Persuasive Writing

Although this model project uses the topic of places to visit as a springboard for teaching persuasive writing, the teaching process here can be adapted to many other persuasive topics and forms. The Power Writes in this section will give you ideas for several such adaptations in addition to those that follow.

Possible Topics

Topics may correlate with content in your science and social studies standards, current events, or class interests.

Should we squash bugs?

Do aliens exist?

Should we be scared of snakes?

Which planet is the best?

What is the best toy?

Writing a letter to a friend, family member, or person in the school to ask for something

What is the best sport?

Should we have to clean up our rooms?

Which are better, dogs or cats?

What makes the best pet?

Does school go for too long?

Should we help our parents with housework?

Why should we brush our teeth?

What would be some good rules to have in our classroom?

What is the best drink?

Possible Forms

Some of these forms are invariably persuasive (like advertisements or book reviews) while others (like letters or signs) can be used for a variety of purposes, including persuasion.

Letter	Debate
Poster	Review
Bumper sticker	Advertisement
Sign	Diagram
Note	Illustration
E-mail	Photograph
Written argument	Poem
Speech	

Setting Up Your Research Stations

For the *class project*, you will need to gather books, articles, pictures, and bookmarked websites about your students' city or area—enough material that the whole class can research and take notes simultaneously. You could include fact sheets and flyers from the chamber of commerce, local attractions, and so on. Try to provide books or other resources recorded on tapes or CDs. You might find people who work in the town, such as a parks administrator, coach of a local team, or local events coordinator, who are willing to be interviewed by your students.

For Session 1, you will need photographs of various locations around the city, such as parks, museums, places for recreation, and so on.

For Session 5, you will need an example of a tri-fold brochure.

For the *individual project*, gather similar materials on a few other cities of interest to your students. You will have an easier time providing materials if you limit student choices to four or five cities. This limited approach will allow you to organize small-group meetings and lessons for students who are writing about the same city. Your social studies curriculum may provide suitable topics for this assignment, or you might choose four or five cities from your state for which you can find adequate research materials.

Please refer to page xiii of the introduction to this book and page 285 in the Resources section at the end for additional information on setting up and using research stations.

Focusing on Standards

This extended writing unit is designed to teach students about the form and content of persuasive writing as they apply basic writing strategies. Each of the lessons provides you with suggested demonstrations, but you may wish to tailor your instruction based on the common needs of your own students. The pre-assessment from Session 1 will help you identify these needs.

Before introducing the unit, carefully review the list below so you can keep the lesson objectives in mind as you teach, coach, and monitor students' growth as writers of persuasive texts.

KEY SKILLS AND UNDERSTANDINGS: PERSUASIVE TEXTS GRADE 2
Purpose
• Understands the purpose for writing a persuasive piece
Ideas/Research
• Reflects research and planning to support a goal
• Bases writing on research and personal opinion
• Includes facts from research to support opinions
• Gathers and uses information from multiple sources
Organization/Text Features
• Includes a title that reflects the topic and goal
• Begins with an opening statement that reveals the goal
• Provides at least one supporting reason or argument
• Supports arguments with opinions
• Supports arguments with facts
• Ends with a sentence or statement that restates the goal
• Includes visuals that help persuade readers
Language/Style
• Shows a clear, consistent opinion throughout the piece
• Uses persuasive, descriptive language
• Sums up personal feelings and opinions in the ending
Conventions and Presentation
• Uses headings for categories of information
• Uses capital letters for specific names
• Uses strategies for spelling tricky words
• Uses an editing checklist

The list on the previous page is the basis for both the Individual Evaluation Record and the Ongoing Monitoring Sheet shown in Figure 4.1. Both forms can be found in the Resources section at the back of this book and also on the *Resources* CD-ROM. Use the Individual Evaluation Record if you want to keep separate records on individual students. The Ongoing Monitoring Sheet gives you a simple mechanism for recording information on all your students as you move around the class, evaluating their work in progress. Use this information to adapt instruction and session length as needed.

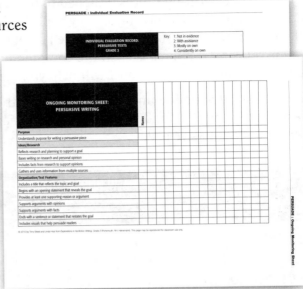

Figure 4.1

You will also use the Ongoing Monitoring Sheet and/or the Individual Evaluation Record at the end of the unit to record students' growth as writers after comparing their published work from the individual project with the pre-assessment they will complete in Session 1 of the class project.

Planning and Facilitating the Unit

Students will need preparation, coaching, prompting, and support as they move through this extended writing unit. Use the following tips and strategies as needed to ensure each child's success.

Before the Unit:

▸ When planning your teaching, bear in mind that each session in this unit is designed to be completed in a day. However, you will likely find that your students need more time for certain activities. Take the time you need to adequately respond to the unique needs of your students.

▸ Begin building background knowledge about persuasive texts in general as well as your students' city or town at least a week in advance. Shared reading, guided reading, and read-aloud experiences as well as group discussions will ensure that students are not dependent exclusively on their own research.

▸ As you share persuasive texts with students, be sure to highlight the goal of the text, reasons, facts, opinions, beginning and ending statements, and convincing illustrations.

During the Class Project:

▸ Begin each session with a focused minilesson to demonstrate traits in persuasive writing. The mentor text "Washington, D.C." acts as the model to show students the structure and features of a persuasive text. You may wish to use other mentor texts to assist you with your demonstrations.

▸ Be sure to model note taking for students as you think aloud about information in reference materials. Use chart paper to capture your notes, and display the model prominently as students work independently in research stations.

▸ Some students may benefit from a sentence frame written on each page of their notebooks. Read the sentence frames with students. Then, help students locate information to complete the frames.

▸ Provide templates (found on the *Resources* CD-ROM) for students who need extra support when writing their brochures. Include spaces for the title (city name), opening statement, headings, and ending statement. Allow room for persuasive illustrations.

▶ As students work independently on their research and writing, note those who are struggling and bring them together in small groups for think-alouds. As needed, demonstrate how you begin with a goal, write headings for categories of information, find supporting facts, and craft an ending statement. When it's time to revise, show how you choose descriptive words, use capital letters for specific names, use an editing checklist, and add supporting illustrations.

▶ Students who seem very confident and who have clearly grasped all of the concepts taught so far can be brought together in a small group to extend their understanding to more challenging work, such as thinking of interesting beginnings for each category of information.

▶ Students who finish their brochures early can think about adding color to set off their headings and categories of information. They can be research and writing partners for students who are still drafting.

▶ Although the lessons provide suggested demonstrations for each session, you may wish to tailor your instruction to meet the common needs of your students. The Ongoing Monitoring Sheet, together with the Individual Evaluation Record found on the *Resources* CD-ROM, will help you keep track of each student's unique needs. Refer to the section on assessment and ongoing monitoring on page xxx in the introduction to this book for further information.

▶ Use the Daily Planner (Figure 4.2) to plan your own class projects for future explorations based on the needs of your students.

Figure 4.2

During the Individual Project:

▶ Continue to use the Ongoing Monitoring Sheet and the Individual Evaluation Record to identify topics you'll want to address in the focused minilesson that begins each session. Continue to use the Daily Planner to lay out future explorations based on student needs.

▶ Keep your modeled writing charts on display so students can refer back to each feature as they plan, draft, and publish their brochure.

▶ Have students select topics from a small number of choices for which you can provide plenty of information at research stations. Four topics are suggested in Session 6.

▸ Guide students to include opinions and facts in their reasons. Some students may publish just one reason; some may publish a series of reasons. Remind students that illustrations can be just as convincing as text.

▸ Some students will benefit from saying their reasons and opening and closing statements aloud to a partner before writing them.

▸ Remind your insecure illustrators that this is not an art project and they will not be graded on the quality of their drawing. Emphasize that simple line drawings are perfectly adequate. Students may be able to cut photographs and other illustrations out of magazines, flyers, or other publications to support their own persuasive texts.

▸ Encourage students to label their illustrations if time allows. This may be especially helpful to English language learners.

▸ Have writing partners conference with each other often in order to check one another's work for sense, clarity, and persuasiveness.

After the Unit:

▸ Be sure to give students opportunities to share and celebrate their individual writing projects.

▸ Distribute copies of the Student Self-Reflection Sheet (on the *Resources* CD-ROM). Students will benefit greatly from the chance to reflect on their progress during the unit and to hear their classmates' feedback.

▸ Compare students' final writing products with their pre-assessments to evaluate their growth as writers of persuasive text.

▸ Look at common needs of the class and address these when planning future explorations on persuasive writing, or through the Power Writes.

▸ Reflect on the strengths and challenges of implementing this series of lessons. How might it be adjusted to maximize student learning?

SESSION 1
Immersion and Pre-Assessment

Students are introduced to persuasive writing and draft a simple persuasive text for the pre-assessment.

MATERIALS
- Photographs of various locations around your city or town, such as parks, museums, and places for recreation
- Paper and pencils

FOCUSED MINILESSON *(prewriting)*
20 MINUTES

- Focus the learning: *Today I'm going to introduce you to a special kind of writing called "persuasive writing," and we'll do some persuasive writing of our own.*

- Introduce the concept of persuasion: *Have you ever asked your parents for a special privilege, like staying up late? How did you try to convince them? Did you have good reasons for staying up late? What are you doing when you try to convince someone to think or feel a certain way? You are trying to persuade! Persuasion is all around us. If you've seen ads in magazines or on television, you've seen persuasion. Advertisers want us to buy something, and they give us reasons to convince us to make the purchase.*

  TURN &TALK *Tell your partner about an ad you have seen. Describe how it tried to persuade you.*

- Introduce travel brochures as one type of advertising: *Most of you have seen ads that tell you that some product is going to make your life better. Have you ever seen a travel brochure? This is a special kind of persuasive writing. A travel brochure uses pictures and words to convince you to visit a particular place, such as a city, a state, or an attraction such as a zoo or an amusement park.*

  TURN &TALK *Partners, think together. What place is your favorite? Discuss some reasons that this place is the best place to spend your free time.*

- Introduce the topic for the pre-assessment: *It sounds as if you have all had some great adventures in many places. Today you're going to write persuasively about your favorite place. Your job is to persuade—or convince someone to visit that place.*

WRITING and COACHING *(drafting)*
20 MINUTES

- Allow time for students to draft their pre-assessment pieces.

- If students have trouble getting started, suggest that they make quick sketches of their favorite places and then label their sketches with phrases or sentences that tell why these places are so fantastic.

- Some students may struggle with spelling as they draft their pre-assessment pieces. Encourage them to try their best, and always praise their efforts.

SHARING and REFLECTING
10 MINUTES

TURN &TALK *Partners, put your heads together as you read each other's persuasive texts. What do you see in your partner's writing that will make people want to visit the place?*

- Lead a discussion about students' experiences with persuasive writing. Help them sum up what they've learned so far about the purpose for writing a persuasive text: *You've all worked hard to convince your classmates to visit your favorite place. You're beginning to understand that the purpose of persuasive writing is to make another person think or act a certain way. In the next few sessions, we'll learn some strategies that can help you do that better.*

- After class, evaluate each students' writing using the Ongoing Monitoring Sheet (in the Resources section and also on the *Resources* CD-ROM). Use the results to revise instruction and personalize the lessons in this unit. If you want to keep individual records on students, use the Individual Evaluation Record in the Resources section and on the CD-ROM. Do not make corrections or marks on students' work. For more information on pre-assessment, see page xxx of the introduction to this book.

TIP Provide encouragement for students who struggle with the task: *This is a practice try at persuasion. As the week goes on, we'll learn more about persuasive writing, and you'll be able to come back and work on what you started today. We want to find out today what you already know. Then we can build on that and improve your work.*

SESSION 2
Beginning to Research

Students identify features of persuasive writing and begin to conduct research for their own writing.

MATERIALS
- *Big Book of Mentor Texts:* "Washington, D.C.," pages 38–41
- Research notebooks
- Pencils
- Research stations (books, pictures, bookmarked websites about your city or town)
- Chart paper

FOCUSED MINILESSON *(prewriting)*
20 MINUTES

- Focus the learning: *In this session, we'll explore the features of a travel brochure, which is a special type of persuasive writing. Then we'll start our research for the travel brochures we'll write ourselves to convince readers that our town is a great place to visit.*

- Introduce the mentor text: *Let's read the travel brochure in the Big Book. By looking at the way this author organized her writing, we will get some great ideas for our brochures.* Look through the text together.

  TURN &TALK *What are some features you saw in the mentor text? Discuss these features with your partner.*

- Lead a discussion of the major features of the mentor text. As students name features, begin a list on chart paper. Hang the chart to use as a reference throughout your exploration of persuasive text. By focusing on features, you help students develop a framework for their own writing.

- Lead a discussion about how to organize the information in the brochure into categories: *The "Washington, D.C." text is organized into categories, such as places to learn and places to visit outdoors. Let's think of categories we can use in our brochures about our hometown. That way we will know what kinds of information to look for while we research.*

  TURN &TALK *What are some categories we can use to organize our information? Discuss some ideas.*

- As students share ideas, list them on the board. Narrow the list to five categories on which your students can focus their research.

- Ask students to write the five categories in their research notebooks, one category per page.

Features of a Great Travel Brochure

It includes the name of the place.

It captures your attention with a catchy opening sentence.

It has a powerful ending.

It is organized into chunks or categories of text.

■ To introduce note taking, think aloud as you discover a fact about your town in one of the references you have identified: *Wow—our town has 300 days of sunshine a year! I will write that down on the weather page in my research notebook so I will have the fact when I write my brochure. People who love sunny weather will definitely be persuaded to come visit!*

WRITING and COACHING *(prewriting, drafting)*
20 MINUTES

■ Introduce students to each of the research sources you have identified. To assist students with their research, you could provide books, pictures, bookmarked websites about your town, fact sheets from your chamber of commerce or local attractions, and so on. You could even invite people who live in your town—such as a parks administrator, the coach of a local team, or your town's special events coordinator—to visit your classroom. Students could then interview these people to find out amazing facts about your town.

■ Direct students to begin researching. Circulate around the room, helping students locate usable information and take effective notes in the correct categories in their research notebooks.

■ Encourage students to tell their peers at the research station the information they have discovered before recording it in note form. This will help them put the information in their own words instead of copying it verbatim from the source.

SHARING and REFLECTING
10 MINUTES

TURN &TALK *Share your notebooks with your partners. As you read through your research, identify a fact that would persuade someone to visit our town.*

■ *From listening to your conversations, I can tell that you have discovered many new facts about our town. In the next few days, we'll figure out how to use these facts to persuade people to visit here.*

TIP Students are likely to come up with a variety of categories, depending upon their experiences in your town. Tailor the list to your town and to categories that you believe students can research effectively. To complete their research notebooks, students will need to collect information in five categories suitable for a travel brochure. Some categories to consider include the town's history and local museums, natural beauty and wildlife, tourist sites and shopping, weather, and other facts.

TIP for Conferring with Individuals and Small Groups

English language learners may benefit from a sentence frame written on each page of their research notebooks. For example, on a "Weather" page, you might write, *The spring weather is ___. The summer weather is ___,* and so on. Read the sentence stems with students, asking them to repeat after you. Then help students locate information to complete the frames.

SESSION 3
Drafting Facts from Research

As they continue their research, students focus on using descriptive words and persuasive language to write and revise facts in their research notebooks.

MATERIALS
- *Big Book of Mentor Texts:* "Washington, D.C.," pages 38–41
- Research notebooks
- Pencils
- Research stations
- Features chart from Session 2

FOCUSED MINILESSON *(drafting, revising)*
20 MINUTES

■ Introduce the session: *In our last session, we looked at how the mentor text was organized and added those ideas to our features chart. In this session, we'll look at the mentor text again to explore more features of a great travel brochure, and we'll learn how writers use language to persuade.* Read aloud page 39 in the mentor text.

TURN &TALK *Partners, think together. What do you notice about the language the writer uses on this page of the brochure?*

■ *That's a great observation! You noticed some strong words that might persuade readers to visit Washington, D.C. The writer could have said these places are "nice," but that wouldn't tell us very much. Instead, she uses words that give readers a much more positive feeling about visiting this city.* Have students identify exciting and descriptive words and write them on a class chart. Examples include *fun, cool, amazing, important, fascinated,* and *famous.*

■ Discuss how the use of descriptive words makes the piece persuasive. *I loved the description of the zoo on page 40. The writer could simply have said that there are many animals at the zoo. Instead, she gave a huge number that intrigued me. She added a playful and specific description of an exhibit. And ending with the sentence "What a wild world!" made me want to see this amazing place!*

> **Features of a Great Travel Brochure**
>
> It includes the name of the place.
>
> It captures your attention with a catchy opening sentence.
>
> It has a powerful ending.
>
> It is organized into chunks or categories of text.
>
> It uses descriptive words that help persuade.

■ Add this feature—descriptive words—to the features chart.

■ Talk about revising sentences to make them more persuasive and interesting: *This is a fact from my research that I wrote in the last session. There are many trees in the park. But watch as I make that more exciting and persuasive:* Tall, majestic trees line the shady park. *Doesn't that sound inviting? I would love to go to a park like that!*

■ Model "stretching" a word to figure out how to spell it: *I want to add the word* majestic, *but it is a tricky word to spell. When you write with powerful persuasive words, you will sometimes think of words you do not know how to spell. When that happens, say each word slowly, stretching the word, and listen for the sounds you know.*

TURN &TALK *Open up your research notebooks. Identify a place where you can add a more powerful descriptive word to your research. Share your idea with your partner.*

WRITING and COACHING *(prewriting, drafting)*
20 MINUTES

■ Direct students to continue researching. Remind them to write their facts on the correct pages of their research notebooks.

■ Remind students to focus on descriptive words: *You can add persuasive words to the facts you've already written. As you record new facts, think about how you can make them exciting for your readers.*

SHARING and REFLECTING
10 MINUTES

TURN &TALK *Take a look at your sentences and find one that has descriptive words that jump right out at you. Share that sentence with your partner and talk about what makes it persuasive.*

■ Ask a few students to share persuasive sentences: *Those descriptive words really made a difference! They turned facts into reasons that make readers want to visit our town.*

TIP As you pass out research notebooks, you can do an informal assessment by flipping quickly through the pages to see the progress students have made. This will help you organize small-group instruction for students who are struggling with a particular category of information or with note taking in general.

SESSION 4
Revising and Editing Facts

Students complete their research, revise their facts to include more descriptive words, and edit for correct capitalization of place names.

MATERIALS
- *Big Book of Mentor Texts:* "Washington, D.C.," pages 38–41
- Research notebooks
- Pencils
- Research stations

FOCUSED MINILESSON *(revising, editing)*
20 MINUTES

- Focus the learning: *You've collected some fascinating facts from your research and you've used descriptive words when writing those facts in the five categories in your research notebooks. In this session, we'll look through our notebooks to be sure we have enough facts in each category, and we'll polish our writing by editing for capital letters. Flip through your notebooks now to see where you need to add more information.*

- Review the research stations so that students will know where to look to find more information in the various categories. Use think-aloud language to demonstrate where you would look to find information for each category.

- Help students focus on the correct use of capital letters when writing or editing their notes. Show students the mentor text. Alert them to words that begin with capital letters, apart from those at the beginnings of sentences. Examples include: *Washington, D.C., United States Capitol,* and *Washington Monument. Why do these words begin with a capital letter?* Lead students to understand that words that tell the name of a specific person, place, or important object start with capital letters.

    TURN &TALK *Partners, think together. Take a look in your research notebooks to find a word that should be capitalized. Explain to your partner why that word should begin with a capital letter.*

- Focus students on their tasks for their writing time: *Make sure today that you have enough information for each category of your brochure. When you name specific places in our town, like Phillips Park or Vaughn Center, be sure their names start with capital letters.*

WRITING and COACHING *(drafting, editing)*
20 MINUTES

- Direct students to add new research to any categories in their notebooks that are currently lacking. They should also edit their writing to include descriptive words and to capitalize the names of people, places, and important objects.

- As students are writing, note those who may need additional help adding persuasive words and using capital letters correctly. Organize small-group teaching around these instructional needs.

- If you find that most of your students are struggling with the same task, stop the class and reteach as needed.

SHARING and REFLECTING
10 MINUTES

TURN &TALK *Talk with your partner about how you revised your work. What did you improve most about your writing?*

- After sharing a few examples, sum up the minilesson: *You capitalized specific places in your writing—just look at all the great places you wrote about! And you have enough information to make each section of your brochure detailed enough so that your readers will want to visit.*

TIP for Conferring with Individuals and Small Groups

Encourage your more capable writers to think of interesting beginnings for each category: *I've noticed that in travel brochures, the writer starts each section with a catchy sentence like "Washington, D.C., is a place for the whole family to do it all!" How might you introduce your section on museums?*

SESSION 5

Publishing and Adding Illustrations

Students begin to publish their travel brochures, adding drawings or photographs to match each category of information.

MATERIALS

- *Big Book of Mentor Texts:* "Washington, D.C.," pages 38–41
- Research notebooks
- Pencils
- Research materials with pictures of your city or town
- 11" x 17" white paper
- Rulers
- Colored pencils, markers, crayons

FOCUSED MINILESSON *(publishing)*
20 MINUTES

- Introduce the session: *In this session, we'll begin to publish our travel brochures. We will choose one or two favorite facts about each category and publish them on that page of the brochure. Then we will add illustrations that support our writing and make it even more persuasive.*

- Show students a tri-fold brochure. *When you publish your travel brochures, each category will go on a separate section. The front page is the cover. This is where you will put the name of our town. The cover should also include a picture that makes your readers want to open the brochure and find out more.*

- Discuss the importance of illustrations in a travel brochure: *Let's take a look at the mentor text again. If we covered up the text, what would you notice? Pictures! The photographs on these pages show us more about the place and make us excited to go there. The pictures need to match the text, too. I don't think I would put a picture of a zoo in a section about a sports team!*

   TURN &TALK *Pick one of our categories. Discuss with your partner some pictures you could draw to illustrate that category in our town.*

- Pass out paper. Model how to fold the paper into thirds. Point to the various categories and help students as they write each category heading on one section of the brochure.

- Explain how to complete the brochure: *Think about how you want each section to look. Do you want one picture or two? Do you want the picture at the top, middle, or bottom? You need to plan where you want your picture before you write. You may even want to make a box to save a spot for it.*

- *Now you are ready to publish. Read the heading. Then find that heading in your notebook. Write sentences from that page of your research notebook on the same section in your brochure.*

WRITING and COACHING *(publishing)*
20 MINUTES

- Have students begin working on their brochures. Consider having them work on two or three categories during this session and the rest of the categories in another session.

- Stop the class occasionally to congratulate students on their work. Highlight the efforts of specific students: *I love how Melissa decided to go back and reread the last section of her brochure. Now she can be sure that what she wrote makes sense. That's what good writers do!*

- Consider enlisting parent helpers for this phase of the class project. They can be a wonderful, enriching resource in your classroom.

SHARING and REFLECTING
10 MINUTES

TURN & TALK *Share the writing you've done today with your partner. How do your illustrations and text go together to create a persuasive brochure? What do you like most about your partner's work?*

- If you created a travel brochure yourself, model for students as you reflect on your work: *I think the picture I chose to illustrate my section on recreation really does the trick. That soccer field is so special; I know people would love to watch a game there. But my favorite part of my brochure is the section on education. Can you guess why?*

- Preview the work students will do in the next session: *We've nearly completed our persuasive brochures! In the next session, you can publish the rest of the categories.*

TIP Most children enjoy the autonomy that comes from designing their own creations. Other students, however, might benefit from a template that already has headings, frames for illustrations, and write-on lines. Using the template, students can add illustrations and research facts for each section. You might also use the template on the *Resources* CD-ROM so that students can polish their brochures. Encourage students to consider adding photographs and clip art to enhance their brochures.

SESSION 6
Publishing and Celebrating

Students finish publishing their travel brochures, then share and celebrate their work.

MATERIALS

- *Big Book of Mentor Texts:* "Washington, D.C.," pages 38–41
- Research notebooks
- Pencils
- Research materials with pictures of your city or town
- 11" x 17" white paper
- Rulers
- Colored pencils, markers, crayons
- Features chart

TIP Students should have an authentic purpose for writing. Consider placing the final, published brochures at a local library to help residents find ideas for great things to do in town. You might also scan brochures or have students publish them on the computer and share them with a faraway sister school.

FOCUSED MINILESSON *(publishing)*
20 MINUTES

■ Focus the learning: *You've done a great job so far of publishing your travel brochures. You are using descriptive words and correct capitalization, and you've drawn illustrations that really match your text. In this session, we'll finish publishing and then we'll celebrate all the really great work we've done.*

TURN &TALK *Which categories do you have left to publish today? Discuss your action plan with your partner!*

■ Remind students to think about how they want each section to look. How can they place the pictures to go with their text? Return to the mentor text to refresh students' memories: *Take a look at this travel brochure again. Do you notice that each photograph has a sentence or two that goes with it? Remember that your illustrations should show something about our town. Words need to support the illustrations—and illustrations need to support the words!*

■ *In the last session, you wrote your headings on your brochure. Remember to match these headings to the headings in your research notebook. This will keep the information organized!*

■ Students should have an authentic purpose for writing. Remind them that their brochures are written to influence families to visit their town, so the pictures should reflect things that would appeal to families.

WRITING and COACHING *(publishing)*
20 MINUTES

■ Have students finish the rest of their categories in this session and put the finishing touches on their brochures and the accompanying illustrations.

■ Consider having students work in pairs to finish publishing their brochures. Pair students who are lagging behind with those who are likely to finish early, and instruct the early finishers to assist their buddies as needed.

■ Don't hesitate to add an additional session for publishing if a majority of your students seem to need more time for illustrating and adding color to their sketches.

SHARING and REFLECTING
10 MINUTES

■ Plan a time of celebration. Students could share their brochures with another class. You might invite the mayor, an alderperson, or another town dignitary to help students celebrate the work they did showcasing their town.

TURN &TALK *What have you learned about what makes a great travel brochure? As you discuss your ideas, point out those features in each other's brochures.*

■ *We had a lot to celebrate today. Let's compare our finished work to our features chart. Do you see that you wrote great openings, included reasons, and gave specific facts? Your persuasive descriptions sparkled on the page. Our town seems very exciting, thanks to your great brochures!*

TIP If students finish early, have them think about adding more color to their brochures: *We have some great headings in our brochures that match our categories. What can we do to set these categories off in our brochures? Color is a great idea! You could put the headings in a different color to set them off and make them easy for your readers to find.*

SESSION 7
Launching the Individual Project

Students review the features of a great travel brochure, select their own topics, and begin their research.

MATERIALS
- Features chart from class project
- Research stations (books, photos, travel brochures)
- Research notebooks

TIP You will have an easier time providing research materials if you limit student choices to four or five cities. This limited approach will also allow you to organize small-group meetings and lessons for students who are writing about the same city. Your social studies curriculum may provide suitable topics for this assignment. You might also choose four or five cities in your state for which you can find adequate research materials.

FOCUSED MINILESSON *(prewriting)*
25 MINUTES

- Focus the learning: *In our class project, you learned about the features of persuasive text as we wrote travel brochures for our town. Now you'll choose a different city to research, and you'll create your own individual travel brochure, booklet, or flyer about it.*

  TURN &TALK *Think back to what you learned about persuasive texts. What features of persuasive texts make them different from other texts that you know?*

- As students share features, remind them of the purpose of persuasive texts: to convince readers to think or act a certain way. A persuasive text has a goal—like "Visit our town!"—and strong reasons to support that goal. Review the features chart created during the class project.

- Brainstorm topics with students, writing them on the board.

- Review using categories to record notes: *When we wrote about our own town, we divided our research notebook into categories. Then we took notes about each category.*

  TURN &TALK *Let's evaluate how recording our notes in categories helped us with our writing. Share your thoughts with a partner*

- *You shared some great thoughts about research! Putting the information under the correct category helped you find the information you needed when it was time to publish your work. Revisit the categories that you used for the class project and give students the opportunity to suggest additional categories that came up as they researched. Then have students write headings in their research notebooks, as they did in the class project.*

WRITING and COACHING *(prewriting, drafting)*
20 MINUTES

- Direct students to the research stations. Show them the materials you've gathered, and use think-aloud language to demonstrate how you would gather information: *I can see that this station has books and magazines about Dallas, Texas. This book looks like it has lots of information about fun things to do in Dallas. I'm going to use the words and pictures to help me gather facts for my research notebook, and I'm going to write the facts I find in the section of my notebook labeled "Fun for All."*

- Have students research and begin drafting information in their notebooks. As students work, check their notebooks for understanding of the research process. If students need assistance, give them some direction: *You found a great fact about the Rose Garden. Should that go in the "Museum" category or "The Great Outdoors"? Think about where you are when you go to the garden—that's definitely an entry for "The Great Outdoors"!*

- Remember: You don't have to restrict your coaching to this particular session. Look for other opportunities during the day to pull together students who are struggling, and support them with another quick minilesson or some guided writing.

SHARING and REFLECTING
10 MINUTES

TURN &TALK *Share your notes with your partner. Think together. Which facts so far are the most persuasive? Explain why you think so.*

- After allowing a few students to share their facts, sum up the session's work as you set the stage for the next session: *You have already identified some great facts to include in your persuasive texts, and your research is organized in your notebooks to help you focus on what else you need to find. In our next session, we'll continue our research. Think about what you'd like to find out next!*

TIP for Conferring with Individuals and Small Groups

More capable students may be ready for a lesson in summarizing when taking notes. Pull together a group of students and model how to read a paragraph and write a summary of the information. Emphasize that their summaries tell the facts in their own words. Share summaries from student notebooks and talk about how those summaries include only the most important information from the research.

SESSION 8
Drafting from Research

Students continue writing facts from their research, focusing on using persuasive words and correct spelling.

MATERIALS
- Research stations
- Research notebooks
- Features chart from class project

FOCUSED MINILESSON *(prewriting, drafting)*
15 MINUTES

■ Introduce the session: *Today you'll have more opportunities for research so you can include fascinating facts in your work. Remember, your goal is to persuade. If you find out that your city has something that people wouldn't like, such as a lot of air pollution, you should probably leave that out! Instead, focus on something great, like an awesome museum or a fun place to play. Each part of your research should support a reason for visiting the town or city you chose—that's what persuasive writing is all about!*

■ Redirect students to the persuasive word chart you created during the class project (Session 3): *Remember the exciting words we came up with to persuade? Let's think about how to make a sentence even more persuasive by adding description. Let's practice on this sentence I'll write on the board:* You can walk on the beach and see the ocean.

> **TURN &TALK** *Partners, think together. If you want people to flock to the beach, what can you do to make that sentence more persuasive?*

■ As you take a few suggestions from students, model how to use a caret to add descriptive words: *Listen to our sentence: "You can play in the gentle surf and glimpse blue ocean waves for miles from the sandy white beach." Doesn't that make you want to come to the beach? These are the kinds of words that will persuade your readers. Add those kinds of descriptive words to your reasons for visiting.*

■ Introduce strategies for spelling unknown words: *When we do research for a travel brochure, we might use words that aren't familiar to us. Some of these words are tricky to spell! You can check to see if the word is on a chart in our room, such as our persuasive words chart or the word wall. Then you can copy the word from the chart. Sometimes when I want to do that, I take a sticky note to the wall so I can copy the word up close. What if my word is not on the wall? Then I might check a dictionary or ask a learning partner for help.*

TIP Place a high-frequency word chart in students' writing folders. Students may add words that they frequently misspell or words that they want to remember. This can be placed inside a clear plastic sleeve so students can easily store and update the list. When students have word lists at their disposal, it increases their independence and pride as writers.

TURN &TALK *Find a sentence in your research that will be more persuasive with added describing words. Work with your partner to make it more descriptive.*

■ As students discuss their work, walk around the room and listen for words that can be added to the chart. Ask students to model how to use these words for their classmates.

WRITING and COACHING
(prewriting, drafting, revising)
20 MINUTES

■ Be sure to have students' research notebooks waiting at their tables before the writing session begins. This way they'll have maximum time for researching and writing.

■ Direct students to any resources that might be useful for finding information on their topics.

■ As students write, watch for students who need to add more information to certain categories. Direct these students to the appropriate resources, including other students, to help them find information: *I noticed that Keisha is working on Houston as well. I think she had quite a few ideas listed for outdoor activities. You might ask her to direct you to some resources she used to find those great places.*

SHARING and REFLECTING
10 MINUTES

TURN &TALK *What tricky word did you encounter today? Share a strategy you used with your partner to spell it.*

■ Listen in and praise great strategies that you hear. Validating students' use of strategies not only gives them pride in what they are able to accomplish, but also fosters independence.

TURN &TALK *Share your work with your partner. Identify in each other's work a strong example of an engaging persuasive word.*

■ As students identify persuasive words, have them write great examples on sticky notes to place on the class word wall: *Your choices of persuasive words really make your work sparkle! In our next session, we'll continue to research and look for more reasons to visit our selected cities.*

TIP To foster independence with spelling, place a "try-it" sheet in writing folders. This consists of three columns. Ask students to make two attempts to spell a word before asking you for help. When a student comes for assistance, point out the parts of the word he or she spelled correctly. Then help the student spell the word correctly in the third column. The student can then add this word to his or her personal word list.

SESSION 9
Revising Drafts

Students continue to research, draft, and revise what they have written, focusing on clarity and sense.

MATERIALS
• Research stations
• Research notebooks

TIP Students sometimes think that good writers write perfectly on the first try. Minilessons focusing on revision not only show students how to revise, but also why to revise. Students need these lessons to see how revising improves writing. Create confident writers not by focusing on "mistakes," but by showing through your own modeling that revising strengthens the message and assists readers with their understanding.

FOCUSED MINILESSON *(drafting, revising)*
15 MINUTES

■ Focus the learning: *When I write, I revise for meaning. I reread my work carefully to be sure that it makes sense. If it doesn't make sense to me, it definitely won't make sense to my readers! In our last session, we revised for persuasive words. In this session we'll revise our work again to be sure it says exactly what we want it to say.*

■ Model revising for meaning. On the board, write this sentence and then read it aloud: The Golden Gate Bridge one of most famous in the world. *This sentence doesn't make sense, does it?. When I read it out loud, I can tell I missed some words.* Model using a caret to add missing words to the sentence.

> **TURN &TALK** *Partners, work together. Choose a section of your work to read aloud for your partner. Partners, suggest a revision that might help the writing make more sense.*

■ Listen in on partner conversations to offer suggestions on revising. Help frame students' thinking as you think aloud: *I heard you tell your partner that you wanted to hear more detail about why the lake is such a great place to visit. That's great feedback! Let's make it even more helpful. What kind of detail would help? I heard you talking about how it's fun to visit the lake when it's hot outside. Maybe it would help to add a detail about how refreshing the cool water is on a hot summer day. That's such a persuasive reason to visit the beach!*

WRITING and COACHING
(prewriting, drafting, revising)
20 MINUTES

■ As you pass out students' research notebooks, do a quick progress check. Form small groups of students who need help finding and taking notes on similar information. You can form groups based on students who are writing about the same city, or you can form groups based on students who need to find information in the same categories.

■ Direct students to continue researching, writing, and revising in their notebooks. As students work, ask questions such as "What does this mean?" and "Why do you think that?" to make students aware of opportunities to revise while allowing them to retain ownership. Allow them to make their own "final decisions."

SHARING and REFLECTING
5 MINUTES

TURN &TALK *Partners, share the work that you did today with your partner. Which facts were most persuasive? What made them convincing?*

■ Reinforce students' great work: *I saw several of you using a great strategy. As you wrote, you read your writing aloud to yourself. That's a fantastic way to find missing words and to make sure that your writing makes sense. You are making your writing more powerful and more persuasive.*

TIP for Conferring with Individuals and Small Groups

For more fluent writers, this is a great opportunity to introduce the word *because* to join sentences. Show students how to use *because* to provide reasons in their sentences: *Good persuasive writers give reasons to convince their readers. They use words such as* because *to link their reasons. Would you like to try that with your writing? I'll start the sentence, and you finish it: "The Empire State Building is awesome because_____." What can you add to make your writing more persuasive? How can you turn this into a reason to visit the Empire State Building?*

SESSION 10
Writing Openings and Closings

Students review the mentor text to learn what makes a persuasive opening and closing. Then they apply what they learn to their individual travel brochures.

MATERIALS
- Research notebooks
- *Big Book of Mentor Texts:* "Washington, D.C.," pages 38–41
- Persuasive words list

FOCUSED MINILESSON *(drafting)*
15 MINUTES

■ Introduce the session: *We know how important it is to include great reasons when we persuade someone. But how do we capture the readers' attention in the first place? How do we end our work so that it leaves a strong impression? We'll find out in this session. Let's take a look at the mentor text and see how one writer did it.*

> **TURN &TALK** *Focus on the opening and the closing. What did the writer do that grabbed your attention? How did the ending sum up the information? Talk it over with your partner.*

■ *You noticed a great beginning, one that draws readers in with the promise of fun! The ending has some catchy words to persuade us that Washington, D.C., is a place with many, many things to do that appeal to the whole family. When you focus on your beginning and your ending, think "How will I get my readers' attention? What feelings do I want to leave them with?"*

> **TURN &TALK** *Work with a partner who is writing about the same city. Think together as you create a powerful beginning or a catchy ending.*

■ Allow time for students to share some of their great beginnings and endings. Then summarize the learning from this session: *Powerful beginnings are important because they grab the readers' attention and make them want to read more. Powerful endings are important because they leave readers with strong feelings about what they should do. As you are writing today, think about how to grab your readers' attention and how to leave them with a strong desire to visit your chosen city or town.*

WRITING and COACHING *(drafting)*
20 MINUTES

■ Display the mentor text in a prominent spot so students can refer to the author's technique when writing their own beginnings and endings. Also keep your list of powerful persuasive words visible for reference.

■ If students struggle with openings, provide a sentence frame in which they can list three unique things about their city, such as *Where else can you see ____, ____, and ____?* or *Imagine visiting ____, ____, and ____!*

■ If students struggle with the concept of a final impression, ask them to think about how they usually feel after watching a television commercial for an exciting new toy or theme park.

SHARING and REFLECTING
5 MINUTES

TURN &TALK *Read your opening and closing to a partner. Partners, identify something that you find amazing in the work! Talk about how you might make the beginnings and endings more powerful, too.*

■ As you listen in to conversations, praise students' powerful beginnings and endings: *Your beginnings draw your readers in, and your endings sum up your information and will make your readers want to visit. That's how great persuasive writers work—they hook their readers and leave them ready to act!*

TIP For more capable students, introduce persuasive techniques such as the following:

Star Appeal: Wouldn't you like to walk in the footsteps of Abraham Lincoln?

Bandwagon: Every year, over 20 million people visit San Diego. Wouldn't you like to be one of them?

Emotional Appeal: Imagine your children's laughter and excitement as they ride their first roller coaster.

You can show students examples of these techniques in actual advertising and work with small groups to insert sentences into their work that use one or more of these techniques.

SESSION 11
Editing, Publishing, and Celebrating

Students will work independently to edit their writing for mechanics and revise illustrations before publishing. Then they'll celebrate their accomplishments as a class.

MATERIALS

- *Big Book of Mentor Texts:* "Washington, D.C.," pages 38–41
- Research notebooks
- Paper and pencils
- Crayons, colored pencils, and so on
- *Resources* CD-ROM
- Features chart

TIP The expectation for editing will change as you go through the year. As you teach new grammar and mechanics skills, add them to an editing checklist. Involve students in revising the checklist, and reinforce the importance of using the checklist to edit. Post the list in a prominent place in the room or in a plastic sleeve inside students' folders to make updates manageable.

FOCUSED MINILESSON *(editing, publishing)*
15 MINUTES

- Focus the learning: *In our last session, we revised our writing to make our beginnings and endings powerful and persuasive. In this session, we're going to polish our work by editing the rest of our sentences and adding illustrations that will really grab our readers.*

- Explain the importance of editing: *Editing is an important step in writing. When we edit, we make sure our work is easy for readers to understand and that it looks polished and complete. What do you look for when you edit?* Students may mention capitalization, spelling, and so on. Choose a few ideas to focus on and add them to your class editing checklist.

- Remind students that illustrations should match the text: *A really good illustration helps get the reader's attention. Is it colorful and bright? Does it get the reader interested in your writing? Most important, does it match the text?* Revisit the mentor text to look at strong examples of photos that match the text: *How do the pictures in the mentor text support the writing?*

  TURN &TALK *Describe for your partner an idea you have for an illustration that will match your text. Partners, how will the illustration make the text even better?*

- Suggest to students that they can include maps to show where their cities are located. If possible, help students print maps from preselected websites. Otherwise, help them locate state maps that show their cities. They can use these to draw. Ask students what other illustrations or photos they may want to include.

- Pass out paper. Model how to create a booklet, brochure, and flyer. Refer to the sample flyers on the *Resources* CD-ROM for assistance. *Now you're ready to publish!*

- Explain how students should organize their text: *Your flyer, brochure, or booklet will be divided into sections or categories that have the same headings you used in your research notebook. Think about how you want each section to look. Then plan where you want to place your pictures before you write. You may even want to make a box or two in each section to save a spot for illustration.*

WRITING and COACHING (publishing)
40 MINUTES

■ Circulate around the room and support students as they begin the process of publishing their brochures. If they struggle to get started, remind them to use the headings they wrote in their research notebooks to tell them what facts belong in each section: *Now you are ready to copy your text. Read each heading. Then find that heading in your notebook. You can copy the sentences from that page onto the same section in your brochure.*

■ Have early finishers go back and double-check their work before handing it in. Then allow them to help other students.

SHARING and REFLECTING
10 MINUTES

TURN &TALK *Assess what makes your travel writing so persuasive. Tell your partner which of the persuasive features in your work is your favorite.*

■ Sum up this session's learning: *Wow! What an exciting day! As I look over our features chart and your work, I see that you included all the important features. You have a clear message, and you gave reasons to support that message, too! That's the essence of what we want to do with our persuasive writing—convince our readers. You should be proud of how convincing and how organized your work turned out to be.*

■ Remember to look back at the students' pre-assessment pieces and to use the Ongoing Monitoring Sheet or the Individual Evaluation Record (in the Resources section and also on the *Resources* CD-ROM) to document growth and areas for improvement. Pass out copies of the Student Self-Reflection Sheet (on the CD-ROM) to assist students as they reflect on their own growth. Finally, be sure to make notes on what worked and what didn't during the unit so you can make adjustments for next time. See "After the Unit," page 197, for more information about post-assessment and self-reflection.

TIP Creating the brochures may take more than one day. Plan the time needed for students to finish their work. If some students finish early, have them double-check their work against the features chart you created during the class project. Then they can help their partners.

TIP Providing an audience will add even more to students' sense of pride and accomplishment. You can invite a neighboring class to listen to your students' presentations. Divide the class into small groups of three or four presenters and three or four audience members. Sharing the travel brochures with a local library or a travel center will give students an even wider audience.

Written Argument

A written argument uses opinions and facts to persuade others to take action.

FEATURES

- Strong opening argument that tells your opinion
- Reasons that support the argument
- Inspiring conclusion that repeats your opinion

FOCUSED MINILESSON

Our school is sponsoring a TV turn-off week, and I think you should participate. You might think, "No way. I would never keep my TV off for one week!" *Let me see if I can persuade you that it's a good idea with a written argument.*

Persuasion makes readers take action. Watch as I start by writing: You should . . . *The word* should *tells what I want my readers to do. I'll finish:* You should turn off the TV for a week! *That's a statement of opinion. Now, to convince my readers with reasons.*

TURN &TALK *Partners, think together. What reason can you think of to turn off the TV for a week?*

I heard some of you talk about fun activities you can do outside. You also mentioned exercise and being healthier. Watch as I add these great ideas to the argument: With the TV off, you'll have even more time to play outside. You can't play basketball in front of the TV! Exercise and fresh air are good for your health.

One of my favorite reasons for turning off the TV is to have more time for reading. I'm going to add that to my argument, too.

A persuasive argument needs a strong conclusion that inspires action. I don't want to just repeat my opening. I want it to be different, but convincing. Watch as I write my conclusion: Turn off your TV for a week . . . and get a better life!

Dear Mr. Bryson, I want you to make the children laugh that will be helpful. but I can not make the children laugh

You should turn off the TV for a week! With the TV off, you'll have even more time to play outside. You can't play basketball in front of the TV! Exercise and fresh air are good for your health. Do you love reading? Turning off the TV will allow you to devour book after book! You'll learn so much.

Turn off your TV for a week . . . and get a better life!

Modeled Writing

Write the features of a persuasive argument on a chart as you focus on the modeled writing: *Let's take a close look at this argument. It starts with a strong opinion that's followed by reasons to support it. The conclusion restates the call for action in a new and fresh way. Do you think readers will be persuaded to turn off the TV? I hope so!*

WRITING and COACHING

Now it's your turn to write a persuasive argument! Think of an issue that you feel strongly about. Write an argument to convince others to take action! If students struggle with the "freedom" in this assignment, craft an assignment that centers on an argument. Some writers may benefit from a form, such as *I think _____. Why do I think so? Because _____.*

SHARING and REFLECTING

Writers, your written arguments are so convincing! You've included opening arguments that tell your opinions and give supportive reasons. You've also included inspiring conclusions that repeat your opinions and call for action.

ASSESS THE LEARNING

As students work, check to see if they include all the features of a written argument. If necessary, review the difference between fact and opinion and discuss how to support persuasion.

SELF-ASSESSMENT

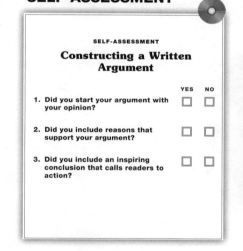

SELF-ASSESSMENT

Constructing a Written Argument

	YES	NO
1. Did you start your argument with your opinion?	☐	☐
2. Did you include reasons that support your argument?	☐	☐
3. Did you include an inspiring conclusion that calls readers to action?	☐	☐

PERSUADE

S U P P O R T I N G   A N D   E X T E N D I N G

▸ See if students can use written argument to persuade their parents to change a family rule, such as early bedtime or dinner before dessert.

▸ Ask students to craft written arguments from the perspective of their school's principal. Students might take the position that homework should be given over every school vacation or that every school day should be two hours shorter!

▸ Challenge students to use a strong written argument to convince the principal to allow five more minutes for recess each day.

Persuasive E-mail

An e-mail can persuade readers with a strong argument and reasons.

To: Susie@BuildaBear.net
Cc:
Bcc:
Subject:
Attachments:
Importance: Normal
Options: None

Career day on May 15th

Dear Susie,
Fearn School is having a career day on May 15th, please join us! We are learning about responsibility, so it would be great if you could teach us how to take care of a Build a Bear like it's living person. Another reason why we want you to come is to have you tell us about all the new Build a Bear features. It would be great if you could come!

FEATURES

- Subject line
- Friendly greeting
- Opinion or request with supporting reasons
- Persuasive ending
- Closing and signature

FOCUSED MINILESSON

This lesson focuses on convincing the principal to allow students to eat lunch in their room once a month, but you should choose a topic that is significant to your class. Lay the groundwork for persuasive success by seeing if a request can be granted. Create on chart paper an e-mail "form" to show how to write the e-mail, or work on your computer as it is projected onto a screen.

Wouldn't it be great if we could eat lunch in our classroom once a month? I need to ask the principal for permission to do this, so I'm drafting an e-mail to send. First I'll write the subject line. A subject line is for summing up the message so that the reader will know what the e-mail is about before he or she opens it. Watch as I write in the subject line: Permission to Eat Lunch in Room 2B. *I want my e-mail to convince our principal to allow us to eat lunch together.*

Notice that I start my e-mail with Dear Mr. Woods. *That is called a greeting. This is like saying "hello" when you see somebody.*

The first part of the e-mail will tell Mr. Woods exactly what we want. Watch as I write: Please allow our class to eat lunch together in Room 2B once a month. *I used* please *to be polite as I made our special request. Now I want to include some great reasons to support that request. Watch as I write a reason:* One reason we would like to do this is that it would give us a chance to get to know each other better. *Mr. Woods will like this!*

TURN &TALK *Partners, think together. How would eating lunch together in our room make a difference to you?*

Watch as I write another persuasive reason: Another reason we would like to eat lunch in our room is that we could spend the time discussing special class projects or solving class problems.

Subject: Permission to Eat Lunch in Room 2B

Dear Mr. Woods,

Please allow our class to eat lunch together in Room 2B once a month. One reason we would like to do this is that it would give us a chance to get to know each other better. Another reason we would like to eat lunch in our room is that we could spend the time discussing special class projects or solving class problems. Please allow our class to eat lunch in our room!

Thank you,

Mrs. Brown

Modeled Writing

Now I'm almost finished. My last sentence repeats my request in a way that lets Mr. Woods know how excited we'll be if we get permission. Please allow our class to eat lunch in our room!

Now I write the end of my e-mail: Thank you, Mrs. Brown. *That's a polite way to close!*

After writing: *This is a very convincing e-mail! Let's take a look at its features. The e-mail has a subject line for previewing the message, a greeting, and a closing. Even more important is the message itself. It's a polite request followed by convincing reasons to grant it.* Write these features on a chart for student reference.

WRITING and COACHING

Writers, now it's your turn. Write a persuasive e-mail to convince someone who has an interesting job to come to class for Job Day. Plan your e-mails on a piece of paper first, and we'll send them using the computer later. Remember to include the features we created in our modeling.

SHARING and REFLECTING

Writers, you wrote some very persuasive e-mails today. You included subject lines, greetings, your opinion or request, reasons, a closing, and a signature. Now let's see what responses you get!

ASSESS THE LEARNING

Gather persuasive e-mails and assess understanding. Determine whether students understand how to use a subject line to sum up the message and prepare readers.

SELF-ASSESSMENT

SELF-ASSESSMENT
Persuading with an E-mail

	YES	NO
1. Did you include features such as a subject line, greeting, and closing?	☐	☐
2. Did you start with a request or opinion?	☐	☐
3. Do clear reasons support your request?	☐	☐
4. Did you end with a sentence that repeats your request in a different way?	☐	☐

PERSUADE

S U P P O R T I N G   A N D   E X T E N D I N G

▶ Create persuasive e-mails to send to a fifth-grade class asking if your class can watch them practice for an upcoming play.

▶ Have students send persuasive e-mails to the local zoo suggesting a name for the latest newborn animal.

▶ Have students write persuasive e-mails convincing a favorite author to write a sequel to a story they like.

Friendly Letter

A friendly letter can persuade readers with an argument and supporting reasons.

Dear Ms. White,

As you know, everybody loves candy but kids are eating to much! I would like you and and all the cafateria laddies to put more healthy foods in the lunch line.

Eating sugary snacks will make your teeth rot. But eating apples and carrots are good for your whole body. Healthy foods will also help kids get good grades.

Sincerely,

Georgia

FEATURES

- Greeting, body, closing, and signature
- Persuasive argument
- Reasons to support the argument

Dear Mr. Petzke,

The only thing that's better than a cool book is a cool treat! I would like to hold a special party for my students called "Cool Books and Cool Treats" to celebrate their work as readers.

The students in my class have worked very hard to read lots of cool books. I like to reward them for their hard work, and a cool treat is just a small reward that is still so much fun!

Sincerely yours,

Ms. Johansen

Modeled Writing

FOCUSED MINILESSON

You have done an amazing job with your reading this quarter! I want to hold a special celebration in class and bring in frozen treats to enjoy while we talk about books. I need to ask permission for this, so I'm writing the principal a letter to persuade him that this is a great idea!

Let's take a look at a persuasive letter to get some ideas for writing. Turn to pages 42–43 in the Big Book of Mentor Texts. A boy wrote to his teacher to ask her for a special field trip. Let's look at the beginning of the letter.

TURN &TALK *Partners, think together. As you followed along, what features really stood out for you?*

You noticed the greeting. That's the part with Dear. *I'll start my writing the same way. Watch as I write on the top line of the paper:* Dear Mr. Petzke. *Notice that I put a comma after the greeting. The first paragraph of the letter in the mentor text starts with the reason for writing the persuasive letter. Can you tell this writer's goal? He wants to go the ballpark for a field trip! Taking a cue from this mentor text, watch as I write:* The only thing that's better than a cool book is a cool treat! I would like to hold a special party for my students called "Cool Books and Cool Treats" to celebrate their work as readers.

I notice that each paragraph of the mentor text has a reason to support the argument. Here, Andre tells his teacher that going to a ballgame can be a great math lesson. That's convincing!

TURN &TALK *Writers, what do you think might be a great reason I can use to persuade Mr. Petzke that the cool treat party is a good idea?*

I heard great reasons! Students deserve rewards for great work. Frozen treats can be pretty healthy. When we talk about books, students may be motivated to read even more. Wow! These reasons are convincing. Watch as I develop one into a paragraph: The students in my class have worked very hard to read lots of cool books. I like to reward them for their hard work, and a cool treat is just a small reward that is still so much fun!

I am going to leave space for more reasons in my letter, but I want to close the letter. How does Andre close his letter in the mentor text? Andre uses the closing Sincerely yours. *That's a great closing for my letter, too. Watch as I write the closing, followed by a comma. Then my name goes on the next line.*

After writing: *Writers, this is a great start to a persuasive letter. Notice the letter features—a greeting, closing, and signature. The first paragraph includes an argument, and the second paragraph supports the argument with a reason. The letter is still polite and respectful.* Write these features on a chart for student reference.

WRITING and COACHING

We listed other reasons that support a cool treat party! Now it's your turn. Develop one of these reasons to add to our letter. Students can use one of the reasons listed in the focused minilesson or develop one of their own. More confident writers may want to write persuasive letters about other topics.

SHARING and REFLECTING

Writers, your letters are very convincing! You used the features of letters in your writing. You also crafted solid reasons to support your argument.

ASSESS THE LEARNING

As you assess students' letters, look for features of letters as well as persuasive elements. If students struggle, reteach persuasion and help students match reasons to arguments.

SELF-ASSESSMENT

SELF-ASSESSMENT

Pursuading with a Letter

	YES	NO
1. Did you include letter features—greeting, closing, and signature?	☐	☐
2. Did you craft a persuasive argument?	☐	☐
3. Do reasons support your argument?	☐	☐

PERSUADE

SUPPORTING AND EXTENDING

▸ Students can write persuasive letters to parents to ask for a special pet, a new bedtime, or permission to do something special with their families.

▸ Have students write letters to the school librarian, convincing him or her to purchase a particular book for the school library.

▸ Have students write letters that persuade others to eat healthy foods or go outside and play.

Book Review

A book review persuades readers with convincing reasons to read a certain book.

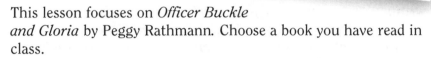

it was a good book but the End was. a little Yucke but I still liked it.

FEATURES

- Title and author
- Star rating that shows the writer's opinion
- Reasons that support the star rating
- Persuasive language

FOCUSED MINILESSON

This lesson focuses on *Officer Buckle and Gloria* by Peggy Rathmann. Choose a book you have read in class.

Writers, I loved Officer Buckle and Gloria *so much, I want to convince other people to read it! One way I do that is to write a persuasive book review.*

Show students a chart with this information: ★ = I did not like the book. ★★ = I liked it, but not much. ★★★ = I really liked it! ★★★★ = I loved it!

Watch as I write the title and author at the top of my paper: Officer Buckle and Gloria *by Peggy Rathmann.*

TURN &TALK *Partners, think together about the book. What star rating would you give the book? Why?*

Help students appreciate logical relationships between star ratings and reasons: *What if somebody gave this book two stars? Would you expect them to say something good about the book or something not so good? This is a book I really loved, and I want to share my opinion. Since I loved it so much, I'm putting four stars on my paper! A book review includes my opinion and reasons to persuade other readers to feel as I do about the book.*

TURN &TALK *I gave the book four stars. Talk with your partner. What reasons might support this rating?*

I'm with you! I had a lot of fun looking for the hidden clues in the illustrations. Plus, the ending message about teamwork really inspired me. Look at my persuasive language! I could have just said, "I like the clues." But instead I am writing: I had a lot of fun looking for the hidden clues in the illustrations. *That shows my reader how excited I am, and it might persuade my reader to get excited and read the book, too!*

Officer Buckle and Gloria
by Peggy Rathmann
★★★★

This is an amazing book! I had a lot of fun looking for the hidden clues in the illustrations! They are fun to discover. Plus, the ending message about the importance of teamwork really inspired me. Read Officer Buckle and Gloria today!

Modeled Writing

TURN &TALK *Writers, what might be a good ending for my review? Share an idea with your partner.*

Great suggestions! Since I really liked this book, I am going to end with my recommendation: Read <u>Officer Buckle and Gloria</u> today!

After writing, discuss the model and list the features on a chart: This is a very convincing book review! Let's take a look at its features. It has the book's title and author at the top. It has a star rating that shows my opinion. I gave reasons to support the rating, and I used persuasive words. I think my review will convince others to read this amazing book!

WRITING and COACHING

Writers, it's your turn to create persuasive book reviews. Write a review to persuade others to agree with your opinion about any book you have read. Be sure to give a star rating and reasons for your rating.

After writing: Provide students with an audience for their book reviews by having students share their reviews with a student who has not yet read the same book.

SHARING and REFLECTING

Writers, your book reviews are going to be great additions to our classroom library and will help build a community of readers! You each included a star rating that gives an at-a-glance rating, as well as a strong opening opinion with reasons to support it.

ASSESS THE LEARNING

Have students gather around the model and compare their work to the review you created. As necessary, reteach the difference between fact and opinion and ensure that students are giving opinions about books, not just retelling the plots.

SELF-ASSESSMENT

SELF-ASSESSMENT

Writing a Book Review

	YES	NO
1. Did you tell the title and the author's name?	☐	☐
2. Did you use a star rating to show your opinion?	☐	☐
3. Did you give at least 2 reasons for your opinion?	☐	☐

PERSUADE

SUPPORTING AND EXTENDING

▶ Have students write persuasive reviews of movies or television shows. Build excitement for writing reviews by having a "critics corner" where students can share reviews with classmates.

▶ Have students write a book review to help a kindergarten reading buddy pick out a great book.

▶ Read several nonfiction books about the same topic. Have students create persuasive book reviews explaining which book was the best for helping them learn about the topic.

VISUAL LITERACY

Persuasive Flyer

A flyer can persuade others by stating an opinion and giving strong reasons for it.

FEATURES

- Single page
- Attention-getting opinion statement
- Reasons to support the opinion
- Eye-catching art
- Inspiring conclusion

FOCUSED MINILESSON

Writers, today I'm going to make a flyer to convince as many people as I can to contribute to the food drive we are having for the local homeless shelter. I'm going to use exciting words to capture readers' attention and persuade them to contribute. Watch as I first write my opinion statement: Stop hunger now! *Did you notice that I wrote large letters at the top of the flyer? Large letters and exciting words capture attention. Now, I need to provide reasons. Persuasive writing needs to have reasons that support opinions. I will write:* Just one can of soup will make a great meal because it has vegetables and meats that are very nutritious.

TURN &TALK *Evaluate my reason. Is this reason strong enough to convince people to bring food for our food drive? Are there any other reasons that would be good additions to this flyer?*

As we continue to think of reasons why people should contribute, we also need to tell them where they can take the food. I am going to draw two children and use speech bubbles. That will capture attention. In the speech bubbles, I will write: Bring in cans! Please! *Because this is a flyer, I can use art along with my writing to grab attention! I also think our flyer will show up better if we add a red border around the edges and add some real labels from canned food.*

TURN &TALK *Evaluate my persuasive flyer. Do you think this flyer would convince someone to bring food to our food drive? What suggestions do you have to make it even better?*

I have one more important job to do. I need a conclusion that restates the goal and tries one more time to persuade a reader. Watch as I draw a text box at the bottom of the page.

Modeled Writing

Inside I'm writing: Take a bite out of hunger. Send some soup today! *See how this captures the idea in the main opinion but with different words? In my conclusion, I try to inspire my readers to take action!*

After writing: Let's look at this flyer and create a chart of its features. It has an exciting title, reasons why people should contribute, eye-catching art, and a strong conclusion that restates the goal.

TURN &TALK *If you were going to teach a friend how to create a persuasive flyer, what would you say?*

WRITING and COACHING

Now, it's your turn to work with a partner to create a flyer. Our homeless shelter needs food but they also need books, clothes, and toys. They even need toothpaste, shampoo, and hairbrushes. Decide with your partner which items you would like to encourage people to contribute. Share your ideas by creating a persuasive flyer.

SHARING and REFLECTING

Writers, today you remembered to use the features of a persuasive flyer. You gave your opinion and then added reasons and an inspiring conclusion to clarify the information. Your art really grabs attention and you had a terrific conclusion! Your flyers can really make a difference by persuading others to help!

ASSESS THE LEARNING

Assess which students have included all of the features of a persuasive flyer. Reteach as necessary, using persuasive flyers for mentor texts.

SELF-ASSESSMENT

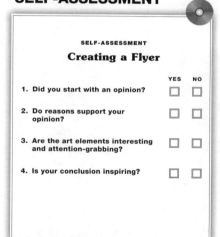

SELF-ASSESSMENT
Creating a Flyer

	YES	NO
1. Did you start with an opinion?	☐	☐
2. Do reasons support your opinion?	☐	☐
3. Are the art elements interesting and attention-grabbing?	☐	☐
4. Is your conclusion inspiring?	☐	☐

PERSUADE

SUPPORTING AND EXTENDING

▸ Ask students to create persuasive flyers to promote their favorite books. Share flyers with the class next door. Then ask the other class to create flyers of their own to send back to your class.

▸ Ask students to create persuasive flyers about their favorite pets. Put them in a binder to be shared in the reading corner.

▸ Have pairs of students create persuasive flyers about recycling. Distribute the flyers to other classrooms.

Graphic Organizer

A graphic organizer shows both an argument and reasons to support it.

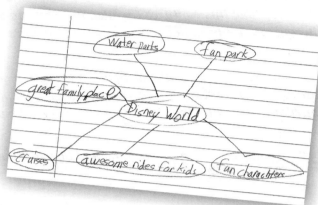

FEATURES

- Title
- Boxes and connecting lines
- Persuasive argument with reasons

FOCUSED MINILESSON

This lesson focuses on the best place to visit. Adapt the sequence for content in your classroom.

Writers, today I want to persuade you to visit one of my favorite places—the beach! I am going to show my argument and reasons in a graphic organizer. Creating a visual like a graphic organizer shows connections between ideas and helps me organize my thoughts.

Watch as I write a title at the top of the page: The Beach: The Best Place to Visit! *That title definitely prepares readers for my message! Now it's time to write my persuasive argument. I'm writing it in a box:* You should visit the beach as soon—and as often—as possible.

Notice that this is a strong statement. It tells readers what they should do. Now comes the part where I need to convince readers with strong reasons.

TURN &TALK *Share with your thinking partner one reason you think might convince someone to head for the beach.*

I heard some very convincing reasons. Watch as I write one reason in a box: Sand and water are great toys! You can build and sculpt all day long. *To show the connection between ideas, I'm drawing a line between the boxes. Now the organizer shows that this argument supports my opinion about the beach. I heard another great reason, that beaches are great places to search for treasures.*

TURN &TALK *Partners, think together. What should I do next with my graphic organizer?*

Watch as I follow your advice! I'm writing the reason in a box: Beaches are great places to search for treasure. Who knows what will wash up on the sand? *Then, to show the relationship between the argument and reason, I'll draw a connecting line.*

The Beach: The Best Place to Visit!

You should visit the beach as soon—and as often—as possible.

Sand and water are great toys! You can build and sculpt all day long.

Beaches are great places to search for treasure. Who knows what will wash up on the sand?

After writing, create a features list with students based on the graphic organizer: *Let's take a look at the graphic organizer. A title tells the topic. The persuasive statement, or argument, is in a large box. Boxes with supporting reasons are connected to the main argument.*

WRITING and COACHING

Writers, it's your turn to create your own persuasive graphic organizer. Convince the class to visit a place you think is great. It can be somewhere you have been or somewhere you want to go. Make sure that your reasons are persuasive! Writers who struggle may benefit from having a form to use to note reasons.

SHARING and REFLECTING

Writers, these organizers do such a great job of showing relationships between the argument and the reasons. Your arguments are convincing. Now I want to visit all sorts of places. That means you were persuasive!

ASSESS THE LEARNING

Have students gather around the graphic organizer you created to compare their work to the model. As necessary, reteach how to use strong arguments to convince someone of a position.

SELF-ASSESSMENT

PERSUADE

SUPPORTING AND EXTENDING

▸ Have students create persuasive graphic organizers on a unit of study, such as Most Exciting Planet, Best Environment to Live In, Most Important Insect, Best Invention, Most Daring Explorer, and so on.

▸ Have students create graphic organizers designed to persuade another class to read a particular book. Have readers note whether they were persuaded or not.

▸ Have students use graphic organizers to explore their thinking before writing a persuasive letter or argument.

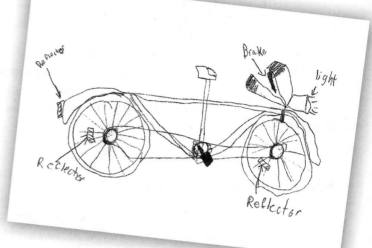

Investigation

An investigation combines convincing words and supporting pictures in a powerful layout.

FEATURES

- Headings and text boxes
- Two facing pages form a "spread"
- Labels and captions

FOCUSED MINILESSON

This lesson focuses on the issue of bike safety. Use the lesson format and adapt it to other content you are teaching.

Writers, after taking a course on bicycle safety at the community center, I'm convinced that everyone should learn the rules of bike safety. Now I want to convince other people of the same thing. I know I can make them feel just as sure about this as I do! I'm going to create a persuasive investigation.

First, I want to take a look at an investigation to get an idea of what it might look like. Turn to page 22 in the *Big Book of Mentor Texts. Let's take a look at this investigation. It has a clear persuasive message: Make some healthy switches to have a healthy life! But how does this investigation make the message clear?*

TURN &TALK *Partners, think together. What do you notice in this investigation that makes the persuasive message stand out?*

You've identified many great features! A text box has the main message right at the top. Then each part of the argument has a box with text and photographs that capture our attention. A text box on the bottom sums up the message. The message is powerful, and it's lively and interesting, too.

Taking a cue from the mentor text, watch as I title my investigation: Bike Safety Is Important for All.

TURN &TALK *Writers, why do you think that bike safety is so important? Describe a persuasive idea with your partner.*

Yes, it's true that many children are injured in bike accidents every year because they don't wear a helmet. That's something you would learn about in a course on bike safety.

Modeled Writing

After writing, list features of an investigation as you point them out on the model: *Let's take a look at the investigation so far. A persuasive title sets the stage to convince our readers. I've started with a text box and illustration with one reason that supports the argument. We can definitely add more, but it's a great place to begin!*

WRITING and COACHING

It's your turn to add some reasons! Work with partners to add reasons to the investigation. What makes bike safety so important? Have students work independently or with partners to create reasons to add to the investigation. They might also add visual elements such as bikes, bike helmets, and reflectors or reflective clothing that will bring the issue to life and convince their readers.

SHARING and REFLECTING

Writers, we've created an amazing investigation. It shows information about bike safety and sends the message that bike safety is important for everyone. Your use of text boxes, illustrations, headings, and color makes the valuable safety information pop from the page!

ASSESS THE LEARNING

Assess which students need additional support to lay out ideas, combine pictures with text, and use features such as titles and colors to support ideas. If necessary, review how to support a persuasive argument.

SELF-ASSESSMENT

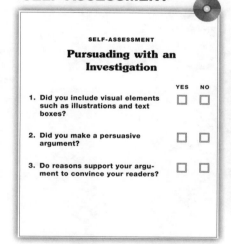

SELF-ASSESSMENT

Pursuading with an Investigation

	YES	NO
1. Did you include visual elements such as illustrations and text boxes?	☐	☐
2. Did you make a persuasive argument?	☐	☐
3. Do reasons support your argument to convince your readers?	☐	☐

PERSUADE

SUPPORTING AND EXTENDING

▶ Have students create persuasive investigations based on other topics, such as using recyclable bags for lunches, adopting pets from the animal shelter, or joining certain clubs or activities at school.

▶ Taking a cue from the mentor text, have students create their own "Switch It Up" investigations to persuade others to adopt healthy habits.

▶ Have students think of historical figures they've studied in class or learned about on their own, such as George Washington, Betsy Ross, Martin Luther King, Jr., explorers, scientists, inventors, and so on. Have them create investigations that share why one or more of these people would be the most fascinating to meet.

Response Writing Projects

Responses express a factual, critical, or personal response to a prompt or text. Students might be asked to respond to a piece of literature by writing or drawing what they liked or disliked about it, what they want to ask the author, what they think about a character, or what they learned from a piece of nonfiction. Academic prompts might ask students to answer questions or write about what they did or observed during a class activity. Responses can take many forms such as learning logs, sketches, diagrams, descriptions, written reflections, quick writes, book reviews, and reaction pieces. The writer responds to the piece of literature or prompt by expressing opinions backed up with examples from the text or facts.

. . . .

CONTENTS

EXTENDED WRITING UNIT

▸ Class Project: Poster Responses to *Black Whiteness: Admiral Byrd Alone in the Antarctic* by Robert Burleigh (about 6 days)

▸ Individual Project: Poster Response to a Book (about 5 days)

POWER WRITES

▸ Response to a Poem

▸ Fact/Opinion Chart

▸ Two-Word Strategy

▸ Friendly Letter

▸ Information Equation

▸ Sketch to Stretch

▸ Fact-And-Response Grid

▸ Investigation

The Big Picture: Class and Individual Projects

During the *class project*, students create poster responses to *Black Whiteness: Admiral Byrd Alone in the Antarctic* by Robert Burleigh. The mentor text "Response to *Diary of a Worm*" acts as a model to show students the structure and features of a response. Note that the mentor text is a response to *Diary of a Worm* by Doreen Cronin, not a response to *Black Whiteness*. This is to ensure that students will actively respond to the book they have read and not just copy the mentor text directly. You may want to read different books and create a different mentor text to fit with content you are teaching. No matter which book you choose for students to respond to, allow time to read it aloud to them before writing time. Note that students do not need to read *Diary of a Worm* to understand the mentor response. Students observe features in the mentor response that will help them write their own responses. Then they reflect on *Black Whiteness*, talk about it with a partner, and draft, revise, and publish their responses. Students share their thinking about response writing with classmates and display the published responses in the classroom library.

During their *individual project*, students review the features of a response, choose a book to respond to, and draft, edit, and publish their own response. Writing partners share ideas, read each other's drafts, and give feedback to improve response qualities. Students share their published responses with partners, check the features chart to see what features they included, and display their finished responses.

CLASS PROJECT		
Session	**Focused Minilesson**	**Writing and Coaching**	**Sharing and Reflecting**
1	Introduce response writing; read book for pre-assessment response	Draft pre-assessment response	Share your response with your partner. How are your responses the same and different?
2	Study "Response to *Diary of a Worm*"; list features; read *Black Whiteness*; write response title; think about likes/dislikes	Begin drafting what you like and dislike about the book; include specific details	Share your draft with your partner. Did you like or dislike any of the same things?
3	Study "Response to *Diary of a Worm*"; focus on connections; learn to use linking words (*and, then, because*)	Draft connections; use linking words	Share your draft with your partner. Did you make any similar connections? What linking words did your partner use?
4	Study "Response to *Diary of a Worm*"; focus on endings, feeling/describing words	Write an ending	Share your ending with your partner. What would you say to teach someone how to write a great response?
5	Study "Response to *Diary of a Worm*"; focus on revising and editing	Edit and revise response	Share your draft with your partner. Point out a change you made. How did it make your work better?
6	Learn how to create a response poster	Plan and publish response poster	How are the responses similar and different? What generalizations can you make about good response writing?

INDIVIDUAL PROJECT		
Session	**Focused Minilesson**	**Writing and Coaching**	**Sharing and Reflecting**
7	Review response features; choose book; focus on title, likes/dislikes, details	Draft, revise, and edit reasons why you liked/disliked the book	Read what you wrote to your partner. What response features did you include in your writing?
8	Focus on writing connections; learn to use linking words	Draft connections using linking words; reread, revise, edit	Compare connections. What linking words did you and partner use?
9	Focus on endings; learn to use powerful adjectives and exclamation points	Draft ending with powerful adjectives; reread, revise, edit	Share draft with partner. What words did your partner use to make the ending exciting?
10	Review editing and publishing strategies for poster responses	Edit final draft; publish text on poster	Share what you've published. What edits are you most proud of?
11	Study sample posters; focus on illustrations	Finish publishing by adding illustrations	Share; celebrate. What features made your responses wonderful?

Other Topics and Forms for Response Writing

Although this model project uses poster responses to books as a springboard for teaching response writing, the teaching process here can be adapted to many other response topics and forms. The Power Writes in this section will give you ideas for several such adaptations in addition to those that follow.

Possible Topics

Topics may correlate with content in your science and social studies standards, current events, or class interests.

What do you think about this book?
What did you like and dislike about the book?
What connections can you make to the poem?
What did you learn from that part of the book?
What are you wondering about what you just read?
What would you like to ask the author?
What is the big idea in this book?
How do the illustrations support the text?
Would you recommend this book/movie/restaurant/TV show? Why?
What was the best part of the field trip?
How did you solve that problem?
What did you learn from the experiment/activity?
What is your opinion of this book/picture/piece of music?
How are these two things similar? How are they different?
Who does this character remind you of?
What do you think the main character should do?
What is the problem in this story and how is it solved?
Why is this book worth reading?
Do you agree with the author? Why or why not?

Possible Forms

Some of these forms are invariably responses (like book reviews or reaction pieces) while others (like letters or diagrams) can be used for a variety of purposes, including responses.

Reading journal	Letter
Two-column journal	Poster
Interactive journal	Summary
Learning log	Written reflection
Observation log	Writer's notebook
Illustration	Quick write
Description	Book review
Labeled diagram	Reaction piece
Venn diagram	Poem

Gathering Your Materials

You will not need to assemble research materials for this unit because students will be writing responses to books they have read. However, you will need to have several books available for students to respond to.

For Session 1, you will need to provide or create an example of a poster response such as a poster that reviews a book, movie, show, or musical event. You will also need to choose a piece of literature to read to students for the pre-assessment response. The example suggested in Session 1 is a short story from Arnold Lobel's *Mouse Tales*. Be sure to allow time to read the book with your students before the class session.

For the *class project,* students will read and respond to *Black Whiteness: Admiral Byrd Alone in the Antarctic* by Robert Burleigh. Be sure to allow time to read *Black Whiteness* to your students during Session 2. Students will also read the mentor text, "Response to *Diary of a Worm*" from the *Big Book of Mentor Texts.* You will want to have *Diary of a Worm* by Doreen Cronin available for students to read. Note that you may want to choose different books to fit with content your class is studying. If you use different books, be sure to use one of the books to create your own response mentor text for students to analyze and identify the features of a good response to literature.

For the *individual project,* students will respond to a nonfiction book of their choice. Have students select a title from books that you have gathered or a title from their personal independent reading selections. Make sure they have chosen this piece of literature ahead of time and reread it during independent reading time so that they are ready to begin their responses.

Focusing on Standards

This extended writing unit is designed to teach students about the form and content of response writing as they apply basic writing strategies. Each of the lessons provides you with suggested demonstrations, but you may wish to tailor your instruction based on the common needs of your own students. The pre-assessment from Session 1 will help you identify these needs.

Before introducing the unit, carefully review the list below so you can keep the lesson objectives in mind as you teach, coach, and monitor students' growth as writers of responses.

KEY SKILLS AND UNDERSTANDINGS: RESPONSE WRITING GRADE 2
Purpose
• Understands the purpose for writing a response piece
Ideas/Research
• Responds directly to a piece of literature or prompt
• Expresses an opinion (e.g., likes or dislikes)
• Supports the response with details from the text or facts
• Includes wonderings about the piece of literature or prompt
• Makes a personal connection to the piece of literature or prompt
Organization/Text Features
• Includes a title that reflects the purpose or task
• Uses text features that match the purpose or task
• May include illustrations that support the response
Language/Style
• Shows a clear point of view
• May express personal opinion or feelings
Conventions and Presentation
• Uses a variety of sentence structures: declarative, interrogative, imperative; simple, compound
• Leaves spaces between words
• Uses spelling strategies to help with spelling
• Uses capital letters to start sentences
• Uses appropriate end punctuation

The list on the previous page is the basis for both the Individual Evaluation Record and the Ongoing Monitoring Sheet shown in Figure 5.1. Both forms can be found in the Resources section at the back of this book and also on the *Resources* CD-ROM. Use the Individual Evaluation Record if you want to keep separate records on individual students. The Ongoing Monitoring Sheet gives you a simple mechanism for recording information on all your students as you move around the class, evaluating their work in progress. Use this information to adapt instruction and session length as needed.

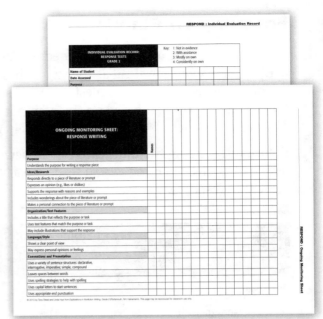

Figure 5.1

You will also use the Ongoing Monitoring Sheet and/or the Individual Evaluation Record at the end of the unit to record students' growth as writers after comparing their published work from the individual project with the pre-assessment they will complete in Session 1 of the class project.

Planning and Facilitating the Unit

Students will need preparation, coaching, prompting, and support as they move through this extended writing unit. Use the following tips and strategies as needed to ensure each child's success.

Before the Unit:

▸ When planning your teaching, bear in mind that each session in this unit is designed to be completed in a day. However, you will likely find that your students need more time for certain activities. Take the time you need to adequately respond to the unique needs of your students.

▸ Obtain or create an example of a poster response such as a poster that reviews a book, movie, show, or musical event.

▸ Begin building background knowledge about response writing in general as well as the books students will respond to at least a week in advance. Shared reading, guided reading, and read-aloud experiences as well as group discussions will ensure that students have read the books and are well prepared to write responses.

▸ As you share responses with students, be sure to highlight the purpose of the response, details or facts the writer provides from the piece of literature or prompt, connections the writer makes to the piece of literature or prompt, wonderings, and illustrations that support the writer's point of view.

▸ You may want to use texts other than *Mouse Tales, Diary of a Worm,* and *Black Whiteness* to fit with content you are teaching. If you choose different books, be sure to use one of the books to create your own response mentor text for students to analyze and identify the features of a good response to literature. No matter which books you choose, be sure you have set aside time for reading the texts with your students.

During the Class Project:

▸ Begin each session with a focused minilesson to demonstrate traits in response writing. The mentor text "Response to *Diary of a Worm*" acts as the model to show students the structure and features of responses. You may wish to use other mentor texts to assist you with your demonstrations.

▸ Help students get started by suggesting how to organize their notebook: title page followed by pages for likes, dislikes, wonderings, and connections.

▸ If students struggle as they write their responses, encourage them to draw their response first (what they like, dislike, wonder, or connect to) and then add a sentence to their picture.

▸ Begin a chart with words students will need to help them write their responses. Use the mentor text to point out words and phrases such as *favorite, like, illustration,* and *because.* You can add to this list throughout the unit.

▶ As students work independently on their writing, note those who are struggling and bring them together in small groups for additional support. If they are struggling to write details, model how to make a like or dislike more specific. Pose questions to help them make connections. Help them expand their thinking to write more than one sentence for their ending.

▶ Provide a minilesson on different types of connections: text-to-self, text-to-text, and text-to-world. Work with students to reread *Black Whiteness* and create a chart with examples of each type of connection.

▶ If you have English language learners struggling to write in English, suggest that they draw their response to the book and add labels as they are able.

▶ Make a short checklist of conventions for students to focus on as they edit their work. If students are struggling, suggest they focus on editing their work for only one convention on the list at a time.

▶ When students publish their posters, help early emergent writers so that readers can understand their finished work. If they have used pictures to respond or spelling that cannot be understood, you can use sticky notes to write their thoughts and attach to the bottom of their work.

▶ Students who seem very confident and who have clearly grasped all of the concepts taught so far can be brought together in a small group to extend their understanding to more challenging work, such as making deeper connections and using more describing words.

▸ Students who complete their responses early can work on adding illustrations that support their text. They can be partners for students who are still writing.

▸ Although the lessons provide suggested demonstrations for each session, you may wish to tailor your instruction to meet the common needs of your students. The Ongoing Monitoring Sheet, together with the Individual Evaluation Record, will help you keep track of each student's unique needs. Refer to the section on assessment and ongoing monitoring on page xxx in the introduction to this book for further information.

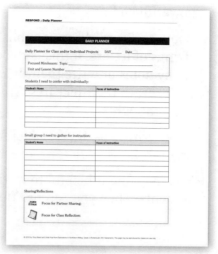

Figure 5.2

▸ Use the Daily Planner (Figure 5.2) to plan your own class projects for future explorations based on the needs of your students.

During the Individual Project:

▸ Continue to use the Ongoing Monitoring Sheet and the Individual Evaluation Record to identify topics you'll want to address in the focused minilesson that begins each session. Continue to use the Daily Planner to lay out future explorations based on student needs.

▸ Have students select a nonfiction title from literature that you have gathered or from their personal independent reading selections. Make sure they have pre-selected and read this book ahead of time so that they are ready to begin their responses.

▸ Post the word chart from the class project so students can see the words and use the chart as they draft and revise. Continue to add words and phrases to the chart as they come up in the individual project sessions.

▸ Have students share their ideas with a partner before writing. Have them reread their writing to make sure it makes sense and includes enough detail.

▸ To encourage and assist students with the revising process, create a revision checklist that you add to each day.

▸ Provide support for English language learners and students with limited oral language through focused questioning and models. Prompt them to express their ideas, and record what they say so they can copy correct sentences.

▸ If students are struggling with the editing process, provide a short checklist with one or two conventions particular to their needs.

▸ If students are ready for more challenging work, have them create a chart that categorizes adjectives by degree of positive or negative connotation. Encourage them to make different types of connections and to write powerful endings.

▸ Some early writers may publish their responses using only pictures or strings of letters. If this is the case, record their thinking for them on sticky notes or write their dictation directly onto their published pieces underneath their pictures. This will ensure that others will be able to read their thoughts.

▸ Have writing partners conference with each other often in order to check one another's work for sense and clarity.

▸ You may find it helpful to work on your own response along with your students. Then you can use this model as an example during think-alouds.

After the Unit:

▸ Be sure to give students opportunities to share and celebrate their individual writing projects.

▸ Distribute copies of the Student Self-Reflection Sheet (on the *Resources* CD-ROM). Students will benefit greatly from the chance to reflect on their progress during the unit and to hear their classmates' feedback.

▸ Compare students' final writing products with their pre-assessments to evaluate their growth as writers of responses.

▸ Look at common needs of the class and address these when planning future explorations on response writing, or through the Power Writes.

▸ Reflect on the strengths and challenges of implementing this series of lessons. How might it be adjusted to maximize student learning?

SESSION 1
Immersion and Pre-Assessment

Students are introduced to response writing, then write a simple response to a book for the pre-assessment.

MATERIALS
- A book to read aloud to evoke student response
- Examples of reviews (reviews of books, movies, music, and so on)
- Paper and pencils

FOCUSED MINILESSON *(prewriting)*
20 MINUTES

- Introduce the unit: *Over the next several days, we will learn about and practice a special kind of nonfiction writing called* response writing. *When we write responses, we tell what we think and feel about something we have read, seen, or heard, such as books, movies, plays, or music. Response writing is important because when people read a writer's response, they may decide to read the same book or to see the same movie!*

- Discuss a popular movie, book, or television show that you know will evoke strong responses in your students. Ask them to share what they thought of it. Explain that they just responded to something by telling what they thought or felt when they read, saw, or heard it: *Our responses came easily and naturally, didn't they? It isn't hard to say what you think and feel!*

- Provide or create an example of a poster response such as a poster that reviews a book, movie, show, or musical event. Point out that there are many formats for responses and that children are going to have the chance to create their own response poster about a book you will read together.

  TURN &TALK *What does it mean to create a response to a book? Share with your partner a characteristic of a response.*

- *You really paid attention to the responses we looked at! Telling what you liked or didn't like about the book is a response, because it lets other people know your opinion.*

- Read aloud a book to the class, such as a short story from Arnold Lobel's *Mouse Tales*. Choose a text that will evoke strong responses in your students.

  TURN &TALK *What would you include in a response to this book? Turn to a partner and share your response.*

- *We just responded by talking with each other, but we can write our responses, too. We'll do that next!*

TIP To help students connect meaningfully with the purpose of response writing, give them personal examples of how you use responses. *Sometimes, if I am thinking of seeing a new movie, I will go online and read a few responses called* reviews *that tell what the writers thought of the movie. Or, I might look at the newspaper to check out the movie reviews. If there are a lot of good reviews, then I may decide to go and see the movie.*

WRITING and COACHING *(drafting)*
10 MINUTES

■ Direct students to write a response about the book that you read aloud: *Remember some of the things you talked about with your partner, and put those in your written response.*

■ If you find that certain students are having trouble remembering the story, pull them together in a small group and have a quick "book talk" to refresh their memories.

■ Circulate around the room while students write, but try not to offer too much direct support for the pre-assessment. Your goal is to find out what students do and don't know about writing a response.

SHARING and REFLECTING
10 MINUTES

TURN &TALK *Share your response with your partner. Compare and contrast your responses. Did you notice anything similar about them?*

■ Help students reflect on the purpose of a response: *How is this kind of writing similar to or different from other writing we have done?* Invite volunteers to share their ideas. When you give students time to reflect on what they've learned, they can begin to apply that understanding to their own writing.

■ Explain that you're going to put this first group of responses in students' writing folders and that students may revisit them later in their exploration of responses.

■ After class, evaluate each student's writing using the Ongoing Monitoring Sheet (in the Resources section and also on the *Resources* CD-ROM). Use the results to revise instruction and personalize the lessons in this unit. If you want to keep individual records on students, use the Individual Evaluation Record in the Resources section and on the CD-ROM. Do not make corrections or marks on students' work.

TIP for Conferring with Individuals and Small Groups

If students struggle as they write their responses, point out that most writers struggle when they are trying out a new kind of writing. Reiterate that this first draft is just a way for them to show what they already know about writing a response. If you have beginning or early intermediate English language learners struggling to write in English, suggest they draw their response to the book and include labels as they are able.

SESSION 2
Drafting a Response

Students analyze features of the mentor text, then begin to draft their own responses to a book they read together.

MATERIALS
- *Big Book of Mentor Texts:* "Response to *Diary of a Worm*," pages 44–46
- *Diary of a Worm* by Doreen Cronin
- *Black Whiteness: Admiral Byrd Alone in the Antarctic* by Robert Burleigh
- Research notebooks
- Pencils

TIP In the interest of time, you should plan to read *Black Whiteness* aloud during your reading block, not during the twenty minutes allotted for the minilesson. As you read the book, encourage students to note things that they like and don't like that they can include in their response writing.

FOCUSED MINILESSON *(prewriting)*
20 MINUTES

■ Introduce the session: *In this session, we will begin drafting our responses to a book we will read together. First, we will look at a great example of this new kind of writing so we can get an idea of how to write responses of our own.*

■ Display the mentor text and the book *Diary of a Worm.* Explain that the person who wrote this response read *Diary of a Worm* and responded to it. Invite volunteers to predict what they think *Diary of a Worm* may be about. Then read the mentor text aloud.

TURN &TALK *Talk about the response with your partner. What did you notice about it? Are there features in this response that we could apply to our own response writing?*

■ As you highlight features in the mentor text, lead students to understand that responses often begin with the book's title and reasons the writer liked or didn't like the book: *The writer tells us several things she likes. She writes about how funny the story is and includes examples of some of the funniest parts. Then she mentions not liking a few of the diary entries.* List features on chart paper: *This chart will guide us as we write our responses.*

■ Explain that students will get to write what they think of a new book. Display the book *Black Whiteness* or another book of choice, and remind students that this is the book you read aloud during the reading block earlier. Ask students to remember what they did and did not like about the book.

TURN &TALK *What did you like about the book? Was there anything you didn't like? List some ideas that you might include in your writing today.*

Features of a Great Response

It includes the title and author.

It tells what the writer likes about the book.

It may tell what the writer dislikes about the book.

■ Explain that over the next few days, students will draft their responses in their notebooks and then turn them into posters: *When visitors come, they can view our posters to find out our thoughts and feelings about this book!*

■ Help students get started by suggesting how to organize their notebooks: *Your readers need to know the book you're responding to, so write the title on one page. On the next page, write what you liked about the book. If there was anything you didn't like, begin another page and include your dislikes there. This way, you will have enough space if you think of more details to add later.*

TIP You may wish to begin a chart with words students will need to know how to spell as they write their responses. Words such as *like, favorite, because, illustration,* and so on are often included in responses. Ask students what other words might be helpful to know as they write their responses today. You can add to this word bank chart throughout the class project.

WRITING and COACHING *(drafting)*
20 MINUTES

■ Have students begin their drafts. Early finishers can work on pictures for their responses: *When you finish, start thinking about a picture you might want to include on your poster. You can practice your drawing in the extra space on your title page.*

■ To facilitate the revision and editing process that comes later, have students write on lined paper, leaving at least one blank line between each line of text.

■ Some students may struggle with the difference between a response and a summary. You might pull these students together in a small group for another look at the mentor text and a quick review of the features chart.

TIP for Conferring with Individuals and Small Groups

If students are struggling to write specific details, bring them together in a small group. Use the mentor text to help them recognize details. *The writer of this response didn't just say she liked the pictures. She gave examples and wrote that they were colorful and funny.* Then page through *Black Whiteness* and ask students to pinpoint a few things they liked or didn't like and the reasons why.

SHARING and REFLECTING
10 MINUTES

TURN &TALK *Share your draft with your partner. Did you like or dislike any of the same things? Compare your ideas.*

■ Give students time to reflect on how their writing was similar to or different from the other responses they heard today. If students are given opportunities to compare and contrast their writing with their peers, they can expand their thinking as writers and build a strong community in the process.

SESSION 3
Drafting and Revising

Students analzye the mentor text to note connections the author makes, then add connections to their own responses.

MATERIALS
- *Big Book of Mentor Texts:* "Response to *Diary of a Worm*," pages 44–46
- Features chart from Session 2
- *Black Whiteness: Admiral Byrd Alone in the Antarctic* by Robert Burleigh
- Research notebooks
- Pencils

TIP Making connections is a reading strategy that students should practice before they attempt to add this feature to their response. To assist students with making different types of connections (text-to-self, text-to-text, and text-to-world), review the strategy during shared reading time. Reread *Black Whiteness* and have students help you create a list of examples of each type of connection.

Features of a Great Response

It includes the title and author.

It tells what the writer likes about the book.

It may tell what the writer dislikes about the book.

It may tell connections that the writer made to the book.

FOCUSED MINILESSON *(drafting, revising)*
20 MINUTES

■ Focus the learning: *Our features chart is looking good! In this session, we'll talk about another feature of a great response and we'll add it to our work from the last session.*

■ Display the mentor text: *Listen as I reread this response so we can get some more ideas about what we can include in our responses.*

TURN &TALK *In addition to writing about what she liked and didn't like, what else did you notice that this writer included in her response? Talk it over with your partner.*

■ Explain that in this session you will focus on one feature they noticed—how response writers sometimes include different connections to the book. Display the chart you began in the previous session and add this feature.

■ Ask students to identify what words the writer used in the mentor text to write her connections *(this book reminded me of . . .)*. Then do a minilesson on common linking words to help students express their connections clearly: *When we write connections we make to a book, we often have more than one thought about the connection. We may want to explain why we connected to the book in this way or tell more about our connection to give our readers details. To show how these thoughts are linked together, we can use special linking words.* Write *and, then,* and *because* on the board.

■ Ask volunteers to share a few connections they made to *Black Whiteness.* Use one of the examples to model how to use *because* to link thoughts together with an example, such as: Black Whiteness *reminded me of the book* I, Matthew Henson (by Carole Boston Weatherford) *because both books are about brave people who survived in very cold places.* Use other examples of connections students made to model how to use *and* and *then* to link together related thoughts.

TURN &TALK *What connections will you include in your response? Tell your partner what you are thinking of writing. Can you name a linking word you will use in your writing?*

■ Tell students that they will add to the responses they started in the last session: *Today, begin a new page in your notebook and add connections that you made to the book there. Remember, there are many ways to connect to a book.*

WRITING and COACHING *(drafting)*
20 MINUTES

■ Have students add connections to their drafts. When they are finished, encourage them to read back through their work to ensure it makes sense and includes enough detail.

■ As you circulate around the room, support students who are struggling by asking leading questions: *Does this book remind you of any other stories you have read or seen in a movie or on television? Was there ever a time in your life when you were in a very cold place?*

■ To strengthen your community of writers, have early finishers help other students with writing their connections.

SHARING and REFLECTING
10 MINUTES

TURN & TALK *Share your draft with your partner. Did you make any similar connections? Name linking words you heard as your partner read his or her work.*

■ Discuss some connections students included and call out some examples of masterful use of linking words.

■ Then draw students' attention to the features chart. Help students sum up what they have learned by reflecting on the features of a response. Giving students opportunities to reflect will help them begin to internalize the features of response writing.

TIP for Conferring with Individuals and Small Groups

Pose specific questions to assist students who are struggling to write a connection. You may be able to use their likes or dislikes to help them make a connection: *I see you didn't like that Admiral Byrd got sick, but you liked how the men came and helped take care of Admiral Byrd. Have you ever been sick? Maybe you could write about a time when someone helped you get better. That would be a great connection to the book!*

TIP If time permits, you may wish to have volunteers share their drafts with the class. Encourage other students to make positive comments about the writing. As students are encouraged to recognize and comment about details in other students' writing, it builds awareness and confidence and will give them the opportunity to support others as they learn ideas to incorporate into their own writing.

SESSION 4
Drafting the Ending

Students finish drafting their responses, focusing on strong endings that summarize their thoughts and feelings.

MATERIALS

- *Big Book of Mentor Texts:* "Response to *Diary of a Worm*," pages 44–46
- Features chart
- *Black Whiteness* by Robert Burleigh
- Research notebooks
- Pencils

Features of a Great Response

It includes the title and author.

It tells what the writer likes about the book.

It may tell what the writer dislikes about the book.

It may tell connections that the writer made to the book.

It has an ending that summarizes what the writer thought of the book.

TIP Have students help you create a list of feeling words to use in a positive review, such as *fantastic, exciting,* and so on. Then have them create a list of words to use if they didn't like what they reviewed, such as *boring, horrible,* and so on. Encourage students to try out new words in their writing.

FOCUSED MINILESSON *(drafting)*
20 MINUTES

- Introduce the session: *You have done a terrific job writing your responses to* Black Whiteness. *In this session, we are going to learn how we can write great endings for our responses.*

- Show students the mentor text. Reread the last paragraph to focus students on how the writer ended her response to *Diary of a Worm.*

  TURN &TALK *What did you notice about how the writer ended her response? Why do you think it is important to include a strong ending? Talk about the ending with your partner.*

- Sum up the thinking you heard: *Those are very smart details to notice about the ending. It does give a summary of what the writer thought of the book. It also tells that the writer recommended the book.*

- Display the *Features of a Great Response* chart. Add the ending/summary to the chart.

- Provide students with a modeled writing experience to help them see the different ways they can end a review. For example: *I really loved this book. At the end of my response, I want to make sure the people who read the response understand that. I will write a sentence that sums up what I thought of the book:* This book was excellent. Excellent *is a strong word that will tell readers what I thought of the book. Then I could finish with a sentence or two that says something more to my readers. I know they are reading this review to see if they might be interested in also reading the book, so I will write a sentence that addresses this:* You will really enjoy reading this exciting account of survival!

  TURN &TALK *Tell your partner how you are thinking of ending your response.*

WRITING and COACHING *(drafting)*
20 MINUTES

■ Tell students that they will add an ending to their responses. Have students begin a new page in their notebook and write their endings.

■ As students finish, remind them to read back their work to make sure it makes sense and says what they want it to say.

■ Encourage early finishers to use the extra time to go back and check that they included enough detail when they wrote about their likes, dislikes, and connections.

SHARING and REFLECTING
10 MINUTES

TURN &TALK *Read and show your partner what you wrote today. Did your partner's ending help you think of another way you could end your response?*

■ Give students a sense of success by praising them for their effort: *You must be so proud of your responses. You have worked really hard, and the endings you wrote today are marvelous!*

TURN &TALK *Imagine you had to teach someone how to write a great response. Tell your partner what you would say.*

■ As volunteers share their ideas, reinforce their responses by directing the class to the features listed on the features chart.

TIP for Conferring with Individuals and Small Groups

If some students are struggling to write more than one sentence for their endings, help them expand their thinking and include another interesting sentence: *I see you really loved this book. Would you recommend this book for others to read? You would. Why is that? That is a wonderful reason to recommend this book. Perhaps you could add another sentence to your ending about how readers will enjoy reading this suspenseful and true story.*

TIP Before students share their writing, take the time to reiterate why it is so important for writers to share their work with each other: *Writers can inspire each other when they share their work. A great idea may pop into your head as you listen to your classmates share their writing.*

SESSION 5
Revising and Editing a Response

Students revise their responses to include the appropriate features. Then they edit their work, focusing on proper use of conventions.

MATERIALS

- *Big Book of Mentor Texts:* "Response to *Diary of a Worm*," pages 44–46
- Features chart
- *Black Whiteness: Admiral Byrd Alone in the Antarctic* by Robert Burleigh
- Research notebooks
- White poster paper
- Pencils and markers

TIP If you have the time, you may want to take this opportunity to elaborate and do a quick minilesson on editing for a particular convention that your students really need to focus on, such as using uppercase letters in titles.

FOCUSED MINILESSON *(editing)*
10 MINUTES

- Focus the learning: *We're almost ready to publish our responses. But first we need to make sure they are the best that they can be. In this session we'll revise and edit so our responses can shine!*

- Display the mentor text. Point out that before this response was published, the writer went through an editing process to make sure we could understand the writing.

  TURN &TALK *What can we do today to make sure our responses are the best they can be?*

- Use students' responses to focus on editing for a few particular conventions appropriate to the needs of your students—such as including appropriate end punctuation and checking for the correct use of capital letters.

- Ask volunteers to share strategies about how they will check spelling, and praise them for their resourcefulness: *Yes—great thinking! You can ask a friend to help with spelling or to help you edit your sentences for capital letters and punctuation. You can also use our word wall and your word lists.*

- Use this opportunity to also focus on the features chart: *Let's take a look at this chart. We want our responses to include what we like about the book, what we don't like, and our connections. I can use this chart like a checklist. I reread my draft to be sure I've included each part. And, if I've included each part, I reread to check that each part is complete and detailed enough.*

- Share a revision example with students: *I wrote that I like* Black Whiteness *because Admiral Byrd survives in dangerous conditions. That's a great detail! But I can make it even more detailed:* Can you imagine the air around you so cold that it could shatter plastic? Those are the dangerous conditions in which Admiral Byrd survives!

WRITING and COACHING *(editing, revising)*
30 MINUTES

■ Have students revise and edit their responses. As they work, remind them to focus on the features of a great response and correct spelling, punctuation, capitalization, etc.

■ If your students are ready for it, you might want to have them exchange papers and edit one another's work. Peer editing is a powerful technique that generally works well at second grade.

■ As you assist students, praise them for specific changes they are making: *You really can be proud of your editing—changing that capital letter to lowercase is a great change!*

TIP Some students may feel overwhelmed when editing their work for more than one convention at a time. Help students make a short checklist of what they will look for, and suggest they focus on editing their work for only one convention on the list at a time.

SHARING and REFLECTING
10 MINUTES

TURN &TALK *Share your draft with your partner. Point out a change that you made as you revised and edited. Explain how that change made your work better.*

■ After discussing the editing and revising process, preview the work students will do in the next session: *Now that we have polished our responses, we are going to use our finished work to make response posters that we will display in our library!*

SESSION 6
Publishing and Sharing

Students publish and share their responses.

MATERIALS

- *Black Whiteness: Admiral Byrd Alone in the Antarctic* by Robert Burleigh
- Research notebooks
- White poster paper
- Pencils and markers

TIP If you have the time, you may want to take this opportunity to do a minilesson on creating an illustration that matches the text. *A poster with striking visuals would really capture our readers' interest! Think about* Black Whiteness. *What might be a great picture that you could add to your poster? Think about illustrating a main scene from the book or drawing something that you really liked about the text.*

FOCUSED MINILESSON *(publishing)*
10 MINUTES

- Preview today's work: *We're going to finish our responses by creating posters from the drafts we wrote in our notebooks. Then we will share and display our work. This will help other readers decide if they want to read* Black Whiteness.

  TURN &TALK *What can we do today to make sure our poster responses will look and be their very best for our readers? Share your thoughts with a partner.*

- Use students' responses to focus on the importance of using clear handwriting, writing large enough so that the main ideas can be seen from across the room, and so on.

  TURN &TALK *Tell your partner what steps you will take to transform the draft in your notebook into your poster response.*

- Ask volunteers to share their processes. Then, you may wish to suggest that students plan how to organize the space on their posters before they begin writing their final copy: *Look at the amount of text you have written and see if a picture will fit. Also, decide how big you want your title to be—you want your readers to be able to clearly see the title of the poster, but you need to leave yourself enough room to include everything for your response.*

- Model for students how you would plan your own poster: *Watch as I organize the space I will use for my response poster. I am writing my title in the center at the top of the poster, and I'm using nice big letters. Now I'll draw a box under the title that's big enough to hold the body of my response. That gives me just enough room for two drawings on either side. I can decide what to draw later.*

WRITING and COACHING *(publishing)*
30 MINUTES

■ Have students create their posters. Offer assistance as needed.

■ Students at this age often have trouble composing and filling a large space. If this happens, pass out plain printer paper and let the students practice drawing large circles over and over on both sides of the page. This simple exercise can go a long way toward helping them feel more confident about writing and drawing "big."

SHARING and REFLECTING
15 MINUTES

■ Have students share their work. Students can share in small groups or with the whole class. If time allows, invite another class to come and listen to groups of students share their responses.

> **TURN &TALK** *Reflect with your partner about the terrific responses you heard today. In what ways were they similar or different? What generalizations can you make about good response writing?*

■ Invite volunteers to share their thoughts. Discuss how response writing is interesting, because everyone responds to the same book differently. Connect students' thoughts to the features chart you created throughout the project. Reiterate that students can use the chart as a guide when they write another response.

■ Celebrate students' efforts as you deliver finished posters to the librarian for display. (Alternatively, you can display the finished posters near your class library.) *You all did a wonderful job with your responses. It will be so interesting to read each other's responses to see what different people thought of the book!*

TIP Some students may focus more on the drawing than on the writing or find the drawing difficult. Remind them that their purpose is to respond to the book. Show students examples of book jackets to help them see how text and illustrations work together.

TIP If time allows, follow up with a discussion that allows students to reflect on and evaluate the process of response writing. Have them talk about what they really enjoyed and anything that they found frustrating about their experience writing this past week. Encourage students to think about anything they might do differently when they write another response.

SESSION 7
Launching the Individual Project

Students review the features of a great response, choose nonfiction books for the individual project, and begin to draft their responses.

MATERIALS

- A selection of nonfiction books you've read together recently in read-alouds or shared readings
- Features chart from class project
- Research notebooks
- Pencils
- Student-selected nonfiction books

TIP Have students choose their books ahead of time and reread them during independent reading time. Remind them that as they reread their books today, they should focus on discovering what they really like or don't like.

FOCUSED MINILESSON *(prewriting)*
15 MINUTES

■ Introduce the session: *Today we'll each choose a nonfiction book that we've recently read, and we'll begin to draft our individual responses. We'll want to think about the features of a great response as we write our own, and try to include as many of those features as possible.*

■ Reflect on the key features of what makes a good response. Refer students to the features chart if they need prompting. If students have not already chosen nonfiction books for their individual responses, have them do so now.

TURN &TALK *Evaluate the book you chose for your response. Tell your partner what you like or don't like about your book.*

■ Praise students for mentioning specific details: *Writing that you thought the author used beautiful words to describe the snow is a wonderful detail to include in a response about* Snowflake Bentley (by Jacqueline Briggs Martin).

■ Do a brief minilesson to remind students how to add details by justifying their likes and dislikes: *It is important to make sure our readers get plenty of interesting information. Readers will want to know why you liked or didn't like something.*

■ Choose a book and model this process: *I really loved this book because the pictures were fantastic. If I want to make my response really excellent, I should explain why I found the pictures so wonderful. So, I could write a few sentences that tell what I liked and why I liked it:* The illustrations were fantastic. Looking at the pictures made me feel like I could actually see Wilma Rudolph running. The illustrations were colorful and dramatic. *When I write reasons why I liked or didn't like something, I help my reader get a sense of what reading the book was like.*

TURN &TALK *Tell your partner something you liked in your book. Name a detail from the book that supports your feelings.*

WRITING and COACHING
(drafting, revising, editing)
20 MINUTES

■ Have students begin drafting their responses. Remind them to begin with the title of their book. Then students should focus on writing what they liked and/or disliked about it, referring back to the book itself as often as needed.

■ When students are finished writing, suggest that they read back their work to make sure it makes sense and includes enough detail, particularly reasons why they liked or disliked the book.

■ After students have made revisions, encourage them to edit their work. Create a community of writers by suggesting that students work together and help each other edit.

■ Students will have other opportunities to revise and edit their work before publishing, but encouraging them to improve and polish their work as they go may make the process less overwhelming for some students.

SHARING and REFLECTING
10 MINUTES

TURN &TALK *Read what you wrote today to your partner. List important features of a response that you included in your writing today.*

■ Have a few students share with the class: *Great responses tell what we liked and didn't like about the book. They also tell why we liked or didn't like something.* Give students time to reflect on why it is important to justify thinking in a response. Have volunteers share their ideas.

■ Preview the next session: *Can anyone tell us another feature we could add to our responses the next time we work on them? Yes, connections are another feature of a good response.*

TIP To encourage and assist students with revising, you may wish to create a revision checklist chart that you add to each day during the individual project. You might include questions such as: "Did I explain my thoughts clearly to my readers?" and "Have I expanded on why I liked or disliked the book?"

TIP for Conferring with Individuals and Small Groups

To assist students with the editing process, provide one or two conventions particular to their needs, such as the correct use of upper- and lowercase letters and checking end punctuation. Giving students responsibility for using an editing checklist gives them ownership of the work and ensures that they think carefully about the conventions of powerful writing.

SESSION 8
Drafting and Revising

Students continue to draft and revise their responses, focusing on making connections and using linking words.

MATERIALS
- Features chart from class project
- Research notebooks
- Pencils
- Student-selected nonfiction books

TIP While you want to encourage students to use the word *and* to link thoughts together, you may want to explain that good writers only use *and* once or twice in a sentence. Point out that if you use the word *and* too many times, readers can get tired. If you notice some of your students using *and* too many times in a sentence, suggest they begin another sentence and challenge them to use the words *also* and *another*.

FOCUSED MINILESSON *(drafting)*
15 MINUTES

- Focus the learning: *During our last session, we wrote about what we liked and disliked about our books. In this session, we are going to write connections and review words that will help us write our connections more clearly.*

  TURN &TALK *Partners, put your heads together. Discuss different ways that readers connect with the text. What connections did you make as you were reading the book you chose?*

- Highlight a few interesting connections you heard as you listened to students' conversations. To set students up for successful writing, quickly review the different ways to connect to a book (text-to-text, text-to-self, text-to-world).

- Do a minilesson to remind students how to use common linking words such as *and, but, so,* and *because* as they write their connections. Write the words on a chart and explain why good writers use them: *When we write about our likes, dislikes, or connections, we can use words such as* because, and, so, *and* but *to link our ideas and to help our readers understand how those ideas are related.*

- Model how to explicitly combine two thoughts using each of the linking words. Write two sentences about a connection to a book and then think aloud as you choose a linking word to combine the sentences appropriately. For example: *Here I wrote about my connection. I see that one of the sentences really elaborates, or tells more, about the first sentence. I can use a linking word such as* so *or* because *to show the relationship between these thoughts. I could revise these sentences to say:* This book reminded me of how important it is to never give up. So, I found this book inspiring. *Or I could write:* I found this book inspiring because it reminded me of how important it is to never give up.

  TURN &TALK *Tell your partner a connection you are planning on writing about today. Use one of the linking words to connect your thoughts together and expand on your connection.*

- Listen in and assist partners who need help using linking words to put their thoughts together.

WRITING and COACHING
(drafting, revising, editing)
30 MINUTES

- Have students get started adding connections to their responses, referring to their chosen book as needed.

- Explain that when they are finished drafting, they should read back their work and check to make sure they linked the information together. After making revisions, encourage students to edit their work for spelling and correct use of capital letters.

- Build a community of writers by encouraging early finishers to help other writers with their connections or to engage in peer editing.

- If you don't have a strong corps of parent volunteers to assist you, it can be difficult to conference with every student who needs support during writing and coaching time. Look for other opportunities during the day to sneak in a few quick conferences with students you haven't gotten to yet.

SHARING and REFLECTING
10 MINUTES

TURN &TALK *Look at your partner's work. Compare and contrast the way you both connected to your books. What linking words did you and your partner use today?*

- Have students reflect on how they used linking words as they wrote during writing time today.

- Celebrate students' success: *A response lets people know how we connected with a book. So, including different connections and linking together your thoughts is important. You should be proud of the work that you did!*

TIP for Conferring with Individuals and Small Groups

If you have some students who are only making text-to-self connections, help them expand their thinking by encouraging them to see how they can also make a text-to-text connection. For example: *Gita, I see you have written about how the book reminded you of learning about lizards at the zoo. Have you seen any television programs or read other books about lizards? You've read* What Do You Do With a Tail Like This? (by Steve Jenkins) *That would be a fantastic text-to-text connection to write down.*

SESSION 9
Drafting and Revising the Ending

Students draft and revise strong endings for their responses, focusing on their use of powerful adjectives.

MATERIALS
- *Big Book of Mentor Texts,* "Response to *Diary of a Worm,*" pages 44–46
- Features chart from class project
- Research notebooks
- Pencils

TIP You may wish to create a chart that categorizes the adjectives by degree of positive or negative connotation. For example, if students would give the book 5/5 stars they might use words from the first column (*sensational,* and so on); if they just thought the book was pretty good (3/5 stars), they could use words from another column (*pretty good, mediocre,* and so on); if they thought the book was not good, they could use words from a final column.

FOCUSED MINILESSON *(drafting)*
20 MINUTES

- Preview the session: *Today we are going to write powerful endings for our responses, and we'll focus on choosing adjectives that can help us describe our thoughts and feelings more clearly.*

- Display the mentor text and refer students back to the class project. Reread the ending in the mentor text as well as some great examples of student endings that are displayed around the room.

  TURN &TALK *Why do you think it's important to have a great ending? Put your heads together as you talk about what makes an ending excellent.*

- Invite volunteers to share their ideas. Provide positive reinforcement: *Yes, a great ending sums up your thoughts about the book and powerfully communicates your feelings about the book to your readers.*

- Do a minilesson on how to use adjectives to make the ending powerful: *The writer of this response to* Diary of a Worm *used the word* wonderful *in her ending. Using words like* wonderful *sends a powerful message to her readers. What are some other words we can use in our endings to describe a book we really loved?* Create a list of adjectives with students that includes exciting words such as *amazing, wonderful, sensational, fantastic, excellent, superb, incredible, terrific,* and so on. Repeat the process for adjectives that students could use if they didn't like their books.

- Point out the use of an exclamation point in the ending of the mentor text. Discuss how and why writers use exclamation points. Ask students to help you write a summary sentence that includes a strong adjective and an exclamation point. For example: *This book was marvelous!*

  TURN &TALK *Tell your partner how you are going to end your response. Share some powerful describing words you are thinking of using when you write your ending today.*

- Ask volunteers to share, and praise them for using various adjectives: *Your readers will really get a sense of how you felt about this book if you use the word* sensational. *Great thinking!*

WRITING and COACHING
(drafting, revising, editing)
30 MINUTES

- Have students begin drafting their endings.

- Explain that when they are finished drafting, they should read back their work and revise to be sure they used adjectives to create a powerful ending.

- Encourage students to help each other edit their work for spelling, punctuation, and correct use of capital and lowercase letters.

SHARING and REFLECTING
10 MINUTES

TURN &TALK *Share your draft with your partner. Identify at least one word your partner used to make his or her ending exciting.*

- Invite a few volunteers to share their drafts and celebrate their efforts: *Great responses have powerful endings. These endings pack a punch and sum up your feelings!*

- Give students time to reflect on how they incorporated adjectives into their writing today. If students are given opportunities to reflect on how they successfully used new describing words, then they will be more likely to continue to select appropriate adjectives for future writing.

- Praise students' efforts: *Good writers find the right words to communicate their feelings to their readers. You carefully chose words to get just the right effect!*

TIP If you notice that one of your students has come up with a really creative and powerful ending, you might consider asking the group to stop writing and listen to the ending. This will encourage other students to expand their thinking and perhaps spark their creativity as they take the opportunity to try out something new.

SESSION 10
Editing and Publishing

Students review editing techniques and publish their responses on poster paper, leaving room for illustrations.

MATERIALS
- Features chart from class project
- Student drafts
- Poster paper
- Pencils and markers

TIP You may wish to review and make a list of strategies your students can use to improve spelling, such as stretching out the sounds in words, using your word wall and other word charts you have developed with your class (blends charts, high-frequency word chart, response writing word chart), creating personal word lists, and referring to dictionaries.

FOCUSED MINILESSON *(editing)*
15 MINUTES

■ Introduce the session: *You have come a long way in drafting and revising your responses. Think of how much you have learned since your first response writing! Today, we are going to review ways to be sure our writing looks right and is ready to be published. Then we will publish our responses on posters.*

■ Do a minilesson to help students edit and publish their work. Touch on areas such as: making sure sentences begin with capital letters and end with appropriate end punctuation, checking for spelling, writing legibly, and using enough space between words. Begin by showing some excellent student examples from the class project. (Be sure these examples demonstrate legible handwriting and good spacing between words. If possible, also choose one that shows good use of an exclamation point.)

TURN &TALK *What do you notice about the way the writing looks on these fantastic response posters? How do you think these writers edited their work before publishing their responses on the posters?*

■ Use students' responses to discuss and create a list that they can use to edit their work before publishing: *Yes! These posters show words that are spelled correctly. The sentences have correct end punctuation. Did you notice that Mira included an exclamation point in one of her ending sentences? You might also check to see where you could change a period to an exclamation point in your writing. Where did Mira and Dominic use capital letters? You're right! They only used capital letters in their titles and at the beginning of their sentences.*

■ Revisit the student examples and ask the class to explain why they are able to read the words on these posters so easily. Praise students' analysis: *The words are written in the writers' very best handwriting. Mira and Dominic took their time forming the letters and made sure they left enough space between words. If you are unsure about how much space to leave between words, remember you can place your finger at the end of a word you wrote to know where to start the next word.*

TURN &TALK *Look at your work from the last session. Tell your partner how you will edit your response before publishing today and what you will do as you publish to be sure your work is readable.*

WRITING and COACHING
(revising, editing, publishing)
30 MINUTES

■ Have students make final edits on their drafts and then publish their work on the poster paper. Be sure to explain that they will have the chance to add illustrations in the next session, so they should leave blank space on their posters for one or two drawings.

■ Remind students to refer frequently to the editing list you developed as a class when they review their work.

■ Strengthen your community of writers by encouraging students to ask each other for help with editing or with the spelling of a particular word. If you have some really good spellers, you might think of appointing them "spelling captains" so other students can consult with them on various strategies they might use for spelling more difficult words.

SHARING and REFLECTING
10 MINUTES

TURN &TALK *Share what you have published so far with your partner. What edits are you most proud that you made before publishing?*

■ Give students time to reflect on why it is important to do a final edit before publishing: *I saw many of you catching spelling mistakes and adding end punctuation. Good writers do their best to make sure their readers understand their message.*

■ Preview the next session: *Wonderful work today! The next time we write, we will finish publishing our posters and share them.*

TIP You may wish to explain that good editors usually read through their drafts several times and edit for one particular convention at a time. They might read through their drafts and first check to see that they have the correct end punctuation for their sentences. Then, they will go back and read their drafts again—this time looking for errors in spelling. Encourage students to see editing as a fun process of discovery and detective work to catch ways they can improve their writing for their readers.

TIP If you have students who really struggle with writing legibly, praise their efforts and connect their effort to the purpose of publishing: *Wow! Your handwriting is getting better and better! Your readers will really be able to focus on the message of your response now. You have really come a long way—reading your work is a breeze!*

SESSION 11
Publishing and Celebrating

Students add illustrations to their published responses before sharing them with classmates and celebrating all that they've learned.

MATERIALS
• *Big Book of Mentor Texts,* "Response to *Diary of a Worm,*" pages 44–46
• Features chart
• Students' responses from Session 9
• Pencils
• Crayons or markers

TIP To help activate students' thinking about how to choose something appropriate to illustrate for their responses, display and discuss a few really great student examples from the class project or revisit the mentor text so students can analyze further why these pictures were good choices.

FOCUSED MINILESSON *(publishing)*
15 MINUTES

■ Focus the learning: *Today we are going to review what makes a great illustration and then we'll add pictures to our response posters.*

■ *Take a look at our posters for* Black Whiteness—*what other feature can we include that would make our posters really exciting for our readers? Yes! Pictures are great features to include in a response— they make your piece interesting.*

■ Give a minilesson on how to help create great illustrations: *Pictures help give our readers information. Different kinds of writing use different kinds of pictures—remember when we wrote our procedural texts? We included pictures to help our readers understand our directions. Think about the kind of pictures that would work well for a response.*

TURN &TALK *What kind of pictures would be great to include in a response? Explain your thinking to your partner.*

■ Validate students' thinking: *Yes, a picture of our favorite part in the book would be a great idea—it's important that our pictures match the words we wrote so we don't confuse our readers. Since we wrote about our likes, something we like would be an excellent choice for a picture.*

TURN &TALK *Tell your partner a great picture you could draw that would work well with your response.*

■ Invite volunteers to share their ideas. Give students a sense of success by praising them for specifically connecting their picture ideas to their text: *That is a marvelous idea. A picture like that will really help readers understand why you liked your book.* Inform students that they will have the chance to look back at their published pieces and add illustrations.

WRITING and COACHING *(publishing)*
20 MINUTES

■ Have students work on their illustrations and finish their responses. Remind them to also include the titles of their books and to put their names on their posters.

■ Offer assistance as needed. Celebrate all efforts to create great published pieces: *Your picture is excellent! If I saw your poster, I would really be drawn to it and would want to read it more closely.*

SHARING and REFLECTING
15 MINUTES

■ Have students share their work in pairs or in small groups. Create a community of writers by encouraging students to comment on something they liked about their classmates' responses.

TURN &TALK *Reflect with your partner about the terrific responses you heard today. What features did you include that made your responses so exciting for your readers?*

■ Invite volunteers to share. Link students' thoughts back to the features chart as they share. To encourage further reflection, you might also invite students to share what they enjoyed most about response writing.

■ Celebrate students' efforts and display the finished posters in your classroom or outside in the hallway so other classes can see the responses: *You all did an excellent job. It will be interesting to read each other's responses! If you read these responses, it may make you want to read or reread the books your classmates wrote about.*

■ Now that the unit is over, remember to look back at students' pre-assessment pieces and to use the Ongoing Monitoring Sheet or the Individual Evaluation Record to document growth and note areas for improvement. Pass out copies of the Student Self-Reflection Sheet found on the *Resources* CD-ROM to help students reflect on their own growth. Finally, be sure to make notes on what worked and what didn't during the unit so you can make adjustments for next time. See "After the Unit," page 245, for more information about post-assessment and self-reflection.

TIP If some students have written a lot of text and do not have much space left for an illustration, have them create their drawings on separate pieces of paper. Then, provide students with two pieces of poster paper taped together. They can cut and paste their text and their pictures onto the new, enlarged posters.

Response to a Poem

A poetry response reveals reactions, opinions, connections, and questions.

I like this poem because it made me feel like going outside to hear silence. So I did but all I heard was cars and birds. NO silence. I wonder what she hears in the silence. I also wonder what she means when she says bits of moonglow drift over me.

I think this poem sounds like two different poems and I like the top part best.

FEATURES

- Title and author
- Reactions, opinions, and connections with support
- Questions

"Tremendously Tough Tooth"

I adore this poem! Action words like wiggled, jiggled, and slammed made me feel like I was actually trying to pull out my tooth. The poem reminds me of how proud I was when I lost my first tooth. I also like the way the poet uses alliteration. Repeating the t sound in the title — "Tremendously Tough Tooth" — gives the poem a rhythm. This poem left me wondering if the girl ever found her tooth after it shot across the floor.

FOCUSED MINILESSON

Writers, I love reading poems. Their descriptions and clever words engage me! I want to write a response to a great poem today. Then you'll have a chance to respond, too!

Turn to the *Big Book of Mentor Texts,* page 47. *Listen as I read this poem.*

TURN &TALK *What did you think of the poem? Share with a partner whether you liked it or not and tell why. What connections did you make?*

I liked this poem too. Watch as I start my response with the title: "Tremendously Tough Tooth." *Then I am going to share my reactions. Watch as I write:* I like it.

TURN &TALK *Writers, what do you think of this response so far? Evaluate it with a partner.*

Many of you said that my response wasn't very specific or detailed. Rereading it now, I agree! Watch as I revise for more detail: I adore this poem! Action words like *wiggled, jiggled,* and *slammed* made me feel like I was actually trying to pull out my tooth.

I also like how the poet used alliteration in the poem. Notice how she repeats the sound t *in the title:* "Tremendously Tough Tooth." *Watch me add that reason to my response.*

I also want to share a great connection I made to the poem. Watch as I write: The poem reminds me of how proud I felt when I lost my first tooth. *I heard many of you share that same connection earlier! A connection helps make our responses more complete.*

TURN &TALK *Great poems often leave me wondering. As I read the poem one more time, listen and think. What do you wonder? Share with a partner what questions were in your brain at the end of the poem.*

Modeled Writing

I wondered the same thing—did the poet ever find her tooth after it flew across the floor? Watch as I end my response with my wondering.

After writing: *Let's take a look at my response. It starts with the title. Then I wrote my reaction to the poem and explained why I felt that way. I included a connection and questions I had after reading.*

TURN &TALK *Partners, think together. If you were going to share with a friend the steps to create a poetry response, what would you include?*

Use students' ideas to generate a features list.

WRITING and COACHING

Now it's your turn to respond to a poem. Pay close attention as I read "Listen" by Linda Hoyt. Read the poem on page 48 of the *Big Book of Mentor Texts.*

What did you think of the poem? Why did you feel that way? Now write your response! Be sure to include all of the important features of a poetry response.

After students complete their writing, provide an opportunity for partners to share their responses with one another.

SHARING and REFLECTING

Writers, your poetry responses show your own reactions, opinions, connections, and questions. You also included evidence from the poem to support your responses. It was interesting to see so many different interpretations!

ASSESS THE LEARNING

Gather poetry responses and assess understanding. Reteach features as necessary. Be sure students have responded rather than retold the poems or put them in their own words.

SELF-ASSESSMENT

SELF-ASSESSMENT

Responding to a Poem

	YES	NO
1. Did you include the title and author?	☐	☐
2. Does your response include reactions, opinions, and connections?	☐	☐
3. Did you include something you wondered about?	☐	☐

SUPPORTING AND EXTENDING

▸ Have students respond to poems written by writing partners. Allow time for partners to share responses.

▸ Read multiple poems to the class about the same topic (e.g., whales, worms, plants). Place the poems in a binder. Have students write their responses on sticky notes and place them on the poems to which they responded.

▸ Have students use the format to respond to other texts, such as songs, short stories, and essays, and to forms of media, such as television, movies, and websites.

VISUAL LITERACY

Fact/Opinion Chart

A good response can include both facts and opinions about a topic.

FEATURES

• Detailed statement of fact

• Detailed statement of opinion

• Supportive illustrations

Koalas

Fact

Koalas spend most of their time in trees. They try to stay off the ground as much as they can to avoid predators.

Opinion

Koalas are smart to stay away from the ground. I hope they stay safe from danger.

FOCUSED MINILESSON

This lesson focuses on desert plants.
Choose a topic your class has recently studied.

I was so interested in our unit on desert plants! Today I want to capture a fact and an opinion about what I learned. I am going to start with a fact, or a statement that can be proven.

TURN &TALK *Partners, put your heads together. Share a fact about desert plants. Remember, a fact is a statement that can be proven to be true.*

I heard Ashley say, "The Joshua tree grows in the desert." This is an interesting fact. It can be proven. Watch as I write my fact on a note card and add an interesting detail: The Joshua tree lives in the desert. It has sharp pointed leaves that protect it from animals. *The detail gives even more information about the fact for my readers. Now I will staple my note card to the top of my construction paper. I can write a message underneath. I want to add a supportive drawing that illustrates my fact.*

TURN &TALK *Share with a partner what I could draw at the bottom of my paper to support my statement of fact.*

Listen for drawing ideas that you can add to the model.

After writing: *Examine my fact writing. Do you think readers will guess it is a fact? Watch as I write* Fact *under my note card so my readers can check whether my statement is a fact or an opinion.*

Next I'll write an opinion. Remember, an opinion is a statement that tells what you think or feel about something. It is not something you can prove. Instead, it's your own idea or belief.

TURN &TALK *Share with your partner an opinion you have about desert plants.*

Repeat the steps above, modeling forming an opinion.

The Joshua tree lives in the desert. It has sharp pointed leaves that protect it from animals.

Fact

Modeled Writing

After writing: *Examine my opinion writing. I included a detailed statement that reflects my personal view and an illustration to support it. I wrote opinion under the flap.*

Review both models and generate a list of the features: *Now I've created the two parts of a fact/opinion chart. I've written a fact with details that can be proven. I've written my opinion with details to support my view. And I provided supportive illustrations.*

The cactus is the most interesting desert plant because it has prickles.

opinion

Modeled Writing

WRITING and COACHING

Writers, now it's your turn to write a fact and an opinion. On your first note card, write a fact and craft an interesting detail. Remember, facts can be proven. On the second note card, write a detailed statement that is an opinion. Remember, an opinion is your personal view. Be sure to illustrate both statements.

As students work, offer support by reminding them of the features of facts and opinions and the differences between them. Allow students to share their statements in small groups. Classmates can guess whether each statement is a fact or an opinion.

SHARING and REFLECTING

Writers, your fact statements gave interesting information that can be proven, and your opinion statements really revealed your personal thoughts. Your illustrations were not only supportive, they were also creative.

ASSESS THE LEARNING

Gather students' work to assess their understanding of *fact* and *opinion*. If students need assistance, provide facts and opinions and have them classify.

SELF-ASSESSMENT

SELF-ASSESSMENT

Creating a Fact/Opinion Chart

	YES	NO
1. Did you write a fact—a statement that can be proven?	☐	☐
2. Did you write an opinion—a statement that tells your personal view?	☐	☐
3. Is each statement supported by an illustration?	☐	☐

RESPOND

S U P P O R T I N G   A N D   E X T E N D I N G

▸ Ask students to create fact/opinion charts about animals or another topic of study. Bind the illustrated charts into class books.

▸ Have partners create fact/opinion charts about a famous person you are studying. Post them on a classroom wall to be shared.

▸ Extend the fact/opinion charts by having students create a multimedia slide show in which a statement appears on one slide and the word *fact* or *opinion* appears on the following slide. Present the show to another class. After each statement, students can classify it as fact or opinion before you reveal the next slide.

Two-Word Strategy

Choosing two important words can help us focus our thinking as we respond to text.

> common   intricate
>
> Willie's neighbors thought that snowflakes were **common**. They laughed when he said he wanted to take pictures of them. But Willie was fascinated by the **intricate** patterns he saw when he took a closer look at snowflakes. Each one was different. They weren't common at all!

FEATURES

- Two words at the top of a piece of paper
- Focus words used in sentences

FOCUSED MINILESSON

This lesson uses Jacqueline Briggs Martin's *Snowflake Bentley* as a mentor text. Choose a text your class has recently read and follow the lesson sequence.

The two-word strategy helps us think more deeply about text. If I were thinking about Snowflake Bentley, *for example, I would choose the word* persistent. *Why would I choose that word? Snowflake Bentley was persistent. He never stopped working hard to take pictures of snowflakes.*

Watch as I reflect my thinking using the two-word strategy. First, I'm recording the word persistent *at the top of the page. Now watch as I write a few sentences that explain why I chose the word:* Snowflake Bentley was <u>persistent</u> when he took pictures of snowflakes. It was hard work to take so many pictures with the equipment he had, but he didn't give up. *I want you to notice something about my work. The author didn't tell me that Snowflake Bentley is persistent. I thought about clues from the book to come up with the word and to write the sentences. I underlined the word so it would stand out.*

TURN &TALK *Now it's your turn! Partners, put your heads together. Name another word that reflects your thinking about the book.*

As I was listening, I heard some great ideas! I am going to capture one of them as I write another word about the book: unique. *Now I need to write a sentence that explains why I chose that word:* The book *Snowflake Bentley* is <u>unique</u>.

TURN &TALK *Partners, what do you think of my sentence? Evaluate my writing.*

> persistent   unique
>
> Snowflake Bentley was <u>persistent</u> when he took pictures of snowflakes. It was hard work to take so many pictures with the equipment he had, but he didn't give up.
>
> Snowflake Bentley discovered that each and every snowflake has a <u>unique</u> shape.

Modeled Writing

As I was listening, I heard some of you say that my sentence doesn't give much information about the book. Thinking about it, I agree! Many books are unique to their readers. So, I am going to write a sentence that reflects some deeper thinking.

TURN &TALK *Writers, what sentence would you write to show that something about Snowflake Bentley is unique? Think together.*

Great suggestions! Watch as I finish: Snowflake Bentley discovered that each and every snowflake has a <u>unique</u> shape.

After writing: Let's read my writing. Notice how I placed my special words at the top of the page. I used them again when I told why these words reflect my thinking. I underlined my special words so they would stand out. List the features on a chart for student reference.

ASSESS THE LEARNING

Analyze written responses for the presence of two words that reflect students' thinking about the text. Provide reteaching for students who used only literal words or wrote two-word phrases.

WRITING and COACHING

Depending on their readiness, students can use the two-word strategy to write two more words with sentences about *Snowflake Bentley,* or they can use the strategy to write about other books that you choose. *Remember, choose two words that reflect your thinking. They may or may not be words from the text. Then write about the words you chose.*

SELF-ASSESSMENT

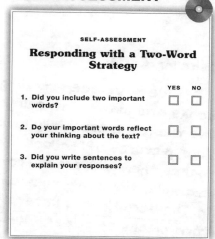

SELF-ASSESSMENT
Responding with a Two-Word Strategy

	YES	NO
1. Did you include two important words?	☐	☐
2. Do your important words reflect your thinking about the text?	☐	☐
3. Did you write sentences to explain your responses?	☐	☐

SHARING and REFLECTING

You thought deeply about the text when you chose your two words. Then you crafted sentences to reflect your thinking, and you underlined the words so they would stand out. Your two-word responses show very powerful thinking!

S U P P O R T I N G A N D E X T E N D I N G

▸ Have students make "important books" about content you are studying, such as "The Most Important Things About Whales." Each student should contribute a page for each class book.

▸ Have students each choose two words and write them on index cards, with their support sentences on the back. Have them add their words to a word wall, sorting words to help them discuss relationships between ideas.

▸ Students can use the two-word strategy to contribute to an electronic slide show. For a unit about the seasons, for example, each student can choose two words, write about them, and illustrate them with clip art. Group the slides by season to create a class show.

Friendly Letter

A friendly letter is one way to respond to a text or to an author's work.

Dear Mrs. Hayt,

Thank you for coming to our classroom. We injoied hearing how to punch up our sentenses. I love Syl- ster and the Magic Pebble. Thanks for helping me get a good mentel picter. I also liked when we did the list of descibing words for our

FEATURES

- Greeting
- Body with reactions, opinions, and connections
- Closing with signature

FOCUSED MINILESSON

Letters are a great way to share our thoughts with others. We have really enjoyed reading several Eric Carle books, so I thought it would be fun to tell him that. I am going to write a letter from our class. (Choose an author your class has studied or another purpose for writing a letter.)

I know that letters always start with a greeting. Watch me as I write Dear Mr. Carle, *at the top. Did you notice the comma? It is important to put a comma after the greeting. Next, I need to write the body of the letter. This will be the main part of the letter in which I can share my reactions, opinions, and connections relating to Mr. Carle's work.*

TURN &TALK *Put your heads together, partners. Talk about your reactions and connections to the books we've read by Eric Carle.*

I heard a lot of great ideas! Evan said, "I love the illustrations. They look like a collage, which makes them different from most books." I'm capturing that idea to write in the body of the letter. I can make this even better if I give an example from a specific book. Watch as I add: The circle eyes on the caterpillar in The Very Hungry Caterpillar look like little torn pieces of paper. These illustrations are unique and really captured our attention. *This specific example makes our writing sparkle!*

I also heard Tatiana say that she loves the special endings in the book. I will write about that, too.

TURN &TALK *Share with a partner an example of a special ending in one of Eric Carle's books. What connections did you make to this ending?*

Dear Mr. Carle,

We have been reading many of your books and wanted to tell you how much we like them. We especially love the illustrations. Your pictures often look like a collage, which makes them different from most books. For example, the circle eyes on the caterpillar in The Very Hungry Caterpillar look like little torn pieces of paper. These illustrations are unique and really captured our attention. We also truly enjoyed your special endings. The chirping crickets at the end of The Very Quiet Cricket were so cool. It made us feel like we were outside in nature listening to them sing. Your glowing fireflies at the end of The Very Lonely Firefly reminded us of fun summer nights chasing fireflies.

Thanks so much for writing such interesting books.

Sincerely,

(add signatures)

Modeled Writing

I hear some great ideas about endings! Watch as I add those statements to the body of our letter.

The last important feature in a friendly letter is a closing. Let's end by thanking Mr. Carle for writing such great books. Then we'll add our signatures.

Capture the features of a friendly letter in a chart as you discuss them: *We opened our friendly letter with a greeting. Then, in the body, we shared our reactions and connections. Last, we wrote our closing and signed the letter. I think Eric Carle will really enjoy reading our friendly letter!*

WRITING and COACHING

Now it is your turn to write your own friendly letter. There are several authors whose books we have loved, such as Kevin Henkes, Jan Brett, and Tomie DePaola. Choose one of these authors. Write a friendly letter sharing your reactions, opinions, and connections.

Set out a basket of books written by each author for students to use as a reference as needed. Remind students to refer to the features chart as necessary.

SHARING and REFLECTING

Writers, these letters will make a great impression! You remembered to start with a greeting, add your reactions and connections in the body, and end with a closing. I especially liked all the evidence you stated to support your thoughts.

ASSESS THE LEARNING

Have students compare their letters to the class model to check for inclusion of features. As necessary, reteach citing specific examples from text to support responses.

SELF-ASSESSMENT

SELF-ASSESSMENT

Responding with a Friendly Letter

	YES	NO
1. Did you begin with a greeting?	☐	☐
2. Did you include a body with reactions, opinions, and connections?	☐	☐
3. Does your letter end with a closing and signature?	☐	☐

RESPOND

SUPPORTING AND EXTENDING

▸ Have students write a friendly letter to an author who visits the school for an assembly or the local bookstore for a book signing.

▸ Ask an older class to partner with your class. Have the older students read stories they have written to your second-grade students. Then ask each of your students to write a friendly letter to the older student who shared a story with him or her.

▸ Ask students to write friendly letters to you to share their responses to a new topic they've learned about in class. If time allows, reply to the letters to start a dialogue about class content.

Information Equation

Math symbols can connect ideas about a topic and reveal deeper understanding.

Puddles + heat = evaporation This is important because it takes heat to make water evaporate and turn into a gas.

FEATURES

- Words or phrases
- Math symbols
- Relationships between ideas and concepts
- Writing stem: *This is important because ____.*

FOCUSED MINILESSON

Students can create information equations for many purposes. Adapt the lesson for content in your class.

Writers, you already understand how to write and solve math equations. Today we are going to write a different type of equation. Watch as I think like a writer and a mathematician at the same time to create an information equation.

I want to create an equation about rainbows. Watch me as I write what I know in an equation: Rain + sunlight = rainbow. *Notice that I did not use sentences. I needed only individual words or phrases. I used math symbols like "plus" and "equals" to create an equation. Can you see how my information equation shows an important concept about a rainbow?*

TURN &TALK *Let's write another information equation. Think about water. We know we can change its state of matter. Can you come up with an information equation that shows the relationship between a liquid and a solid?*

I heard a really great real-life connection! Watch as I write: Juice + freezer = frozen treat. *The equation has individual words connected with math symbols. Now that we have written the equation, it is time to add a sentence below telling why it is important. I want to fill in the answer for the writing stem:* This is important because ____.

TURN &TALK *Why do you think it is important to know how to freeze juice to make a frozen treat? Turn to your partner and share what you think I should write on this line.*

Juice + freezer = frozen treat

This is important because knowing how to change states of matter lets us use things in different ways.

Modeled Writing

What great ideas! Watch as I write Marcus's idea: This is important because knowing how to change states of matter lets us use things in different ways.

After writing: *Take a look at our information equation about frozen treats. We used individual words and math symbols in our equation. We showed the relationship between liquids and solids. We also answered "This is important because ____." Wow! Information equations are a really fun way to respond!*

TURN & TALK *An information equation uses words or phrases and math symbols to show relationships between ideas and concepts. If you were going to teach someone how to create an information equation, what would you say?*

Use students' ideas to generate a features list.

WRITING and COACHING

Now it is your turn to write! Create information equations about anything you have learned about matter. You can write about states of matter, properties of matter, changing matter, mixing matter, evaporation, and so on. As students work, circulate and provide support as needed.

SHARING and REFLECTING

Writers, your awesome information equations show relationships and connections you made. The math symbols make the information easy to understand.

ASSESS THE LEARNING

Have students compare their information equations to the ones you created during modeling. Help students understand connections between ideas.

SELF-ASSESSMENT

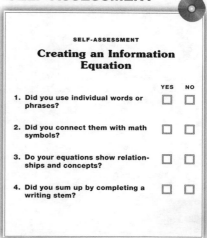

SELF-ASSESSMENT

Creating an Information Equation

	YES	NO
1. Did you use individual words or phrases?	☐	☐
2. Did you connect them with math symbols?	☐	☐
3. Do your equations show relationships and concepts?	☐	☐
4. Did you sum up by completing a writing stem?	☐	☐

SUPPORTING AND EXTENDING

▸ Ask students to create information equations to describe characters in a book you are reading or real-life figures from history.

▸ Ask students to create information equations about a topic you are studying. Have them write their equations on sentence strips and display them on a bulletin board.

▸ Partner your students with students from another class. Ask your students to read just the beginnings of their information equations. Partners can infer the answers to their equations. Encourage partners to discuss why each equation is important.

RESPOND

VISUAL LITERACY

Sketch to Stretch

A simple sketch with labels on it captures thinking about a topic.

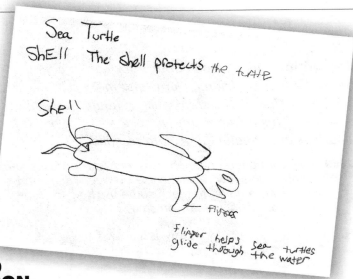

FEATURES

- Simple one-color sketches
- Labels
- Facts about a topic

FOCUSED MINILESSON

This lesson centers on sea turtles. Choose a topic that your class is currently studying.

Writers, when I read, I sometimes make a sketch about important facts in the reading. When I sketch and label, I can more easily remember what I've read. Sketching helps me stretch my thinking, so I call this kind of writing "sketch to stretch."

During a read-aloud, pause often to share your thinking. As you sketch your simple line drawings with labels, think out loud about key ideas and how the drawings can help you remember them. Emphasize the thinking about content—not the art!

I was really interested to learn about how sea turtles use seaweed. The way seaweed is like a pantry of foods for hatchlings is amazing! Imagine being able to find your favorite snacks—jellyfish and crab— in the same place where you make your first bed. So, I am going to sketch some seaweed with jellyfish and little fishes and crabs. I'm labeling this Seaweed pantry. I will also label the jellyfish, fishes, and crabs.

It's also really interesting how the loggerhead finds its way back to the very same beach where it hatched to lay its own eggs. Watch as I sketch the beach.

TURN &TALK *Partners, think together. Is there anything I might want to add to my sketch?*

Adding labels would definitely be helpful! Watch as I label the beach: birthplace, nest. *This sketch will help me remember something I find really fascinating!*

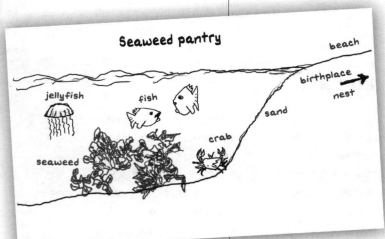

Modeled Writing

After writing: *Let's take a look at my sketches. I sketched things from my reading that I wanted to remember about sea turtles. I wrote labels to help me remember important ideas.*

TURN &TALK *A "sketch to stretch" helps us remember important ideas with drawing and writing. What are the most important things to remember when you use this strategy?*

Help students generate a list of the features of a "sketch to stretch."

WRITING and COACHING

What did you think of the things I chose to draw? What things would you have sketched?

Now it's your turn to sketch about sea turtles. Think about the key things you remember. Make sure you draw your ideas with simple sketches and write labels where you can. Remind students of the features of a "sketch to stretch" as you confer with and support individuals in creating their own sketches. Provide an opportunity for partners or small groups to share their sketches with one another. Have them focus on why they drew what they did.

SHARING and REFLECTING

Writers, your sketches do a great job of capturing your thinking with simple drawings and labels. No doubt these sketches will help you remember important facts and ideas!

ASSESS THE LEARNING

Gather sketch-to-stretch writing and assess understanding. Note which writers used the sketches as a vehicle for collecting thoughts about content. If necessary, reteach the use of labels.

SELF-ASSESSMENT

SELF-ASSESSMENT
Responding with Sketch to Stretch

	YES	NO
1. Did you make simple drawings?	☐	☐
2. Did your drawings focus on important ideas?	☐	☐
3. Did you use labels to call out important concepts?	☐	☐

RESPOND

S U P P O R T I N G   A N D   E X T E N D I N G

▸ Have students "sketch to stretch" with articles from periodicals or electronic media that tie into your science or social studies curriculum.

▸ Have students write about their key ideas from the sketches. If necessary, ask open-ended questions: *What did you learn? What key ideas stayed with you? What was the most important part of what we read?*

▸ As students begin a new unit, assign each group a question to explore through their reading or research. Each group can answer its question using a "sketch to stretch."

Fact-and-Response Grid

A fact-and-response grid captures responses based on prompts.

The moon travls around the Earth.
I wonder how long it taks to go around once.
I think the moon is prety.
I feel the moon is following us when we drive the car.
I'd like to know if the moon is made out of chees.

FEATURES

- Single fact about content
- Sentence stems to launch responses about the topic

FOCUSED MINILESSON

This lesson focuses on the sun and moon. Adapt the lesson for content your class is studying.

Writers, today we are going to create a fact-and-response grid. A fact-and-response grid is a great way to explore topics and think more deeply about our learning. All our writing today will stem from one fact, so we'll start by choosing a fact—a statement that can be proven true.

TURN &TALK *Writers, think together. What fact have we learned about the sun? List one together.*

You remembered many facts about the sun that will give us a great start. Watch as I write one of your facts at the top of a piece of paper: FACT: The sun is a star.

Now we need to add stems that will spark our writing. Watch as I write four different stems beneath the fact: I wonder . . . I think . . . I feel . . . I'd like to know. . . .

I will start our grid by responding to the first stem. I am thinking about the fact that the sun is a star. I wonder why we always draw stars with five points when the sun doesn't seem to have any points at all. I'm recording what I wonder. If you were completing this, you might wonder something different.

Now, how about I think . . .

TURN &TALK *What do you think about the fact that the sun is a star? Share your idea with your partner.*

This fact led to a lot of great thinking! Watch as I capture a thought by completing the stem: I think we're lucky that the sun is close to Earth. The sun provides all our energy.

FACT: The sun is a star.

I wonder . . . why we always draw stars with five points when the sun doesn't seem to have any points at all.

I think . . . we're lucky that the sun is close to Earth. The sun provides all our energy.

I feel . . .

I'd like to know . . .

Continue the process to complete the grid, having students contribute ideas to complete the stems as you guide their thinking.

TURN &TALK *What do you notice about our writing? Talk with your partner about our fact-and-response grid. What stems would you have answered differently?*

Capture the features of a fact-and-response grid in a chart as you take another look at the model: *Writers, let's take a look at the writing. A fact is listed at the top. That fact can be proven true. Underneath, we've completed each sentence stem. Notice that each sentence relates directly to the fact.*

WRITING and COACHING

Now it is your turn to create your own fact-and-response grid. I think we should select a fact about the moon for your grid. At the top of your paper, write: FACT: The moon travels around Earth. *Beneath the fact, write the four stems you see on our class grid:* I wonder . . . I think . . . I feel . . . I'd like to know. . . . *Make sure you leave enough room to complete the stems.* Some students may benefit from a pre-printed form with the fact at the top and sentence stems underneath.

SHARING and REFLECTING

Nice work, writers! You placed your fact at the top as your heading, and you responded to the four stems we used today with fantastic ideas. Responding to a single fact is a great way to reflect more deeply on the content.

ASSESS THE LEARNING

Collect fact-and-response grids and note which students had difficulty completing the sentence stems. Be sure that stem responses relate directly to the fact.

SELF-ASSESSMENT

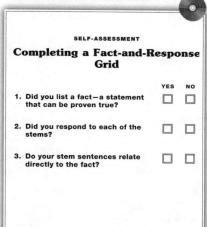

SELF-ASSESSMENT

Completing a Fact-and-Response Grid

	YES	NO
1. Did you list a fact—a statement that can be proven true?	☐	☐
2. Did you respond to each of the stems?	☐	☐
3. Do your stem sentences relate directly to the fact?	☐	☐

RESPOND

S U P P O R T I N G   A N D   E X T E N D I N G

▸ Have students work together to generate a master list of additional stems they could select for their own fact-and-response grids.

▸ Use the fact-and-response grid after any science or social studies unit as preparation for partner or small-group discussions.

▸ When you start a new unit, write a fact that students will explore throughout the unit on a bulletin board. As students work through the unit, they can choose stems, respond, and place their responses around the anchoring fact.

VISUAL LITERACY

Investigation

A visual investigation combines words and pictures to capture a response to a text.

FEATURES

- Two facing pages that form a "spread"
- Text features such as text boxes, headings, illustrations, and boldfaced words
- Opinions as well as facts

FOCUSED MINILESSON

Writers, we've read a lot of amazing books. I want to collect responses to those books to share with other readers. One of my favorites is William Steig's Sylvester and the Magic Pebble. *Watch as I create an investigation to respond to the book. I'll design this investigation so that it looks like a piece in a magazine, with a lot of features.*

Watch as I start by folding this large piece of paper in half so it looks like two pages. I'm writing a title in big letters that goes across both pages: Sylvester and the Magic Pebble. *These two pages are a "spread."*

I'm also sketching one big illustration across the spread. My illustration shows a favorite scene in the book. Watch as I write a caption underneath in a text box: I love that Sylvester has a collection! It reminds me of my own collections.

TURN &TALK *Partners, think together. What else might you include in an investigation to respond to something you've read?*

You have great ideas for a response! Watch as I leave space for the different parts you've suggested. On this part of the page, I'm leaving room to write about my favorite detail from the book. Over here, I'm drawing a box that looks like a picture frame to hold a sketch of my favorite character. In this text box under it, I'll write about why that character is my favorite. I'm creating another feature here called "Puzzler"! Watch as I draw a puzzle piece. In it, I'm going to write something about the book that confused me.

Modeled Writing

Notice that I am sketching and thinking about how close or far apart I want things to be on the page. Once I like the way everything looks, I can start filling in my text boxes. I'll be sure to boldface important words in the writing. And remember, since this is a response to the book, I'm sharing my opinion and the reasons for it.

Capture the features of an investigation in a chart as you examine the model with students: *Writers, this investigation isn't complete, but I got a great start planning it! The purpose of a response is to show how we feel about a book. I chose to use text features—text boxes, illustrations, and headings—to present my response. My response will share my feelings—and it will be interesting to read!*

WRITING and COACHING

Provide sheets of 11" x 17" paper. Have students fold their papers to create a "spread." Guide students in selecting a favorite author or series and planning the space. *Where should your text boxes go? How will you share your opinions? What would be interesting to include? Favorite words? Favorite characters? Should you add drawings or illustrations? Where can you add color?* Allow time for students to share their completed investigations.

SHARING and REFLECTING

Writers, your responses show deep thinking about the books you read! Your opinions shine through as you use all the space for features, text boxes, illustrations, and so on. Your texts will guide readers, helping them decide if they want to read these texts themselves.

ASSESS THE LEARNING

Observe closely as students are planning and drafting their investigations to determine which students need additional support. You might review the difference between fact and opinion and show students the informational and persuasive investigations in the *Big Book of Mentor Texts* (pages 20 and 22). Although the content will vary, the investigations show text features.

SELF-ASSESSMENT

SELF-ASSESSMENT

Responding with an Investigation

	YES	NO
1. Did your investigation use the entire space?	☐	☐
2. Did you plan out the way you wanted things to look?	☐	☐
3. Does your investigation share a response with ideas to support it?	☐	☐

RESPOND

SUPPORTING AND EXTENDING

▸ Have students create investigations to respond to movies or other media.

▸ Have students create investigations to respond to nonfiction. What did students learn? What did they like about the texts? What made them exciting?

▸ When you start an author study or a unit centered on a theme, start a response investigation on a bulletin board. Have students record their feelings in response to their reading and thinking.

Resources for Teaching Nonfiction Writing

CONTENTS

Research Tools
▸ Research Stations
▸ The R.A.N. Strategy

Index of Model Lessons by Subject Area

Index of Lessons by Writing Form

Index of Lessons by Mentor Text

Handwriting Guide

Tools Researchers Use

Additional Resources

Inform
▸ Topic Selection Sheet
▸ Ongoing Monitoring Sheet
▸ Daily Planner
▸ Individual Evaluation Record

Instruct
▸ Ongoing Monitoring Sheet
▸ Daily Planner
▸ Individual Evaluation Record

Narrate
▸ Ongoing Monitoring Sheet
▸ Daily Planner
▸ Individual Evaluation Record

Persuade
▸ Ongoing Monitoring Sheet
▸ Daily Planner
▸ Individual Evaluation Record

Respond
▸ Ongoing Monitoring Sheet
▸ Daily Planner
▸ Individual Evaluation Record

Research Tools

Research is a unique requirement of writing nonfiction. All nonfiction texts, from personal narratives to informational reports, are based on information, and research is the process of gathering that information. Research can involve searching one's own memory for personal narrative; trying out a procedure in preparation for writing instructions; or observing, reading, viewing, or listening in order to write an informational text. All of these inquiries yield the facts that are the basis of nonfiction writing.

There is a multitude of research tools that students can use during class and for individual units of study. *Explorations in Nonfiction Writing* for kindergarten to grade 2 depends on two primary tools: research stations and the R.A.N. chart.

RESEARCH STATIONS

Research stations are an excellent way to get students actively engaged in locating information. Students use a variety of sources dynamically and interactively as they search, question, and locate information. In addition, research stations are a particularly effective means of organizing the resources you have gathered for classroom research. Research stations can:

▸ explicitly support your curriculum and content standards

▸ provide students with a variety of age-appropriate resources

▸ actively engage children in discovering information for themselves, thus developing their sense of inquiry

▸ make it easy for children to access information related to their topic

▸ focus writers' attention on content and writing rather than searching for sources

▸ provide a forum for student collaboration and enhance learning

▸ make an exploration manageable in the classroom

If your classroom is small, don't worry! You can still utilize research stations by placing resources in tubs that teams can take to their tables or place on the floor while engaging in a "station."

GATHERING RESOURCES

Before beginning a curriculum unit or an exploration, you need to assemble curriculum and standards-based resources—textbooks, reference books, and the like. At the same time, you'll want to alert your school and community librarian(s). They will be able to identify available resources—print as well as other media—for you to borrow or catalog in a reference list. In addition, they may be able to set aside a cart containing these topic-specific sources for your class to use.

Ensure that the material you gather is not too challenging for students to read or understand. They need to be able to access facts easily and gain the information to record in their research notebooks, on sticky notes, or on individual R.A.N. charts. If students find some of the material too challenging, encourage them to use pictures or video to gather information.

> "Initially, there's a lot of prep work with the research stations, but once they are up and running, they will be a powerful means for having students locate information for themselves, rather than being spoon-fed facts by the teacher."
>
> —FROM A PILOT TEACHER

When resources on each topic are limited, it can be helpful to set up stations that focus on specific topics. With this orientation, students select a research topic and then sign up to work at the station that provides resources on that topic. This forms a collaborative team of researchers who may work together for several days at a single station, gathering facts about their subject.

Articles, Books, and Magazines

Ensure that the material at each station is accessible so your writers can comfortably access information while working independently. Select texts with detailed, enticing photographs and diagrams. Offer brief, interesting articles from magazines and newspapers or adapted from the Internet. Paste them onto the front and back of poster board, heavy card stock, or even cereal boxes. Laminate these and place them into baskets with books on the topic being explored. (Lamination will ensure that they last for many years.) It is also a good idea to include leveled nonfiction books at reading levels that are comfortable for your students.

Make sure you don't have too many books and magazines on a single topic. You don't want students to spend all their time trying to select appropriate resources. To make it easy for researchers to find information, tab specific pages of books that contain lots of information. Then students won't have to sift through too much information to locate relevant facts. Students should spend their research time reading and writing information, not trying to locate it.

If students from previous years have published their own books on the topic, save some of these to add to the basket. In addition, make available big books and mentor texts that you have introduced in whole-class settings for students to review to gather relevant facts.

Encourage students to tell their fellow researchers at the research station the information they have learned before recording it. This will help them put the information into their own words and not simply copy the new facts they are learning.

Realia or Observations

If a topic lends itself to students' being able to make direct observations, gather the necessary items for a classroom research station. For example: If students are studying insects, you could set up an ant farm. If students are studying pioneer America, create an observation station featuring artifacts with brief descriptions that students can observe, discuss, and record information about. If students are studying African animals, provide realistic toy animals to hold and study. Provide magnifying glasses to help students observe live animals, plants, and other artifacts brought in for observation.

Sometimes observations outside the classroom are helpful. These can be as simple as looking out the window to study weather conditions or opening the door to take an observational nature walk, or as involved as taking field trips to community services, museums, or other cultural, research-related locations.

As always with research stations, encourage students to discuss with each other what they are observing before recording the information.

Computer and Internet

Internet research needs to be streamlined, both to protect students and to assure that relevant information is easy to locate. You may wish to begin by organizing texts, visuals, and Internet links in topic-labeled folders on your classroom computers to make it easy for writers to access appropriate materials. To provide online content, look for sites that are kid-friendly and easy to navigate. Narrow down the field of available websites on the topic being explored. Adding the words "for children" when you type in the topic will help narrow the field considerably. Then bookmark appropriate sites, including any relevant video clips you find, so that students are not overwhelmed with too many sites to select from.

If you have access to only a limited number of computers, pair students so that two can use a station at the same time. Pairing students to work on one computer is a great way to get them to talk to each other about what they are learning. This makes it easier for them to write their information.

Pictures, Photographs, and Models

Collect and laminate a variety of pictures and photographs from magazines, books, and websites for students to observe and mine for information. Studying graphic information is a great way for students to hone their inferencing skills—drawing conclusions and figuring out information without being directly told.

Encourage students to discuss what they are seeing with their peers, to raise questions about what they are seeing, and to record what they see—in pictures or in words—in their research notebooks or on the R.A.N. chart. Be sure to check in with each group from time to time to make sure their thinking has not gone astray.

Enhance children's visual comprehension by using a masking tool (such as a piece of cardboard or paper with a circular cut-out) to focus in on smaller sections of a picture, then zoom out to reexamine the whole in view of the details they've studied.

Listening Station

Although commercially produced audiotapes and CDs do not often explore nonfiction topics, you can get around this lack by making your own. During read-alouds of favorite nonfiction texts or mentor texts, flip on the recorder as you read to create a lasting audio resource. Alternatively, encourage your best readers to practice enough to create expressive read-aloud recordings—or have students from higher grades make them for you. Keep the read-aloud books with the audiotapes at the listening station so children can both look at and hear the information.

You also might want to make topic-specific audiotapes or CDs for students to listen to. Narrate a collection of photographs, for example, or read aloud a tabbed section of an article or book that might be too difficult for students to read. This is a good way to assure that students "discover" important information required by your curriculum or standards.

Have students listen to only a small portion of the audio, stop and talk, and then record what they have learned. They can then go back and listen to the next small portion of information. By breaking up the listening, students will gather far more information and not become overwhelmed with large volumes of facts in one hearing.

DVDs and Videos

Bookmark video clips on the Web or locate commercially produced DVD documentaries on the topics of your students' research.

For inspiration, consider recording videos of students presenting their individual explorations and making them available for students in future years—or savoring them again in the current year. These not only boost the morale of your current students but also give subsequent classes something to aim for.

As with audio resources, have students view small portions of the DVD, stop and talk, then record what they have learned. They can then go back and view more information. Breaking up the viewing makes information less overwhelming and assures that students will gather far more information.

MANAGING RESEARCH STATIONS

A strategy for managing participation at research stations and a few guidelines for students will help your research stations work smoothly.

Set Up a Task Management Board

When setting up small-group research stations, it is advisable to have a task management board so that students know which station they are attending each day. Assigning a particular set of children to each station allows you to keep the research groups to a reasonable number, to group students across genders and abilities, and to make sure students progress to their stations in an orderly manner.

Chart or Poster with Names

One way to set up a task management board is to write the name of each station on a card, display the cards in a pocket chart, and slip the names or pictures of the children in each research team next to the appropriate card. Simply change the station cards each day to signify the new station that each group of students will be attending. (Alternatively, use sticky notes for stations and students, and display these on a large piece of poster board.)

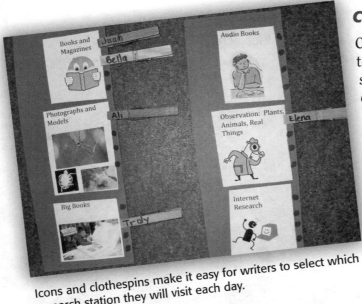

Icons and clothespins make it easy for writers to select which research station they will visit each day.

Clothespin Organizer

Clothespins provide an alternative organizing tool to link nonfiction writers to research stations. For this format, place the name of each student on a clothespin. Determine how many individuals may be at each station, and then invite writers to attach their clothespins next to the picture of the station they wish to visit. (Notice the dark circles next to each station indicating the number of writers allowed at that station.) If that station is full for the day, then writers know to select another option. Or, if you need to identify in advance which writers will go to which stations, you can easily arrange the clothespins yourself to ensure that students attend particular stations.

Use Research Notebooks or Folders

To keep each student's research information in one place, consider beginning a new research notebook for each topic students are studying—one for the class project and another for the individual project—or make a research folder or individual R.A.N. chart for each child.

While research is always a good idea, it will be particularly crucial in the Extended Writing Units focused on informational reports. In a report, writers need to have a system for collecting and organizing facts. While there are many ways to do this, we find that research notebooks, research folders, concept webs, and R.A.N. charts (see page 295) are all powerful tools for writers.

From research notebook to finished project, this writer has kept turtle information organized by topic.

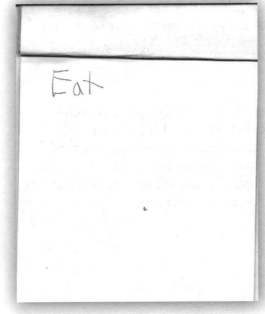

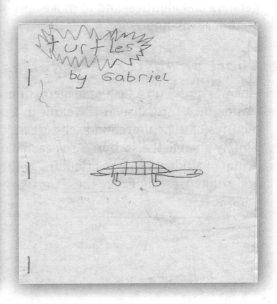

Research Notebooks

A research notebook is made from half-size sheets of plain paper that are stapled together into a small journal. Like a content web, the research notebook serves as an organizer where facts can be inserted with other related information. For research on bears, individual pages in the research notebook might have headings such as *Eat, Live, Look,* and *Interesting Facts*. For kindergarten and early first-grade writers, it is helpful to have each page pre-labeled with a category so that valuable time isn't wasted copying the headings for the pages.

With a research notebook in hand, young writers interact with research stations by collecting facts from books, magazines, videos, audio books, and so on. Because facts related to a concept such as "What a bear looks like" all go on the same page, facts are gathered in an organized manner that is highly supportive of the writing that will follow.

Research Folders

Research folders are an alternative to research notebooks. Simple to create, they are file folders with envelopes glued inside. Each envelope carries a category such as appearance, habitat, food, and so on. As researchers gather facts—in the form of sketches, single words, or phrases—they jot their information on small pieces of paper. The notes then are slipped into the appropriate envelopes. When the writer is ready to construct a text, it is easy to arrange the notes in an order that supports sentence and paragraph development.

Research folders offer another way for writers to organize information.

Concept Webs

Concept webs, especially when they include sketches and small pictures to support emergent learners, are helpful tools for organizing facts and information. They can be part of either a research folder or a research notebook. The web shown here was modeled by the teacher during a read-aloud of Gail Gibbons's book *Spiders* to show writers how a web can assist them in organizing information.

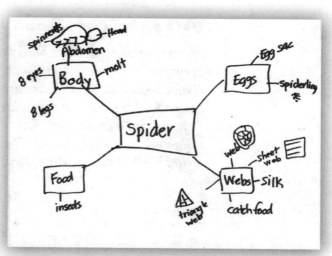

Concept webs that include both words and small sketches support nonfiction writers as they gather and organize facts for their writing.

Individual R.A.N. Charts

Individual R.A.N. (Reading and Analyzing Nonfiction) charts may be used in conjunction with the class R.A.N. chart during a class project or to organize a writer's independent project. We recommend that you guide children several times through the R.A.N. strategy's thinking analysis in a whole-class setting before expecting them to use it on their own. See the complete explanation of both class and individual uses of the R.A.N. chart in *A Guide to Teaching Nonfiction Writing, Grades K–2.* (For information about the guides, refer to page xvii of the introduction to this book.)

All writers will benefit from the use of any of these research organizers. What is critical is that they learn to categorize information so that facts can be clustered together in a meaningful way when they write.

Demonstrate How to Record Information

While engaging with research stations, nonfiction writers record their learning in sketches, in words, and in sentences, ending up with a research notebook filled with facts on their topic. But it is essential to scaffold success by showing children how to interact at the station and how to transfer their facts and learning onto paper. For all stations, show students the materials at the station and use think-aloud language to demonstrate how you would gather information. For the computer, audio, and video stations, you will also need to set guidelines and procedures for use of the equipment as well as teaching students how to use these media as research tools.

The following think-alouds offer some examples of how explicit modeling can pave the way for success at research stations.

Important Note: Writers use a research notebook to gather facts on a single topic. The examples below are not meant to suggest that one writer is researching several topics simultaneously.

Using the Books and Magazines Station: Think-Aloud

At this station there are books and magazines about bears. Watch as I select a book and find interesting facts. In this book it says that some bears are black. It also says that some bears are brown and that polar bears are white. The pictures also show me the color of the bears. We can learn a lot from pictures. I am ready to write some facts. Notice how I turn to the page in my research notebook that says "Look." This is the page for what bears look like. I will write: black, brown, white. *Bears come in those three colors.*

Using the Listening Station: Think-Aloud

Watch as I show you how to use the listening station. I am going to listen to the book being read and then I will use sketches and words to record my facts. [We listen to a recording of a book excerpt about turtles' eating habits, and then I turn off the tape.] *At the listening station, it is really helpful to stop the tape recorder each time the reader tells me to turn the page. While the recorder is stopped, I can think about what I have heard and decide if I want to write or draw any facts in my research notebook. I am not going to try to write it all down. That would be too much. Watch as I turn to the page in my research notebook that says "Eat." I am going to draw some of the things that I learned turtles eat. I will also add labels. The labels will help me remember what I drew.*

Using Realia or Observation: Think-Aloud

I am at the station with the shell of a turtle and the big labeled diagram. I can tell this station will help me find information for the page that says "Look." With this shell, I can really think about the turtle's body and create a sketch that includes detail. Watch as I use the labeled diagram to find the words that describe different parts of the turtle's body. I definitely need to add some of those words to the diagram in my research notebook.

Recording Information with Sketches, Labels, and Notes: Think-Aloud

Monitor the entries writers make in their research notebooks to ensure that they are focusing on sketches, labels, and notes rather than writing lengthy sentences. Sketches and labels are particularly important as facts are gathered. Sketches and labels allow writers to collect data quickly and are an accessible communication system for writers at all developmental levels.

Researchers, here is a trick that can help you create great sentences. I use the Key Word strategy and I write down the key words on sticky notes in my research notebook. I have just read this page about frogs and I want to select some key words. The page tells me that tadpoles start with gills and then they grow lungs. Watch as I use sticky notes and write: tadpoles,

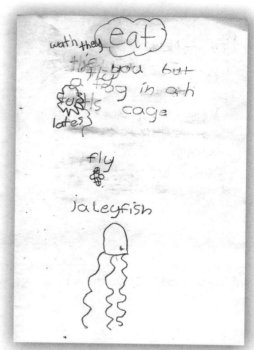

Sketches and labels help writers remember facts from their research.

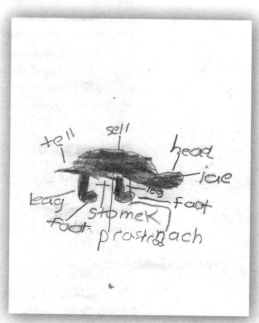

Realia and diagrams help writers create scientifically accurate diagrams of their own.

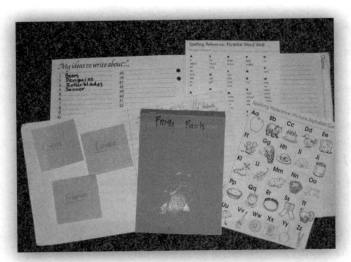

Organizing sticky notes by topic in a notebook helps writers think logically and facilitates the drafting process.

gills, lungs. *Those are the key words I want to remember. Now, watch how I can take my sticky notes out of the research notebook and arrange them so they help me make a sentence.* Tadpoles start with gills and then they grow lungs. *The Key Word strategy helped me use facts from the books but write them in my own words!*

Working Together: Think-Aloud

Encourage writers to tell their peers at the research station the information they have learned before recording it. This will not only increase their knowledge by letting them learn from each other but will also help them put information into their own words and not simply copy the new facts from the sources.

Writers, one of the most important things you can do at a research station is talk to your thinking partners. I have asked Marina to be my thinking partner so we can show you how it works. We are at the research station with big books. Watch how we read and think together before we write facts. "Marina, this page about the shark is amazing. It says that the great white shark weighs as much as a car. I am thinking that I could draw a picture of a car on the page about what the shark looks like. That would help me remember how much it weighs. What facts do you think are important on this page? What are you going to write in your research notebook?"

Accommodating Beginning Writers

Early in the year, if parent helpers or older students are available during research time, you may want to consider adding an "expert" at one or two of the research stations. The guiding expert can do additional modeling with the materials of the station, take a bit of dictation, coach writers on creating detailed sketches, and so on.

If beginning writers have difficulty recording the information they have discovered, let them tell you what they have learned. Then write it for them on sticky notes that they can put into their notebooks. This will ensure that their thinking is not lost when they want to share and/or publish it later.

See the DVD *Nonfiction Writing: Intentional, Connected, and Engaging* (in the resources list on page 307 and the Power Writes for additional ways to teach researching.)

THE R.A.N. STRATEGY:
READING AND ANALYZING NONFICTION

The strategy for reading and analyzing nonfiction, or the R.A.N. strategy, is an excellent tool for students to use as writers when researching a specific topic for either class or individual projects. Researchers collect information and organize their ideas on a chart to make their thinking visible. The chart is used throughout a research project to record and categorize information on the go. The R.A.N. helps writers in two critical ways: first, to be aware of and critically examine their thinking, and second, to organize their research information in preparation for writing.

The R.A.N. strategy is a modification of the KWL strategy—What We Know, What We Want to Know, What We Learned (Ogle, 1986)—and expands KWL into a critical research process. The comparison between the two strategies can be seen below.

KWL STRATEGY		
What We Know	**What We Want to Know**	**What We Learned**
Children state information they know or think they know about the topic.	Children come up with questions they want answered.	Children research to answer specific questions raised.

R.A.N. STRATEGY				
What we think we know	**Yes, we were right, or Confirmed information**	**We don't think this anymore, or Misconceptions**	**New learning, or New facts**	**Wonderings**
Children state information they believe to be correct about the topic (prior knowledge).	Children read to confirm prior knowledge.	Children read to discard incorrect prior knowledge.	Children read to locate additional information not part of prior knowledge.	Children raise questions based on the new information gathered.

Comparison of the KWL and R.A.N. Strategies

OVERVIEW OF THE R.A.N. CHART

A R.A.N. chart—a large board for working with a whole class or a folder or simple graphic organizer for an individual—is divided into columns labeled with thinking-analysis headings. Facts about the topic are recorded under the appropriate headings—first, under "What we think we know," and later, after researching, under any one of the other headings.

Headings → Categories ↓	**1** What we think we know	**2** Yes, we were right or Confirmed information	**3** We don't think this anymore or Misconceptions	**4** New learning	**5** Wonderings
What bears look like	Children state information they think to be correct about bears (prior knowledge)	Children read to confirm prior knowledge about bears	Children read to discard incorrect prior knowledge about bears	Children read to locate additional information about bears	Children raise questions about bears based on the new information gathered
Where bears live					
What bears eat					
Other great facts					

R.A.N. chart for a class report on bears

1 "What we think we know" is similar to the KWL first step. This heading acknowledges that students come to school with background knowledge and that this background knowledge may not be correct.

2 "Yes, we were right" or "Confirmed information" gives students an opportunity to confirm prior knowledge as they research a given topic. It gives them a sense of success as they confirm facts that they already know.

3 "We don't think this anymore" or "Misconceptions" helps students understand that when researching, the information they locate may be different from or even contradict their prior knowledge. It encourages students to rethink what they previously thought to be correct.

4 "New learning" or "New facts" encourages students to think about information that is new learning, and to gather new literal understandings. This helps deepen their content understandings about a topic.

5 "Wonderings" is the same as the KWL heading "What We Want to Know." In the R.A.N. strategy, this heading is applied after students have researched and not before. This is because researchers raise questions during and after they explore a topic, not just before. It is difficult for students to raise questions about a topic they have little prior knowledge about.

In addition to the thinking-analysis headings, the R.A.N. chart may specify categories of information. Content categories are derived from the specific content you want to cover as well as your research sources—you may want to identify subtopics for which you have the most information available. These categories help writers sift through and organize their research notes in preparation for writing. In this sample, a class R.A.N. chart for a report about bears, the content categories are "What bears look like," "Where bears live," "What bears eat," and "Other great facts." Illustrations help young researchers identify and remember both headings and categories.

CONSTRUCTING A CLASS R.A.N. CHART

For class projects, you will need to construct a large, sturdy R.A.N. chart as the centerpiece of your whole-group instruction. Begin with a basic chart containing the appropriate thinking-analysis headings. (See below for suggestions for tailoring these to beginning researchers.) Laminating the chart will enable you to use it again for future explorations. If you are using sticky notes for students to record their ideas, the R.A.N. chart may be displayed anywhere. If you use index cards or paper for recording information, you'll need to mount the R.A.N. chart on a bulletin board and affix the ideas with tacks. Information will be re-categorized during instruction, so it is important to use sticky notes or other means of moving information around the board easily.

The next step is to determine the categories of information you want students to look for as they research. (On the R.A.N. chart for the bear report, these were appearance, habitat, food, and other facts.) Three or four subtopics are enough for beginning writers. These categories will become the subtopics or internal headings of the written report. Be sure that the resources in your research stations provide adequate information on all of your subtopics. Include a category like "Other great facts" to give writers a chance to share something that excites them but may not fit elsewhere.

When first introducing the R.A.N. strategy or when using it with younger children, it is advisable to create your R.A.N. chart using only headings 1, 2, and 4 ("What we think we know," "Yes, we were right," and "New learning"). This way, students won't become overwhelmed on their first attempt at working with this new research strategy. As students become more comfortable working with the R.A.N. strategy, headings 3 and 5 can be introduced. For beginning researchers, you may also want to use the R.A.N. chart without the categories. This works well for a relatively narrow, focused topic and eliminates the challenge of categorizing information under the correct subtopics.

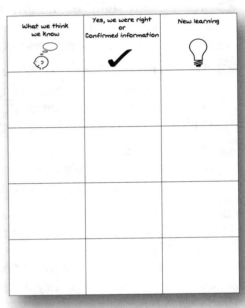

Introducing the R.A.N. strategy

IMPLEMENTING THE CLASS R.A.N. CHART

Working collaboratively with children on a class R.A.N. chart is an excellent way to model and guide young researchers' thinking. The chart helps students keep track of the facts they are gathering while still giving them the freedom to discover information on their own. It also shows writers how to begin organizing the various sections of their writing.

Introduce the R.A.N. Chart

Provide an overview of the chart by explaining its purpose and how each of the thinking-analysis headings supports research.

We're going to put some of our most important research information on this chart as we study for the next couple of weeks. [Point to the first heading.] This first heading says "What we think we know." I have put a picture of a brain here to remind me that this is where we will put information that is already in our brains before we start researching. We're going to write down what we already know about bears on sticky notes and put them on this chart under "What we think we know."

After we've researched for a while, we'll look at our sticky notes and decide if we found facts to prove that [point to the second heading] *"Yes, we were right" or that maybe what we thought before isn't true, so* [point to the third heading] *"We don't think this anymore."*

Continue this process with the remaining headings on your class R.A.N. chart.

Then explain the categories and the illustrations you have chosen for your topic. For example, an introduction to the categories for the bear report above might begin this way: *One thing I hope we find out when we research is what bears look like. That's why I included this category: "What bears look like." You can see I have drawn a pair of eyes next to this category to remind me that it's about what bears look like, or their appearance. If I think I know something* [point to the "What we think we know" heading] *about what bears look like* [point to the "What bears look like" category], *this is where I'll put it.* [Indicate the square under "What we think we know" and beside "What bears look like."]

Continue explaining the remaining categories. After a few categories, children should be able to chime in or show you where you would put your researched facts.

What We Think We Know

Begin research by asking children to share their prior knowledge about the topic. Introduce the topic you will explore together and model the thinking you expect children to engage in.

The first thing we're going to do is share all the information we already have about bears. [Point to the "What we think we know" column.] *Well, one thing I think I know is that bears eat fish. I remember seeing a picture once of a bear standing in a stream reaching for a leaping fish. I'm going to write* fish *on my sticky note and put it in the "What we think we know" column, next to "What bears eat."*

Then ask writers to tell you what they think they know about the selected topic. Accept all students' background knowledge, whether it is accurate or not. This is their prior thinking. Having them share is a wonderful way to assess their content knowledge on a particular topic and will help you extend their content understandings.

Chart students' responses using sticky notes, slips of paper, or index cards. Alternatively, allow each student to write his or her own fact onto a card or sticky note and then post it on the chart in the "What we think we know" column next to the appropriate category. This will ensure that all students have their thinking recorded. However, limit each child's information to what they consider to be their best or "Wow!" fact. This will help you avoid filling the class R.A.N. chart with too much information to process.

If you find that your students possess little background knowledge on a topic, introduce the topic through a read-aloud, a shared reading, or a field trip before asking again for "What we think we know." This will give all students some accurate prior knowledge to contribute and will give them a sense of success when they confirm their prior thinking through research.

	What we think we know	Yes, we were right or Confirmed information ✔	We don't think this anymore or Misconceptions ✗	New learning	Wonderings ?
What bears look like (eye)	furry, long tall, tall and fat, big feet with claws, 2 ears, sharp teeth				
Where bears live (house)	cave, in trees, sleep in the grass, house in the woods, in snow				
What bears eat (person)	fruit, honey, fish, campers' food, donuts				
Other great facts (star)					

Children record prior knowledge on sticky notes under "What we think we know."

If students come up with similar background knowledge, place the sticky notes or cards on top of each other, or write the initials or names of the students who came up with the same information on one note and discard the others. This will signify that more than one person was thinking the same idea.

Assist students who have trouble putting their information in the correct category by involving the group in a think-aloud: *Harvey's note says "Bears eat berries." Hmmm . . . Where would I put that? Here, next to "What bears look like"? No; "Bears eat berries" doesn't talk about what bears look like. Does it go next to "Where bears live" or "What bears eat"?*

Use the R.A.N. Chart to Record Researched Information

Continue working with the R.A.N. chart throughout the research project, adding and moving sticky notes to reflect students' growing knowledge. Make time for writers to research the chosen topic. (See the section on research stations, page xiii, for ways to manage this process.) Come together as a group after each research session to share a "best fact" using the R.A.N. chart. Each heading on the chart prompts children to examine and evaluate their information. Following are tips for engaging their thinking and making it visible on the R.A.N. chart.

Yes, We Were Right or Confirmed Information

As students research, encourage them to look for facts to confirm the prior knowledge that has been posted on the class R.A.N. chart. Use think-aloud language to demonstrate this process: *I wrote in my research notebook under what I think I know that "Bears eat fish" and "All bears climb trees." Well, I did some research and I found that bears do eat fish. So, I put a check mark next to that fact in my notebook. This means "Yes, I was right." I didn't find out that all bears climb trees, so I can't put a check mark next to this piece of information yet.* On the R.A.N. chart, locate the appropriate sticky note and move it from "What we think we know" to "Yes, we were right" to show children that a fact has been confirmed.

To convey the importance of factual accuracy, ensure that each researcher is responsible for confirming her or his own prior knowledge. If other students locate information that confirms another researcher's prior thinking, encourage them to share this information so that the sticky note can be moved across to the "Yes, we were right" column.

When moving facts from "What we think we know" to "Yes, we were right," encourage students to provide evidence for their information by citing their sources. For example: *Dwain, you wrote on your sticky note in the "Other great facts" category that bears like to sleep in the winter. Now you want to move it to "Yes, we were right." How do you know that it's right? Oh, you read it in the book about bears at the books and magazines station! That's great, Dwain. Good writers always make sure their information is accurate.*

If students are unable to confirm their prior thinking and your class R.A.N. chart still has a lot of facts in the "What we think we know" column, you may need to guide researchers toward specific sources or look for additional resources that will help them achieve this goal.

For more advanced learners, have them write the source from which they were able to confirm the information on the back of the sticky note or card. This is a valuable way to begin teaching students how to cite sources as they research.

We Don't Think This Anymore or Misconceptions

In addition to finding information to confirm their prior knowledge, encourage students to look for information that contradicts any facts they thought they knew: *I was looking at a website trying to confirm my information that all bears climb trees, and I found out something I didn't know. Bears can climb trees, sometimes to get away from danger, but some bears—like grizzlies and polar bears—are really too big to climb, so they run away instead. I don't think all bears climb trees anymore, so I'll move my sticky note to the "I don't think this anymore" column, but I'll keep it in the row next to "Other great facts."*

If students identify misconceptions posted on the R.A.N. chart, encourage them to share information with the "owner" of the relevant fact so that the sticky note can be discussed during class time and moved to the "We don't think this anymore" column.

Be alert to any misconceptions you see in the "What we think we know" column, and try to provide students with adequate resources to correct these misconceptions. If important sources are not easily accessible to young researchers—they require too much reading or are too sophisticated—use your read-aloud time to highlight specific information.

You may also encourage older or more advanced learners to correct misconceptions. Have them cite the source of the correct information on the back of the sticky note or index card containing the original information.

With younger learners, some misconceptions should be left alone even if they are incorrect. If, for example, you are studying deer and the children come up with "Rudolph flies" under "What we think we know," do not deem this a misconception. We need to respect the fantasies that young students bring to certain topics. To the young learner, this piece of information is a fact and should be treated as nonfiction.

New Learning or New Facts

Although confirming and refuting prior knowledge is an important research skill, locating new information is at the heart of research. New information builds new learning and broadens students' knowledge base. Give students ample opportunities to research together to locate and record new facts. Refer to the section on research stations (page 285) to assist students with this task.

Fan the flames of children's excitement at learning new things. Encourage researchers' amazement, curiosity, and engagement. *Wow! I just found out about sun bears. They are the smallest bears in the world, but they are still almost twice as big as one of you kids! And they are kind of a mystery because no one has studied them much. This is my favorite bear so far. I'm going to put my sketch of a sun bear and its weight on the R.A.N. chart next to "What bears look like" because it tells what the sun bear looks like. What interesting facts have you found?*

When the class comes together to share new information on the R.A.N. chart, continue to limit students' contributions to what they consider to be their best or "Wow!" facts to keep the volume of information on the chart manageable. This will also ensure that there is not too much information for young learners to process.

If your more advanced learners are recording the sources for their information, make sure that their source information is complete. At the conclusion of the unit, you can demonstrate how to use this information to create a bibliography or reference page.

Wonderings

One way to assure learners' engagement with information and ideas is to teach them to wonder about them. Learning doesn't stop with gathering, recording, and evaluating facts. It is fueled by taking the next step toward further research: raising questions, or "wonderings," about the facts students researched.

	Wonderings ?
What bears look like 👁	I wonder what color sun bears are. How long is a sun bear's fur?
Where bears live 🏠	Where do sun bears live? In trees? In caves? I wonder where sun bears sleep.
What bears eat	I wonder what sun bears eat.
Other great facts ★	I wonder why no one has studied sun bears. How do scientists study bears?

Wonderings about sun bears.

Demonstrate how to raise wonderings by posing questions that use the standard "WH" question words—*who, what, when, where, why,* and *how*—and prompting children to do the same. Select a fact, confirmed or new, from your R.A.N. chart and use a think-aloud to model wondering or questioning with the question words. Use this opportunity to reinforce categorizing the questions by placing your questions next to the relevant subtopics on your R.A.N. chart. For example: *I'll look at my sticky note on sun bears. All I know is how much they weigh. Here are some other things I wonder about.*

Use students' wonderings to stimulate further research. Have researchers find answers to their wonderings and chart these answers under the heading "New learning." Also, encourage students to look at the wonderings raised by other students to see if they can find the answers.

Once the research is done, any information remaining under the heading "What we think we know" that has not been confirmed or deemed a misconception can be moved across to the "Wonderings" column. This helps students understand that not all of their prior knowledge can be verified and that unverified facts become unanswered wonderings.

	What we think we know	Yes, we were right or Confirmed information ✓	We don't think this anymore or Misconceptions ✗	New learning	Wonderings ?
What bears look like 👁		2 ears; furry; big feet with claws; sharp teeth	tall and fat; long tall	brown black and white; most have small ears; some fur is long some is short; some have markings on their fur; many SIZES	I wonder how much a brown bear weighs.
Where bears live 🏠		in trees; cave; in the snow	house in the woods; sleep in the grass	swamps; on a glacier in the Arctic; rains; all over the world; some bears hibernate in winter; burrows in the ground	How do polar bears keep their feet warm?; Why do bears live near water?; Where do bears spend the winter?
What bears eat 🧍	donuts	fish; fruit; campers' food; honey		plants; flowers and grasses; berries; seals; honey; birds	Why do bears go into camp grounds?
Other great facts ⭐					Grizzly bears are huge!; Polar bears can swim.; Bears can climb trees fast!; A koala isn't really a bear.

Organizing thinking on a R.A.N. chart

IMPLEMENTING INDIVIDUAL R.A.N. CHARTS

After regular use of the class R.A.N. chart, first- and second-grade students may become familiar enough with the thinking to use a personal version of the R.A.N. chart to organize their notes, either in conjunction with or instead of their research notebooks or folders. Use of an individual R.A.N. chart can go hand in hand with the class R.A.N. chart. That is, individuals can record prior knowledge in their R.A.N. chart as the class is doing so. They can confirm and collect new facts on their own and bring their results to the class discussion.

Individual R.A.N. charts can be constructed in many ways. One option creates a sturdy folder that can store and organize sticky notes and can be reused again and again. It is advisable to laminate the file folders before you put them together. This will ensure that the R.A.N. folder will last for the entire school year.

If you do not have access to file folders, you can use paper or card stock as an alternative.

File-Folder R.A.N. Chart

Step 1: Start with two file folders. Place the left half of folder 2 on top of the right half of folder 1.

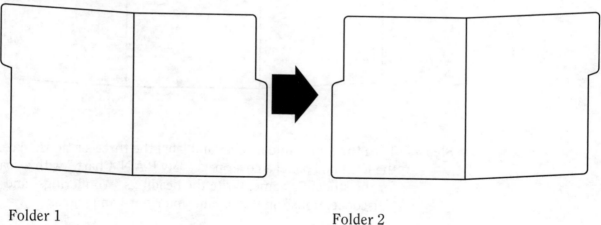

Folder 1   Folder 2

Step 2: Staple, glue, or tape the overlapped sections together.

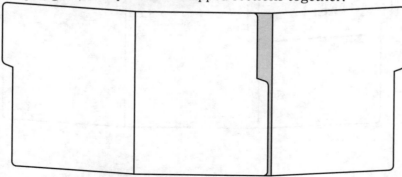

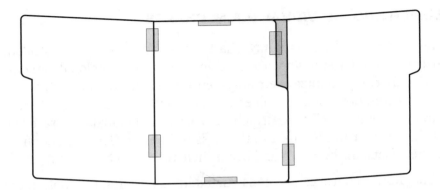

Step 3: Label the three sections at the top: "What I think I know," "Confirmed information," and "New learning."

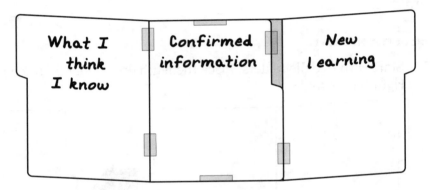

Step 4: Turn the joined folders over and label the three sections. Make the left-hand panel a cover page, "My R.A.N. Chart," with a space for the student's name. Write the headings "Wonderings" and "Misconceptions" on the middle and right-hand panels.

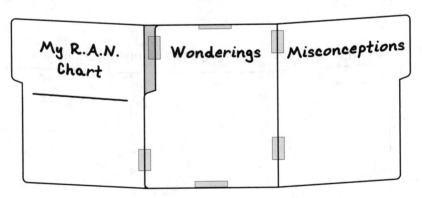

Step 5: Turn to the first side again. Fold "What I think I know" over "Confirmed information." Then fold the cover panel to the front.

Simplified R.A.N. Organizer

Beginning writers may struggle using the R.A.N. folders as shown above. One simplified method is to use an organizer with just one or two headings: "What I think I know" and "New facts I learned." Look for a template on the *Resources CD-ROM*.

If you feel that personal R.A.N. charts are too complex for your students to navigate, you can instead provide them with research notebooks to record their information. A research notebook is simply a collection of blank pages with a cover.

More R.A.N. Resources

For further information on using the R.A.N. strategy, see the following resources.

Hoyt, Linda, and Tony Stead. 2011. *Nonfiction Writing: Intentional, Connected, and Engaging* DVD. Portsmouth, NH: Heinemann.

Stead, Tony. 2009. *Good Choice! Supporting Independent Reading and Response.* Portland, ME: Stenhouse Publishers.

Stead, Tony. 2006. *Reality Checks: Teaching Reading Comprehension with Nonfiction,* Chapter 2. Portland, ME: Stenhouse Publishers.

Grade 2
Index of Model Lessons by Subject Area

Art

Topic	Writing Form	Lesson or Unit	
Clay Pot	Procedural Letter (how to make a clay pot)	Instruct Power Write, page 104	
Crab Drawing	Procedural Text (how to draw a crab)	Extended Writing Unit, page 84	
Scarecrow	Investigation (how to make a scarecrow)	Instruct Power Write, page 116	VL
Spider Craft	Art Project Directions (how to make a googly-eyed spider)	Instruct Power Write, page 108	

Math

Topic	Writing Form	Lesson or Unit
Shapes	Friendly Letter to Summarize	Inform Power Write, page 54

Reading

Topic	Writing Form	Lesson or Unit	
Author Study	Friendly Letter (Eric Carle)	Respond Power Write, page 274	
Author Tea	Eyewitness Account	Narrate Power Write, page 180	
Biography	Biography (Amelia Earhart and a self-selected hero)	Narrate Extended Writing Unit, page 154	
	Biography (Wilma Rudolph)	Inform Power Write, page 64	
	Response Poster (Admiral Byrd)	Respond Extended Writing Unit, page 246	
	Two-Word Strategy (Wilson "Snowflake" Bentley)	Respond Power Write, page 272	
Book Party	Friendly Letter	Persuade Power Write, page 224	
Book Review	Book Review	Persuade Power Write, page 226	
Respond to What You Read	Fact-and-Response Grid	Respond Power Write, page 280	
	Fact/Opinion Chart	Respond Power Write, page 270	VL
	Friendly Letter	Respond Power Write, page 274	
	Information Equation	Respond Power Write, page 276	
	Investigation	Respond Power Write, page 282	VL
	Response Poster	Respond Extended Writing Unit, page 246	
	Response to a Poem	Respond Power Write, page 268	
	Sketch to Stretch	Respond Power Write, page 278	VL
	Two-Word Strategy	Respond Power Write, page 272	

Science

Topic	Writing Form	Lesson or Unit	
Animals	Column Graph (favorite zoo animals)	Instruct Power Write, page 114	VL
Antarctica	Response Poster (Admiral Richard Byrd)	Respond Extended Writing Unit, page 246	
Bats	Venn Diagram	Inform Power Write, page 66	VL
Birds	Venn Diagram	Inform Power Write, page 66	VL
Crabs	Procedural Text (how to draw a crab)	Instruct Extended Writing Unit, page 84	
Deserts	Fact/Opinion Chart (desert plants)	Respond Power Write, page 270	VL
Earth's Rotation	Class Newsletter	Inform Power Write, page 68	
Food	Cross-Section Diagram (lemon)	Instruct Power Write, page 112	VL
	Persuasive Flyer (food drive)	Persuade Power Write, page 228	VL
	Recipe (how to make a salad)	Instruct Power Write, page 110	
Flight	Biography (Amelia Earhart)	Narrate Extended Writing Unit, page 154	
Habitats	Fact/Opinion Chart (desert plants)	Respond Power Write, page 270	VL
	Graphic Organizer (beach)	Persuade Power Write, page 230	VL
	Report (habitats)	Inform Extended Writing Unit, page 14	
	Response Poster (Antarctica)	Respond Extended Writing Unit, page 246	
Insects	Friendly Letter (insect books)	Respond Power Write, page 274	
Machines	Investigation (bicycles)	Persuade Power Write, page 232	VL
	Readers Theater (simple machines)	Inform Power Write, page 62	
Matter	Information Equation	Respond Power Write, page 276	
	Informational Poem	Inform Power Write, page 70	
Moon	Fact-and-Response Grid	Respond Power Write, page 280	
	Timeline (moon phases)	Narrate Power Write, page 184	VL
Ocean	Graphic Organizer (beach)	Persuade Power Write, page 230	VL
	Sketch to Stretch (sea turtles)	Respond Power Write, page 278	VL
Owls	Venn Diagram	Inform Power Write, page 66	VL
Rain Forest	Report	Inform Extended Writing Unit, page 14	
Rainbow	Information Equation	Respond Power Write, page 276	
Relationships in Science	Information Equation	Respond Power Write, page 276	
Science Fair	E-mail to Summarize	Inform Power Write, page 58	
Seeds	Eyewitness Account (planting seeds)	Narrate Power Write, page 180	
Senses	Response to a Poem ("Listen" by Linda Hoyt)	Respond Power Write, page 268	
Snakes	Personal Narrative	Narrate Extended Writing Unit, page 132	
Snow	Response Poster (Admiral Richard Byrd)	Respond Extended Writing Unit, page 246	
	Two-Word Strategy (Wilson "Snowflake" Bentley)	Respond Power Write, page 272	
Sun	Fact-and-Response Grid	Respond Power Write, page 280	
Teeth	Response to a Poem ("Tremendously Tough Tooth" by Linda Hoyt)	Respond Power Write, page 268	

Tigers	Nonfiction Narrative	Narrate Power Write, page 178	
Tornadoes	Retell from a Different Point of View	Narrate Power Write, page 176	
Turtles	Sketch to Stretch (sea turtles)	Respond Power Write, page 278	VL
Weather	Information Equation (rainbow)	Respond Power Write, page 276	
	Retell from a Different Point of View (tornado)	Narrate Power Write, page 176	
	Two-Word Strategy (snow)	Respond Power Write, page 272	
Whales	Investigation	Inform Power Write, page 72	VL

Social Studies

Topic	Writing Form	Lesson or Unit	
Class Events	Class Newsletter	Inform Power Write, page 68	
	E-mail to Summarize (science fair)	Inform Power Write, page 58	
	Eyewitness Account (author tea)	Narrate Power Write, page 180	
	Factual Recount (science lesson)	Narrate Power Write, page 182	
	Friendly Letter (book party)	Persuade Power Write, page 224	
	Note to Invite (open house)	Inform Power Write, page 56	
	Personal Narrative (animal visit to classroom)	Narrate Extended Writing Unit, page 132	
Class Routines	Map (fire drill)	Inform Power Write, page 60	VL
	Persuasive E-mail (lunch)	Persuade Power Write, page 222	
	How-to List (fire drill)	Instruct Power Write, page 106	
Communication	Class Newsletter	Inform Power Write, page 68	
	E-mail to Summarize	Inform Power Write, page 58	
	Eyewitness Account	Narrate Power Write, page 180	
	Factual Recount	Narrate Power Write, page 182	
	Friendly Letter	Persuade Power Write, page 224	
	Graphic Organizer	Persuade Power Write, page 230	VL
	Investigation	Persuade Power Write, page 232	
	Note to Invite	Inform Power Write, page 56	
	Persuasive E-mail	Persuade Power Write, page 222	
	Persuasive Flyer	Persuade Power Write, page 228	
	Travel Brochure	Persuade Extended Writing Unit, page 198	
	Written Argument	Persuade Power Write, page 220	
Community	Graphic Organizer (best place to visit)	Persuade Power Write, page 230	VL
	Investigation (bike safety)	Persuade Power Write, page 232	VL
	Persuasive Flyer (food drive)	Persuade Power Write, page 228	VL
	Travel Brochure (our town)	Persuade Extended Writing Unit, page 198	
Fire Drill	Map (how to get to a safe place in a school fire drill)	Inform Power Write, page 60	VL
	How-To List (how to do a fire drill)	Instruct Power Write, page 106	

Food	Recipe (salad)	Instruct Power Write, page 110
	Persuasive E-mail (eat lunch in classroom)	Persuade Power Write, page 222
	Persuasive Flyer (food drive)	Persuade Power Write, page 228 **VL**
Heroes	Biography (Amelia Earhart and a self-selected hero)	Narrate Extended Writing Unit, page 154
	Biography (Wilma Rudolph)	Inform Power Write, page 64
	Response Poster (Admiral Richard Byrd)	Respond Extended Writing Unit, page 246
	Two-Word Strategy (Wilson "Snowflake" Bentley)	Respond Power Write, page 272 **VL**
Personal Story	Personal Narrative	Narrate Extended Writing Unit, page 132
	Personal Narrative	Narrate Power Write, page 174
Safety	Investigation (bike safety)	Persuade Power Write, page 232 **VL**
	Map (how to get to a safe place in a school fire drill)	Inform Power Write, page 60 **VL**
	How-To List (how to do a fire drill)	Instruct Power Write, page 106
Scarecrow	Investigation (how to make a scarecrow)	Instruct Power Write, page 116 **VL**
Thanksgiving	Investigation (the first Thanksgiving)	Narrate Power Write, page 186 **VL**
TV	Written Argument (turn off the TV for a week)	Persuade Power Write, page 220

Grade 2
Index of Lessons by Writing Form

Writing Form		Lesson
Account	Eyewitness Account	Narrate Power Write, page 180
Argument	Graphic Organizer	Persuade Power Write, page 230 **VL**
	Written Argument	Persuade Power Write, page 220
Biography	Biography	Inform Power Write, page 64
	Biography	Narrate Extended Writing Unit, page 154
Book Review	Book Review	Persuade Power Write, page 226
Brochure	Travel Brochure	Persuade Extended Writing Unit, page 198
Chart	Fact/Opinion Chart	Respond Power Write, page 270 **VL**
	Fact-and-Response Grid	Respond Power Write, page 280
Description	Two-Word Strategy	Respond Power Write, page 272
Diagram	Cross-Section Diagram	Instruct Power Write, page 112 **VL**
	Venn Diagram	Inform Power Write, page 66 **VL**
E-mail	E-mail to Summarize	Inform Power Write, page 58
	Persuasive E-mail	Persuade Power Write, page 222
Equation	Information Equation	Respond Power Write, page 276
Flyer	Persuasive Flyer	Persuade Power Write, page 228 **VL**
Graph	Column Graph	Instruct Power Write, page 114 **VL**
Graphic Organizer	Graphic Organizer	Persuade Power Write, page 230 **VL**
	Venn Diagram	Inform Power Write, page 66 **VL**
Investigation	Investigation	Inform Power Write, page 72 **VL**
	Investigation	Instruct Power Write, page 116 **VL**
	Investigation	Narrate Power Write, page 186 **VL**
	Investigation	Persuade Power Write, page 232 **VL**
	Investigation	Respond Power Write, page 282 **VL**
Letter	Friendly Letter	Persuade Power Write, page 224
	Friendly Letter	Respond Power Write, page 274
	Friendly Letter to Summarize	Inform Power Write, page 54
	Procedural Letter	Instruct Power Write, page 104
List	How-To List	Instruct Power Write, page 106
Map	Map	Inform Power Write, page 60 **VL**
Newsletter	Class Newsletter	Inform Power Write, page 68
	Eyewitness Account	Narrate Power Write, page 180
Nonfiction Narrative	Biography	Inform Power Write, page 64
	Biography (Nonfiction Narrative)	Narrate Extended Writing Unit, page 154

	Nonfiction Narrative	Narrate Power Write, page 178
	Retell from a Different Point of View	Narrate Power Write, page 176
	Timeline	Narrate Power Write, page 184 **VL**
Note	Note to Invite	Inform Power Write, page 56
Organizer	Graphic Organizer	Persuade Power Write, page 230 **VL**
	Venn Diagram	Inform Power Write, page 66 **VL**
Personal Narrative	Eyewitness Account	Narrate Power Write, page 180
	Factual Recount	Narrate Power Write, page 182
	Personal Narrative	Narrate Extended Writing Unit, page 132
	Personal Narrative	Narrate Power Write, page 174
Poem	Informational Poem	Inform Power Write, page 70
Poster	Response Poster	Respond Extended Writing Unit, page 246
Procedure	Art Project Directions	Instruct Power Write, page 108
	Column Graph	Instruct Power Write, page 114 **VL**
	Cross-Section Diagram	Instruct Power Write, page 112 **VL**
	Investigation	Instruct Power Write, page 116 **VL**
	Procedural Letter	Instruct Power Write, page 104
	How-To List	Instruct Power Write, page 106
	Procedural Text	Instruct Extended Writing Unit, page 84
	Recipe	Instruct Power Write, page 110
Readers Theater	Readers Theater	Inform Power Write, page 62
Recipe	Recipe	Instruct Power Write, page 110
Recount	Eyewitness Account	Narrate Power Write, page 180
	Factual Recount	Narrate Power Write, page 182
Report	Report	Inform Extended Writing Unit, page 14
Response	Fact-and-Response Grid	Respond Power Write, page 280
	Fact/Opinion Chart	Respond Power Write, page 270 **VL**
	Friendly Letter	Respond Power Write, page 274
	Information Equation	Respond Power Write, page 276
	Investigation	Respond Power Write, page 282 **VL**
	Response Poster	Respond Extended Writing Unit, page 246
	Response to a Poem	Respond Power Write, page 268
	Sketch to Stretch	Respond Power Write, page 278 **VL**
	Two-Word Strategy	Respond Power Write, page 272
Retell	Factual Recount	Narrate Power Write, page 182
	Retell from a Different Point of View	Narrate Power Write, page 176
Review	Book Review	Persuade Power Write, page 226
Sketch	Sketch to Stretch	Respond Power Write, page 278 **VL**
Summary	E-mail to Summarize	Inform Power Write, page 58
	Friendly Letter to Summarize	Inform Power Write, page 54
Two-Word Strategy	Two-Word Strategy	Respond Power Write, page 272

Grade 2
Index of Lessons by Mentor Text

Mentor Text	Corresponding Lesson Resource	Pages
The Sonoran Desert	Inform EWU: Report	14–53
Science Learning!	Inform PW: Friendly Letter to Summarize	54–55
Trail Guide **VL**	Inform PW: Map	60–61
Designed for Survival	Inform PW: Readers Theater	62–63
Nancy Lopez	Inform PW: Biography	64–65
	Inform EWU: Biography	154–173
Goods and Services	Inform PW: Informational Poem	70–71
The Telephone: An Amazing Invention **VL**	Inform PW: Investigation	72–73
	Narrate PW: Investigation	186–187
Switch It Up! **VL**	Inform PW: Investigation	72–73
	Persuade PW: Investigation	232–233
How to Draw a Dolphin **VL**	Instruct EWU: Procedural Text	84–104
Make Your Own Cajon **VL**	Instruct PW: Investigation	116–117
Grandma's Surprise	Narrate EWU: Personal Narrative	132–154
On the Beach	Narrate PW: Nonfiction Narrative	178–179
Washington, D.C.	Persuade EWU: Travel Brochure	198–219
Take Me Out to the Ballgame	Persuade PW: Friendly Letter	224–225
Response to *Diary of a Worm*	Respond EWU: Response Writing	246–267
Tremendously Tough Tooth	Respond PW: Response to a Poem	268–269
Listen	Respond PW: Response to a Poem	268–269

HANDWRITING GUIDE

Handwriting or penmanship is an important skill for students to master to give them fluency in recording their thoughts. Every student's handwriting is different; however, there is a standard way that each letter is formed that students need to be taught. Figure 1 (here and on the next page) shows the correct formation of both lowercase and uppercase letters.

Figure 1. Correct formation of letters

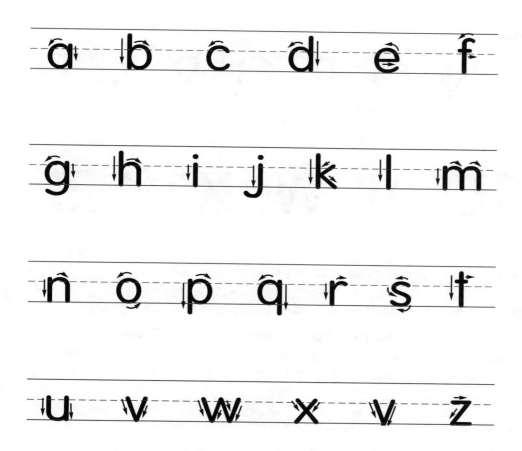

© 2010 by Tony Stead and Linda Hoyt from Explorations in Nonfiction Writing, Grade 2 (Portsmouth, NH: Heinemann). This page may be reproduced for classroom use only.

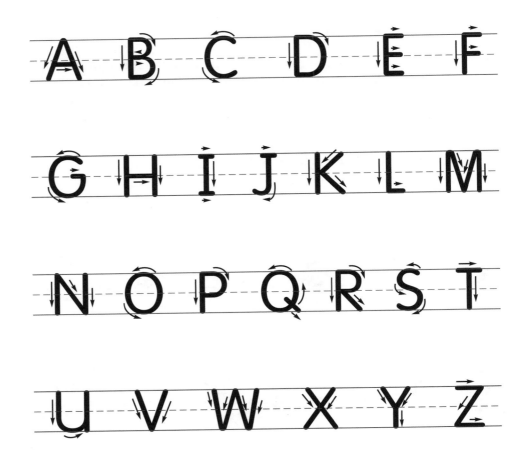

Tips and Considerations for Teaching Handwriting

▶ Discuss with students the importance of legible handwriting.

▶ Assist students with correct pencil grip as they write. Demonstrate how you hold a pencil, and have them practice. That is, hold the pencil between the thumb and first finger, resting on the second finger.

▶ Make sure students' pencils are always sharp.

▶ Encourage students to keep their paper straight when writing.

▶ Give beginning writers a multitude of writing materials such as crayons, pencils, paintbrushes/paint, and markers to help develop their fine motor skills.

▶ Encourage students not to grip pencils too hard. This will help them with writing fluency.

▶ Have students practice forming letters in the air with their index finger.

▶ Give students opportunities to practice tracing letters that they are having problems forming.

▶ Praise students' attempts to form letters but always demonstrate the correct method at point of need.

▸ When students are publishing their work, give them support with letter size by either providing lined paper or showing them how large the letters need to be. This is very important when publishing as many students will begin to write their information too small for others to clearly read.

▸ Provide opportunities for students to write class signs, cards, and letters.

▸ Display alphabet charts around the classroom. Make copies of the alphabet and place them on students' tables for reference.

▸ Provide support in whole class, small group, and individual settings based on need.

▸ Left-handed students may encounter difficulties forming some letters. Provide support as needed.

▸ Teach students letters that have a similar formation. Once students learn how to form one specific letter, it is much easier for them to form letters within the same group. Refer to Figure 2. Note: You do not need to teach all the letters that have a similar formation at the same time.

Similar Letter Formations	
Lowercase	
Counterclockwise	a, c, d, e, f, g, o, s, q
Downwards	i, j, k, l, t, u
Downwards then up	b, h, m, n, p, r
Diagonal	v, w, x, y, z
Uppercase	
Straight lines	E, F, H, I, L, T
Straight and diagonal lines	A, K, M, N, V, W, X, Y, Z
Straight lines and curves	B, D, J, P, R, U
Counterclockwise	C, G, O, Q, S

Figure 2. Similar Letter Formations

MONITORING STUDENTS PROGRESS

Use the Checklist for Handwriting in Figure 3 to record each student's skills in handwriting. This checklist will also help you provide whole class, small group, and individual support based on needs.

Checklist for Handwriting			
Student's Name		**Grade**	**Year**
Lowercase Letters	✔	**Uppercase Letters**	✔
a		A	
b		B	
c		C	
d		D	
e		E	
f		F	
g		G	
h		H	
i		I	
j		J	
k		K	
l		L	
m		M	
n		N	
o		O	
p		P	
q		Q	
r		R	
s		S	
t		T	
u		U	
v		V	
w		W	
x		X	
y		Y	
z		Z	

Figure 3. Checklist for Handwriting

© 2010 by Tony Stead and Linda Hoyt from *Explorations in Nonfiction Writing, Grade 2* (Portsmouth, NH: Heinemann). This page may be reproduced for classroom

Tools Researchers Use

- Label and sketch.

- Jot notes.

- Record ideas in a research notebook.

- Save ideas in a research folder.

- Talk to a thinking partner.

© 2010 by Tony Stead and Linda Hoyt from *Explorations in Nonfiction Writing, Grade 2* (Portsmouth, NH: Heinemann). This page may be reproduced for classroom use only.

TOPIC SELECTION SHEET

Student name: _____

My First Choice: _____

My Second Choice: _____

My Third Choice: _____

© 2010 by Tony Stead and Linda Hoyt from *Explorations in Nonfiction Writing, Grade 2* (Portsmouth, NH: Heinemann). This page may be reproduced for classroom use only.

ONGOING MONITORING SHEET: INFORMATIONAL WRITING

Names

Purpose

Understands the purpose for writing an informational piece

Ideas/Research

Reflects research and planning

Bases writing on research and prior knowledge

Includes facts and details from research

Gathers and incorporates information from multiple sources

Organization/Text Features

Includes a title that tells what the piece is about

Provides a table of contents

Presents categories of information with headings

Includes labeled illustrations that support the text

Language/Style

Puts information in her or his own words

Uses linking words (*and, when, but, that, so,* etc.)

Uses adjectives to describe information

Conventions and Presentation

Begins sentences with capital letters

Uses correct end punctuation

Uses appropriate spelling

© 2010 by Tony Stead and Linda Hoyt from *Explorations in Nonfiction Writing, Grade 2* (Portsmouth, NH: Heinemann). This page may be reproduced for classroom use only.

DAILY PLANNER

Daily Planner for Class and/or Individual Projects   DAY_____   Date_____

Focused Minilesson: Topic _____

Unit and Lesson Number _____

Students I need to confer with individually:

Student's Name	Focus of Instruction

Small group I need to gather for instruction:

Student's Name	Focus of Instruction

Sharing/Reflections

TURN &TALK   Focus for Partner Sharing:

Focus for Class Reflection:

© 2010 by Tony Stead and Linda Hoyt from *Explorations in Nonfiction Writing, Grade 2* (Portsmouth, NH: Heinemann). This page may be reproduced for classroom use only.

INDIVIDUAL EVALUATION RECORD: INFORMATIONAL TEXTS GRADE 2	Key: 1: Not in evidence 2: With assistance 3: Mostly on own 4. Consistently on own					
Name of Student						
Date Assessed						
Purpose						
Understands the purpose for writing an informational piece						
Ideas/Research						
Reflects research and planning						
Bases writing on research and prior knowledge						
Includes facts and details from research						
Gathers and incorporates information from multiple sources						
Organization/Text Features						
Includes a title that tells what the piece is about						
Provides a table of contents						
Presents categories of information with headings						
Includes labeled illustrations that support the text						
Language/Style						
Puts information in her or his own words						
Uses linking words (*and, when, but, that, so,* etc.)						
Uses adjectives to describe information						
Conventions and Presentation						
Begins sentences with capital letters						
Ends sentences with periods						
Uses appropriate spelling strategies						

© 2010 by Tony Stead and Linda Hoyt from *Explorations in Nonfiction Writing, Grade 2* (Portsmouth, NH: Heinemann). This page may be reproduced for classroom use only.

	Names																			

ONGOING MONITORING SHEET: PROCEDURAL WRITING

Purpose

Understands purpose for writing a procedural piece

Ideas/Research

Reflects research and planning

Bases writing on research and prior knowledge

Includes facts and details from research

Gathers and incorporates information from multiple sources

Organization/Text Features

Includes a title that tells what is to be done or made

Provides a list of materials

Presents steps in a logical sequence

Supports the text with illustrations or diagrams

Language/Style

Uses descriptive words to make directions clear

Includes time-order words (*first, next, then, last*)

Begins each step with an action verb (*put, mix, cut, take, etc.*)

Conventions and Presentation

Begins sentences with capital letters

Uses correct end punctuation

Begins each step in the process on a new line

© 2010 by Tony Stead and Linda Hoyt from *Explorations in Nonfiction Writing, Grade 2* (Portsmouth, NH: Heinemann). This page may be reproduced for classroom use only.

DAILY PLANNER

Daily Planner for Class and/or Individual Projects   DAY_____   Date_____

Focused Minilesson: Topic _____

Unit and Lesson Number _____

Students I need to confer with individually:

Student's Name	Focus of Instruction

Small group I need to gather for instruction:

Student's Name	Focus of Instruction

Sharing/Reflections

TURN &TALK   Focus for Partner Sharing:

Focus for Class Reflection:

© 2010 by Tony Stead and Linda Hoyt from *Explorations in Nonfiction Writing, Grade 2* (Portsmouth, NH: Heinemann). This page may be reproduced for classroom use only.

INDIVIDUAL EVALUATION RECORD: PROCEDURAL TEXTS GRADE 2	Key:	1: Not in evidence 2: With assistance 3: Mostly on own 4: Consistently on own					
Name of Student							
Date Assessed							
Purpose							
Understands the purpose for writing a procedural piece							
Ideas/Research							
Reflects research and planning							
Bases writing on research and prior knowledge							
Includes facts and details from research							
Gathers and incorporates information from multiple sources							
Organization/Text Features							
Includes a title that tells what is to be made or done							
Provides a list of materials							
Presents steps in a logical sequence							
Supports the text with illustrations or diagrams.							
Language/Style							
Uses descriptive words to make directions clear.							
Includes time-order words (*first, next, then, last*)							
Begins each step with an action verb (*put, mix, cut, take,* etc.)							
Conventions and Presentation							
Begins sentences with capital letters							
Uses correct end punctuation							
Begins each step in the process on a new line							

© 2010 by Tony Stead and Linda Hoyt from *Explorations in Nonfiction Writing, Grade 2* (Portsmouth, NH: Heinemann). This page may be reproduced for classroom use only.

	Names																	

ONGOING MONITORING SHEET: NARRATIVE WRITING

Purpose

Understands the purpose for writing a narrative piece (a true story)

Ideas/Research

Generates ideas

Tells about event/s or time

Gives the reader factual information

Includes engaging related details

Organization/Text Features

Includes a title that relates closely to the narrative

Relates an event or sequence of events in time order

Includes a beginning, middle, and end

Includes pictures that match text

Includes labels and captions on pictures

(continued on next page)

© 2010 by Tony Stead and Linda Hoyt from *Explorations in Nonfiction Writing, Grade 2* (Portsmouth, NH: Heinemann). This page may be reproduced for classroom use only.

ONGOING MONITORING SHEET: NARRATIVE WRITING	Names																
Language/Style																	
Uses first person for personal narratives																	
Uses third person for nonfiction narratives																	
Uses a consistent verb tense																	
Uses interesting action words																	
Uses descriptive words and phrases																	
Uses sequence words and phrases *(at first, soon, etc.)*																	
Conventions and Presentation																	
Uses complete sentences																	
Uses regular and irregular verb forms correctly																	
Uses strategies to help with spelling																	
Capitalizes the pronoun *I*																	
Uses capital letters to start sentences																	
Uses punctuation marks to end sentences																	

© 2010 by Tony Stead and Linda Hoyt from *Explorations in Nonfiction Writing, Grade 2* (Portsmouth, NH: Heinemann). This page may be reproduced for classroom use only.

DAILY PLANNER

Daily Planner for Class and/or Individual Projects   DAY_____   Date_____

Focused Minilesson: Topic _____

Unit and Lesson Number _____

Students I need to confer with individually:

Student's Name	Focus of Instruction

Small group I need to gather for instruction:

Student's Name	Focus of Instruction

Sharing/Reflections

TURN &TALK   Focus for Partner Sharing:

Focus for Class Reflection:

© 2010 by Tony Stead and Linda Hoyt from *Explorations in Nonfiction Writing, Grade 2* (Portsmouth, NH: Heinemann). This page may be reproduced for classroom use only.

INDIVIDUAL EVALUATION RECORD: NARRATIVE TEXTS GRADE 2	Key: 1: Not in evidence 2: With assistance 3: Mostly on own 4: Consistently on own					
Name of Student						
Date Assessed						
Purpose						
Understands the purpose for writing a narrative piece						
Ideas/Research						
Generates ideas						
Tells about event(s) or time						
Gives the reader factual information						
Includes engaging related details						
Organization/Text Features						
Includes a title that relates closely to the narrative						
Relates an event or sequence of events in time order						
Includes a beginning, middle, and end						
Includes pictures that match text						
Includes labels and captions for pictures						
Language/Style						
Uses first person for personal narratives						
Uses third person for nonfiction narratives						
Uses a consistent verb tense						
Uses interesting action words						
Uses descriptive words and phrases						
Uses sequence words and phrases (*at first, soon,* etc.)						
Conventions and Presentation						
Uses complete sentences						
Uses regular and irregular verb forms correctly						
Uses appropriate spelling strategies						
Capitalizes the pronoun *I*						
Uses capital letters to start sentences						
Uses punctuation marks to end sentences						

© 2010 by Tony Stead and Linda Hoyt from *Explorations in Nonfiction Writing, Grade 2* (Portsmouth, NH: Heinemann). This page may be reproduced for classroom use only.

	Names

ONGOING MONITORING SHEET: PERSUASIVE WRITING

Purpose

Understands purpose for writing a persuasive piece

Ideas/Research

Reflects research and planning to support a goal

Bases writing on research and personal opinion

Includes facts from research to support opinions

Gathers and uses information from multiple sources

Organization/Text Features

Includes a title that reflects the topic and goal

Begins with an opening statement that reveals the goal

Provides at least one supporting reason or argument

Supports arguments with opinions

Supports arguments with facts

Ends with a sentence or statement that restates the goal

Includes visuals that help persuade readers

© 2010 by Tony Stead and Linda Hoyt from *Explorations in Nonfiction Writing, Grade 2* (Portsmouth, NH: Heinemann). This page may be reproduced for classroom use only.

ONGOING MONITORING SHEET: PERSUASIVE WRITING

	Names						
Language/Style							
Shows a clear, consistent opinion throughout the piece							
Uses persuasive, descriptive language							
Sums up personal feelings and opinions in the ending							
Conventions and Presentation							
Uses headings for categories of information							
Uses capital letters for specific names							
Uses strategies for spelling tricky words							
Uses an editing checklist							

© 2010 by Tony Stead and Linda Hoyt from *Explorations in Nonfiction Writing, Grade 2* (Portsmouth, NH: Heinemann). This page may be reproduced for classroom use only.

DAILY PLANNER

Daily Planner for Class and/or Individual Projects   DAY_____ Date_____

Focused Minilesson: Topic _____

Unit and Lesson Number _____

Students I need to confer with individually:

Student's Name	Focus of Instruction

Small group I need to gather for instruction:

Student's Name	Focus of Instruction

Sharing/Reflections

TURN &TALK   Focus for Partner Sharing:

Focus for Class Reflection:

© 2010 by Tony Stead and Linda Hoyt from *Explorations in Nonfiction Writing, Grade 2* (Portsmouth, NH: Heinemann). This page may be reproduced for classroom use only.

INDIVIDUAL EVALUATION RECORD: PERSUASIVE TEXTS GRADE 2	Key: 1: Not in evidence 2: With assistance 3: Mostly on own 4: Consistently on own					
Name of Student						
Date Assessed						
Purpose						
Understands the purpose for writing a persuasive piece						
Ideas/Research						
Reflects research and planning to support a goal						
Bases writing on research and personal opinion						
Includes facts from research to support opinions						
Gathers and uses information from multiple sources						
Organization/Text Features						
Includes a title that reflects the goal and topic						
Begins with an opening statement that reveals the goal						
Provides at least one supporting reason or argument						
Supports arguments with opinions						
Supports arguments with facts						
Ends with a sentence or statement that restates the goal						
Includes visuals that help persuade readers						
Language/Style						
Shows a clear, consistent opinion throughout the piece						
Uses persuasive, descriptive language						
Sums up personal opinions and feelings in the ending						
Conventions and Presentation						
Uses headings for categories of information						
Uses capital letters for specific names						
Uses strategies for spelling tricky words						
Uses an editing checklist						

© 2010 by Tony Stead and Linda Hoyt from *Explorations in Nonfiction Writing, Grade 2* (Portsmouth, NH: Heinemann). This page may be reproduced for classroom use only.

ONGOING MONITORING SHEET: RESPONSE WRITING

	Names

Purpose

Understands the purpose for writing a response piece

Ideas/Research

Responds directly to a piece of literature or prompt

Expresses an opinion (e.g., likes or dislikes)

Supports the response with reasons and examples

Includes wonderings about the piece of literature or prompt

Makes a personal connection to the piece of literature or prompt

Organization/Text Features

Includes a title that reflects the purpose or task

Uses text features that match the purpose or task

May include illustrations that support the response

Language/Style

Shows a clear point of view

May express personal opinions or feelings

Conventions and Presentation

Uses a variety of sentence structures: declarative, interrogative, imperative; simple, compound

Leaves spaces between words

Uses spelling strategies to help with spelling

Uses capital letters to start sentences

Uses appropriate end punctuation

© 2010 by Tony Stead and Linda Hoyt from *Explorations in Nonfiction Writing, Grade 2* (Portsmouth, NH: Heinemann). This page may be reproduced for classroom use only.

DAILY PLANNER

Daily Planner for Class and/or Individual Projects   DAY_____   Date_____

Focused Minilesson: Topic _____

Unit and Lesson Number _____

Students I need to confer with individually:

Student's Name	Focus of Instruction

Small group I need to gather for instruction:

Student's Name	Focus of Instruction

Sharing/Reflections

TURN &TALK   Focus for Partner Sharing:

Focus for Class Reflection:

© 2010 by Tony Stead and Linda Hoyt from *Explorations in Nonfiction Writing, Grade 2* (Portsmouth, NH: Heinemann). This page may be reproduced for classroom use only.

INDIVIDUAL EVALUATION RECORD: RESPONSE TEXTS GRADE 2	Key: 1: Not in evidence 2: With assistance 3: Mostly on own 4: Consistently on own					
Name of Student						
Date Assessed						
Purpose						
Understands the purpose for writing a response piece						
Ideas/Research						
Responds directly to a piece of literature or prompt						
Expresses an opinion (e.g., likes/dislikes)						
Supports the response with reasons and examples						
Includes wonderings about the piece of literature or prompt						
Makes a personal connection to the piece of literature or prompt						
Organization/Text Features						
Includes a title that reflects the purpose or task						
Uses text features that match the purpose or task						
May include illustrations that support the response						
Language/Style						
Shows a clear point of view						
May express personal opinions or feelings						
Conventions and Presentation						
Uses variety of sentence structures: declarative, interrogative, imperative; simple, compound						
Leaves spaces between words						
Uses spelling strategies to help with spelling						
Uses capital letters to start sentences						
Uses appropriate end punctuation						

© 2010 by Tony Stead and Linda Hoyt from *Explorations in Nonfiction Writing, Grade 2* (Portsmouth, NH: Heinemann). This page may be reproduced for classroom use only.